The rate of settlement of disputes in international arbitration is strikingly low, especially as compared to settlement rates in national court generally. Pedro Martínez-Fraga convincingly shows that this cannot be as heavily attributed as it commonly is to tribunals' simple failure to promote it. This brilliant book adopts a broader lens and finds that many central elements of the arbitral process itself – some of them paradoxically introduced in the interest of economy in time and cost – contribute importantly to the problem. Energetically promoting settlement may require rethinking some of international arbitration's most standard features.

George A. Bermann, Gellhorn Professor of Law & Jean Monnet Professor of European Union Law, Director, Center for International Commercial and Investment Arbitration (CICIA), Columbia University School of Law

A bold and brilliant reframing of settlement in international commercial arbitration. Pedro Martínez-Fraga's latest book offers a powerful critique of international commercial arbitration's failure to embrace settlement as a core objective. He convincingly argues that without clear evidentiary rules enabling parties to assess risk, meaningful settlement remains out of reach. With scholarly rigor and elegant prose, he challenges traditional perspectives and places settlement at the very heart of arbitral efficiency. Through a compelling critique of current norms and a visionary call for reform, Martínez-Fraga offers a transformative blueprint for broadening arbitration's dispute resolution potential. The book persuasively promotes the advantages of moving dispute resolution beyond zero-sum outcomes toward results based on informed, equitable settlement.

Margaret L. Moses, Mary Ann G. McMorrow Professor of Law, Loyola University Chicago

A thoughtful and necessary analysis that delves into the underlying factors contributing to the relatively low settlement rate in international commercial arbitration, in general and in contrast to the significantly higher settlement frequently observed in the US civil judicial proceedings. Mr. Martínez-Fraga offers a substantive evidential approach that is novel and considers the structural, procedural, and strategic differences between international arbitration and litigation. By examining these elements, the analysis aims to illuminate why parties in international arbitration may be less inclined to settle early, and how this trend diverges from the more settlement-driven dynamics of domestic litigation in the US courts.

Gary Born, WilmerHale (Partner)

Professor Martínez-Fraga has given us a rigorous and insightful work compellingly demonstrating the link between settlement and risk assessment in international arbitration. Bringing his considerable experience to bear in a most thought-provoking manner, he identifies along the procedural timeline the incremental adjustments needed to sharpen the parties' respective understanding of the dispute in which they find themselves, better enabling them to bargain toward settlement. The book warrants careful study by anyone wishing to improve international arbitration's efficiency in ending disputes.

Jack J. Coe, Jr., PhD, Faculty Director of the LLM Concentration in International Commercial Arbitration, Pepperdine University – Caruso Schol of Law

SETTLEMENT AND RISK ASSESSMENT IN INTERNATIONAL COMMERCIAL ARBITRATION

International commercial arbitration has failed to redeem its promise to be efficient. Approximately 27 percent of all international commercial arbitral proceedings are settled before issuance of a merits-based award. This book asserts that legacy international commercial arbitration is based on the economic efficiencies arising from a zero-sum-game approach to dispute resolution pursuant to which the most efficient result is one that yields a prevailing (winning) and non-prevailing (losing) party. This emphasis on process efficiency has caused international commercial arbitration to lose its standing as the premier dispute resolution methodology for cross-border commercial conflicts. Historically, settlement has not been perceived as an element of the culture of international commercial arbitration. Only recently has a consensus arisen acknowledging that arbitrators have an obligation to facilitate settlement. This book explains that, through timely risk assessment, voluntary settlement of arbitral proceedings will become the rule, not the exception, leading to optimal efficiency.

Pedro J. Martínez-Fraga is Global Co-Leader of the International Arbitration Practice for Bryan Cave Leighton Paisner LLP (BCLP). He is Distinguished Visiting Practitioner of International Law and Adjunct Professor of Law at New York University Law School. He has represented eleven sovereign states as lead counsel, and published over fifty academic articles and eleven books on public and private international law.

Settlement and Risk Assessment in International Commercial Arbitration

PEDRO J. MARTÍNEZ-FRAGA
Bryan Cave Leighton Paisner (Law Firm)

CAMBRIDGE
UNIVERSITY PRESS

CAMBRIDGE
UNIVERSITY PRESS

Shaftesbury Road, Cambridge CB2 8EA, United Kingdom

One Liberty Plaza, 20th Floor, New York, NY 10006, USA

477 Williamstown Road, Port Melbourne, VIC 3207, Australia

314–321, 3rd Floor, Plot 3, Splendor Forum, Jasola District Centre, New Delhi – 110025, India

Cambridge University Press is part of Cambridge University Press & Assessment, a department of the University of Cambridge.

We share the University's mission to contribute to society through the pursuit of education, learning and research at the highest international levels of excellence.

www.cambridge.org
Information on this title: www.cambridge.org/9781009756495
DOI: 10.1017/9781009756532

When citing this work, please include a reference to the DOI 10.1017/9781009756532

First published 2026

Cover image: Attic black-figured amphora. Attributed to: *The Lysippides Painter.* Circa 530BC, Greece. The British Museum.

A catalogue record for this publication is available from the British Library

A Cataloging-in-Publication data record for this book is available from the Library of Congress

ISBN 978-1-009-75649-5 Hardback

To my wife, Liza, my daughters, Alejandra Sofía and Valentina Lucía, and to the memory of my parents, Ana Nuñez Aragón and Pedro Julio Martínez-Fraga. If words could express what you mean to me, they would be the instruments of the gods and not of mere mortals.

Si vis pacem, para bellum
(If you want peace, prepare for war)

Flavius Vegetius, *De re militari* (c. 4th or 5th century AD)

***

[A]s a litigant, I should dread a lawsuit beyond almost anything else short of sickness and death.

Judge Learned Hand to the Association of the Bar of the City of New York, 1921

Contents

Figures and Tables

FIGURES

TABLES

Foreword

I find that we do much more talking than thinking about settlement of the disputes that come to arbitration. When they occur, discussions of settlement tend to dwell on whether, to what extent, when, and how arbitrators should promote it. These are unquestionably important questions that warrant our continuing attention and concern. But should the role of settlement be viewed solely through that lens? Pedro J. Martínez-Fraga thinks not.

Pedro begins where he should. Why, he asks are settlement rates as low as they are in international arbitration? Based on scattered evidence, those rates in international commercial arbitration are in the neighborhood of 27 percent and even slightly lower in investor–state arbitration. Settlement rates are considerably higher in national courts – not that one should emulate the United States, where it is due to the ills of litigation that settlement rates reach over 90 percent.

Before considering the reasons for settlement's undersized role in international arbitration, Pedro points out the irony that a greater incidence of settlement would seriously address the problem of inefficiency in time and cost that has long been and remains the international arbitration community's central preoccupation. The correlation between settlement and efficiency should be self-evident.

Turning to explanations, Pedro finds an overall lack of a "settlement culture" in international arbitration. But what in turn are the reasons for that? One explanation is what Pedro calls the system's preoccupation with "process efficiency," that is the efficiency that comes (or does not come) from the introduction of procedural devices, like accelerated proceedings or summary disposition of claims. But attaining efficiency requires a wider lens. Another factor is our supposition that, as in litigation, there must be in any arbitration a "winner" and a "loser." That mentality does not lend itself to settlement. We rightly disfavor the notion of arbitrators disposing of disputes by compromise, but surely there's nothing wrong with the parties doing exactly that.

Still another – and especially pervasive – factor is the profound uncertainty with which international arbitration operates. The greater the uncertainty in the arbitral process, the less able we are to assess risk. "Procedural uncertainty," he writes, "is inimical to risk assessment," and yet it is precisely risk assessment on which parties' willingness or unwillingness to settle is based.

Closely related to this uncertainty is the high degree to which international arbitration privileges the exercise of discretion by arbitrators, an exercise that is largely unguided. Discretionary decision-making on the part of others is not the best laboratory in which to conduct reliable risk assessment. (Ironically, arbitrator discretion is also a bit at war with party autonomy.) Pedro finds that even the Prague Rules, which made efficiency their absolute touchstone, do no better than what we now have.

It may not be particularly fashionable these days to favor rules over standards, but that is where Pedro is heading. He focuses principally on evidentiary practices in international arbitration which, he says, suffer from profound indeterminacy. These practices operate in what he calls a "doctrinal void in the taking and presentation of evidence." Occasionally, other more discrete features of international arbitration also come in for criticism due to their contribution to uncertainty. One example is the overly prized institution of *iura novit curia*. Another is due process paranoia itself, which positively thrives on process uncertainty.

In closing, Pedro has ten prescriptions to offer. Some of these are eminently sensible, such as prioritizing materiality over relevance in the assessment of evidence. Others stand to garner less support, such as the introduction of exclusionary rules of evidence (the "best evidence" rule, for example) to mitigate the prevailing "free assessment" of the evidence by tribunals. He welcomes having much needed rules on cross-examination, the treatment of objections, and the use of expert testimony. Though Pedro does not use the term "discipline," that is essentially what he finds missing in our approach to evidence, and of this the settlement of disputes is a major casualty.

Substance aside, the book is beautifully written. It is deeply learned and amply documented. Pedro's source material is nothing short of prodigious. And yet the book is a pleasure to read.

Like many, I welcome more robust efforts by tribunals in promoting the settlement of disputes. But it is not enough for arbitrators themselves to encourage parties to settle (essential though that is). Parties need to feel comfortable with the settlement of their disputes. That requires us to examine the environment in which arbitration is conducted and identify how it may be changed to better equip parties to perform the risk assessment on which informed decisions to settle or not depend. Among the key dividends would be efficiency, tools for which the international arbitration community is chronically striving. Settlement's contribution to efficiency has been woefully overlooked. After *Settlement and Risk Assessment in International Commercial Arbitration*, that will no longer be the case.

George A. Bermann[*]
Columbia University School of Law
Walter Gellhorn Professor of Law and
Jean Monnet Professor of European Union Law

[*] *The Director of the Center for International Commercial & Investment Arbitration at Columbia Law School, George A. Bermann '75 LL.M. is a world-renowned authority on comparative law, EU law, international trade contracts, WTO dispute resolution, and transnational litigation and arbitration. For more than four decades, he has been an active international arbitrator in commercial and investment disputes in all sectors, including general commercial contract, construction, intellectual property, energy, oil and gas, competition law, insurance, telecommunications, pharmaceuticals, distributorship and franchising, transportation, and employment. He also serves regularly as an expert witness before international arbitral tribunals, as well as before courts in arbitral-related cases.*

Acknowledgments

Acknowledgments are obligatory. The thoughts and contributions of my students at New York University School of Law during the last fourteen years (as of the date of this writing), and the University of Navarra in Pamplona, Spain (seventeen years), have played a decisive role in the development of this text. These students have taught me more than I will ever fully comprehend. Special gratitude is extended to Sharon McCann, Commissioning Editor Academic Books, Law, at Cambridge University Press, who supported and believed in this project, and without whom this work would not have been possible. I also want to acknowledge the contribution and valuable insights of Michael H. Graham, Professor of Law (Ret.) and Dean's Distinguished Scholar for the Profession at the University of Miami School of Law, who offered extremely valuable suggestions, particularly regarding the text's structural organization for the U.S. Federal Rules of Evidence, as well as advising on conceptual evidential approaches.

I am particularly grateful to Professor George A. Bermann, Walter Gellhorn Professor of Law and Jean Monnet Professor of European Union Law, Director of the Center for International Commercial & Investment Arbitration at Columbia University School of Law, who was generous and patient in writing the foreword to this text. Quite frankly, the foreword alone justifies the entire book's publication.

Special gratitude is extended to C. Ryan Reetz, with whom I have had the privilege of continuously practicing law and discussing (literally over a lifetime) many of the central propositions underlying this contribution. His practical and theoretical insights have been invaluable to the central thesis of this text.

Professor Linda Silberman, Clarence D. Ashley Professor of Law Emerita and former Director of the Center of Transnational Litigation, Arbitration, and Commercial Law at New York University School of Law, was extremely generous with her time in reviewing half-baked preliminary drafts of the manuscript: a true labor of love. Her guidance and suggestions proved to be decisive in adding clarity and cohesion.

Professor Franco Ferrari, Clarence D. Ashley Professor of Law, Director, Intesa Sanpaolo Center for Transnational Litigation, Arbitration, and Commercial Law at New York University School of Law, demonstrated that there is such a thing as *infinite* patience residing within *finite* human beings. Professor Ferrari spent countless hours discussing the culture of arbitration and its relationship to settlement. His input was central.

A version of the manuscript comprising this text constituted the Special Course that I delivered in the summer of 2023 at The Hague Academy of International Law. The students attending the Special Course taught me much more about risk assessment than I ever could have aspired to teach them during the week-long presentation of lectures on the subject. They caused me to think and to rethink many of the text's foundational propositions and to present them with greater lucidity.

I wish to express gratitude to Professor José E. Alvarez, Herbert and Rose Rubin Professor of International Law at New York University School of Law. Professor Alvarez always made time in his busy schedule to discuss procedural aspects of international arbitration generally that found their way to this contribution's final iteration.

My law Partner, Craig S. O'Dear, wrestled with the extent to which US federal and state court procedural practice incorporating the mandatory mediation can, would, and should find an analogue in international commercial arbitration (ICA). He invested countless hours revising those sections of the text addressing this concern. Likewise, Mr. Dionisio ("Dennis") Pastrana, Sr., Certified Public Accountant (CPA). Mr. Pastrana's longstanding experience as a CEO of one of Miami-Dade County, Florida's largest employers and dealings with the identification and quantification of risk assessment, was particularly helpful in understanding the value of optimal efficiency in a continuing operational framework.

Finally, Victoria (Vicky) Clark, Knowledge Counsel, Bryan Cave Leighton Paisner LLP (BCLP), and my Legal Assistant, June E. Foyo-Lorenzo, deserve this recognition and the honor of a Purple Heart. Regrettably, I can only provide them with the former.

It is important, however, to add a disclaimer. Whatever inconsistencies or ill-witted propositions may be present, are all of the author's doing and have nothing to do with the valuable contributions of those mentioned.

Table of Cases

Landau v. St. Louis Public Service Co., 364 Mo. 1134, 273 S.W. 2d 255 (Mo. 1954), 10
Lee v. Chica, 983 F.2d 883 (8th Cir. 1993), 53
Legg v. Chopra, 286 F.3d 286 (6th Cir. 2002), 149
Lessin v. Merrill Lynch Fenner, 481 F.3d 813 (D.C. Cir. 2007), 50
LLC Komstroy (successor to LLC Energoalliance) v. Republic of Moldova, 2019 WL 3997385 (D.D.C., Aug. 23, 2019), *aff'd.* on appeal, *LLC SPC Stileks v. Republic of Moldova* 985 F.3d 871 (D.C. Cir. 2021), 47, 48, 49, 50
Luis Dreyfus S.A. v. Holding Tusculum B.V., Quebec Superior Court (December 8, 2008), 172
Major League Baseball Players' Ass'n. v. Garvey, 532 U.S. 504 (2001), 141
Marine Transit Corp. v. Dreyfus, 284 US 263 (1932), 24
Marsh v. Green, 782 So.2d 223 (Ala. 2000), 149
Maryland Casualty Co. v. Kador, 225 F.2d 120 (5th Cir. 1955), 164
Matthews v. Eldridge, 424 U.S. 319 (1976), 46, 51, 53
McCullough v. Clinch-Mitchell Const. Co., 8 Cir., 71 F. 2d 17, 24
Metal-Tech Ltd. v. Republic of Uzbekistan, ICSID Case No. ARB/10/3, Award ¶ 287 (October 4, 2013), 172
Miller v. Coffeen, 365 Mo. 204, 280 S.W.2d 100 (Mo. 1955), 10
Mirjan Damaška, *Evidence Law Adrift* (Yale University Press 1997), 201
Mitsubishi Motors Corp. v. Soler Chrysler-Plymouth, Inc., 473 US 614 (1985), passim
Monarch Insurance Company of Ohio v. Spach, 281 F.2d 401 (5th Cir. 1960), 148
Montgomery Ward & Co. v. Steele, 352 F. 2d 822 (8th Cir. 1965), 195
National Wrecking Co. v. Int'l Bhd. of Teamsters, Local 731, 990 F.2d 957 (7th Cir. 1993), 49
Olin Holdings Ltd. v. State of Libya, 73 F. 4th 92 (2nd Cir. 2003), 11
Ostroski v. United States, 2007 WL 9701868 (S.D. Fla. August 23, 2007), 146
Park Const. Co. v. Independent School Dist., 209 Minn. 182, 296 N.W. 475, 135 A.L.R. 59 (1941), 22, 23
Parker v. United Mexican States, Award in U.S. & Mexico General Claims Commission of 31 March 1926, IV R.I.A.A. 35, 39 (1952), 139
Parsons & Whittemore Overseas Co. v. Societe Generale de L'Industrie du Papier (RAKTA), 508 F.2d 969 (2nd Cir. 1974), 45, 46
Petroleum Separating Co. v. Interamerican Refining Corp., 296 F.2d 124 (2nd Cir. 1961), 142
Podraza v. Comm'r of Internal Revenue, T.C. Summ. Op. 2015-67, 2015 WL 7423525 (T.C. Nov. 19, 2015), 196
Pointer v. Texas, 380 U.S. 400, 85 S. Ct. 1065, 13 L. Ed.2d 923 (1965), 234
Preston v. Ferrer, 128 S. Ct. 978 (2008), 174
Purus Plastics GmBH v. Echo-Terr Distributing Inc., 2018 WL 3064817 (W.D. Wash. June. 21, 2018), 152
Quiborax S.A. and Non-Metallic Minerals S.A. v. Pluri National State of Bolivia, ICSID Case No. ARB/06/2, Award ¶ 92 (September 16, 2015), 172

Table of Statutes

TREATISES

Abbreviations

ADR	Alternative Dispute Resolution
ALJ	Administrative Law Judges
CTS	Caseload Table of Statistics
DIS	German Arbitration Institute
ECT	Energy Charter Treaty
FAA	Federal Arbitration Act
FRCP	Federal Rules of Civil Procedure
FRE	Federal Rules of Evidence
HKIAC	Hong Kong International Arbitration Centre
IBA	International Bar Association
ICA	international commercial arbitration
ICC	International Chamber of Commerce
ICDR	International Centre for Dispute Resolution
ISDS	investor–state dispute settlement
LCIA	London Court of International Arbitration
NCSC	National Center for State Courts
OED	*Oxford English Dictionary*
SCC	Stockholm Chamber of Commerce
SIAC	Singapore International Arbitration Centre
SSA	Social Security Administration
UNCITRAL	United Nations Commission on International Trade Law

Introduction

International commercial arbitration (ICA) cases suffer from a low settlement rate. This metric is between 23 and 32 percent of all ICA cases. The vast majority conclude pursuant to issuance of a merits arbitral award.

The low settlement rate of ICA stands in high relief to its judicial adjudication counterpart. Indeed, in the United States, in both state and federal courts for several decades now, between 76 and 90 percent of all civil cases settle. Approximately 1 percent or less of all US civil cases in state and federal fora are actually concluded pursuant to a jury trial, the judicial equivalent to an arbitral final hearing.

Why do ICA cases generally not settle? Does the low ICA settlement rate raise existential concerns regarding ICA's future? If so, why? These questions were once ignored but have now been made relevant because the universe of consumers of arbitral services has raised serious concerns over the strategic merits of selecting ICA over carefully crafted judicial choice of law and choice of venue clauses.

Questions abound regarding the many reasons why ICA proceedings mostly advance to the issuance of a merits award. Seven salient factors comprise *part* of the principal reasons why ICA proceedings settle in the exception and not the rule. As to be expected, some of these grounds are subtler than others.

First, particularly during the early days of arbitration, and then extending as far back as its origins, the consensus was that arbitration *itself* was a kind of "settlement process." The term "Alternative Dispute Resolution" formally and substantively was understood as a non-judicial means for the settlement of disputes, and not involuntary and unilaterally imposed adjudication. Arbitration was deemed an amicable (non-adversarial) approach to dispute settlement. Embryonic understandings of efficiency and *party-autonomy* contributed to this non-adversarial prospective premised on bilateralism.

Arbitration's origins contemplated a dispute resolution methodology that would lead to a flexible non-adversarial agreement to bring to closure a difference of opinion. Arbitrators were not necessarily lawyers. To the contrary, "industry experts" such as "engineers," populated arbitral tribunals as part of an effort to bring to an end, that is to say, to settle, a particular dispute arising within the framework of a specific industry. Ideally, so this line of reasoning suggests, once the dispute was "settled," the parties would return to working together to maximize profits.

This approach was supplemented with the notion that expediency and efficiency would pervade the process, and therefore, minimize business interruptions while maximizing the likelihood of a resolution to the dispute. Far from foremost was the notion that the arbitration process would yield a "winning" and "losing" party.

From this framework's perspective, it is not difficult to understand why "settlement" within a "settlement process" literally would be unthinkable. Hence spawned an arbitration culture without settlement, because arbitration itself was deemed a settlement methodology rife with equity and bilateral concessions. The point was to solve a problem and to move on from the tribunal's findings.

Second, the concept of "*party-autonomy*" historically has enjoyed a very narrow definition that would not foster a culture of settlement in ICA. The ICA cornerstone principle of *party-autonomy* has been circumscribed to the authority accorded to parties to fashion the rules and elements governing an ICA proceeding. Thus, the selection of (i) seat, (ii) venue, (iii) language, (iv) applicable substantive law, (v) party appointment of a neutral arbitrator, (vi) governing arbitral rules, and of course, (vii) actual consent to arbitration, all represent core elements and *indicia* of a very specific understanding of the principle of *party-autonomy*.

Indeed, the majority of ICA institutional arbitration rules qualify most phases of an arbitral proceeding's management as "subject to the parties' agreement." Notably, however, all of these elements share one common denominator; namely, a concern for stages of the arbitral process that are indispensable to the issuance of a binding and enforceable award.

In this writing, it is suggested that the most meaningful expression of *party-autonomy* is related to the disputing parties' ability to settle their differences *before* issuance of a final merits award. Put plainly, this contribution invites consideration of the proposition that an arbitral tribunal's merits disposition of a claim actually in certain circumstances, is contrary to the principle of *party-autonomy* in its strictest sense of this term. An arbitral tribunal's adjudication of the merits wrests from the parties their individual ability to settle the case in a manner that is not conducive to yielding a zero-sum result.

A merits adjudication of an ICA proceeding constitutes a paradigmatic *zero-sum-game* yielding a *prevailing* and *non-prevailing* party: a euphemism for a "winner" and a "loser." A more authentic understanding within the arbitral framework premised on *party-autonomy* (i) allows for the parties themselves to reach a settlement of the merits and (ii) such agreement necessarily would *not* give rise to an "all-or-nothing" disposition.

The narrow understanding of *party-autonomy* circumscribing this principle to procedural adjudication pitted one of ICA's core concepts against settlement. To the contrary, *party-autonomy* under the legacy understanding exclusively concerns the parties' participation in constructing the proceeding's architecture, and to limit *arbitrator discretion* in the conduct of the arbitration. The narrow conceptualization of *party-autonomy* in part foreclosed the development of non-merits determination settlement as an intrinsic constituent of ICA and its culture.

Third, historically and within ICA's cultural ambit, (i) arbitrators were not trained to facilitate settlements and (ii) they did not see themselves as having such responsibility. Even exhorting the parties to consider settlement seemed to exceed an arbitral tribunal's process driven purview.

The idea of an arbitrator acting as a mediator, or more broadly as an actor encouraging and facilitating settlement, would have been understood as nothing short of heretical. An arbitral tribunal is charged with issuing a binding and enforceable award. This activity, so the argument went, is unrelated to the settlement of a dispute in any way other than pursuant to a merits determination yielding a zero-sum outcome.

In addition, the settlement culture was hampered by the perception that arbitrators would face multiple preclusive conflicts of interest were they to wear two hats: arbitrator and mediator. Navigating such conflicts, or so it was perceived, would be akin to walking through raindrops and not getting wet.

It also was thought that introducing "the facilitation of settlement" into the arbitral proceeding would blur the line separating *arbitration* and *mediation*, thus yielding a hybrid proceeding that altered arbitration's very fiber.

Here it is suggested that multiple approaches and techniques can reconcile the duties and ethical obligations of an arbitrator who also views her role as mandating the encouragement and facilitation of the dispute pursuant to the parties' agreement and not a merits adjudication.

Fourth, only recently has mediation been introduced to the ICA process. And it has been a *soft* introduction that is not mandatory, unlike the role of mediation in most US federal and state courts. Moreover, the workings of mediation within in the ICA framework, in addition to being optional, present challenges. Who will be the mediators? What could be the procedure of such mediations? Is there a place for inadmissible evidence and *ex parte* communications in such mediation efforts? And will mediation take place during a procedural phase of the arbitral process that would allow the parties to understand their respective evidential positions?

It seems to follow that the president of an arbitral panel likely would be best placed to conduct a meaningful mediation that, among other things, would provide the parties with a realistic and transparent understanding of the tribunals' assessment of the merits as of the critical time that the mediation is to take place. This approach is promising. It already has been institutionalized by a modest handful of arbitral institutes.

It does, of course, require the parties' consent to mediation along with a waiver of defenses arising from the tribunal president's involvement in the mediation or settlement facilitation process should the case fail to settle. Even with such guardrails, it remains unclear whether caucusing would be practically viable.

Despite *some* progress mediation, and even settlement facilitation, still are far from comprising part of ICA's histology. This tense relationship between mediation and ICA further contributes to the lack of ICA's settlement culture.

Fifth, ICA faces structural impediments to the development of a culture that embraces settlement. The entire ICA framework is driven by the overarching objective of yielding (i) a binding and (ii) enforceable award. Thus, the appropriate merits determination leading to an award comporting with the Convention on the Recognition and Enforcement of Foreign Arbitral Awards ("the New York Convention") constitutes ICA's polestar. This objective by definition is inimical to settlement.

Certainly these "structural impediments to settlement" represent ICA's most meaningful features because in both theory and *praxis* they contribute to what should be an efficient disposition of a dispute that is final and globally enforceable pursuant to the New York Convention. In fact, however, as is established in this writing, ICA proceedings have grown in complexity. They no longer conclude expeditiously and efficiently.

To the contrary, both (i) legally complex arbitral cases and (ii) ICA proceedings where the amount in controversy is substantial tend to lead to protracted and seemingly endless proceedings that maximize inefficiencies. This state of affairs to some extent can be addressed by adjusting to account for the advantages of a more expansive understanding of the principle of *party-autonomy*, and the introduction of settlement as an imperative forming part of the arbitral tribunal's objectives. Such structural reconfigurations certainly would help.

The culture of primarily yielding a binding and enforceable award will have to create space for procedural structures premised on the proposition that *settlement* constitutes an ICA objective in *pari materia* with issuance of a binding and enforceable award.

Sixth, as to the more notable ICA features that militate against a culture of settlement, ICA administering institutions themselves must (i) train arbitrators to serve as mediators, (ii) instill in arbitrators through institutional rules the responsibility and objective of encouraging settlement, and (iii) underscore pursuant to institutional rules precepts that harmonize mediation and the management of a process also designed to lead to a binding and enforceable award. From an arbitral administering institution's perspective, processing an arbitration claim must be understood in its actual workings as an effort to resolve the dispute *also* beyond the framework of a *zero-sum-game* leading to "winners" and "losers." These six separate but deeply related observations speak to settlement and ICA's culture.

Seventh, and most importantly, awareness of the *actual principal reason* why ICA proceedings do not mainly settle will dissipate the referenced culture barriers to settlement. The *procedure* for settlement is quite distinct from settlement's *substantive* subject matter. The single most important reason why settlement is foreign to ICA is simple. It concerns the parties' failure on a timely basis (i) to identify, (ii) to quantify, and (iii) to communicate risk internally (to itself in the process of ascertaining a comprehensive understanding of the value of a parties' own case) and to the opposing party. Risk assessment is settlement's fulcrum.

The efficiency and success of settlement methodologies depend on a comprehensive understanding of the stakeholder's *liability* and *damages* risks. Absent this understanding, meaningful settlement is only accidentally possible. This assessment in turn simply is not possible without according the parties an opportunity to quantify the admissibility, relevance, materiality, and weight of evidence on a timely basis. Risk assessment is the *only* language of substantive settlement negotiations and of any serious mediation effort. There is no other.

Appropriate evidence disclosure and evidence gathering together with clear rules on the presentation of evidence governing a prospective final hearing, all constitute necessary predicates to the viability of settlement within the existing ICA framework. A necessary return to the original meaning of the concept of efficiency within ICA's historicity must be revisited and implemented. This contribution identifies *optimal efficiency* within the framework of ICA as the efficiency arising from a non-merits determination of the dispute, that is to say, settlement pursuant to the parties' negotiation.

Optimal efficiency also compels a reexamination of *party-autonomy* pursuant to which the parties in fact, and not derivatively (semiotically), in the context of having an arbitral panel consisting of two party-appointed arbitrators, bring a negotiated closure to the dispute.

These views on *efficiency* and *party-autonomy* lead to a revision of current perceptions regarding the present status of the concept of *efficiency* in ICA. The efficiency conducive to the issuance of a binding and enforceable award, without more, is here defined as *process efficiency*.

A new paradigm needs to view *process efficiency* as subordinate to *optimal efficiency*. This paradigm does not represent a realistic aspiration so long as rules rendering *optimal efficiency* possible are not developed. The *optimal efficiency* arising from settlement will require revisions to existing procedural rules governing (i) self-disclosure, (ii) the taking, and (iii) the presenting of evidence in ICA. Cornerstone terms such as "relevance" and "material" will need to be dislodged from the relativistic arbitral orbit of *arbitrator discretion*. Objective rules/standards are imperatives. These adjustments are hardly cataclysmic in scope or altogether foreign to ICA. They do, however, call for revisions that will introduce *optimal efficiency* to ICA.

The contemplated rulemaking will allow for risk assessment. Thereby enhancing the viability of settlement. Consequently, eventually only a modest percentage of ICA cases will proceed to a final hearing.

It is here suggested that:

(i) the introduction of mediation (settlement facilitation) into ICA frameworks,
(ii) the training of arbitrators to encourage and to process settlement,
(iii) exhorting settlement discussions, and

(iv) creating an expansive understanding of *party-autonomy* comporting with settlement and a non-zero-sum disposition of arbitral proceedings, command the ability to engage in *quantifiable risk assessment*. Risk assessment itself necessitates a new approach to evidential thinking and application conducive to transparency. This writing's aspiration is to take a modest step toward identifying settlement as the optimal objective of an arbitral proceeding, the teleology of arbitration.

1

Structuring the Framework for the Identification of a Problem

International Commercial Arbitration Cases Settle Only in a Minority of Instances

1.1 EXPLORING A PROMISE THAT HAS NOT BEEN KEPT: INTERNATIONAL ARBITRATION IS YET TO REDEEM ITS HALLMARK PROMISE TO BE EFFICIENT

Whose woods these are I think I know.
His house is in the village though;
He will not see me stopping here
To watch his woods fill up with snow.

My little horse must think it queer
To stop without a farmhouse near
Between the woods and frozen lake
The darkest evening of the year.

He gives his harness bells a shake
To ask if there is some mistake.
The only other sound's the sweep
Of easy wind and downy flake.

The woods are lovely, dark and deep,
But I have promises to keep,
And miles to go before I sleep,
And miles to go before I sleep.

Robert Frost, "Stopping by Woods on a Snowy Evening"

Robert Frost's lonely traveler resists the seductive and compelling invitation of the lovely woods to take a detour from what appears to be a forced march in the middle of winter. He does so in order to fulfill a promise the lone traveler believes must be kept, notwithstanding the allure of the inviting woods. The promise, of course, is not disclosed. The poet wants the reader to understand the promise as generically as possible and free from any taint of particularity that may otherwise cloud our thinking.

The lonely traveler is redeeming the very concept of a promise. The image invariably leads the reader to wonder why, as human beings, we collectively break rather than keep promises, at all. Obviously, there is no single answer to the query, which itself suggests the multiple answers likely are as complex as the nature of human beings and promises themselves.[1]

As a dispute resolution mechanism that purports to be the dispute resolution or legal counterpart to economic globalization, ICA has advanced a very daring promise upon which its very legitimacy and workings rest – and it has promised efficiency. And in the very name of efficiency it has sacrificed seemingly sacrosanct principles, not the least of which is second instance review, among many others (see Section 8.5), so compelling is efficiency within the ICA framework.

This promise, however, raises more questions than perhaps the promise itself can ever aspire to answer. By way of example, is it possible for ICA to be efficient if only a small percentage of cases settle? Is *settlement* the proper teleology of ICA? If the answer to this second query is in the negative, how then is a merits-based adjudication more in keeping with the ICA core principle of *party-autonomy*, instead of resolution pursuant to a settlement by mutual accord? Is there a *principal* reason or root cause that ICA settlements constitute the exception and not the rule? Assuming there is such a *principal* reason or root cause, can it be identified and addressed?

Equally pressing is the extent to which ICA can be rendered more susceptible to settlements within its existing rubric. More plainly, if in fact there is a discernable principal, overarching reason that tends to preclude settlements in ICA, as opposed to, for example, judicial proceedings in a number of US jurisdictions (Section 1.1.1), can this deficit be addressed without altogether radically altering the nature of ICA itself?[2]

1 The late Professor E. Allan Farnsworth taught me as a student at Columbia University Law School the connection between (i) promises, (ii) the law of contract, and (iii) the poetry of Robert Frost. Indeed, approximately sixteen years *before* sharing this gem, he had spilled some ink on the subject, at least preliminarily, in a law review article titled "Legal Remedies for Breach of Contract," 70 *Colum. L. Rev.* 1145 (1970). It is an honor to reflect on his teachings yet again.

2 *Party-autonomy*, flexibility, process transparency, and *process efficiency* are central tenets that must be both preserved and enhanced. These principles must find balance and reach equipoise with broad arbitral discretion (inherent powers), transparency, and predictive value. *See, e.g.*, Maxi Scherer, "The Fate of Parties' Agreements on Judicial Review of Awards: A Comparative and Normative Analysis of Party-Autonomy at the Post-Award Stage," in *Arbitration International* Vol. 32, Issue 3 (William W. Park ed.) (2016), 437–457 ("Party-autonomy is one of the most fundamental principles in international private law concerning contractual relations on a global and comparative level"); Nigel Blackaby, Constantine Partasides, and Alan Redfern (eds.), *Redfern and Hunter on International Arbitration*, 6th ed. (Oxford University Press 2015):

> Party-autonomy is the guiding principle in determining the procedure to be followed in an international arbitration. It is a principle that is endorsed not only in national laws, but also by international arbitration. It is a principle that is endorsed not only in national laws, but also by international arbitral institutions worldwide, as well as by international instruments such as the New York Convention and the Model Law.

Julian D. M. Lew, Loukas A. Mistelis, & Stefan M. Kröll, *Comparative International Commercial Arbitration* (Kluwer Law International 2002), 28 ("Party-autonomy is the primary source of the

It follows that because arbitral disputes are not most commonly settled, they necessarily proceed to a merits-based adjudication. In this book, the reader is invited to consider adopting the assumption that merits-based adjudications are time-consuming and inefficient. Moreover, they necessarily take the form of a "zero-sum-game,"[3] meaning that there is a prevailing party and non-prevailing party. And that is, I dare say, a euphemism for "a winner" and "a loser."[4]

Thurow for the first time introduced the concept of a zero-sum-game to describe economic models providing for specific solutions that would lead to medium-to-long-term economic gains, but that necessarily and inevitably would cause segments of the population to suffer from economic losses arising from the salutary adjustments:

> This is the heart of our fundamental problem. Our economic problems are solvable. For most of our problems there are several solutions. But all these solutions have the characteristic that someone must suffer large economic losses. No one wants to volunteer for this role, and we have a political process that is incapable of forcing anyone to shoulder this burden. Everyone wants someone else to suffer the necessary economic losses, and as a consequence none of the possible solutions can be adopted.
>
> Basically we have created the world described in Robert Ardey's *The Territorial Imperative*. To beat an animal of the same species on his home turf, the invader must be twice as strong as the defender. But no majority is twice as strong as the minority opposing it. Therefore we each veto the other's initiatives, but none of us has the ability to create successful initiatives ourselves.
>
> Our political and economic structure simply isn't able to cope with an economy that has a substantial zero-sum element. A *zero-sum-game is any game where the losses exactly equal the winnings*. All sporting events are zero-sum-games. For every winner there is a loser, and winners can only exist if losers exist. What the winning gambler wins, the losing gambler must lose.
>
> When there are large losses to be allocated, any economic decision has a large zero-sum element. The economic gains may exceed the economic losses, but the losses are so large as to negate a very substantial fraction of the gains.

Applied to the ICA model, a party to a dispute may secure a favorable award. The cost in terms of resources (funds, company time, the time value of money)

arbitration and the procedure."); Gary B. Born, *International Commercial Arbitration*, 3rd ed. (Kluwer Law International 2020); and Martin Domke, Gabriel Wilmer, & Larry E. Edmonson § 1:2 *Domke on Commercial Arbitration* (West 2023) ("Arbitration is a creature or matter of contract. It is a contractual procedure. Thus, the FAA lets parties tailor some, even many features of arbitration by contract, including the way arbitrators are chosen, what their qualifications should be, and which issues are arbitrable, along with procedure and choice of substantive laws.").

3 See Lester C. Thurow, *The Zero-Sum Society: Distribution and the Possibilities for Economic Change*, 11–12 (Basic Books, Inc. 1980); and Lester C. Thurow, "The Zero-Sum Solution: An Economic Political Agenda for the 80s," in *The Zero-Sum Society: Distribution and the Possibilities for Economic Change* (Simon & Schuster 1985).

4 *See* Thurow's writings, which are specific to the concept.

may not at all be compensated in terms of the award, and it often is not. Even more importantly, in the business context, losing a strategic partner or investor with company and industry sector know-how may far negate the value of the award over time.

The adjudicative act in an ICA environment differs meaningfully from its counterpart judicial adjudication. The latter is charged with the equitable application of organic law that in turn is implementing sovereign-national policy. The same is not the case with an ICA arbitral panel. The ICA arbitral panel is charged with the resolution of a dispute, notwithstanding the foundational role that applicable law plays in the process. It is for this reason, in part, that an arbitral panel can err as a matter of law, fact, and the application of law to fact, and still yield a binding and enforceable award. Second instance merits review, however, ensures that the same does not hold true for the exercise of *judicial* adjudication.

An intrinsic part of resolving disputes in a commercial context should and must entail exploration of the possibility of reaching a resolution that *may* allow the parties to obviate the transactional costs and the expense of securing new strategic partners or investors lacking the expertise and experience in the particular business and industry sector had by the non-prevailing party. Zero-sum-game adjudication altogether forecloses this possibility. Only *optimal efficiency* in the form of settlement tenders any hope.

The proposition that *merits-based adjudications are not preferable to settlement* itself can be viewed as hardly conclusive and little more than an untested assumption that is subject to critical discursive reasoning, and which leads to diametrically opposite conclusions. Certainly, it can be forcefully and elegantly asserted that parties to a contract are entitled to nothing less than a merits-based determination that rewards the prevailing party, that is to say, the nonbreaching stakeholder, by placing that stakeholder in the position that he or she was in prior to the breach, or otherwise with the entitlement to lost profits arising from noncompliance. The specter of specific performance may also loom as an attractive measure of remedies to be attained.[5]

Hence, so *this* argument says, ICA's genuine teleology is a merits-based adjudication where damages are established and awarded to the prevailing party. Indeed, this proposition further contends that nothing short of a merits-based adjudication was contemplated by the stakeholders at the time the relevant arbitration clause was

5 Parties lacking an adequate *remedy* at law have a right to seek specific performance. It is generally held in the context of a judicial proceeding in the US that specific performance is largely within the sound discretion of a trial court. *See, e.g., Landau v. St. Louis Public Service Co.*, 364 Mo. 1134, 273 S.W. 2d 255, 259 (Mo. 1954). However, this discretion is actually very restricted; and it has been held that the court's equitable rules have been met and the contract is fair and plain as "specific performance goes as a matter of right." *Miller v. Coffeen*, 365 Mo. 204, 280 S.W.2d 100, 102 (Mo. 1955) quoting *Berberet v. Myers*, 240 Mo. 58, 77, 144 S.W. 824, 830 (mo. 1912) (emphasis omitted).

(i) presumably negotiated[6] and (ii) drafted in its final iteration. This assertion further advances that a "settlement" by definition is a "compromise" that deprives the nonbreaching party of the right to be made whole based upon economic models of *risk assessment* and costs that have nothing to do with the actual equities underlying the particular dispute at issue.

There is no empirical evidence from which to infer or to conclude that contracting parties consider economic settlement models as part of a bargaining process or in the allocation of rights and obligations in a contract. The closest that contracting parties get to any such consideration, and it is still far from any serious economic modeling, would be the inclusion of mediation provisions in an arbitral clause or in a self-standing provision. This much is insufficient to sustain the assertion that parties to a contract contemplate the likelihood of being made less than whole in the event of a breach.

The question of whether a merits-based adjudication is preferable to a settlement shall pervade this writing. It will be looming in an invisible and silent background: but ever present.

The assumption upon which this journey, however, is based is that settlements are more efficient, and therefore less expensive to the stakeholders than a merits-based adjudication that takes place approximately three years *after* a *Request for Arbitration* is filed, and yielding an "all-or-nothing" result at the end of this timeframe. Moreover, it is further asserted that notwithstanding the efficiencies endemic to the absence of second instance plenary review,[7] the proliferation of New York Convention stakeholders,[8] and the narrow grounds for setting aside an award

6 I say "presumably" for the now extremely obvious reason that arbitration clauses are still referred to as "midnight clauses." Unsophisticated transactional lawyers somehow have concluded that arbitration clauses are boilerplate in nature and not worthy of consideration as a genuinely negotiable item of true consequence.

7 Article III of the United Nations Convention on the Recognition and Enforcement of Foreign Arbitral Awards (New York, June 10, 1958) (New York Convention), reads:

> Each Contracting State shall recognize arbitral awards as binding and enforce them in accordance with the rules of procedure, of the territory where the award is relied upon, under the conditions laid down in the following articles. There shall not be imposed substantially more onerous conditions or higher fees or charges on the recognition or enforcement of arbitral awards to which this Convention applies than are imposed on the recognition or enforcement of domestic arbitral awards.

Article III makes clear that awards are final and, therefore, not subject to review on appeal. *See, e.g.*, *Olin Holdings Ltd. v. State of Libya*, 73 F. 4th 92, 104 (2nd Cir. 2003) holding,

> [i]n sum, we conclude that a binding agreement to arbitrate was formed between the parties, when Olin submitted its request for arbitration to the ICC. Because Libya's jurisdictional arguments implicate Olin's right to arbitrate under a binding arbitration agreement, not the existence or formation of the agreement in the first place, the district court was not required to independently review the tribunal's decision on jurisdiction.

8 As of the time of this writing (September 2024), there are 172 state parties to the New York Convention. The UN currently has 193 Member States. Hence, 89 percent of all Member States recognized by the UN are signatories to the New York Convention.

set forth in modern national arbitration laws,[9] at the conclusion of a final hearing and subsequent issuance of an award,[10] the execution phase merely commences.

Here as well, time and resources will be consumed without necessarily a promise that the award shall be satisfied. Risk also is present, and often dominant, in the recognition and enforcement phase. Please bear in mind that we are not factoring into the time and resources equation complexities and problems that inevitably would be compounded and multiplied by counterclaims and multiparty arbitrations.[11] Such considerations also are present at the recognition and enforcement stage.

1.1.1 *ICA Lacks a Settlement Culture*

Accepting the premise that settlements are more efficient than merits-adjudication, it necessarily follows that ICA has failed to keep and redeem its promise to be an efficient cross-border dispute resolution methodology. This difficulty is made worse because conciliation and mediation only constitute a perfunctory role in the actual culture of ICA, notwithstanding parallel Mediation Rules offered by many of the leading arbitral institutes,[12] and fairly recent guides on facilitating settlement in international arbitration published as recently as July 2023.

Indeed, the International Court of Arbitration of the International Chamber of Commerce (ICC), more specifically the ICC's Commission on Arbitration and

[9] Article 34(2)(a)(b) of the UNCITRAL Model Law, which has in whole or in large measure been adopted by the majority of Member States sets forth the following eight grounds for setting aside an award:

> (2) An arbitral award may be set aside by the court specified in article 6 only if: (a) the party making the application furnishes proof that: (i) a party to the arbitration agreement referred to in article 7 was under some incapacity; or the said agreement is not valid under the law to which the parties have subjected it or, failing any indication thereon, under the law of this State; or (ii) the party making the application was not given proper notice of the appointment of an arbitrator or of the arbitral proceedings or was otherwise unable to present his case; or (iii) the award deals with a dispute not contemplated by or not falling within the terms of the submission to arbitration, or contains decisions on matters beyond the scope of the submission to arbitration, provided that, if the decisions on matters submitted to arbitration can be separated from those not so submitted, only that part of the award which contains decisions on matters not submitted to arbitration may be set aside; or (iv) the composition of the arbitral tribunal or the arbitral procedure was not in accordance with the agreement of the parties, unless such agreement was in conflict with a provision of this Law from which the parties cannot derogate, or, failing such agreement, was not in accordance with this Law; or (b) the court finds that: (i) the subject-matter of the dispute is not capable of settlement by arbitration under the law of this State; or (ii) the award is in conflict with the public policy of this State.

[10] The average international commercial arbitration has a two-year duration.

[11] ICA proceedings are more complex than at any time in its modern history, mostly as a result of economic globalization *and* the success of the New York Convention. It is no surprise that the complexity of these disputes has led to a proliferation of claims and counterclaims, which have now replaced the "traditional" embryonic kinds of simple contractual disputes that characterized ICA's advent.

[12] Jus Mundi, "ICC Facilitating Settlement in International Arbitration" (2023), 4, https://shorturl.at/1JFgt (last accessed November 2023).

Alternative Dispute Resolution (ADR) in July 2023, launched guides on *Effective Conflict Management* and *Facilitating Settlement in International Arbitration*. The publication on Facilitating Settlement in International Arbitration observes that the historical role of arbitrators "in most jurisdictions has been that the role of the Arbitral Tribunal is to decide the case in an enforceable award."

It adds that in keeping with this understanding of arbitrator objectives,

> the parties remain free to negotiate and to settle their dispute should they wish to do so, but that was not something the Arbitral Tribunal should seek to encourage, facilitate, or, least of all, become directly involved with. This view was motivated by concerns that taking on such a role would negatively impact the Tribunal's neutrality vis-à-vis the merits of the dispute or the party's perception of it.[13]

The ICC's Commission on Arbitration and ADR further observed in the *Introduction* of the *Facilitating Settlement in in International Arbitration* guidelines that "[t]he debate has now moved from whether arbitrators (and arbitral institutions) should take steps to facilitate settlement, to how that should be done."[14] This publication, of course, is a modest step in the right direction. In fact, the publication itself includes the disclaimer that the views contained "should not be thought to represent views and recommendations of the ICC International Court of Arbitration or the ICC International Centre for ADR, nor are they in any way binding on either body."[15]

Addressing the question of settlement in ICA, however, will require far more than just educating arbitrators in most jurisdictions on helpful settlement facilitation techniques. Structural procedural amendments, together with the development of a new arbitral culture, shall be necessary. The task is daunting.

This analysis is based on a second proposition that is accepted as true for purposes of this writing. It may seem as heretical as the principle that settlements are more favorable to arbitral parties than merits adjudication. The inevitable question

[13] London Court of International Arbitration (LCIA) Mediation Rules (2020); German Arbitration Institute (DIS) Mediation Rules (2010); and the International Centre for Dispute Resolution (ICDR), International Dispute Resolution Procedures (including Mediation and Arbitration, 2014).

[14] ICC, *Facilitating Settlement in International Arbitration*, at p. 4, 3 July 2023.

[15] *Id.* (first para.). In addition, the report further tempers the workings of its content, promoting settlement ICA as follows:

> 68. This Report describes techniques that are known to be effective in facilitating settlement in arbitration proceedings. Not all of these techniques will be appropriate for every case or for all parties, counsel or arbitrators. A careful selection of the most appropriate technique should be made, considering all of the circumstances, including the skills and experience of the arbitrators in implementing each technique.
>
> 69. The Report reflects current thinking and practice. It is anticipated that new approaches and practices will continue to develop in the coming years, just as we have seen the development over the past 10–15 years (as described in paras. 1–11 above). It is therefore hoped that this will be a living report, which will be updated in the future to provide further assistance on settlement facilitation to all involved in the arbitration process.

arises. Is there a principal reason why ICA cases do not settle with greater regularity? Perhaps more precisely stated, why is it that in some jurisdictions (most notably the US) an overwhelming percentage of all civil judicial cases settle, while in ICA the diametrically opposite proposition holds true?

The vast majority of ICA proceedings do not settle. Certainly, even generally speaking, there are multiple legitimate reasons why this is the case. Arbitrators are not trained to encourage settlement. And only recently in the 2021 ICC Arbitration Rules was the wording of Appendix IV changed from merely *informing* parties that they were free to settle their disputes, to arbitrators who were empowered to "encourage the parties to consider settlement."[16] And the culture of arbitration generally does not emphasize settlement in its foundational Arbitration Rules. There is no settlement culture in ICA.

Indeed, in almost all of the major institutional arbitration rules, the term "settlement" does not appear at all, or is hardly even referenced. In ICA, mediation is not compulsory. And any settlement effort using the best placed settlement facilitator, the arbitral tribunal itself, necessarily would have to navigate considerable ethical challenges, which certainly are manageable but also quite significant. Almost like walking around raindrops.

In this writing it is assumed that generally a settlement of a dispute is not possible, and certainly not likely, unless and until the stakeholders have been able to: (i) identify, (ii) quantify materially, and (iii) communicate comprehensively their respective risk in proceeding to a final hearing. ICA cases do not settle largely because *risk assessment* either is not possible, or mostly is not viable (if at all) until a procedural juncture is reached when it is simply too late to settle. Why is this the case?

A second assumption underlying this writing is that the analysis presented here does not pertain to a strategic model negotiation process. Such an approach does not contemplate the relative symmetries or asymmetries between the parties in connection with specific norms and the application of law to facts. This strategic model represents a "relatively norm-free process centered on the transmutation of underlying bargaining strength into an agreement by the exercise of power, horse-trading, threat and bluff."[17]

[16] ICC Arbitration Rules, Appendix IV Case Management Techniques, (h)(i) reads:
h) Settlement of disputes:

(i) encouraging the parties to consider settlement of all or part of the dispute either by negotiation or through any form of amicable dispute resolution methods such as, for example, mediation under the ICC Mediation Rules;
(ii) where agreed between the parties and the arbitral tribunal, the arbitral tribunal may take steps to facilitate settlement of the dispute, provided that every effort is made to ensure that any subsequent award is enforceable at law.

[17] Melvin Aron Eisenberg, "Private Ordering through Negotiation: Dispute-Settlement and Rulemaking," 89 *Harv. L. Rev.* 637, 638–639 (February 1976).

Instead, the framework assumed is a law or norm-centered paradigm that is adjudication-centric. Meaning that risk analysis and negotiation are undertaken in the context of a specific understanding of very particular applicable rules and substantive law, together with an understanding of and access to most relevant and material evidence.

These two assumptions are central to the thesis of *optimal efficiency* pursuant to timely and bilateral risk assessment.[18]

The ICA evidence taking, evidence presentation framework, and self-disclosure rules, in addition to omitting compulsory mediation early or throughout the process at strategic junctures, is simply plagued with too many uncertainties. These "uncertainties" lead to a lack of process transparency. In turn, a paucity of process transparency diminishes the parties' negotiating entitlements or bargaining arsenal. What is not known cannot be used as a basis to lead a counter-party to identify commercial risk. Similarly, it cannot give rise to the identification of legal norms that may or may not influence the proceeding's outcome.

As will be more fully discussed, the arbitration rules of *all* major arbitral institutes dedicate all but a few paragraphs (generously assessed) to *evidence taking, self-disclosure*, and *presenting*. The *de facto* effect is to minimize ICA's foundational principle of *party-autonomy* in favor of *arbitrator discretion*. This latter principle (*arbitrator discretion*), nonetheless, is not a central tenet that arbitration stakeholders view as paramount, notwithstanding that the principle of *arbitrator discretion* is often cloaked with the correct and also euphemistic mantle of "the inherent powers of arbitrators."

This term (inherent powers), however, does not wrest from *arbitrator discretion inherent uncertainty* that translates into *unquantifiable* risk and, therefore, lack of predictive value. Likewise, the term "inherent powers of arbitrators" does little to reconcile the need to maximize "*party-autonomy*," a principle that is the fulcrum of ICA's better workings, or to maximize efficiency. *Arbitrator discretion is inversely proportional to* ***party-autonomy***. It equally detracts from process predictive value (see Sections 1.2.2 and 3.2).

The scant treatment of evidence taking and presenting in the rules of all major arbitral institutes is not cured by the International Bar Association Rules (IBA Rules on the Taking of Evidence in International Arbitration) or the Prague Rules (Rules on the Efficient Conduct of Proceedings in International Arbitration).

The interplay between efficiency, *party-autonomy*, *arbitrator discretion*, and existing institutional rules of evidence, as well as the IBA Rules, will have to be closely analyzed within the framework of these very Rules in order to determine whether ICA evidentiary Rules can be framed to provide for *risk assessment* that is conducive to settlement. Can the evidentiary Rules that govern evidence *taking*, *self-disclosure*, and *presenting* in ICA be so framed, (i) so as to preserve the nature of ICA, (ii) while maximizing efficiency, and (iii) minimizing the likelihood of a zero-sum-game (a scenario where one party invariably loses)? Have we really understood efficiency within the rubric of ICA (Section 1.1)?

18 *Id.*

It will be suggested that the legacy understanding of *efficiency* in ICA only has been associated with what is here termed "*process efficiency.*" And for this reason, in large measure, the efficiencies of settlement have mostly been undermined, if not altogether ignored.

1.1.2 *ICA's Promise to Be Efficient and* Optimal Efficiency: *Settlement*

What, then, is the promise to be efficient? Is it possible to discern why settlement has been de-emphasized, or altogether ignored? What is the historicity of efficiency, sometimes expressed as a form of "expeditious streamlining," within the context of ICA? It will be asserted that efficiency in ICA has been limited to "*process efficiency* only." This term ("*process efficiency*") is used to describe efficiency that is only limited or circumscribed to yielding a *binding* and enforceable award.

Some, but not all, of these questions have answers. It is, however, demonstrable that the promise of efficiency in ICA has many faces. None of them, however, concern *settlement*. They all pertain to *process*. The different faces of efficiency in ICA necessarily have to be referenced, even if ever so fleetingly, if we are to understand the various practical and structural challenges that settlement presents to the efficiency equation.

The *Oxford English Dictionary*'s (*OED*) definition of the word "*efficiency*" is connected to "*efficient*," the adjective derives from the Latin *efficientem*, which has the nominative *efficiēns*, a participle of *efficere*, making its way in 1398 to Old French, meaning "making."

The *OED* captures this etymology with a first entry defining *efficient* as "[m]aking, causing; that makes a thing what it is." The second entry under *efficient* de-emphasizes causal connection, while still acknowledging it, but underscores lack of waste. It defines efficiency as "effective," and "producing the desired result with the minimum wasted effort; (of a person) capable, competent; **PHYSICS** characterized by high (or specified) efficiency."

It is, however, the third entry in the *OED* for "efficiency," under "**PHYSICS**" that is most helpful: "**a** [t]he work done by a force in operating a machine; the total energy expended by a machine. **b** [t]he ratio of useful work performed by a device or system to the total energy input."

The appropriate definition must be one that captures *ratios* and *proportions*. The relationship between currency expended as part of the process of arbitral adjudication in relation to the amount in controversy (i.e., damages sought) is absolutely paramount. Therefore, the approach must be one that seeks to embrace and to quantify currency expended as a condition precedent to a process that must culminate with an *enforceable* arbitral award.[19]

[19] At this point, only *process efficiency* is being discussed, thus the reference to an enforceable award. *Process efficiency*, however, can only serve as a point of departure, as shall be illustrated.

More, however, is necessary. A proportion, a relationship between ratios, would be compelled. Any truly serious attempt to explore efficiency in ICA must add to the cost of arbitration in relation to the amount in controversy, the entire duration of the process together with the quantification of business interruption (i.e., the human hours expended directly or indirectly as part of the arbitration process).

Efficiency models also must account for proportionality, as we shall see, (i) in the taking of evidence and (ii) presentation of evidence. The entire arbitration process, and then each procedural phase, should be susceptible to efficiency accountability if in fact arbitration is to redeem its promise.

To be sure, even a proportionality-based definition of efficiency in the context of arbitration shall require further consideration and refinement of factors such as,

(i) the complexity of legal and factual issues,
(ii) the particular kind and extent of technical expert testimony required,
(iii) the factual document intensity of the case,
(iv) the number and location of *expert* and *fact witnesses*,
(v) the configuration of evidence taking,
(vi) the presence or absence of counterclaims,
(vii) the amenability of partial or complete summary disposition,
(viii) the practicality of mediation,
(ix) the parties' resources in both relative and absolute terms,
(x) the nature of the parties, that is, juridic entities or natural persons, and
(xi) the number of parties.

These factors hardly are exhaustive.

The particular nature of the dispute as contextualized by the facts unique to the controversy also must be considered. Arbitrators are being efficient in the context of an actual, and always idiosyncratic controversies. Arbitral panels are not charged with being efficient in the abstract. Efficiency always must be contextualized. Significantly, the "quality" of the outcome, beyond just the inevitable element of participants' satisfaction and dissatisfaction, is ignored. Is the award efficient if it leaves both, prevailing and non-prevailing parties, wanting? Does the award necessarily invite further refinement, or even set aside. Certainly the rigors of efficiency must extend to such considerations.

An understanding of efficiency in the context of ICA that does not consider these basic elements together with a proportionality approach that accounts for (i) resources expended, (ii) in furtherance of an objective, (iii) over time, would be meritless. In fact, one commentator went so far as quite rightfully to observe that the *OED*'s definition of efficiency as "the state or quality of being efficient," as the historical meaning of the word, would lead to the absurd result that

> any arbitration that results in an award would be considered an efficient arbitration. However, perhaps this historical definition does not work well with a modern

business-like approach that many parties expect from arbitration. It is not merely a matter of getting an outcome but also of getting an outcome in a process which itself appears and perhaps also is efficient.[20]

A comprehensive and rigorous definition of efficiency applied to ICA more often than not would demonstrate that settlement in the majority of cases most often comports with a higher efficiency rating than an all-or-nothing (zero-sum-game) merits adjudication. It is unlikely that a merits-based ICA adjudication yielding an award approximately twenty-four to thirty-six months after the filing of a *Request for Arbitration* can lead to an efficient result. Such particularly would be so where the award is challenged and execution on an award reduced to a judicial judgment is required.

1.1.3 *The Emergence of* Process Efficiency *in ICA: A Necessary but Stunting Aspiration*

Efficiency in arbitration historically has been *promised* and *assumed*, but never *defined*. Both its definition and practical application remain elusory, notwithstanding its importance as a defining pillar of ICA, together with *party-autonomy*, and predictive value arising from (i) the enforceability of awards, (ii) the procedural certainty of the process.

It is virtually impossible to identify *when* efficiency surfaced as a principal polestar of ICA. In the US, by way of illustration, the national arbitration law, the Federal Arbitration Act (FAA) (9 U.S.C. §§ 1–307) was first enacted on February 12, 1925, in its initial iteration (43 Stat. 883). Its legislative objective principally was to overcome four badges and vestiges of conceptual prejudice that judicial hostility ascribed to arbitration:

(i) the ousting of jurisdiction from courts of otherwise competent jurisdiction;
(ii) the view that an arbitration proceeding requires judicial supervision;
(iii) the conviction that arbitration was not well-suited for administering complex domestic or international cases; and
(iv) the idea that arbitration is not the appropriate dispute resolution methodology to administer certain types of *statutory claims* providing defendants with rights in situations where they lacked equal bargaining fiat.[21]

Addressing these badges of judicial prejudice unquestionably constituted the FAA's principal objective.[22]

20 Loukas Mistelis, "Efficiency – What Else? Efficiency as the emerging defining value of international arbitration: between systems theories and party autonomy," Queen Mary University of London, *School of Law Legal Studies Research Paper*, No. 313/2019, pp. 4–5.

21 Federal Arbitration Act (FAA) (9 U.S.C. §§ 1–307).

22 *Id.*

Even though these four grounds for "explaining" judicial aversion to arbitration were much vaunted both in England and the US, a deeper analysis of the history of arbitration in England and the US will help to contextualize the totality of the picture with respect to the deep judicial recalcitrance pervading this issue.

1.2 A THUMBNAIL SKETCH OF THE HISTORY OF ARBITRATION IN ENGLAND AND THE US

The "ouster of jurisdiction" argument has a hollow ring to it. Such principle, by way of example, would render it illegal and against public policy for this very same reason (ouster of jurisdiction) to enforceable waivers in the form of known and bargained for intentional relinquishments of known rights. In this same vein, releases of liability generally, but certainly in the form of reciprocal obligations imposed on parties to a judicial settlement, also would seem to fail based upon the identical ground. Indeed, in *United States Asphalt R. Co. v. Trinidad Lake P. Co.*,[23] Judge Jough wisely stated that "the legal mind must assign some reason in order to decide anything with spiritual quiet[.]" Significantly, he stated as much in the context of listing the "causes advanced for refusing to compel men to abide by their arbitration contracts," which the court saw as susceptible to being subdivided into five pithy categories.[24] There is sufficient evidence from which it can be reasonably inferred that ousting the jurisdiction of courts may be more of a pretext than an actual cause.

It certainly is clear that British courts, as would their US counterparts prior to the enactment of the FAA in 1925, recognized arbitration agreements to determine damages and factual questions, so long as liability and legal issues unencumbered with factual questions were left to the province of the judiciary. Breach of executory arbitration agreements, however, were largely non-actionable for a long period of time commencing in the latter part of the seventeenth century.[25]

[23] *United States Asphalt R. Co. v. Trinidad Lake P. Co.*, 222 F. 1006, 1008 (S.D.N.Y. 1915).

[24] The Court stated that "arbitration contracts may apparently be subdivided" into five categories. The contexts suggest none of such categories, or all of them combined, in fact justify the refusal to compel signatories to arbitration clauses to honor such agreements:

(a) The contract is in its nature revocable.
(b) Such contracts are against public policy.
(c) The covenant to refer is but collateral to the main contract, and may be disregarded, leaving the contract keeper to his action for damages for breach of such collateral covenant.
(d) Any contract tending to wholly oust the courts of jurisdiction violates the spirit of the laws creating the courts, in that it is not competent for private persons either to increase or diminish the statutory judicial power.
(e) Arbitration may be a condition precedent to suit, and as such valid, if it does not prevent legal action, or seek to determine out of court the general question of liability. *Id.*

[25] While it is clear from Thucydides' *History of the Peloponnesian Wars* that the Greek city-states relied on nonjudicial dispute resolution mechanisms, much like ICA's counterpart investor–state dispute settlement (ISDS) treaty-based arbitration, ironically we have less certainty regarding the early English

Prior to the enactment of the Statute of Fines and Penalties enacted in 1687,[26] the breach of an executory arbitration agreement was enforceable by posting a penal bond (purportedly provided for purposes of enforcement of the agreement to arbitrate).

A breach of the bond's contingent terms would result of course in a judicial judgment in the amount of the penalty. This rather clever and practical approach had real teeth. Indeed, in the somewhat renown *Vynior's Case*,[27] Coke *in dicta* labored long and hard to square the circle by arguing that the doctrine of revocability would provide a basis for wresting from an arbitrator the authority to act as such, "[b]ut the party cannot revoke his bond or deed of submission [citations omitted] but will be

history of enforcement of executory arbitration agreements. In addition to being able to trace the roots, and therefore the influence, of international arbitration to as early as 431 BC (the Peloponnesian War), and subsequently to Roman law, itself profoundly influenced by Greek law, there is considerable scholarship also pointing to the influence of Ecclesiastical law and its use of arbitration as possibly influencing early English history on the subject.

See Paul L. Sayre, "Development of Commercial Arbitration Law," 37 *Yale L. J.* 595, 597 (1928):

> It seems likely that arbitration became part of the common law through the work of the Ecclesiastical courts, since we find authority for arbitration from the seventeenth century in canon law, and since we know that, in Bracton's time especially, the canon law governed much of the litigation that is now handled by our regular courts. There was a partially developed system of arbitration in Roman law, both during the Classical period and under Justinian. There is apparently no germ of arbitration in Anglo-Saxon law, and the idea of arbitration is not one which the King's courts would favorably entertain at the time we find it making its appearance. Perhaps the main purposes of the King's justice were political and financial, in consolidating and unifying the kingdom and in bringing fees into the royal treasury according to Ashe's Tables, the earliest case involving arbitration is Y.B. 21 Ed. III, f. 15.

Sayre's analysis is deficient in that he totally omits how Greek law influenced Roman law and thereby canon law incorporated principles sufficiently distinct so as to be accurately and credibly identified as arbitration.

For the sake of completeness, Thucydides' first reference to arbitration reads, citing to an original source:

> XXXIV –"But if they say that it is not right for you to receive their colonists, let them know that while every colony honours the mother-city so long as it is well treated, yet that if wronged it becomes alienated; for colonists are not sent out to be slaves to those who are left behind, but to be their equals. And that they were in the wrong is manifest; for when challenged to arbitrate the case of Epidamnus they preferred to prosecute their charges by war rather than by equity." (Bk. I, XXXIII.2–XXXIV.3)

See also, Sabra A. Jones, "Historical Development of Commercial Arbitration in the United States," 21 *Minn. L. Rev.* 240, 243–244 (1928); Harry Baum & Leon Pressman, "The Enforcement of Commercial Arbitration," 8 *N.Y.U.L.Q. Rev.* 238, 239–249 (1930); *Red Cross Line v. Atlantic Fruit Co.*, 1924, 264 U.S. 109, 121, 44 S. Ct. 274, 68 L. Ed. 582 (1924); Julius Henry Cohen, *Commercial Arbitration and the Law* (Hardpress Publishing 1918); Aristotle, *Rhetoric*, Bk. 1, Ch. 13, 1374b; Sir Paul Vinogradoff, 2 *Historical Jurisprudence* 50, 146 (1922); Sir Paul Vinogradoff, "Aristotle and Legal Redress," 8 *Col. L. Rev.* No. 7 548–560 (Nov. 1908); W. W. Buckland, *A Text-Book of Roman Law from Augustus to Justinian* 527–528 (Cambridge University Press 1921); Max Radin, *Handbook of Roman Law* 308 (West Publishing Company 1927).

26 Statute of Fines and Penalties (8 & 9 Wm. 3rd c. 11, s. 8) (1687).

27 Vynior's Case, 8 Coke Rep. 81 b (1609).

liable to be sued upon it."[28] He further adds that "where a judge's order contained not only the submission of the parties, but directed that either party should, under certain circumstances, pay to the other such costs as the court should think reasonable and just; it was held that such order might be made a rule of court after a revocation, in order to enable the court to dispose of the question of costs."[29]

This not-too-circuitous way of skinning the cat was very much dealt with somewhat directly seventy-nine years following Coke's pronouncement when the Statute of Fines and Penalties was enacted in 1687. It was then held that the doctrine of irrevocability of course applied, but the damages for withdrawing the submission of authority to arbitrate would be limited to the actual damages suffered, which in the last quarter of the seventeenth century would be limited only to nominal damages.[30]

The effect that Statute of Fines and Penalties had on executory arbitration agreements hardly escaped notice. Hence, perhaps not too surprisingly, eleven years later in 1698, Parliament enacted a statute (9 Wm. III c. [1698]) intended to address this concern.[31] At this point, an ordinary executory arbitration agreement was practically unenforceable. First, it was held not to constitute a legal basis of a plea in bar in, or a stay of, an action on the original cause of action.[32] Second, an executory arbitration agreement was not specifically enforceable in equity.[33] The rulings were no different in admiralty proceedings.[34]

28 *Id.*

29 *Id., citing to Aston v. George,* 2 Barn, and Aid. 395. S.C. 1 Chitty, 200.

30 *See Kulukundis Shipping Co. v. Amtorg Trading Corp.,* 126 F.2d 978, 982 (2nd Cir. 1942), n. 7, *citing to* 9 C.J. pp. 128, 129; 11 C.J.S. Bonds, § 130; William Holdsworth, *A History of English Law* 519–520 (Methuen 1938).

31 The statute provided that if an arbitration agreement prescribed that it could be made "a rule of law" (i.e., a court order, "in which event it became irrevocable, and one who revoked it would be subject to punishment for contempt of court; but the submission was revocable until such a rule of court had been obtained. This statute, limited in scope, was narrowly construed and was of little help."). *Kulukundis Shipping Co. v. Amtorg Trading Corp.,* at n. 8, *citing to* Sayre, "Development of Commercial Arbitration Law," 606; Annotation, 47 L. R. A., N. S. 436; Zechariah Chafee (Jr.), Sidney Post Simpson, 1 *Cases on Equity, Jurisdiction and Specific Performance* 552–553 (1934).

In 1833, a statute (3 & 4 Wm. IV c. 42) was passed that was intended to reinforce the 1680 statute, but it still left a submission revocable until an action was brought in connection with an arbitration proceeding.

An Act of 1854 (17 & 19 Vict. c. 125) provided that any arbitration agreement could be made the basis of a stay and irrevocable except by leave of court, granted in the exercise of the court's discretion.

The Arbitration Act of 1899 (52 & 53 Vict. c. 49) provided that any such agreement, unless contrary intention is expressed therein, shall be irrevocable, except by leave of court, and shall have the same effect as if it had been made an order of court; it provided adequate court review of questions of law raised in the arbitration hearing. *See* citation in *Kulukundis Shipping Co. v. Amtorg Trading Corp.* of Sayre, "Development of Commercial Arbitration Law," 606–607; 47 L. R. A. N. S., 436 ff; and of Zechariah Chaffee, Jr. & Sidney Simpson, *Cases on Equity* (Published by the Editors 1934) 1942 A. M. C. 364, *id.*

32 *Id.* n. 8a *citing to* 1 Chaffee & Simpson, *Cases on Equity,* 520ff; *Tobey v. County of Bristol,* 23 Fed.Cas. p. 1313, No. 14,065, 3 Story 800; 2 Story, Equity Jurisprudence, Section 670.

33 *Kulukundis Shipping Co. v. Amtorg Trading Corp.,* 126 F.2d 978, 982 (2nd Cir. 1942).

34 *Id.*

An agreement to arbitrate hence occupied an odd legal space. It seemed to hover in abeyance flanked by releases and covenants not to sue on one end, and the domain of the illegal on the other. The elite Second Circuit Court of Appeals panel comprised by no other than Learned Hand, Harrie Bringham Chase, and Jerome Frank described as "a clear instance of what Holmes called a 'right' to break a contract and to substitute payment of damages for non-performance; was, in this type of case, the damages were only nominal, that 'right' was indeed meaningful."[35]

As additional efforts aimed at justifying what still remained as substantively inexplicable judicial hostility to executory arbitration agreements, notwithstanding the surface arguments asserted in furtherance of this visceral rejection of arbitration, it became popular to assert that executory arbitrations simply could not take place absent court supervision. The problem was that such a proposition was not perceived as the appropriate subject matter of the common law, that is to say, judge-made-rules. Legislation setting forth court supervision of arbitral proceedings was identified as a necessary predicate to the perfect workings of executory arbitration agreements.[36]

Of course, the lack of judicial supervision over arbitration also does not completely sound like a deep and comprehensive cause for the judicial aversion. It does not, for example, explain why courts were willing to enforce arbitral awards, whether in the form of awards passing only on factual or damages questions, or actually awards that settled the liability of the parties. The basic lack of symmetry between the argument, namely the need for judicial supervision, and the uniform enforcement presents intriguing and perhaps conceptually irreconcilable propositions.

Instead of protecting parties to arbitrations, the history of English arbitrations during this time (sixteenth and seventeenth centuries) reflects a commitment to interpret as narrowly and as restrictively as possible statutory frameworks that purported to give effect to executory arbitrations.[37]

A more banal but deeply human account of the actual reason explaining judicial hostility toward arbitration was articulated by Lord Campbell, who explained:

> The doctrine had its origin in the interests of the judges. There was no disguising the fact that, as formerly, the emoluments of the judges depended mainly, or almost entirely, upon fees, and as they had no fixed salaries, there was great competition to get as much as possible of litigation into Westminster Hall for the division of the spoil … And they had great jealously of arbitration whereby Westminster Hall was

[35] *Kulukundis Shipping Co.*, at 983.

[36] *Id.* 983 n. 11 *citing to* Sayre, "Development of Commercial Arbitration Law"; Peterson, J., dissenting in *Park Const. Co. v. Independent School Dist.*, 209 Minn. 182, 296 N.W. 475, 478ff, 135 A.L.R. 59 (1941). "Sayre argues that if the courts had really been unfriendly to arbitrations they would not have enforced arbitrators' awards. The real truth, however, seems to be that they were unfriendly but did not carry out their hostility to its logical conclusion." *Id.* at 983, n. 11.

[37] *See* n. 37 in this chapter, *citing to* (i) statute (3 & 4 Wm. IV c. 42) (1680), (ii) Act of 1854 (17 & 19 Vict. c. 125), and (iii) the Arbitration Act of 1889 (52 & 53 Vict. c. 49).

robbed of those cases which came not into Kings Bench, nor the Common Pleas, nor the exchequer. Therefore they said that the courts ought not to be ousted of their jurisdiction, and that it was contrary to the policy of the law to do so. That really grew up only subsequently to the time of Lord Coke, and a saying of his was the foundation of the doctrine.[38]

It is to be expected that whenever a truth of this ilk is made public rarely is the reaction a tempered one. Shedding light on profit motive as the real doctrinal underpinning of the hostility that English judicial courts displayed toward arbitration awoke the ire of those who were most likely to suffer from the indignity of being exposed as asserting a conceptual (albeit a very superficial one) pretext to mask plain and coarse self-interest.[39] Justice Peterson's apology in support of judicial acceptance of arbitration represents a minority view. And it is a very novel and particular reading of history, and more importantly, of the actual jurisprudence.

I side with Learned Hand, Harrie Bringham Chase, and Jerome Frank in noting that: "[p]erhaps the true explanation is the hypnotic power of the phrase, 'oust the jurisdiction' gives a bad dogma a good name and its bite may become as bad as its bark."[40]

In the nineteenth century, the ruling of US courts reflected the inherited English aversion to arbitration and primarily relied on the "ouster" argument that remained rife with untested assumptions. The Supreme Court's pronouncement in *Hamilton v. Liverpool*[41] is emblematic of the incorporation of the English precedent into US

38 *Scott v. Avery*, 25 L.J. Ex. 308, 313; the report of his remarks in 5 H.C.L. 811 is more meager, according to *Kulukundis Shipping Co.*, at 983–984, n. 14.

39 Justice Peterson of the Minnesota Supreme Court, registering his dissent in *Park Const. Cov. v. Independent School Dist.*, 209 Minn. 182, 204, 296 N.W. 475 (1941), attacks the pecuniary self-interest and jealously grounds with verve. He writes:

> Lord Campbell's assertion appears to be groundless. He does not substantiate his statement with any evidence or citation. The available evidence is against him. In 1648, which was just 40 years after the decision in *Vynior's Case*, and over 200 years before the decision in *Scott v. Avery*, 5 H. L. 811, March stated in his treatise on Slander and Arbitraments, p. 262, that the law seemed favorable to arbitration. Referring to the act of 1698, Blackstone said that the legislature encouraged arbitration because of "the great use of these peaceable and domestic tribunals." (2 Blackstone, Bk. 3, pp. 15–17)

The enforcement by common-law judges of contracts to arbitrate in the same manner as other contracts were enforced and of bonds given to secure performance of such contracts is a complete refutation of Lord Campbell's claim of judicial jealousy. *Vynior's Case* and the authorities which it cites illustrate the utter groundlessness of his assertion. If the courts wanted to put an end to agreements to arbitrate and thus terminate arbitration, the result could have been accomplished by simply declaring such contracts illegal as against public policy. Quite to the contrary, the courts recognized the validity of contracts to arbitrate and enforced bonds given to secure their performance. The remedy on the bond of recovery of the full face amount effectually enforced the agreement to arbitrate. The courts so far from showing hostility to arbitration did everything permissible under the then existing law to make it effective [citation omitted].

40 Kulukundis *Shipping Co.*, at 984.

41 *Hamilton v. Liverpool, London & Globe Insurance*, 136 U.S. 242, 10 S. Ct. 945, 34 L. Ed. 419, 1890 U.S. LEXIS 2210 (1890).

jurisprudence concerning judicial aversion to arbitration as a self-standing dispute resolution methodology in *pari materia* with judicial tribunals.[42] The contemporary authority reflects that only nominal damages would be recoverable in cases involving executory arbitration agreements.[43]

Although in the early twentieth century the Supreme Court of the United States *in dicta* fleetingly alluded to a possible new horizon that would construe arbitration agreements in a more favorable light with greater affinity with judicial proceeding as to *standing* and *legitimacy*, the issue was not ripe in those few extraordinary cases.[44]

The Supreme Court, however, in *Marine Transit Corp. v. Dreyfus*,[45] observed that, at least theoretically, the FAA was crafted with the intent to alter the prevailing

[42] *Id.*

[43] *See Williston on Contracts*, 6 Contracts (rev. ed. 1938) Section 1927A (p. 5392, n. 9); *Munson v. Straits of Dover S.S. Co.*, 102 F. 926 (2nd Cir. 1900) *but cf. McCullough v. Clinch-Mitchell Const. Co.*, 71 F. 2d 17 (8th Cir. 1934); Annotation, 47 L.R.A., N.S., 409, 410, as cited in *Kulukundis Shipping Co.*, at 983, n. 20.

[44] In *The Atlanten*, 252 US 313, 315 (1920) there are sparks of a promised change on the question of the enforcement of an executory arbitral agreement. Interestingly, that case has a remarkable cast of judicial characters. At the trial court level (federal district court), none other than Judge Learned Hand presided and found for plaintiff, respondent on appeal, against a Swedish corporation owner of the steam ship *Alanten*, for breach of a charter party executed in Denmark. The Circuit Court of Appeals, Judge Hough speaking for the Court affirmed the district court's finding that where the owner of the vessel repudiated the contract containing an arbitration clause, such agreement to arbitrate did not apply because the repudiation of the charter party (presumably on *force majeure*) did not constitute a breach of the underlying contractual obligation with respect to which, so both the district and appellate courts concluded, did not trigger the application of the arbitration clause. It did, however, cause a liquidated damages clause to apply. Pursuant to this clause liquidated damages would be limited to the estimated amount of the chartered freight.

On appeal, the star-studded proceeding featured Justice Holmes writing for the Supreme Court. The Supreme Court held that the ship owner's refusal was not a "dispute" of the "kind referred to in the arbitration clause." *Id.* at 315. The Court added:

> *With regard to the arbitration clause, we shall not consider the general question whether a greater effect should not be given to such clauses than formerly was done*, since it is not necessary to do so in order to decide the case before us. For this case, it is enough that we agree substantially with the views of Judge Learned Hand in the district court and Judge Hough in the circuit court of appeals. Their opinion was that the owner repudiated the contract, and that the arbitration clause did not apply. It is true that it would be inaccurate to say that the owner repudiated the contract in toto, for the letter that we have quoted assumed that the contract was binding and referred to it as fixing the liability incurred. It meant simply that the owner would not proceed with the voyage. [Citation omitted.] But we agree that such a refusal was not a "dispute" of the kind referred to in the arbitration clause. (Id. at 315) (Emphasis added)

Justice Holmes clearly raised the specter of enforcing executory arbitration agreements. Although the Court made clear the issue was not conceptually ripe for adjudication within the context of the immediate case, raising it, even if without more, provided all arbitration stakeholders with a fleeting glimpse of the Court's view that the issue was one to be addressed, examined, and possibly reexamined.

[45] *Marine Transit Corp. v. Dreyfus*, 284 US 263, 279 (1932) (holding that "[t]he Congress has authorized the Court to direct the parties to proceed to arbitration in accordance with a valid stipulation of a maritime contract and to enter a decree upon the award found to be regular and within the terms of the agreement").

judicial penchant against arbitration. Even though some of the 1925 language in the Congressional Archives (now nearly 100 years ago) is more than a shade anachronistic, it is emblematic because it constitutes the foremost and most forceful Congressional pronouncement demonstrating that Congress rejected the judicial branch's derision of arbitration.

Language from the House of Representatives regarding House Bill No. 68-96 (the number 68 refers to the 68th Congress and the 96 represents the report number) in the first quarter of the twentieth century (1924) is helpful. The FAA's priority was dispelling judicial skepticism concerning arbitration that had been imported wholecloth into US common law from English common law. Certainly, it would not be a complete stretch to argue that the principle of *efficiency* was foremost in the institutionalization of arbitration, at least in the US:

> Arbitration agreements are purely matters of contract, and the effect of the bill is simply to make the contracting party live up to his agreement. He can no longer refuse to perform his contract when it becomes disadvantageous to him. An arbitration agreement is placed upon the same footing as other contracts, where it belongs.
>
> The need for the law arises from the anachronism of our American law. *Some centuries ago, because of the jealously of the English courts for their own jurisdiction, they refused to enforce specific agreements to arbitrate upon the ground that the courts were thereby ousted from their jurisdiction. This jealously survived for so long a period that the principle became firmly embedded in the English common law and was adopted with it by the American courts.* The courts have felt that the precedent was too strongly fixed to be overturned without legislative enactment, although they have frequently criticized the rule and recognized its illogical nature and the injustice that results from it. The bill declares simply that such agreements for arbitration shall be enforced, and provides a procedure in the Federal courts for their enforcement.
>
> ***
>
> *It is particularly appropriate that the action should be taken at this time where there is so much agitation against the costliness and delays of litigation. These matters can be largely eliminated by agreements for arbitration, if arbitration agreements are made valid and enforceable.*[46] (Emphasis added)

While certainly the fulcrum for the enactment of the FAA was to place arbitration in *pari materia* with judicial tribunals, the legislative evidence makes clear that *process efficiency* in contrast with (i) the "costliness" and (ii) the "delays of litigation," appear to have been underscored as a material feature of arbitration warranting its promotion and adoption as a dispute resolution methodology of equal dignity with judicial tribunals. This language represents more than just a marginal comment.

In a Senate Report dated May 14, 1924 that the Committee on the Judiciary submitted, the identical understanding of efficiency in relation to arbitration is identified:

[46] House Report No. 96, 68th Cong., 1st Sess.

> It has been said that "arrangements for avoiding the delay and expense of litigation and referring a dispute to friends or neutral persons are a natural practice of which traces may be found in any state of society." The desire to avoid the delay and expense of litigation persists. The desire grows with time and as delays and expenses increase. The settlement of disputes by arbitration appeals to big business and little business alike, to corporate interests as well as to individuals. The Arbitration Society of America, with offices in the city of New York, has through its arbitration tribunal, *settled* more than five hundred cases during its less than two years of existence.[47]

Quite significantly, this Congressional Report is a particularly rich historical document because it goes on to cite to a contemporaneous newspaper report:

> In the *New York Times* May 11 is found a brief résumé of the work accomplished [referring to the number of cases processed by the *Arbitration Society of America* during a mere two year timeframe]. We quote the following:
>
> > In contrast with the long time required by the courts with their congested calendars to settle a dispute, the records of the society show that the average arbitration required but a single hearing, and occupied but a few hours of the time of disputant, counsel, and witnesses. The cost to the disputants was said to be trifling as compared with the cost of litigation.
>
> "Complicated controversies involving large sums of money which, beyond a reasonable doubt, if taken to the courts would have been fought through years of costly litigation, have been legally determined in this tribunal whose only rule of procedure is the rule of common sense, in from two to three weeks." [The report states,] "the specially significant thing – just as significant as the saving of time and money – is the fact that wide satisfaction has resulted from the procedure. Winners and losers alike bear witness to this in letters on file at the office of the society."[48]

The reference to prevailing and non-prevailing party satisfaction bespeaks a dispute resolution methodology that is engineered to resolve disputes, likely so as to provide for the efficiencies inherent in encouraging the disputing parties to continue doing business together once a difference between them has been reconciled.

The testimony before the Joint Committee of Subcommittees on the Judiciary, US Senate and House of Representatives held on January 9, 1924, similarly underscores the primacy of efficiency as arbitration's foundational pillar. This face of efficiency principally, but not exclusively, is in the form of contrast with litigation. Relatively brief excerpts from a representative of the New York State Chamber of Commerce who also represented the Importers and Exporters Association and the Merchants Association of New York suffice for illustrative purposes:

47 Senate Report No. 536, 68th Cong. 1st Session at 8 (emphasis added).

48 *Id.*

MR. BERNHEIMER: The most unprofitable thing that the merchant and businessman, or anyone engaged in buying and selling, can have confront him is that of litigation. It is unprofitable to him and it is unprofitable to the State and it is unprofitable to the law office.

MR. BERNHEIMER: Speaking for those who have had experience and who are engaged in business, I may say this, that arbitration saves time, saves trouble, saves money. There is no question about that. We know it. *It preserves business friendships*. The usual court atmosphere does not get into the arbitration hearings.... [Arbitration] prevents unnecessary litigation, and eliminates the law's delay by relieving our courts.[49]

Similarly in this connection, industry representatives further testified that, "the objectives of the bill, we are very much in favor of the objectives of an arbitration in commercial matters, believing it will be helpful in speeding business."[50] Testimony likewise contended that while the dollar savings to businesses resulting from passing the FAA could not be quantified, Julius Henry Cohen, a member of the Committee on Commerce, Trade and Commercial Law of the American Bar Association and the then General Counsel for the New York State Chamber of Commerce, testified that:

> If you could get rid of the New York calendars, both in the federal courts and in the state courts, and in the congested centers through the country – if you could get rid of the litigation that these business concerns can prevent by their arbitration committees – you and I would be able to get along without important litigation without waiting for a year or two for it to be reached. In other words, you would take out all these matters of business and leave the courts free to handle the business that ought to be handled with dispatch.

Indeed, the early evidence contemporaneous with the passing of the FAA is simple in its aspiration based upon the principle of efficiency that was viewed as defining arbitration. In the words of a declarant memorialized in the Congressional Records of the House of Representatives, "[t]he result of such a bill will be to do away with a lot of expensive litigation."[51]

Context and perspective matter. The analysis of historical evidence can easily be conflated with "modern" (nonhistorically contemporaneous) cultural facts that pervade all disciplines, and arbitration, international or domestic, is no exception. Seven salient propositions arising from the evidence canvassed compel attention. These premises will render possible the segregation of the historical from contemporary doctrinal assumptions.

49 Statement of Mr. Charles L. Bernheimer, Chairman Committee on Arbitration. Chamber of Commerce of the State of New York, New York City, Joint Hearing before Subcommittees on the Judiciary, Congress of the United States 68th Congress, 1st Session on S. 1005 and H.R. 646, January 9, 1924 pp. 6–7 (emphasis added).

50 *Id.* at 11–12.

51 *Id.*

First, in absolutely *none* of the materials reviewed regarding efficiency in arbitration was there *any* reference to the term "*party-autonomy*." The reason is simple. Contrary to the untested contemporary assumption that the principal premise underlying arbitration during its origins, at least in the US, was *party-autonomy*, the most salient concern was with efficiency. It was the promise of "efficiency" and not of the concept of "*party-autonomy*," as we know it today that was represented as the hallmark and central defining foundational feature of arbitration.

Certainly the references to arbitration as arising from a contractual relationship holds out the implicit, and perhaps explicit, proposition that contracts voluntarily are entered into and therefore the will of the parties to include an arbitration clause is a demonstrable exercise of *party-autonomy*. The reasoning is sound. And does comport with the historical data. Yet, the workings of *party-autonomy* were not detailed in these early writings and the term, textually, literally, and conceptually, is altogether absent. Efficiency, however, is present. The evidence is clear.

The proposition that some commentators have articulated; namely, that "efficiency was not featuring as a typical element of international arbitration some twenty odd years ago,"[52] does not comport with this and most evidence. Efficiency was being emphasized almost one hundred years ago to this very date of publication. *Party-autonomy* of course is central to arbitration. And ICA's most relevant and important regulatory source, the New York Convention, certainly states as much in Article V(1)(d), which reads: "The composition of the arbitral authority or the arbitral procedure was not in accordance *with the agreement of the parties, or, failing such agreement*, was not in accordance with the law of the country where the arbitration took place."

Second, enforceability of an arbitral award, the single most important feature of ICA, nowhere was mentioned. A legitimate counter-argument to both the absence of *party-autonomy* and enforceability as polestar fractures of ICA in the FAA's legislative history can be attributed to the absence of an arbitral enforcement regime, and a timeframe that predated economic globalization by approximately sixty years.

While these two premises do have a surface seductive glitter, however, they do not resist sustained analysis. The International Court of Arbitration of the ICC was founded in Paris in 1923, and the ICC in 1919. Moreover, the Permanent Court of Arbitration was established in 1899 by the first Hague Peace Conference under Articles 20 to 29 of the 1899 Hague Convention for the Pacific Settlement of International Disputes.

Hence, the seemingly ubiquitous reference to *efficiency* as a foundational arbitral precept, in contrast with the paucity of outright explicit references to *party-autonomy* and *enforceability*, cannot be ascribed to the embryonic status of ICA in the first quarter of the twentieth century.

52 Mistelis, "Efficiency – What Else?," 4–5.

As for the proposition that the FAA primarily concerns itself with domestic arbitration and for this reason somehow it emphasized *efficiency* and minimized *party-autonomy* and *enforceability*, the Congressional Records addressing the amendments to the FAA indisputably suggest otherwise.

Even though the FAA was first enacted on February 12, 1925 (43 Stat. 883), it was not codified until July 30, 1947 (61 Stat. 669), and amended on September 3, 1954 (68 Stat. 1233). Critical to this analysis, however, on July 31, 1970 Chapter 2 was added (84 Stat. 692), which incorporated without any revision the entirety the United Nations Convention on the Recognition and Enforcement of Foreign Arbitral Awards of 1958 (the "New York Convention").

Similarly, on August 15, 1990 (PL 101-369), Chapter 3 was added; namely, the Inter-American Convention on International Commercial Arbitration, which is an instrument virtually identical to the New York Convention limited only to the recognition and enforcement of foreign arbitral awards.

Quite remarkably, the Congressional Record concerning the incorporation into the FAA of these two enforcement frameworks actually underscores *efficiency* as ICA's bedrock principle.

The materials pertaining to the New York Convention's wholesale incorporation into Chapter 2 of the FAA includes a Presidential letter of submittal dated April 18, 1968. That correspondence in relevant part states:

> These recommendations for US accession to the convention [the New York Convention] recognize the continually increasing importance of arbitration as an *efficient, expeditious*, and *inexpensive means* of resolving disputes that arise between private parties in carrying on international commerce. They also underline the importance which the convention has assumed in ensuring the carrying out of arbitration awards in cases involving persons of different nationality.[53]

Also illustrative, and forming part of the Congressional Records on this amendment, are private sector correspondence to Mr. Clifford J. Hynning, the then Chairman of the Committee on International Unification of Private Law. One such communication in pertinent part states:

> In brief, I believe that the Convention would be of practical help to American business and that its ratification by the United States would be advantageous. My opinion is based on the belief that the present and future growth and expansion of United States trade and investment overseas will see more frequent resort to arbitration as a means of *expediting the settlement of commercial disputes*. It will prove quite valuable to United States business to be able *to enforce arbitral awards in*

[53] *Convention on the Recognition and Enforcement of Foreign Arbitral Awards* (commonly known as the New York Convention) Message from the President of the United States, June 10, 1958 at 4 (emphasis added).

> *foreign countries*, and there is no reason why we should not support such arbitral awards in this country as a matter of reciprocity.[54]

This language is recurring. In another submission to the Chairman, we read;

> [i]n business litigation, particularly in international business, the only kind of good justice is the one that is *simple, expeditious*, and final. Arbitration if aptly organized can be such kind of justice … a simple arbitration clause which calls for a referee or an umpire to settle any differences that may arise from the contract, takes away much of the sensation of insecurity evoked by the spectre of judicial litigation.[55] (Emphasis added)

Even in the context of "enforcement" efficiency was emphasized:

> We believe that the proposed Chapter 2 [the New York Convention] reconciles the major differences that exist because of the differences between the language and conceptual approach of the convention and of Title 9 and 28 of the United States Codes, and that the proposed system of implementation through the US District Courts *will assist the uniform and efficient enforcement of arbitration agreements and awards in foreign commerce.*[56] (Emphasis added)

In the context of Chapter 3 to the FAA incorporating the Inter-American Convention, *efficiency* is underscored as an organizing principle that renders all other elements singular to ICA and not litigation, viable:

> *Essential to the smooth flow of international commerce is an efficient and flexible method for settling disputes.* As the volume of international commerce accelerates, business parties have increasingly looked to arbitration for settlement of international commercial disputes. Parties who enter into an arbitration agreement can choose the forum, the rules of procedure, and the applicable law. *This flexibility can reduce the need for any party to subject itself to the unfamiliar laws of procedures of the courts of other countries, allows disputes to be settled more expeditiously and enables parties to seek arbitrators with specialized knowledge in appropriate cases.* For arbitration agreements to be effective, however, national courts of law must be able to enforce agreements to arbitrate and the ensuring of arbitral awards. The New York Convention and the Inter-American Convention both seek to do that. This is consistent with US domestic policy as spelled in the Federal Arbitration Act [citations omitted].[57] (Emphasis added)

Third, *efficiency*, as set forth in materials dating from the first quarter of the twentieth century through August 15, 1990, the date on which the FAA was amended to

54 *Id.* at 29 (emphasis added).
55 *Id.* at 36.
56 S.R. 91st Cong., 2nd Sess., No. 91-702 (Calendar No. 695) *Foreign Arbitral Awards* at 8.
57 H.R. Rep. 101-501 1990 p. 2, P.L. 101-368, Inter-American Convention of International Commercial Arbitration House Report No. 101-501. In this report, party-autonomy is linked to efficiency, as explicit reference is made to the parties ability to select the (i) forum, (ii) rules of procedure, and (iii) applicable law.

include Chapter 3 in the form of the *Inter-American Convention on International Commercial Arbitration*, is defined in terms of arbitration's relative cost when compared to litigation.

Fourth, *efficiency* in arbitration during this timeframe also is defined by the seemingly abbreviated time to process an arbitral proceeding from inception to issuance of an award. The reference made to the Association processing approximately 500 cases in just two years grows in stature.[58]

Fifth, efficiency also is explained in terms of time and resource demands on (i) witnesses, (ii) counsel, and (iii) parties.[59]

Sixth, having one hearing only was emphasized as an element of efficiency.[60]

Seventh and finally, reference was made to having "common sense"[61] as the only rule of procedure and, therefore, also as a metric for the promise to be efficient as a core normative feature of arbitration. While efficiency within the arbitral context has not been defined, two general categories from those historical writings stand out: (i) quantitative savings and (ii) qualitative process management.

Although these two categories can be identified with bright-line distinctions, they are profoundly related. Both concern what we have coined to constitute "*process efficiency*."

The value of resources expended in relation to an expeditious process that generates finality within a reasonable to relatively abbreviated timeframe, obviously cannot be altogether severed from quality process and procedural management: a metric for the expeditious processing of disputes. Non-merits adjudication disposition in the form of a settlement was not at all mentioned, and *party-autonomy*, enforceability, and flexibility while fleetingly referenced, certainly appeared to be subordinated to efficiency, or, at minimum, closely related to it.

As early as 1961, Soia Mentschikoff penned a law review article analyzing the findings of a survey extended to different industry sectors concerning ICA. The principal ground for ICA asserted in the survey concerned efficiency in the form of "speed, lower expense, more expert decision, [and] greater privacy[.]"[62] Although hardly a museum piece, this writing certainly can be construed as historical in nature because of its empirical foundation. A quarter of a century after Soia Mentschikoff's historical writing on the subject, the U.S. Supreme Court issued its landmark ruling in *Mitsubishi Motors Corp. v. Soler Chrysler-Plymouth, Inc.*[63] placing ICA as having equal dignity and standing with judicial proceedings.

58 House Report No. 96, 68th Cong., 1st Sess.
59 *Id.*
60 *Id.*
61 *Id.*
62 Soia Mentschikoff, "Commercial Arbitration," 61 *Colum. L. Rev.* 846, 850 (1961).
63 *Mitsubishi Motors Corp. v. Soler Chrysler-Plymouth, Inc.*, 473 US 614 (1985).

1.2.1 *The Supreme Court in* Mitsubishi

The *Mitsubishi* decision was the third of a trilogy of Supreme Court decisions that required discarding the legacy judicial prejudice asserting that ICA was ill-suited for the settlement of complex statutory claims, particularly those concerning anti-trust private rights of action. The case was decided after the FAA's July 31, 1970 amendment incorporating the New York Convention as Chapter 2, but approximately five years before Chapter 3 (the Inter-American Convention on International Commercial Arbitration) had been incorporated into the Act (August 15, 1990).

The issue before the Court was virtually indistinguishable from that which it considered in *Wilko v. Swan* and the holding in that case noting "the intention of Congress concerning the sale of securities is better carried out by holding invalid such an agreement for arbitration of issues arising under the Act [the Securities Act]."[64] The Court reduced an arms-length negotiated arbitration agreement to the status of a "stipulation" within the meaning of 15 U.S.C.A. §§ 77 and 14.[65]

Therefore, the Court again was called to determine whether a statutory cause of action providing for a private remedy would be susceptible to arbitration. It will be pointed out that in addressing this deliciously complex issue, the role of efficiency as a salient element of ICA was duly considered and deemed determinative.

The Supreme Court first framed the question as follows: "The principal question presented by these cases is the arbitrability, pursuant to the Federal Arbitration Act, [citations omitted] and the Convention on the Recognition and Enforcement of Foreign Arbitral Awards ("Convention") of claims arising under the Sherman Act, and encompassed within a valid arbitration clause in an agreement embodying an international commercial transaction."[66] In fact, the Court found it expedient to narrow the issue even further: "We granted certiorari primarily to consider whether an American court should enforce an agreement to resolve anti-trust claims by arbitration when that agreement arises from an international transaction."[67]

This issue was considered within a very simple factual context that commands only cursory recitation. Plaintiff, an automobile manufacturer, filed an action against an automobile dealer alleging, among other claims, nonpayment of stored vehicles, contractual storage penalties, damage to manufacturer's warranties and good will and expiration of distributorship. The dealer filed a counterclaim asserting violations of the Sherman Act, the Automobile Dealer's Day in Court Act, Puerto Rico Dealers' Act, and Puerto Rico Anti-Trust, and Unfair Competition Statutes.

Significantly, the federal district court ordered Mitsubishi (Plaintiff) and Soler (Defendant/Counterclaimant) to arbitrate each of the issues raised in the complaint

64 *See Wilko v. Swan*, 346 US 427, 438 (1953).

65 *Id.*

66 *Mitsubishi*, 473 US at 616 [citation omitted].

67 *Id.* at 624 [citation omitted].

and in all the counterclaims, save two and a portion of a third. With regard to federal antitrust issues, it recognized that the courts of appeals, following *American Safety Equipment Corp. v. J.P. Maguire & Co.*,[68] uniformly held that rights conferred by antitrust laws were "of a character inappropriate for enforcement by arbitration."[69]

The district court, however, following the Supreme Court's arbitration-friendly directive in the *Alberto-Culver*,[70] held that the international component of the claims asserted required adherence to the arbitration agreement even with respect to the antitrust claims.[71]

The First Circuit Court of Appeals, finding analytical foundation in the doctrine announced in *American Safety* (that antitrust claims were not arbitrable), held that antitrust claims are not susceptible to adjudication pursuant to arbitration proceedings and that "neither [the Supreme Court's] decision in *Scherk* [*Alberto-Culver*] nor the New York Convention required abandonment of that doctrine in the face of an international transaction."[72]

For the very first time, the Supreme Court placed arbitration on a level-playing field with judicial proceedings when it reversed the First Circuit on this part of this ruling, and actually challenged and refuted the long-standing badges of prejudice that had nourished judicial hostility against arbitration. Foremost in this case is the fact that arbitration could not *efficiently* process a federal statutory claim providing for a right of action. The majority's opinion surgically focused on the six propositions that had sustained the legacy derisive and diminishing preconception of all arbitral processes.

First, the Supreme Court observed that: "[t]he mere appearance of an anti-trust dispute does not alone warrant invalidation of the selected forum *on the undemonstrated assumption that the arbitration clause is tainted. A party resisting arbitration of course may attack directly the validity of the agreement to arbitrate*."[73]

The parochial and archaic misconception that had been decisive in prior decisions holding that a prospective claimant pursuant to a specially enacted statutory cause of action would be prejudiced by the absence of recourse to challenge a wrongfully issued arbitration award had now been stripped of all legitimacy. Implicit, if not explicit, in the Court's ruling on this critical point is the conviction that arbitration provides parties with ample opportunity to correct wrongs despite the narrow grounds available for such reconsiderations.

Second, the perennial objection to the perceived ill-suited nature of arbitration to process complex commercial disputes is directly questioned and disavowed by the Court's analysis. It is on this critical point that an understanding of the principle of

68 *American Safety Equip. Corp. v. J.P. Maguire & Co.*, 391 F.2d 821 (2d Cir. 1968).
69 *Mitsubishi*, 473 US at 620.
70 *Scherk v. Alberto-Culter Co.*, 417 U.S. 505 (1974).
71 *Mitsubishi*, 473 US at 610 [citation omitted].
72 *Id.* at 623.
73 *Id.* at 632 (emphasis added).

efficiency in arbitration constitutes an important premise in the Supreme Court's reasoning that commentators generally have failed to consider, let alone underscore.

The Court specifically observed that:

> Potential complexity should not suffice to ward off arbitration. We might well have some doubt that even the courts following *American Safety* subscribe fully to the view that anti-trust matters are inherently insusceptible to resolution by arbitration, as these same courts have agreed that an undertaking to arbitrate anti-trust claims entered into *after* the dispute arises is acceptable. [Citation omitted] [Emphasis in original.] And the vertical restraints which most frequently give birth to anti-trust claims covered by an arbitration agreement will not often occasion monstrous proceedings that have given anti-trust litigation an image of intractability. *In any event, adaptability and access to expertise are hallmarks of arbitration.* The anticipated subject matter of the dispute may be taken into account when the arbitrators are appointed, and arbitral rules typically provide for the participation of experts either employed by the parties or appointed by the tribunal. [Citation omitted] *Moreover, it is often a judgment that streamlined proceedings and expeditious results will best serve their needs that causes parties to agree to arbitrate their disputes; it is typically a desire to keep the effort and expense required to resolve a dispute within manageable bounds that prompts them mutually to forego access to judicial remedies. In sum, the factor of potential complexity alone does not persuade us that an arbitral tribunal could not properly handle an anti-trust matter.* (Emphasis added)

The question of efficiency was foremost in an invisible meta-presence in this case. A pronouncement that antitrust claims can benefit from streamlined and efficient arbitral management stands as a most extraordinary proposition. It demonstrates beyond quibble the primacy of arbitration's promise to be efficient.

The flexibility and adaptability of arbitration, two permutations of efficiency itself, comprised the Supreme Court's third premise upon which *Mitsubishi* was decided. It was underscored that it is important to reject

> the proposition that an arbitration panel will pose too great a danger of innate hostility to the constraints on business conduct that antitrust law imposes. International arbitrators frequently are drawn from the legal as well as the business community where the dispute has an important legal component, the parties in the arbitral body with whose assistance they have agreed to settle their dispute can be expected to select arbitrators accordingly.[74]

Fourth, when presented with the premise that parties to an arbitration proceeding are somehow inherently incapable of securing able and competent arbitrators who subscribe to standard ethical norms in the performance of their task, the Supreme Court noted that it would not "indulge the presumption that the parties and arbitral

[74] *Id.* at 633–634.

body conducting a proceeding will be unable or unwilling to retain competent, conscientious and impartial arbitrators."[75]

Fifth, the argument that the Sherman Act promotes national interests, and, therefore, the treble-damages component to rights accorded to private litigants was not susceptible to adjudication in an arbitral context, emphatically was rejected. Here, for the first time, the Court announced that such remedies are remedial in nature despite also playing an important role in penalizing wrongdoers and thus creating a chilling effect with respect to prospective tortfeasors. The Court specifically found that "[t]he importance of the private damages remedy, however, does not compel the conclusion that it may not be sought outside an American court."[76]

Sixth and lastly, the Supreme Court in closing again articulated policy arguments that, in part, were largely bottomed on the principle of efficiency:

> As international trade has expanded in recent decades, so too has the use of international arbitration to resolve disputes arising in the course of that trade. The controversies that international arbitral institutions are called upon to resolve have increased in diversity as well as in complexity. Yet the potential of these tribunals for efficient disposition of legal disagreements arising from commercial relations has not *yet been tested*. If they are to take a central place in the international legal order, national courts will need to "shake off the old judicial hostility to arbitration" [citation omitted] and also their customary and understandable unwillingness to cede jurisdiction of a claim arising under domestic law to a foreign or transnational tribunal. To this extent, at least, it will be necessary for national courts to subordinate domestic notions of arbitrability to the international policy favoring commercial arbitration.[77] [Citation omitted] (Emphasis added)

Accordingly, the First Circuit's ruling was reversed to the extent that it held that statutorily created antitrust claims are not arbitrable. More importantly, however, the Supreme Court disrobed the cloak of legitimacy that had vested the four fundamental badges of judicial hostility against arbitration as grounds for subordinating arbitral proceedings to a role inferior to that of judicial tribunals.[78]

The different faces of efficiency, however, have focused on: (i) time management of the process, (ii) the value of the dispute relative to its cost, (iii) an arbitral panel's reasonable promptness in adjudicating procedural orders and, of course, an award, and (iv) the very configuration and number of arbitrators on a tribunal.

One commentator aptly has suggested that "the value of an award" itself also must be considered, in that the process must yield an enforceable award under the New York Convention if in fact efficiency is to be attained.[79] In this connection, it is

[75] *Id.*

[76] *Id.* at 635.

[77] *Id.* at 639.

[78] *American Safety Equip. Corp. v. J.P. Maguire & Co.*, 391 F.2d 821 (2d Cir. 1968).

[79] See n. 5.

observed that: "The value of arbitral awards is twofold. It lies in the legal framework that allows recognition and enforcement in all these signatory States of the New York Convention. At the same time, arbitral awards maintain an economic value regardless of whether the award has been enforced or not."[80]

Certainly, these different aspects of arbitral efficiency matter. They are important. Yet, even the most surface analysis reveals two distinct features. First, all of them (those just previously mentioned immediately) constitute "*process efficiency*." The culture of ICA in referring to efficiency in institutional rules, the IBA Rules, and the Prague Rules is such that, settlement plays only a token role.[81] The historicity of efficiency bespeaks a process culminating in a (i) binding and (ii) enforceable award. And *process* does not equate to settlement prior to a final hearing, *or* at any point thereafter.

Second, the various categories or faces of efficiency are noted in the context of merits adjudication. They all entail consideration of what is efficient or expeditious within the framework of a zero-sum-game where there is a "winner" and a "loser," or more cynically and euphemistically stated, a "prevailing party" and a "non-prevailing party."

This feature begs the question: Can *optimal efficiency* in a dispute resolution methodology that has as its central core value being efficient actually optimize this value within the framework of a zero-sum-game? Does not simple logic dictate that a zero-sum-game certainly is a "disposition" but not a "solution."

In the scenario of a zero-sum-game, one stakeholder invested resources and by definition lost the investment. Moreover, even though there is no empirical data on this point, it certainly is not beyond man's wit to infer that most likely for all stakeholders, but certainly for the losing party, the business venture relating to the dispute irreparably was ruptured, or at minimum interrupted in an important percentage of cases.

The zero-sum-game categories of efficiency, as we have already fleetingly discussed, place the process in the hands of third parties in the form of an arbitral tribunal. Consequently, the arbitral cornerstone principle of *party-autonomy* altogether is forsaken, albeit by a seemingly voluntary (*party-autonomy* driven) *agreement* of the parties to *disagree*. This scenario only is but a shade away from one where the citizens of a constitutional democracy overwhelmingly agree (pursuant to an ostensibly democratic fiat and process) to abolish constitutional and democratic rule.

Rules primarily relying on a zero-sum-game structure ultimately are at odds with *optimal efficiency*. Such rules only would lead to *optimal efficiency* on an *ad hoc* basis as a matter of statistical happenstance and not system-driven normativity.

Third, all of these expressions of arbitral efficiency fail to account for settlement in furtherance of an economically driven business solution managed by the actual

[80] *Id.*

[81] *See* n. 14 in this chapter.

party stakeholders and not third parties who seek to restore the economic viability of the venture at issue. There are significant economic incentives in generating a settlement of the dispute that preserves the initial human and economic resources forming part of the underlying business concern.

The zero-sum-game efficiency models are important and must be developed with care because some percentage of arbitral proceedings *always* will require a merits adjudication,[82] notwithstanding the multiple economic considerations that render settlement the optimal economic efficiency paradigm. Efficiency's status in ICA remains so unique a promise and extraordinary a defining characteristic that only settlement through appropriate *risk assessment* can at all redeem this promise.

1.2.2 *The Primacy of the Role of the Principle of Efficiency in International Commercial Arbitration: The Interplay between the Due Process Right (i) to Present a Case and (ii) to Be Treated Equally and Fairly*

Due process is the normative source of ICA's legitimacy. This proposition is particularly central to ICA because of the absence of a second instance merits review. Under this unique rubric lacking second instance review, the centrality and primacy of due process is compounded and multiplied.

The indispensable need for the rigorous application of due process in a system of dispute adjudication that lacks second instance review readily can find friction with a seemingly equal defining structural and procedural value by the name of "efficiency." This theoretical and practical tension can only be exponentially increased by the vast discretion accorded to arbitrators under the banner of "inherent powers" with respect to evidentiary matters.[83] Here as well a seemingly irreconcilable squaring of the circle must be undertaken if (i) *arbitrator discretion* is to be consonant with (ii) *party-autonomy* in the taking and presentation of evidence.

A relationship between ratios that hopefully captures these two seemingly conflicting paradigms is a necessary part of this thought experiment:

Due Process: Efficiency:: Party-Autonomy: Arbitrator Discretion.

[82] There will be instances where mathematically it will make more sense to settle. The most evident scenario is where the cost of arbitration to the conclusion of all arbitral labor would be in furtherance of a risk assessment (percentage of likelihood of success multiplied by prospective damages recovery – damages theory) would suggest that the arbitration investment is one worth undertaking in cases where the proposed settlement amount does not justify the assumption of the risk. Likewise, where the end of arbitral labor simply points to a scenario where undertaking risk is a Better Alternative to a Negotiated Settlement, the case rightfully would and should proceed to a merits determination. *See*, Robert H. Mnookin & Lewis Kornhauser, "Bargaining in the Shadow of the Law: The Case of Divorce," 88 *Yale L.J.* 950, 968–69 (1979) ("The range of negotiated outcomes would be limited to those that leave both parents [in the context of family law disputes] as well off as they would be in the absence of a bargain.").

[83] *See* Chapter 3, n. 16 in this volume.

You will note that the denominators in both instances, (i) *Efficiency* and (ii) *Arbitrator Discretion*, have a limiting effect on their corresponding numerators, *Due Process* and *Party-Autonomy*. Therefore, the relationship is expressed not as one of magnitudes, the more classical paradigm of ratios and proportions, but rather of limiting forces and effects by two concepts (*efficiency* and *arbitrator discretion*) on two inherent rights, *due process* and *party-autonomy*.

In the arbitral context, due process provides the parties with two sets of corresponding rights: (i) the right to present a case and (ii) the right to be treated fairly and the same as the opposing party. Both of these elements of due process, the right to present a case and the right to be treated fairly and equally as an opposing party, are in a continuum that moves opposite on that very same continuum to the key principle of efficiency.

Both due process and efficiency in an aspirational state must be at equipoise. Without either principle encroaching on the other. The word "aspirational" is emphasized.

Just as the arbitration rules of all major arbitral institutes are sprinkled with recurring references to *efficient* and *expeditious* practices (Section 3.1), so, too, are they riddled with references to "fair and equal treatment." The connection between due process (the most important normative source for arbitral process legitimacy) and efficiency is central to the conceptual workings of ICA. To be sure, the most eloquent provisions reference both a *due process component* and *efficiency*.

1.2.3 *The Stockholm Chamber of Commerce*

By way of example, the Arbitration Rules of the Stockholm Chamber of Commerce (SCC Arbitration Rules or SCC Rules) in Art. 23, subsection 23.2 provides that: "[i]n all cases, the Arbitral Tribunal shall conduct the arbitration in an *impartial, efficient*, and *expeditious manner, giving each party an equal and reasonable opportunity to present its case*." (Emphasis added.) While simple at first glance, a careful reading of subsection 23.2 brings into sharp relief the tension between "equal and reasonable opportunity to present its case" and conducting the arbitration in an "impartial, efficient, and expeditious manner," sustained analysis suggests that the two principles are deeply related.

At some point, lack of constraints regarding the presentation of a case will doubtless lead to a process that is asymmetrical and driven by the relative resources of the parties rather than the merits. Equal treatment commands the imposition of limits as to the quality and quantity of the proffered evidence. These limits likewise must extend to both the *taking* and *presenting* of evidence. Hence, *process efficiency* directly determines important elements of equitable or fair treatment. The dialectical relationship between efficiency and due process bespeaks more than just contrast.

The squaring of the circle between due process and efficiency is perhaps all the more pronounced in Art. 30 (**Amendments**) of the SCC Arbitration Rules, which reads:

> At any time prior to the close of proceedings pursuant to Article 40, a party may amend or supplement its claim, counterclaim, defence or set-off, provided its case, as amended or supplemented, is still encompassed by the arbitration agreement, *unless the Arbitral Tribunal considers it inappropriate to allow such amendment or supplement having regard to the delay in making it, the prejudice to the other party or any other relevant circumstances*. (Emphasis added)

The textual language of this Article supports the proposition that there may be circumstances pursuant to which the exercise of arbitral discretion in furtherance of efficiency *may* appropriately foreclose a party from continuing to present its case in the form of an amendment or a supplemental filing. The provision is eloquent in raising this concern because, among other considerations, the amendment or supplemental filing that can be disallowed would be "still encompassed by the arbitration agreement," and therefore admissible, relevant, and potentially very much material to the proceeding.

1.2.4 *The UNCITRAL Arbitration Rules*

Comparable provisions abound in the arbitral rules of all major arbitration administering institutions, as well as the United Nations Commission on International Trade Law (UNCITRAL) Arbitration Rules (2021).[84]

[84] *See, e.g.*, ICC Arbitration Rules (2021):

ICC Art. 22 (Conduct of the Arbitration) in relevant part reads:

(1) The arbitral tribunal and the parties shall make every effort to conduct the arbitration in an *expeditious and cost-effective manner, having regard to the complexity and value of the dispute.*

(2) In order to ensure effective case management, after consulting the parties, the arbitral tribunal shall adopt such procedural measures as it considers appropriate, provided that they are not contrary agreement of the parties. Such measures may include one or more of the case management techniques described in Appendix IV.

***

4) In all cases, the arbitral tribunal *shall act fairly and impartially and ensure that each party has a reasonable opportunity to present its case*. [Emphasis added] Article 22 of the ICC Rules foundationally premises the conduct of the arbitration on two principles: (i) efficiency, and (ii) due process, in that order. To the drafters' credit, the arbitral proceedings' stakeholders are compelled (the mandatory "shall" is used) to use the somewhat "objective" metrics of *complexity* and the *value of the dispute* as a standard for the application of process efficiency to each specific case.

See also, **ICDR Arbitration Rules (2021)**, Art. 20 (Conduct of Proceedings) (1)–(3), (7); **DIS Arbitration Rules (2018)**, Art. 27(1), (4), and (7).

Unlike most institutional arbitration rules, the DIS does not address *efficiency* and *due process* in the same rule. Thus, it is in Art. 21, subsection 21.1 that due process is raised in two pithy sentences,

Article 17, subsection 17.1 of the UNCITRAL Arbitration Rules also is particularly clear in illustrating the due process *versus* efficiency musical counterpoint:

> Subject to these Rules, the arbitral tribunal may conduct the arbitration in such manner as it considers appropriate, provided *that the parties are treated with equality* and that at an appropriate stage of the proceedings *each party is given a reasonable opportunity of presenting its case. The arbitral tribunal, in exercising its discretion, shall conduct the proceedings so as to avoid unnecessary delay and expense and to provide a fair and efficient process for resolving the parties' dispute.*[85] (Emphasis added)

This provision captures the virtually unbridled scope of *arbitrator discretion*, due process, and efficiency. The practical workings of the provision, however, make clear that the arbitrator is to exercise its discretion by providing for fairness through the lenses of *efficiency* and the *avoidance of undue delay*, such is efficiency's normative standing within ICA's very fiber. ICA's own foundational basis for legitimacy, due process, amply and without parallel in its judicial dispute resolution counterpart within domestic or international frameworks, is subordinate to efficiency.

Chief Justice Sundaresh Menon of Singapore very compellingly has argued that because there is "common membership of due process and efficiency within the rule of law framework means that both values are, in principle, aligned rather than opposed."[86] The proponent of this proposition then quite reasonably proceeds to conclude that both efficiency and due process stride for legitimacy and "generally correct findings of fact and applications of law," and by sharing these common objectives they cannot be found to be antinomies relative to each other.

which state that "the parties shall be treated equally." And that "[e]ach party shall have a right to be heard."

The DIS Rules, however, much like the ICC counterpart (Art. 22.1), provides guidance to the stakeholders for purposes of determining how efficiency is to be applied by referencing the objective standards of "complexity" and the "economic importance of the dispute."

As more fully discussed in the context of the Prague Rules (Chapter 6), the assumption that shifting initiative from *party-autonomy* to *arbitrator discretion* yields efficiency is untested. This approach largely is driven by cultural concerns and legal tradition rather than empirical data concerned with maximizing *process efficiency*.

LCIA Arbitration Rules (2020) Art. 14(1)(i)–(ii), (2), (5), and (6).

LCIA Art. 14 is especially emblematic of the deep relationship between due process and efficiency. Particularly illustrative is subsection 14.5 because its very textual language purports to broaden even further the inherent powers of arbitrators based upon "the fair, efficient and expeditious conduct of the arbitration." The connectivity between due process and efficiency also is underscored by the very structure of subsection 14.1(i) and (ii).

SIAC Arbitration Rules (2016) Art. 19 (Conduct of Proceedings) (1), (3), and (4).

HKIAC Arbitration Rules (2024) Art. 13 – General Provisions –under Section IV (Conduction of Arbitration), Art. 13(1) and (5).

The HKIAC Rules in subsections 13.1 and 13.5 textually and grammatically display the importance of addressing due process and efficiency together.

85 UNCITRAL Arbitration Rules (2021), Art. 17, subsection 17.1.

86 Sundaresh Menon, "Dispelling Due Process Paranoia: Fairness, Efficiency and the Rule of Law," 17 *Asian Int'l Arb. J.* 1, at 3 (2021).

He goes on to state: "that due process and efficiency are equally essential to achieving both these purposes of the rule of law, and that neither of these values will be sufficient without the other."[87]

One would be hard-pressed to argue against efficiency and due process as somehow being mutually exclusive with respect to having a place within the framework of the rule of law and serving as principles in furtherance of common objective, that is to say, the equitable administration of justice. The tension between the concepts, however, rests with the interplay between the two, within a rubric that vests an arbitral tribunal with practically unbridled discretion, tempered only by general notions of "reasonableness." The intrinsic dialectical relationship between due process and efficiency, like all coherent dialectical dynamics that Hegel has identified,[88] lead to a harmonious resolution. This relationship breaches equipoise with the application of these principles by stakeholders from different and often competing legal cultures.

Hence, only where the exclusion of evidence in furtherance of efficiency would be *unreasonable*, and therefore *irrational*, would a viable due process procedurally based challenge rest. Challenging the boundaries of reason may be a standard too broad to yield meaningful adjudication. The journey to the irrational makes provision for the inequitable.

Before reaching the extreme of the irrational, considerable due process can be legitimately sacrificed at the altar of efficiency without triggering grounds for set-aside or nonenforcement.

1.2.4.1 The False Case of Due Process Paranoia and the True Phenomenon of Qualified Due Process

It is precisely the perceived potential violation of the parties' right to present their case based upon procedural grounds principally premised on some manifestation of efficiency that spawned the term "*due process paranoia*."[89]

The term "due process paranoia" arose in response to the Queen Mary 2015 International Arbitration Survey.[90] The survey chronicled a response observing that there was a "growing concern in international arbitration" regarding a "perceived reluctance by Tribunals to act decisively in certain situations for fear of the award

87 *Id.*

88 *See generally*, G. W. F. Hegel, *The Phenomenology of Spirit*, translated by A. V. Miller (Oxford University Press 1977), pointing to the relationship of coherence between seemingly irreconcilable concepts that in fact are interdependent and indispensable parts of a dynamic that unfolds into an "unassailable principle."

89 *Id.* pp. 1–3; *see also* Section 1.1.1.

90 Queen Mary School University of London, 2015 *International Arbitration Survey: Improvement and Innovations in International Arbitration*, pp. 5, 10, available at: https://shorturl.at/lIT4i (last accessed June 22, 2023); *see also* Menon, "Dispelling Due Process Paranoia" note 73 at 6; and Section 1.1.1.

being challenged on the basis of a party not having had the chance to present its case fully."[91]

The interviewee who cleverly coined the phrase specifically referenced "situations where deadlines were extended repeatedly, evidence was admitted late in the process, and disruptive behavior was accepted given the concern that the award would otherwise be vulnerable to challenge."[92] To be sure, some ink has been spilled suggesting that this concern was to some extent factual.[93]

There is no empirical evidence, however, supporting the phenomenon. And indeed it is likely very well the case that the "paranoia" nomenclature is literally accurate, and little more than general inferences have been drawn from very specific and particular experiences.

Indeed, the converse actually is the case. In the name of efficiency, due process has been qualified and *arbitrator discretion* excluding evidence and abbreviating timeframes prevailed. The primacy of efficiency, notwithstanding arbitration's unkept promise, has been more prevalent than expansive and liberal evidentiary rulings or orders extending timeframes for the presentation of evidence or submission of memoranda.[94]

Moreover, the empirical evidence compellingly demonstrates that challenges to an award on procedural due process grounds predicated on the alleged inability to present a party's case, rarely are granted and constitute the exception to the rule. Courts uniformly uphold such challenges only in the most egregious of circumstances.[95]

[91] Queen Mary School University of London, 2015 *International Arbitration Survey*.

[92] *Id.*

[93] Queen Mary School University of London, 2008 *Corporate Attitudes and Enforcement of Arbitral Awards*, 5, available at: https://arbitration.qmul.ac.uk/media/arbitration/docs/IAstudy_2008.pdf (last visited June 24, 2023).

[94] The proposition that in the name of due *process efficiency* has been sacrificed calls into question the role of the flexibility tenet in international arbitration. Jurisdictional deadlines do not form part of a private adjudicative process not based on the exercise of State sovereignty. The idea that timeframes would be generously enlarged absent bad faith and where doing so does not give rise to strategic or tactical prejudice, perfectly comports with the nature of ICA, and the culture that it has spawned.

[95] Cases giving rise to a set-aside based on lack of due process arising from the preclusion of evidence are sparse. *See, e.g.*, *Tempo Shain Corp. v. Bertek, Inc.*, 120 F.3d 16 (2d Cir. 1997) (in which the Second Circuit Court of Appeals identified "[t]he question on appeal [as] whether the panel's refusal to continue the hearing to allow [respondent's President] to testify amounts to fundamental unfairness and misconduct sufficient to vacate the arbitration award pursuant to Section 10(a)(3) of the Act." The court answered the question in the affirmative and noted that it found "no reasonable basis for the arbitration panel to determine that [respondent's President's] omitted testimony would be cumulative with respect to the fraudulent inducement claims." Indeed, the court restated this proposition; "[s]aid differently, the panel excluded evidence plainly 'pertinent and material to the controversy …'" [citation omitted]). *Id.* at 20.

Notably, as a predicate to its holding, the court focused on the jurisprudence interpreting 9 U.S.C. § 10(a)(3), in part providing that a court may set aside an arbitration award if "the arbitrators were guilty of misconduct in refusing to postpone the hearing, upon sufficient cause shown, or in refusing to hear evidence pertinent and material to the controversy[,] or of any other misbehavior by

1.2.4.2 The Interplay between Efficiency and Due Process

Courts in the US are emblematic of "arbitral due process" that is qualified by the principle of efficiency. The Eleventh Circuit Court of Appeals' analysis in *Scott v. Prudential Securities, Inc.* is helpful.[96] In that case, the respondent non-prevailing party appealed a district court's order confirming the arbitration award entered against respondent and denying its motion to vacate.[97]

which the rights of the party have been prejudiced." In doing so, the Second Circuit observed that "[c]ourts have interpreted Section 10(a)(3) to mean that *except where fundamental fairness is violated,* arbitration determinations will not be open to evidentiary review," *citing to Bell Aerospace Co. Div. of Textron v. Local* 516, 500 F.2d 921, 923 (2d Cir. 1974) (observing that "[i]n handling evidence an arbitrator need not follow all the niceties observed by the federal courts. He need only grant the parties a fundamentally fair hearing."); *Hoteles Condado Beach v. Union de Tronquistas Local* 901, 763 F.2d 34, 39 (1st Cir. 1985) (noting that although not required to hear all the evidence proffered by a party, an arbitral tribunal "must give each of the parties to the dispute an adequate opportunity to present its evidence and argument"); *Teamsters, Local Union 657 v. Stanley Structures, Inc.*, 735 F.2d 903, 905 (5th Cir. 1984) (observing that "[f]ederal courts do not superintend arbitration proceedings. Our review is restricted to determining whether the procedure was fundamentally unfair"); and *Concourse Beauty School, Inc. v. Polakov*, 685 F. Supp. 1311, 1318 (S.D.N.Y. 1988) ("The misconduct must amount to a denial of fundamental fairness of the arbitration proceeding in order to warrant vacating the award.") (*quoting Transit Cas. Co. v. Trenwick Reinsurance Co.*, 659 F. Supp. 1346, 1354 (S.D.N.Y. 1987), *aff.'d mem.*, 841 F.2d 1117 (2d Cir. 1988)).

The Second Circuit's analysis distils the elements for setting aside an award on due process grounds arising from the alleged failure to admit evidence or grant a continuance, to a "fundamentally unfair" standard that would be sufficiently flexible to allow for deviations. Consequently, pursuant to this rubric, a party is not entitled as a matter of a *due process arbitral right* to present all the evidence that the party may deem necessary, appropriate, or adequate. Leaving aside the issue of cumulative and redundant evidentiary submissions, even probative evidence can be excluded where the inadmissibility of the evidence is not conducive to an *inadequate opportunity* to present its case, or fundamental unfairness. *See also Allendale Nursing Home, Inc. v. Local 1115 Joint Board et al.*, 377 F. Supp. 1208, 1214 (S.D.N.Y. 1974) (setting aside award on due process grounds arising from the tribunal's reluctance to grant a rescheduling of a hearing notwithstanding evidence that a material witness would not be able to testify because of a demonstrably established illness); *Vernon-Hunt v. Guzman*, 2021 WL 4950622, *3 (S.D.N.Y. 2021) (holding that "Petitioner has carried the heavy burden of demonstrating that it was denied 'fundamental fairness' because the panel, by its own admission, never considered the documents that he submitted *that formed the exclusive basis for the award.*" (Emphasis added.)). Similarly, a fundamentally fair hearing cannot be had where the evidence upon which the award in whole or in part is based was unduly secured. *Baker Marquart LLP v. R. Kantor*, 231 Cal. Rptr. 3d 796, 804 (Cal. App. 5th 2018) (setting aside award where the arbitral tribunal premised its findings on confidential communications that a party was not able to address or meaningfully challenge).

96 *Scott v. Prudential Securities, Inc.*, 141 F.3d 1007 (11th Cir. 1998).

97 The more precise and prevalent term is "set-aside." The lapidary Art. V.1(e) of the New York Convention provides:

> 1. Recognition and enforcement of the award may be refused, at the request of the party against whom it is invoked, only if that party furnishes to the competent authority where the recognition and enforcement is sought, proof that:
>
> (e) The award has not yet become binding on the parties, or has been *set aside* or suspended by a competent authority of the country in which, or under the law of which, that award was made. (Emphasis added)

The vacatur motion was, in part, based upon the averments that the arbitrators exhibited evident partiality and were guilty of misconduct because they denied respondent's motion to delay the proceeding and precluded respondent from participating in the hearing by telephone. The Eleventh Circuit Court of Appeals affirmed the District Court's order.

As a predicate to its analysis, the Court observed that:

> The FAA permits a district court to vacate an arbitration award in the event that: (1) the arbitrators refused to postpone the hearing upon the showing of sufficient cause; (2) the arbitrators refused to hear pertinent and material evidence; or (3) the arbitrators were guilty of any other misbehavior that resulted in prejudice to the rights of any party. *Citing to* the FAA (9 U.S.C. § 10(a)(3)).[98]

Having established these tenets, in addition to articulating the central feature of arbitral discretion in ICA by stating that "[a]n arbitrator enjoys wide latitude in conducting an arbitration hearing," the Court underscored that any assessment of the basis for vacatur had to be construed within the framework of the principle of efficiency as a foundational policy of arbitration. There can be no substitute for the Eleventh Circuit's own text: "[W]e must recall the basic policy behind arbitration, which is to permit parties to resolve their disputes *in an expeditious manner* without all the formalities and procedures that might attend full-fledged litigation." [Citation omitted] (Emphasis added)

As to the claim that the refusal to delay the hearing merits setting aside the award, the FAA's textual language in 9 U.S.C. § 10(a)(3) requires the movant petitioning for postponement to establish "sufficient cause" for the delay sought. Therefore, the Eleventh Circuit applied the stricture that if there existed "any reasonable basis" for denying the request to postpone the hearing, then such denial cannot rise to the level of justifying a vacatur of the award.[99]

Simply stated, unless the grounds for denying the continuance was unreasonable, that is to say, not sustainable by *reason* and therefore *irrational*, the Tribunal would be justified in its holding. This standard is extremely expansive in relation to *arbitrator discretion* and uncommonly narrow as to due process. *Arbitrator discretion* can be inversely proportional to due process when these inherent powers are exercised exclusively based on efficiency.

Similarly, Article VI of the Convention reads:

> If an application for the *setting aside* or suspension of the award has been made to a competent authority referred to in article V(1)(e), the authority before whom the award is sought to be relied upon may, if it considers it proper, adjourn the decision on the enforcement of the award and also may, on the application of the party claiming enforcement of the award, order the other party to give suitable security. (Emphasis added)

The FAA, however, uses the term "vacatur."

98 *Scott v. Prudential*, 141 F.3d 1007 at 1016.

99 *Id.*

In addition to this reasoning, the Court observed it previously had "held that an arbitration panel's possible reliance on any one of a number of factors, including the desire for an *expeditious resolution of the dispute*, justified its refusal to postpone a hearing to accommodate a party's competing scheduling obligations and, therefore, did not require the vacatur of an arbitration award."[100] (Emphasis added.) The record before the Court demonstrated that respondent merely had a "self-imposed scheduling obstacle" that could not under any analysis constitute a "sufficient cause" to have compelled the Tribunal to postpone the hearing.

As to the Tribunal's refusal to allow respondent to participate in the hearing by telephone, the Court analyzed the argument "as a refusal to consider pertinent evidence or as 'other misbehavior,' under § 10(a)(3) [observing that respondent] must show that the arbitrators' refusal to permit him to participate by telephone caused him some prejudice. [Citations omitted.] An arbitrator need not consider all the evidence the parties seek to introduce but may reject evidence *that is cumulative* or irrelevant."[101] [Citation omitted.] (Emphasis added.)

On this point, the Eleventh Circuit premised its affirmance of the District Court's denial of respondent's motion to vacate on two findings. First, it noted that "[a]lthough the arbitrators refused [respondent's] participation by telephone, the arbitrators did conduct a hearing, of which [respondent] had notice and the opportunity to attend[.]"

Second, the record reflected that the Tribunal considered respondent's fifty-six page affidavit containing respondent's legal arguments and evidentiary proffers.[102] The Second Circuit's venerable chestnut on the issue of arbitral due process, *Parsons & Whittemore Overseas Co. v. Societe Generale de L'Industrie du Papier (RAKTA)*,[103] is helpful. There, an American corporation appealed an adverse entry of summary judgment against it and in favor of an Egyptian corporation confirming a foreign arbitral award holding the American Company liable to the Egyptian claim for breach of contract. The Second Circuit affirmed the district court's confirmation of the award and respondent's challenge, in part, based upon having been denied its right to present its case pursuant to Art. V(1)(b) of the New York Convection.

Specifically, respondent premised its due process challenge on the Tribunal's refusal to reschedule a hearing to allow for respondent's principal witness to testify. Two factual propositions are particularly relevant. First, the witness sought the rescheduling of the hearing based upon an alleged prior commitment to deliver a lecture at a university.

[100] *Id.*

[101] *Id.* at 1017.

[102] *Id.*

[103] *Parsons & Whittemore Overseas Co. v. Societe Generale de L'Industrie du Papier (RAKTA)*, 508 F.2d 969 (2nd Cir. 1974).

Second, the Arbitral Tribunal had "before it an affidavit by [the witness] in which he furnished, by his own account, 'a good deal of the information to which I would have testified.'"[104] The Second Circuit affirmed the District Court's confirmation of the award finding that respondent's due process rights were not violated by initially underscoring the proposition that "inability to produce one's witnesses before an Arbitral Tribunal is a risk inherent in an agreement to submit to arbitration."[105] This proposition merits reading and rereading. *It states in no uncertain terms that arbitration has a singular and qualified due process protection that is narrower than its judicial counterpart.*

The Court proceeded to shed light on the "risk inherent in an agreement to submit to arbitration," in what can only be understood as a remarkably eloquent statement that exemplifies arbitration's qualified due process principle. The Second Circuit noted that "a party relinquishes *his courtroom rights* – including that to subpoena witnesses – in favor of arbitration 'with all of its well-known advantages and draw-backs.'" [Citations omitted.] (Emphasis added.) *Hence, as an analytical point of departure, albeit quite fleetingly, a distinction is drawn between the rights that a party has in the context of a courtroom versus those endemic to an arbitral setting.*

It also observed that "as a matter of fundamental fairness" the postponement of the hearing because of a conflicting speaking engagement cannot be justified, particularly where, as in this case, virtually the entirety of what would have been the declarant's testimony already had been submitted in written form to the tribunal.

It is intriguing that while the Second Circuit plainly acknowledges that arbitral discretion wrests from parties rights that such parties would enjoy in a judicial setting, the opinion views the New York Convention's Art. V(1)(b) language concerning "otherwise unable to present his case," as sanctioning the application of the forum State's standards of due process. In the US, the standard of due process means "the opportunity to be heard at a meaningful time and in a meaningful manner, …"[106]

In substance and not in form, however, the Court analyzed due process through the lenses of arbitration, which in turn qualifies due process by dint of the principles

[104] *Id.* at 975.

[105] *Id.*

[106] *Parsons* (*quoting Matthews v. Eldridge*, 424 U.S. 319, 333 (1976) "[T]he strong federal policy in support of encouraging arbitration and enforcing arbitration awards dictates that [courts] narrowly construe the defense that a party was 'unable to present its case.'") *Gold Reserve Inc. v. Bolivarian Republic of Venezuela*, 146 F. Supp. 3d 112, 128–29 (D.D.C. 2015) (*quoting Rive v. Briggs of Cancun, Inc*, 82 F. App.'x 359, 364 (5th Cir. 2003)). *See also Anderson v. Am. Gen. Life Ins. Co.*, 802 Fed. Appx. 548, 553 (11th Cir. 2020) (holding that arbitrator's refusal to consider evidence deemed irrelevant to the jurisdictional question before the tribunal did not constitute a basis for setting aside the award); *Armont v. K12 (Florida Cyber Charter Academy-FLCCA)*, Slip copy – 3:19-cv-334-MMH-MCR (M.D. Fla. Apr. 23, 2024) ("Assuming *arguendo* that the arbitrator violated a rule or law when he closed the evidence without affording plaintiff the opportunity to call [witnesses] as belated witnesses or object to their withdrawal, it does not automatically follow that he exceeded his powers such that the Court could vacate the arbitration award." Emphasis added).

of efficiency.[107] *Arbitrator discretion* only constitutes the conceptual vehicle for implementing efficiency. Yet, this very inherent authority is charged with enforcing due process.

In a similar case concerning a longstanding dispute between the Republic of Moldova and a Ukrainian energy provider, Energoalliance, the Ukrainian entity filed an investor-State arbitration pursuant to the Energy Charter Treaty (ECT)[108] alleging that a Moldovan State-owned utility with which Energoalliance had entered into an electricity sales purchase agreement, had defaulted and failed to tender payment on an invoice in its entirety. An arbitral award issued in favor of claimant and against Moldova for approximately US$58 million. Moldova challenged a confirmation proceeding that the Ukrainian entity initiated before the U.S. District Court, for the District of Columbia.

Moldova challenged confirmation on the basis of Article V(1)(b) of the New York Convention, in part, asserting that it was "unable to present its case" because the Tribunal (i) refused to admit a proffered expert opinion while holding the absence of an expert opinion against it and (ii) based the arbitral award "on new arguments and evidence advanced by Petitioner [Moldova] for the first time during the hearing and in its written post-hearing final statement."[109]

The District Court rejected both contentions. As to refusal to admit the expert witness testimony and to proscribe witnesses or experts from appearing at the hearing, the District Court observed that the Arbitral Tribunal had

> explained that it would construe the expert opinion "as one and the same as the statement submitted on behalf of the Respondent [Moldova]" because the expert's areas of expertise – "special knowledge of Russian legislation on the capital market and corporate law of the CIS countries" – were not "relevant to this dispute" and because the opinion extended beyond those areas to also address general factual and legal issues.[110]

In this connection, the District Court observed that in fact the Arbitral Tribunal had to have considered the substance of the proffered expert's opinion, and did so as part of Moldova's answer, but merely "discounted its relevance."[111]

Moldova asserted that it was an error not to accord the expert opinion "its own weight,"[112] the District Court, however, noted that the distinction that Moldova drew did not set forth grounds explaining how treating the expert opinion as a

[107] *Id.*

[108] The Energy Charter Treaty (December1994).

[109] *LLC Komstroy (successor to LLC Energoalliance) v. Republic of Moldova*, 2019 WL 3997385, at *7 (D.D.C., Aug. 23, 2019), *aff'd.* on appeal, *LLC SPC Stileks v. Republic of Moldova*, 985 F.3d 871 (D.C. Cir. 2021).

[110] *Id.*

[111] *Id.*

[112] *Id.*

free-standing submission instead of part of the answer, would have yielded a material difference, or the manner in which the alleged error in effect "affected its ability to present its case."[113]

Additionally, the District Court observed that the Arbitral Tribunal "did not criticize the country for failing to produce an expert; rather, the Award simply observes in the 'procedural background' section of its decision that '[t]he Parties have not brought witnesses and experts to produce any statements to the hearing.'"[114] It further added that "the tribunal's unadorned comment merely relays that neither party submitted witnesses or experts subject to cross-examination; the tribunal did not rule against Moldova on the basis that [Moldova] did not submit any expert opinions."[115] On this basis, the Arbitral Tribunal's treatment of the expert report as an answer to the *Request for Arbitration*, and proscribing the expert witness's oral testimony at the hearing, simply did not violate Moldova's Art. V(1)(b) right to present its case through the lenses of US standards of due process, which are qualified by US federal policy strongly encouraging arbitration and consequently requiring courts to construe narrowly the defense that a party was "unable to present its case."[116]

Moldova's second evidentiary-based due process challenge to confirmation based on alleged new evidence and arguments that claimant (petitioner) raised without giving Moldova an opportunity to respond, was denied on factual and technical grounds.

After combing the record, the Court observed that "petitioners [claimant below] post-hearing brief merely elaborated on previous arguments such that Moldova could have reasonably anticipated and responded to them."[117]

The District Court's treatment of the allegedly three new legal authorities on which petitioner (claimant below) allegedly relied for the first time in its post-hearing final statement, however, is less compelling by more than a shade. The analysis is disposed of in three sentences and governed by somewhat facile reasoning. Also, it is relegated to the status of a mere footnote.

The District Court reasoned that legal authorities at issue constituted "well known" awards addressing the scope of the jurisdictional term "investment" (*Ratione Materiae*) within the meaning of the Energy Charter Treaty. It therefore followed,

[113] *Id., citing to Gold Reserve Inc.*, note 113.

[114] *Id., citing to* the Arbitral Award forming part of the District Court's record at ¶ 42.

[115] *Id.*

[116] *See Scott v. Prudential Securities, Inc.*, 141 F.3d 1007 (11th Cir. 1998).

[117] *LLC Komstroy (successor to LLC Energoalliance) v. Republic of Moldova*, 2019 WL 3997385, at *8 (D.D.C., Aug. 23, 2019), aff'd. on appeal; *LLC SPC Stileks v. Republic of Moldova*, 985 F.3d 871 (D.C. Cir. 2021).

For the sake of completeness, it should be noted that the court cited for the inapposite proposition *Flyers Rights Educ. Fund, Inc. v. FAA*, 864 F. 3d 738, 748 n. 6 (D.C. Cir. 2017) declining to find argument waived where "the manner in which [the plaintiff] substantiated [its] argument evolved from its opening to reply brief" because "[w]hat matters is that the core [the plaintiff's] argument … remained the same."

so that District Court reasoned, that petitioner's reliance on commonly known and recognizable authority did not rise to the level of raising new legal arguments that required a response upon penalty of a due process violation.[118]

The District Court also engaged in a hypothetical pursuant to which it reasoned that even had petitioner asserted new arguments in its post-hearing brief, Moldova waived any objections to these procedural irregularities by not raising them before the Tribunal.[119]

The U.S. Court of Appeals for the District of Columbia ("the DC Circuit") confirmed and accepted the lower court's holding and reasoning denying the Art. V(1)(b) New York Convention due process challenge, and merely noted that: "the district court ably refuted Moldova's due process arguments [citations omitted], and we affirm the analysis."[120]

LLC SPC Stileks v. Republic of Moldova is particularly illustrative because of four very specific reasons. First, a party's single expert was foreclosed from testifying at a hearing.

Second, an expert opinion submitted on behalf of a party was treated as an answer, that is, a pleading. This procedural gyration is extremely anomalous and does not make procedural sense. An answer is a pleading, and therefore, asserts allegations. An expert opinion purports to establish evidentiary facts. The two are poles apart.

Third, the proposition that "Petitioner's post-hearing brief merely elaborated on previous arguments such that Moldova could have reasonably anticipated and

[118] The District Court's exact language compels citation in its entirety:

> The same holds true for the three legal authorities on which Petitioner purportedly relied for the first time in its post-hearing final statement. As Petitioner explains, these legal authorities "*were well-known international arbitral decisions*" related to the scope of "investment" under the ECT and decided years ago. [Citations omitted.] Moldova fails to convince the Court that it was unable to present its case simply because the Petitioner cited three well known and relevant legal authorities. (Emphasis added.) *LLC Komstroy (successor to LLC Energoalliance) v. Republic of Moldova*, 2019 WL 3997385, at *7 (D.D.C., Aug. 23, 2019), *aff'd.* on appeal, *LLC SPC Stileks v. Republic of Moldova*, 985 F.3d 871 (D.C. Cir. 2021).

[119] *Id.* *9. The District Court cited to two cases in support of this proposition: *Europcar Italia, S.p.A. v. Maiellano Tours, Inc.*, 156 F. 3d 310, 315–16 (2nd Cir. 1998) (holding that "if [defendant-appellant] failed to raise the issue of the forged 1979 agreement to the arbitrators, the issue is forfeited"); and *Gold Reserve Inc.*, at 125–26 note 93 (finding that respondent in an arbitration waived an argument because the legal and factual points constituting an objection were not sufficiently developed as they were relegated to the status of a mere footnote).

See also National Wrecking Co. v. Int'l Bhd. of Teamsters, Local 731, 990 F.2d 957, 960 (7th Cir. 1993) (issues raised before arbitrator are waived in enforcement proceedings); *Johnson v. Panetta*, 953 F.Supp. 2d 244, 250 (D.D.C. 2013) (holding that "perfunctory and undeveloped arguments, and arguments that are unsupported by pertinent authority, are deemed waived"); and *Thakore v. Universal Mach. Co. of Pottstown, Inc.*, 670 F.Supp. 2d 705, 716 (N.D. Ill. 2009) (holding that "[w]hile the motion cited Rules 402 and 403, it offered no explanation of how the Rules relate to its contention and no cases are cited in support of the conclusion that the summary judgment order speaks for itself. The argument is thus waived").

[120] *LLC SPC Stileks v. Republic of Moldova*, at 883.

responded to them,"[121] in a judicial context would have undermined the settled proposition that perfunctory and embryonic arguments, as well as arguments that are unsupported by appropriate authority are waived even where such contentions raise constitutional issues.[122] This same analysis would apply to the District Court's reasoning that somehow because the authority on which petitioner relied and raised for the first time in its post-hearing final statement allegedly were "'well-known international arbitral decisions,'" therefore justifying respondent's inability to address three arbitral awards, equally circumvents the requirement to flesh out arguments, in part, by citing relevant authority.[123]

Moreover, the premise that somehow "well-known international arbitral decisions," in this case concerning "the scope of 'investment' under the ECT and decided years ago," need not be addressed for this reason by the party against whom the authority is proffered, itself is less than convincing. Equally quizzical is the District Court's unchallenged Petitioner's characterization ("Petitioner explains") of the three "legal authorities" for the first time raised in Petitioner's post-hearing final statement.[124]

The Circuit Court's affirmance and adoption of the District Court's holding and reasoning on these issues is based on a US *attenuated arbitral due process* that narrowly construes the Art. V(1)(b) challenge. It does so because of the FAA's policy to promote arbitration understood as a dispute resolution methodology with the primary objective of rendering a binding and enforceable award. The FAA itself, as noted, was enacted to further arbitration based upon the understanding that *process efficiency* constitutes arbitration's fulcrum.

Accordingly, much of the Arbitral Tribunal's conduct as explained in the *LLC Konstroy* District Court opinion resists an Art. V(1)(b) due process challenge because, under FAA qualified or attenuated due process, "[t]he arbitrator 'need only grant the parties a fundamentally fair hearing.'"[125]

[121] *LLC Komstroy (successor to LLC Energoalliance) v. Republic of Moldova*, 2019 WL 3997385, at *8 (D.D.C., Aug. 23, 2019), *affirmed on appeal*.

[122] *See, e.g., White Eagle Co-op. Ass'n. v. Conner*, 553 F.3d 467, 476 n. 6 (7th Cir. 2009).

[123] *Id.*

[124] *See LLC SPC Stileks v. Republic of Moldova*, at 883.

[125] *Lessin v. Merrill Lynch Fenner*, 481 F.3d 813, 816 (D.C. Cir. 2007), *citing to Bell Aerospace*, 500 F.2d at 923; *accord Sheldon v. Vermonty*, 269 F.3d 1202, 1206 (10th Cir. 2001) (holding that arbitral tribunal's refusal to permit evidence taking notwithstanding institutional rules and code of procedure providing that parties have a right to engage in evidence taking, and arbitral tribunal's dismissal with prejudice solely on allegations in pleadings and the arguments of counsel over a telephonic hearing, found to meet minimum requirements of arbitral due process under the FAA); *Brown v. Coleman Co.*, 220 F.3d 1180, 1182 (10th Cir. 200) (internal quotation omitted), *cert. denied* 121 S.Ct. 1191 (2001) (observing that courts "must give extreme deference to the determination of the arbitration panel for the standard of review of arbitral awards is for the standard of review of arbitral awards is among the narrowest known to law"); and *Hoteles Condado Beach et al. v. Unión de Tronquistas Local 901*, 763 F.2d 34, 40 (observing that "[e]very failure of an arbitrator to receive relevant evidence does not constitute misconduct requiring vacatur of an arbitrator's award").

This qualified arbitral due process in the context of the FAA,[126] has its normative foundation in *process efficiency*.[127] The primacy placed on efficiency commands concessions on the scope of due process. ICA's enshrinement of *efficiency* comes at the expense of *due process*. This allocation of weight accorded to *process efficiency* bolsters the normative standing of *optimal efficiency* within the ICA framework. Efficiency is sufficiently prized so as to carve out the bandwidth of a forum State's due process standard when applied to an Art. V(1)(b) challenge asserting preclusion of evidence.[128]

[126] *See* Section 1.2, noting that on FAA's July 31, 1970 the FAA was amended to incorporate the New York Convention (*see* FAA Chpt.2, 84 Stat. 692).

[127] *See* Section 1.1.2, a, documenting that the FAA's legislative history underscored *process efficiency* as a justification for legislation and a federal policy placing arbitration in *pari materia* with judicial proceedings.

[128] In *Gold Linhas Aereas SA (formerly DRG Linhas Aereas SA) (Respondent) v. Matlin Patterson Global Opportunities Partners (Cayman) II LP and others (Appellants) (Cayman Islands)* from the Court of Appeal of the Cayman Islands Privy Council Appeal No. 0086 of 2020 (Judgment issued on May 19, 2022) in paragraphs 63 through 78 the Privy Council explores the dichotomy concerning the question of whether Art. V(1)(b) of the New York Convention must be construed as (i) constituting a uniform international principle of due process that is self-contained and free standing by itself or (ii) the due process standard governing Art. V(1)(b) must be interpreted in accordance with the due process standard of the recognition forum. In the United States, as noted at Section 1.1, courts sanction the application of the forum State's standards of due process. Yet, it is not the judicial due process that is applied by courts in the context of Art. V(1)(b), but rather qualified arbitral due process arising from jurisprudence interpreting the FAA and its policy to further and to promote arbitration.

In this connection, the Privy Council observed:

The approach of national courts.

65. The case law from a variety of different jurisdictions cited by Born and surveyed in George A. Bermann (ed.), *Recognition and Enforcement of Foreign Arbitral Awards: The Interpretation and Application of the UN Convention by National Courts* (Springer 2017) broadly bears out the statement by Van den Berg of the approach adopted by national courts.

66. Thus, the US courts have held that article V(1)(b) "essentially sanctions the application of the forum state's standard of due process," and therefore US standards of due process: *Parsons & Whittemore Overseas Co. v. Societé Générale de L'Industrie du Papier (RAKTA)*, 508 F.2d 969, 975 (2nd Cir. 1974); *Iran Aircraft Industries v. Avco Corpn.*, 980 F.2d 141, 146 (2nd Cir. 1992). However, this does not require compliance with US court procedure. The relevant standards are the "minimum requirements of fairness" that are fundamental to a fair adjudication, comprising "adequate notice, a hearing on the evidence, and an impartial decision by the arbitrator": *see, e.g.*, *Sunshine Mining Co. v. United Steel Workers of America*, 823 F.2d 1289, 1295 (9th Cir. 1987); *Generica Ltd. v. Pharmaceutical Basics, Inc.*, 125 F.3d 1123, 1129–30 (7th Cir. 1997); *Karaha Bodas Co. LLC v. Perusahaan Pertambangan Minyak Dan Gas Bumi Negara*, 364 F.3d 274, 298–99 (5th Cir. 2004). Courts often cite the seminal decision of the US Supreme Court in *Matthews v. Eldridge*, 424 US 319, 333 (1976) for the proposition that the "fundamental requirement of due process is the right to be heard at a meaningful time and in a meaningful manner."

67. As expressed in the final draft of the new *Restatement of the US Law of International Commercial and Investor-State Arbitration*, approved in May 2019, at p. 602:

In the United States, the relevant principles are generally referred to as "due process" standards, but use of this term does not imply that the domestic constitutional due process protections directly apply in arbitration. The procedural protections that assure fundamental fairness in a consensual arbitral process, particularly ones involving parties from different legal cultures and procedural traditions, are distinct from those that would be required in judicial proceedings in which the Due Process Clause of the Fifth and Fourteenth Amendments of the US Constitution applied.

These cases exemplify the interplay between efficiency and due process in the arbitral context. They demonstrate that efficiency is so foundational to arbitration that it qualifies due process as this principle is interpreted and applied in a judicial context globally.

68. In France, the standards of procedural due process to which foreign arbitral awards are subjected under article V(1)(b) are not domestic law standards. They are drawn from general principles of law that are in turn influenced by a variety of standards, most notably article 6(1) the European Human Rights Convention. In other words, the standards are "denationalized" and reflect l'ordre public international procedural: *see* George A. Bermann (ed.), para. 4.2.2; and also Jean-Louis Delvolvé, Gerald H Pointon and Jean Rouche, *French Arbitration Law and Practice: A Dynamic Civil Law Approach to International Arbitration*, 2nd ed., 254 (Kluwer Law International 2009).

69. In Germany, the prevailing view is that enforcement may be refused under article V(1)(b) of the New York Convention when the decision so deviates from the basic principles of German procedural law that it cannot be deemed, according to the German legal system, to have been rendered in proper legal proceedings. Not all procedural defects are relevant; rather, there must be a violation of minimum standards of procedural justice and the award must be based on that violation: *see* Judgment of 23 April 2004, *Yearbook of Commercial Arbitration* 2005, 557 (Oberlandesgericht Köln); Judgment of 30 October 2008, 2009 SchiedsVZ 66 (Bundesgerichtschof).

70. Commenting on the interpretation and application of the New York Convention in Switzerland, Andrea Bonomi and Elza Raymond-Eniaeva in Bermann (eds.), para. 3.2.2, refer to the controversy over whether the due process concept is an autonomous notion or should be interpreted according to the law of the country in which enforcement is sought, and state:

"While avoiding a clear answer, the Swiss Federal Court seems to take an intermediate stance (domestic standards adapted to the different context of international arbitration and to the transnational standards), although there are scholars supporting an autonomous notion."

71. Sweden adopts the position, in common with a number of other jurisdictions, of being guided by national law but applying a standard of due process adapted to meet the context of international arbitration and the application of an international treaty. Ulf Franke and Annette Magnusson et al (eds), International Arbitration in Sweden: A Practitioner's Guide (Kluwer Law 2013) says at pp 284–285, para. 44 that:

"The provision [article V(1)(b)] aims to safeguard that the parties to the arbitration have had a reasonable opportunity to participate in the arbitral proceedings and to state their case, i.e., to maintain the adversarial principle. It has been argued that the rule of due process is an international provision. However, national courts have on occasion looked at national law for guidance, although noting that a transgression of national law may not necessarily be a transgression of the New York Convention. The provision will in any case be interpreted restrictively."

72. There is little authority on the question in England and Wales. In *Malicorp Ltd v. Government of the Arab Republic of Egypt* [2015] EWHC 361 (Comm); [2015] 1 Lloyd's Rep 423, which involved a claim to enforce an Egyptian arbitration award in England, Walker J, at para. 31, had no doubt that "the test as to ability of the party to present its case involves an application of relevant English principles as opposed to those of Egypt or anywhere else" (citing Cukurova Holdings, para. 32, where on an appeal to the Privy Council from the British Virgin Islands the proposition that the enforcing court must apply its own concept of natural justice was not in dispute).

The Privy Council's survey of the specific question of how courts interpret and apply the defense to recognition and enforcement set forth in Art. V(1)(b) of the New York Convention, authorizing nonrecognition and nonenforcement if "[t]he party against whom the award is invoked was not given proper notice of the appointment of the arbitrator of the arbitration proceedings or *was otherwise unable to present its case*," identifies one common denominator. The alleged due process infringement must be of a foundational nature, and in every instance reflects a very stringent and narrow interpretation of Art. V(1)(b). This fact remains so independently of whether Art. V(1)(b) is understood to be a self-standing principle of international law, or a due process requirement that is construed under national law but with the qualification that it must be tempered for purposes of application in the context of an arbitral proceeding.

Within the framework of US courts addressing the very narrow question of how to interpret and to apply the defense to recognition and enforcement articulated in Art. V(1)(b) of the New York Convention, authorizing nonrecognition and nonenforcement if "[t]he party against whom the award is invoked was not given proper notice of the appointment of the arbitrator or of the arbitration proceedings or was otherwise unable to present his case," the debate concerning the extent to which the Art. V(1)(b) due process defense constitutes an international self-standing principle, or a due process construct that is the product of the due process standard of national courts, becomes irrelevant.

While US courts interpret the due process "unable to present his case" defense through the prism of the FAA's federal policy favoring arbitration, which policy is rooted on *process efficiency*, the net result is indistinguishable from an interpretation of this Art. V(1)(b) defense as a self-standing principle of international law.

The principle of *process efficiency*, while itself the core tenet underlying a national law of arbitration (the FAA), gives rise to a very narrow iteration of due process reduced to the bare elements of "the opportunity to be heard at a meaningful time and in a meaningful manner"[129] Hence, US courts modify the national due process standard in the arbitral context based upon the normative foundation arising from the principle of efficiency. This treatment of a national standard by courts of that jurisdiction curiously yields the most universal and international iteration of due process pursuant to which an arbitrator "need only grant the parties a fundamentally fair hearing."[130]

The US Supreme Court in *Gilmer*, in discussing the differences between litigation and arbitration, reasoned that: "where arbitration is contemplated the courts are not equipped to provide the same judicial review given to structured judgments defined by procedural rules and legal principles. Parties should be aware that they get what they bargain for and that arbitration is far different from adjudication."[131]

Certainly, it would be somewhat extreme to assert that within the ambit of ICA due process is subordinated to efficiency. It is, however, reasonable to conclude that there has been a transnational doctrinal development in the principles that govern the presentation of evidence and due process in ICA such that efficiency together with the principle of *arbitrator discretion* may legally justify denying a motion for continuance or a party's qualified participation at a hearing.

The Honorable Sundaresh Menon, Chief Justice of the Singapore Supreme Court, has written that ICA deliberately has "attenuated" some legal values in

[129] *Matthews v. Eldrige*, 424 US 319, 333 (1976).

[130] *Bell Aerospace Co. Div. of Textron, Inc.*, note 102.

[131] *Gilmer v. Interstate/Johnson Lane Corp.*, 500 U.S. 20, at 30–32, 111 S.Ct. 1647 (1991); *see also Lee v. Chica*, 983 F.2d 883, 889 (8th Cir. 1993) discussing *attenuated arbitral due process* the Court observed: "In the arbitration setting we have almost none of the protections that fundamental fairness and due process [usually] require ... Discovery is abbreviated if at all. The rules of evidence are employed, if at all, in a very relaxed manner. The fact finders (here the Panel) operate with almost none of the controls and safeguards [expected in litigation]."

furtherance of other aspirations, and shares that such attenuation, for example, can be seen

> from arbitration's [i] choice of confidentiality over transparency; [ii] its preference for party-appointment of arbitrators despite the risks to the actual or apparent objectivity of the arbitrators so appointed; [iii] its foundations in consent which limit its ability to manage disputes involving interests beyond those of the consenting parties, [iv] giving rise to the risk of inconsistent findings on overlapping issues; and [v] its restriction of avenues for correction of error, prioritizing finality over the greater assurance of accuracy of outcomes. *But the attenuation is also attributable to arbitration's continuing struggle to control mounting costs and delays, which are inimical to the goals of speed and affordability and hence the rule of law value of accessibility.*[132] (Emphasis added)

I would add that the attenuated rule is that of due process as to the right to present a case and to be treated equally. This qualification represents ICA's greatest attenuation in deference to a private consent-based system of dispute resolution, namely the ICA privatization of dispute resolution.

The judicial authority and empirical evidence are of a single voice in demonstrating that not only is "due process paranoia" a mere inconsequential contrafactual perception (if at all), but also that parties to arbitral proceedings, whether knowingly or otherwise, when agreeing to arbitrate actually embrace a qualified and somewhat diminished set of procedural due process rights that is formed and transformed by the substantive principle of efficiency, which principle has eluded definition and sustained analysis in the academic journal work. This principle is applied pursuant to *arbitrator discretion*. The latter is a source of *unquantifiable risk*.

[132] Menon, "Dispelling Due Process Paranoia" note 93 at 10.

2

Statistical Analyses Establishing the Percentage of Disputes That Settle in Judicial Proceedings in the US

Exploring an Analogy

The presumption that ICA is efficient no longer exists. This fact is so even as concerns *process efficiency*.[1] Efficiency is no longer understood as an essential feature of arbitration in the strict sense of the term "essential feature," that is to say, part of the essence or the fiber of arbitration. Instead, it is, in its most generous light, understood as an aspiration that the contemporary practice of ICA may someday attain.[2]

According to a 2008 study, 85–90 percent of the cost of arbitration is allocated to counsel's legal fees.[3] This figure leaves approximately 10–15 percent allocated to arbitral institutions and to the actual arbitral panel. The allocation of these three expenses in highly technical and specialized disputes is even more unclear.[4]

The 2008 Queen Mary University Survey reflects that as a direct and explicit consequence of this allocation of resources, 41 percent of in-house counsel stated a preference for transnational litigation over ICA to address cross-border disputes.[5]

[1] *Optimal efficiency* is yet to be at all considered.

[2] Queen Mary University of London, 2008 *Corporate Attitudes and Enforcement of Arbitral Awards*, 5.

[3] *Id.* See generally, Richard G. Alleman, "Mind the Settlement Gap: A Call for More Effective Judicialization of International Commercial Arbitration," 38 *Arbitr Int.* 4, 231–248 (December 2022), observing:

> Anecdotal evidence from users and practitioners has long suggested that international arbitration is especially prone to a low incidence of settlement. For instance, a 2008 survey conducted by Queen Mary University London and PriceWaterhouseCoopers revealed that only 32% of participants, including both users and counsel, reported achieving a settlement during arbitration proceedings, either without an arbitral award (25%) or reduced in a consent award (7%). Hard data on settlement rates, in turn, are generally more difficult to come by than in public court litigation, chiefly due to arbitration's confidential and decentralized nature. A 2018 analysis of a sample of around 3,750 international commercial arbitrations result between 2005 and 2018 suggested that 56% of all cases ended in either a settlement or a withdrawal. Not much is known, however, about the composition of that sample other than it includes arbitrations from a wide range of industries and regions that were conducted under a broad variety of institutional and *ad hoc* rules. [Citations omitted.] At 2 of 14 of the 03-06-2025 Kluwer Arbitration published iteration of the referenced article.

[4] Mistelis, "Efficiency," 9–10, citing Queen Mary University of London, 2008 *Corporate Attitudes*. See also n. 6 in this chapter.

[5] Mistelis, "Efficiency," 9–10, citing Queen Mary University of London, 2008 *Corporate Attitudes*.

The cost of arbitration and the incident delays that now constitute the common fare of arbitral proceedings have been amply documented. And the shroud of efficiency has disappeared. In its place, a seemingly infinite number of articles identifying the problem and proposing solutions has arisen.[6] None of them, however, identify settlement as any form of arbitral efficiency, let alone *optimal efficiency*.

[6] See Mistelis, "Efficiency," citing Queen Mary University of London, *2008 Corporate Attitudes*, n. 10; Menon, "Dispelling Due Process Paranoia"; Hermann Bietz, "On the State and Efficiency of International Arbitration: Could the German 'Relevance Method' Be Useful of Not?," 12 *SchiedsVZ* 30, 121 (2014); Michael Dunmore, "Increased Efficiency and Lower Costs in Arbitration: Sole Member Tribunals," IV *Indian J. Arb. L.* 1, 27–33 (2015); Debevoise & Plimpton LLP "Protocol to Promote Efficiency in International Arbitration," at: https://shorturl.at/lqTtJ (2010) (last accessed March 18, 2019); and Diane Desierto, "Rawlsian Fairness and International Arbitration," 36 *U. Pa. J. Int'l L.* 4, 939–993 (2015). David Earnest, Raúl Gallardo, Gardar Vidir Gunnarsson, & Tobiasz Kaczor, "Four Ways to Sharpen the Sword of Efficiency in International Arbitration," (2013), at: https://tinyurl.com/ycj7kx2x (last accessed March 18, 2019); John Fellas, "A Fair and Efficient International Arbitration Process," *PLI Course Handbook*, International Arbitration, No. 10796 (2007); Cristina Florescu, "The Arbitration Agreement and Arbitrability: Towards Achieving Efficiency in International Arbitration," in *Austrian Yearbook Int'l Arb.* (Kluwer Law International 2015), 51–71; Fabricio Fortese & Lotta Hemmi, "Procedural Fairness and Efficiency in International Arbitration," 3 *Groningen J. Int'l L.* 1, 110–124 (2015); Lucy Greenwood, "Does Bifurcation Really Promote Efficiency?," 28 *J. Int'l Arb.* 2, 105–111 (2011); Veijo Heiskanen, "Key to Efficiency in International Arbitration," 30 *ICSID Rev.* 481–485 (2015); ICC Commission on Arbitration and ADR, Task Force on Reducing Time and Costs in Arbitration, at: https://shorturl.at/GEV5L (last accessed March 18, 2019); JAMS International Efficiency Guidelines 2011 for the Pre-hearing Phase of International Arbitrations, at: www.jamsinternational.com/international-arbitration-efficiency-guidelines (last accessed March 18, 2019); Nana Japaridze, "Fair Enough? Reconciling the Pursuit of Fairness and Justice with Preserving the Nature of International Commercial Arbitration," 36 *Hofstra L. Rev.* 4, 1415–1446 (2008); Jennifer Kirby, "Efficiency in Arbitration: Whose Duty Is It?," 32 *J. Int'l Arb.* 6, 689–696 (2015); Elisabeth Leimbacher, "Efficiency under the New ICC Rules of Arbitration of 2012: First Glimpse at the New Practice," 31 ASA *Bulletin* 2, 298–315 (2013); Michael Mcilwrath, "Faster, Cheaper: Global Initiatives to Promote Efficiency in International Arbitration," 76 *Arb.* 532–537 (2010); Michael Moser, "The 'Pre-hearing Checklist': A Technique for Enhancing Efficiency in International Arbitral Proceedings," 30 *J. Int'l Arb.* 155–159 (2013); Christopher Newmark, "Controlling Time and Costs in Arbitration," in *The Leading Arbitrators' Guide to International Arbitration* (Lawrence W. Newman & Richard Hill eds.) (Juris 2008), 81–96; Veit Öhlberger & Jarred Pinkston, "The Arbitrator and the Arbitration Procedure, *Iura Novit Curia* and the Non-passive Arbitrator: A Question of Efficiency, Cultural Blinders and Misplaced Concerns about Impartiality," *Austrian Yearbook Int'l Arb.* (2016), 101–117; Wilson Pimentel, "Efficiency and Equilibrium in the Allocation of Costs," (2015) XII *Revista Brasiliera de Arbitragem* 59–67; Karl Pörnbacher & Alexander Dolgorukow, "Reconciling Due Process and Efficiency in International Arbitration: The Arbitrator's Task of Achieving the One without Sacrificing the Other," LXI *Ann. FLB.* 3, 50–62 (2013); Andreas Respondek, "Five Proposals to Further Increase the Efficiency of International Arbitration Proceedings," 31 *J. Int'l Arb.* 4, 507–513 (2014); Jorg Risse, "Ten Drastic Proposals for Saving Time and Costs in Arbitral Proceedings," 23 *Arb. Int'l.* 3, 5 (2013); Paola Sánchez, "Introducing Efficiency into the 2010 IBA Rules on Evidence: Does This Create a Back Door for Introducing Additional Inefficiencies into the System?," 1 *Int. Commercial Arb. Brf.* 1, 3–4 (2011); Anne-Veronique Schläpfer & Marily Paralika, "Striking the Right Balance: The Roles of Arbitral Institutions, Parties and Tribunals in Achieving Efficiency in International Arbitration," 2 *BCDR Int'l Arb. Rev.* 2, 329–342 (2015); Albert Jan van den Berg (ed.), "Planning Efficient Arbitration Proceedings: The Law Applicable to International Arbitration," *ICCA Congress Series*, No. 7 (Kluwer 1996); Irene Welser, "Efficiency: Today's Challenge in Arbitration Proceedings,"*Austrian Yearbook Int'l Arb.* (2014), 151–166.

Arbitral institutes have reacted to the costs and delays giving rise to inefficiencies by amending their arbitration rules to provide for early disposition and expedited procedure.[7]

The in March 2018 published a report titled *ICC Commission Report Controlling Time and Costs in Arbitration* (the ICC Report). The ICC Report is helpful in promoting *process efficiency*, and can point to significant accomplishments in this regard arising from the workings and application of its first edition.

Notably, however, the eighty-eight-paragraph report only allocates two paragraphs to settlement:

> **Settlement**
>
> 41 *Arbitral tribunal's role in promoting settlement*
>
> The arbitral tribunal *should consider* informing the parties that they are free to settle all or part of the dispute at any time during the ongoing arbitration, either through direct negotiations or through any form of ADR proceedings. For example, mediation proceedings can be conducted under the ICC Mediation Rules, ….
>
> 42 *Settlement initiatives taken with the parties' agreement*
>
> The parties may request the arbitral tribunal to suspend the arbitration proceedings for a specific period of time while settlement discussions take place. The parties may also agree that the arbitral tribunal should take other steps to facilitate settlement of their dispute, provided that such steps are not inconsistent with the tribunal's duty under Article 41 of the Rules to make every effort to make sure that its award is enforceable at law.[8]

Perhaps it is self-evident that the settlement provision does not underscore the decisive advantages of settling a dispute. Moreover, the two paragraphs concerning settlement are but a notice that settlement is a conceptual *possibility* and not a *necessary* predicate (to *optimal efficiency*) or even a *mandatory* consideration.

Indeed, the paragraph 41 reference to settlement is aspirational and not mandatory, stating that "[t]he arbitral tribunal *should consider* informing the parties" regarding the possibility of settlement. This language is poles apart from mandatorily requiring the arbitral tribunal to explain (i) the average cost and (ii) time of an arbitration, without even factoring such foundational considerations as the (iii) cost of business interruption, (iv) expert fees, (v) the clear consequences of a zero-sum-game with only one "prevailing party," and (vi) to propose settlement efforts by party consent that would allow the arbitral tribunal to comment on the relative strength

7 By way of example, the International Centre for Dispute Resolution (ICDR) (2021) Arbitration Rules Art. 23 (Early Disposition) and Art. E-1 (Expedited Procedure), ICC (2021) Art. 30 (Expedited Procedure), London Court of International Arbitration (LCIA) (2020) Art. 22 (Early Determination), Hong Kong International Arbitration Centre (HKIAC) (2018) Art. 42 (Expedited Procedures) and Art. 43 (Early Determination Procedure), and Singapore International Arbitration Centre (SIAC) (2016) Rule 5 (Expedited Procedure) and Rule 29 (Early Dismissal of Claims).

8 *ICC Commission Report Controlling Time and Costs in Arbitration* (ICC 2012) 11 (emphasis added).

of the evidence of record in the context of settlement. In this same vein, the tribunal is not encouraged or required to express its views on the merits and the evidence.

The ICC Report mirrors the status of settlement as a barely cognizable means of marginal significance of efficiently bringing closure to a dispute.

Quite understandably, the ICC Report's suggestions for controlling time and costs in arbitration exclusively deal with *process efficiency*, that is to say, physical logistical concerns, such as determining whether "it is more effective for written submissions to be sequential or simultaneous," "limiting the length of submissions," and "keeping hard copies [of documents] to a minimum," all of which are extremely helpful and practical suggestions. These important concerns, however, pale when contextualized by *optimal efficiency*.

Absent is any reference to risk evaluation and merits assessment. Put simply, the physical logistical techniques for minimizing delays and costs are helpful to the proceeding but are extrinsic to avoiding the expense of the very proceeding in the first instance.

Even though it has been here noted that in July 2023 (just five years after the publication of the ICC Report), the ICC's Commission on Arbitration and ADR published its guide titled *Facilitating Settlement in International Arbitration*, the 2018 ICC Report provides us with a historical document describing the manner in which settlement was being addressed and efficiencies in ICA understood as of that date, that is to say, March 2018. The necessary inference is that settlement was not yet integrated into arbitral culture because its workings as the expression of *optimal efficiency* was not duly recognized as a priority.

2.1 EMPIRICAL ANALYSIS ON SETTLEMENT OF ICA AND US FEDERAL AND STATE COURT PROCEEDINGS

There is no mathematical percentage that can quantify with apodictic certainty what percentage of the total ICA cases filed conclude pursuant to settlement. Only one major institutional arbitral center, the HKIAC, reveals this information.

All major arbitral institutions, however, only publish the number of cases that are filed on a yearly basis. This data, when considered together with (i) the number of cases concluded by award, (ii) all cases submitted to mediation, (iii) cases filed for expedited treatment, and (iv) cases processed pursuant to early dismissal of claims, is in a range of approximately 29–32 percent of all ICA cases filed with the major arbitral institutes appear to be concluded by settlement.[9]

9 The inherently private nature of ICA proceedings renders it difficult to access empirically reliable information. Most arbitral institutes openly address yearly statistics but do not directly publish yearly settlement rates. Most of these institutes reflect rather poor numbers with respect to cases that register just for mediation. Accordingly, much of the data that can be culled is from one of two basic sources. First, arbitral institutes do publish the number of "new cases" registered on a yearly basis. *Some* also make available the number of awards that are issued annually. Within reasonable margins of error,

Significantly, as of this writing, only the HKIAC publishes the actual percentage of cases that settle on a given year. Part of the troubling difficulty is that cases withdrawn are treated as tantamount to having settled. By way of example, the ICC's published statistical records reflect that in 2017, the institute set a record with 512 awards approved. During the 2017 calendar year, however, the ICC registered 810 new cases. These numbers suggest that approximately 30 percent of the cases were withdrawn or settled. It is unclear whether the 512 cases that proceeded to award included those that reached the end of all arbitral labor pursuant to summary adjudication. Moreover, for calendar year 2017, 37 percent were multi-party cases that entailed the registration of several claims within a collective dispute. Hence, here as well it is unclear whether the partial settlements were realized. The settlement percentage likely is slightly higher because the 512 awards also include 33 consent awards. In 2018, the ICC registered 842 new cases and "approved" 599 awards. Understanding that the new cases must be considered in the context of rollovers from previous years (even if it is assumed that the median case has a 28-month life), here as well, it makes sense to project an approximately 29–30 percent settlement rate. This number must also be qualified by noting there were 46 consent awards, and a number of cases (undetermined) that were withdrawn without reaching a settlement.[10]

In calendar year 2020, 946 cases were registered with the Secretariat of the ICC, of which 929 were under the ICC Arbitration Rules and 17 under the ICC Appointing Authority Rules. The ICC Dispute Resolution 2020 statistics (p. 18) effect that the ICC approved 564 awards, 383 final awards, 39 by consent, and 142 partial awards. Using the 525 figure (excluding 39 consent awards), and assuming the "new cases" serve as a general baseline for the number of total cases with respect to which the 525 awards figure applies, then roughly 45 percent of the cases were withdrawn or settled.

this data does provide more than just a "rough" understanding of the percentage of cases that settle, although the figures will be affected by partial awards, consent awards, and cases that simply are not prosecuted.

A second source are the surveys directed at arbitrators and practitioners in the field. Here as well, the methodologies employed, including geographic and specific industry arbitration, to cite only two, are not always as pristine as one would hope. Still, however, in the land of the blind, or so we are told, the Cyclops is king.

It does seem somewhat established that approximately one third settle, which hardly bespeaks *optimal efficiency*. Part of the challenge, in addition to lacking a framework conducive to the necessary risk assessment, the culture of arbitration is yet to embrace settlement as *optimal efficiency*. Arbitrators are only now being sensitized to the importance of settlement as endemic to their responsibilities as arbitrators, and arbitrators acting as *de facto* mediators while processing a case are plagued by a myriad of potential conflicts. See, e.g., Alexandre de Gramont, Michael D. Igyarto, & Tatiana Sainati, "Divergent Paths: Settlement in Us Litigation and International Arbitration," 40 *Fordham Int'l L.J.* 953, 964–66 (2017) addressing these concerns.

Notwithstanding such challenges, ICA must improve in its commitment culturally and operationally to *optimal efficiency* upon penalty of losing process legitimacy.

10 (See "ICC Dispute Resolution Bulletin," 2019, Issue 1, at 17–23; and "ICC Dispute Resolution Bulletin," 2018, Issue 2, "ICC Practice and Procedure," 2018, Issue, 1 at 52.)

The HKIAC, as previously referenced, is the only international arbitration administering center that actually straight-forwardly publishes the percentage of cases that settled. It is noteworthy that their published figures comport with the approximations here analyzed. The HKIAC provides that approximately 45–57 percent of cases registered settle. Figures from 2021 reflect that 43.9 percent settled, with 45 percent in 2022, and 57 percent in 2023. Moreover, the HKIAC states that the rate of amicable settlement constitutes a discernible trend that is increasing.

A study published in 2008 by PriceWaterhouseCoopers and Queen Mary University of London reports that only 33 percent of counsel experienced a settlement either without an arbitral award (25%) or a settlement in connection with a consent award (7%). Of the cases that end in settlements, about 74 percent occur before the hearing on the merits of the case.

Another often cited study is the Straus Institute for Dispute Resolution Survey of Experienced Arbitrators, conducted in cooperation with the College of Commercial Arbitrators and originally published in an article by Thomas Stipanowich and Zachary P. Ulrich in 2014.[11] The survey indicates that a growing percentage of commercial arbitrations are being settled prior to an award, or prior to the start of hearing. Note that the "past 5 years" indicated in Figures 2.1 and 2.2, referring on the chart refer to 2009–2019.

The American Arbitration Association, in the ICDR, also by way of illustration, publishes its yearly caseload (registrations). It is unclear how many of the cases reach the end of all arbitral labor. The ICDR, however, does publish the percentage of cases filed seeking emergency measures of protection and the percentage of such filings that actually settle. These numbers are helpful in charting settlement parameters more generally in ICA. As of December 31, 2019, 106 applications were filed with the ICDR; 16 were withdrawn; and 17 actually settled. Likewise, in 2022 exactly 106 applications for emergency measures of protection were filed. Here 17 percent settled and 14 percent were withdrawn.

The SIAC Annual Report for 2017 reflects that in the 2017 calendar year, 452 new cases were handled by SIAC, with 421 IAC-administered cases. These figures represent without growth from 307 administered cases in 2016 and 343 new cases handled by SIAC in 2016. In 2017, 139 awards issued. Assuming that the 139 wards pertain largely to the average 2014–2015 filings that equals 246 registered cases, then approximately 43 percent of the cases settled or were withdrawn.

In 2018, SIAC issued 141 awards, and registered 402 new cases handled by SIAC, and 375 administered cases, which equaled 93 percent of the total new cases assuming that the 141 awards issued in 2018 relate to the average of cases registered in 2015 and 2016, which equals 275, such that under this scenario, approximately 50 percent of all cases settle.

In calendar year 2021, SIAC handled 469 new cases, and 137 awards were issued. Assuming the 137 awards concern the average of new cases handled for calendar

[11] Thomas Stipanowich & Zachary P. Ulrich, "Commercial Arbitration and Settlement: Empirical Insights into the Rules Arbitrators Play," 6 *Penn State Yearbook on Arb. Mediat.* 1 (2014).

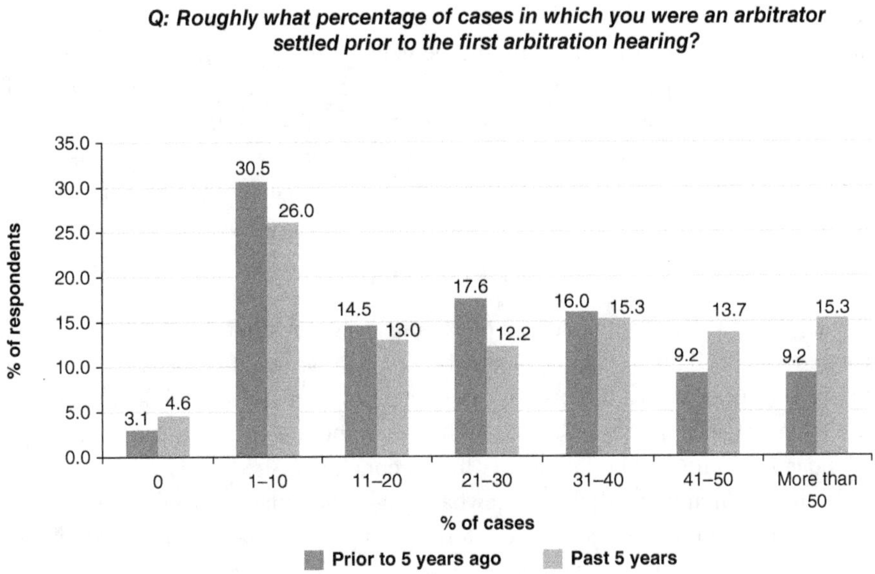

FIGURE 2.1 Settlement prior to hearing

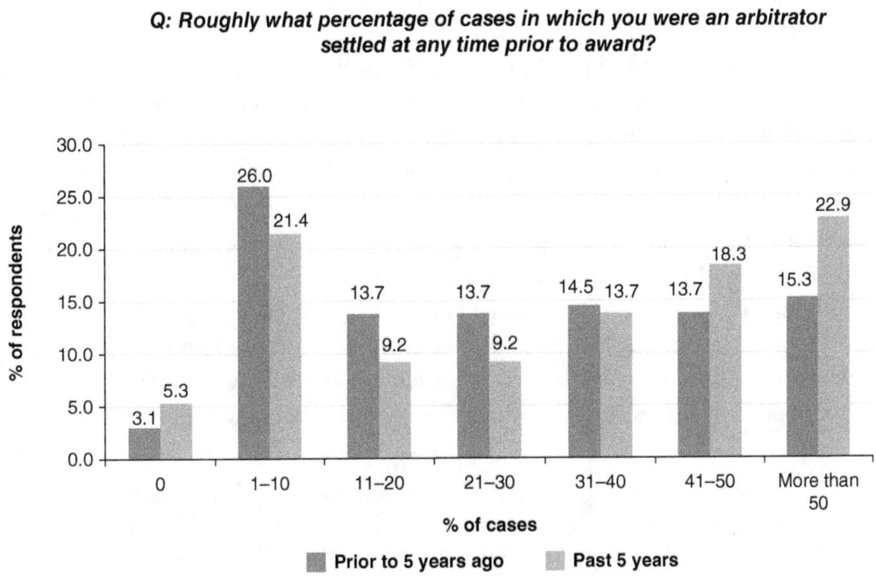

FIGURE 2.2 Settlement prior to award

years 2019 and 2018, which equals 440, 58 percent of cases during the 2021 calendar year were settled or withdrawn. In 2022, SIAC issued 161 awards in a year where 357 new cases were referred, 336 (94%) SIAC administered assuming the 161 awards pertained to the average of cases referred in 2018 and 2019, which equals 440, would yield a 63 percent figure reflecting the percentage of cases settled or withdrawn. (SIAC annual reports for 2017, 2018, 2021, and 2022.) It should be borne in mind that these numbers include consenting awards and partial awards.

Data further clarifying the likely percentage of cases that settle can be gleaned from survey information.[12] This data corroborates the 27–36 percent ICA settlement rate.

2.2 THE HKIAC STATISTICS

In 2021, the HKIAC reported a total of 277 international arbitration cases as having been commenced during this calendar year. That same year, 65 cases concluded by dint of final awards. An additional 51 cases reached the end of all arbitral labor based on settlement. The figures reflecting final awards and settlements during any single calendar year is helpful but altogether hardly conclusive.

While a straightforward and somewhat rough computation would suggest that 45 percent of all the cases concluded during a single calendar year reached finality pursuant to settlement, based on the HKIAC's report for 2021, we would still have 161 cases unaccounted for that were likely still being processed. In any event, however, the mathematically accurate statement based on this specific data point is that of 116 cases that concluded in 2021 under the administration of the HKIAC, 45 percent were concluded pursuant to agreement of the parties.

The HKIAC recorded 344 arbitrations filed during calendar year 2022.[13] Actual specific dates on the filings are not available. The reported statistics reflect that 93.4 of the arbitrations commenced in 2022 were international cases.[14] Notably, only two cases were submitted for early determination,[15] and 20 applications for expedited procedure were reported.[16] During 2022, 56 of the cases submitted were concluded pursuant to final award, while 46 of the filings were settled. Yielding a 45 percent settlement rate, this was the same rate as in 2021.

Although ICA's public international law counterpart, ISDS, presents a more difficult paradigm, often ISDS cases do not settle because of settlement preclusive factors unique to sovereigns that are not present in private ICA commercial disputes between private entities and natural persons render settlement impossible.[17]

[12] Menon, "Dispelling Due Process Paranoia"; Loukas Mistelis, "Article Special Section the 2008 Survey on Corporate Attitudes towards Recognition and Enforcement of International Arbitral Awards: The Settlement-Enforcement Dynamic in International Arbitration," 19 *Am. Rev. Int'l. Arb*. 377 (2008); see also de Gramont, Igyarto, & Sainati, "Divergent Paths," n. 2, 5.

[13] HKIAC, at: www.hkiac.org/about-us/statistics (last accessed January 8, 2024).

[14] *Id.*

[15] *Id.*

[16] *Id.*

[17] Treaty-based international arbitrations concern collateral political considerations that are foreign to most ICA proceedings. Often government administrations opine the payment of millions of dollars in a settlement, although justified pursuant to economic *risk assessment* models, may not be politically

The purely dispute-processing dynamic of an arbitral configuration, including procedural and evidentiary norms governing the taking and presentation of evidence, are shared by both ISDS and ICA stakeholders and processes. In this most important regard, however, the settlement percentage of all ISDS cases filed is instructive and may inform our understanding of ICA settlement percentages.[18]

The entire parabola of the ISDS settlement rate in the context of the International Centre for Settlement of Investment Disputes (ICSID) is very much available. Relevant information during the 1966 through 2021 timeframe is arresting:

(a) For all cases registered with ICSID commencing 1966 through 2021:
- 18%: proceeding discontinued at the request of both parties;
- 8%: proceeding discontinued at the request of one party;
- 4.5%: settlement agreement embodied in an award at the request for all parties.[19]

One generous construction is to surmise that the 4.5 percent figure really is just part of the total 26 percent represented by cases discontinued either at the request of one or both parties. Consequently, the safest reading would assume that these percentages all represent cases concluded by settlement. Yielding a 30 percent settlement rate for the entire history of ICSID arbitrations (ISDS).

This snapshot, however, is somewhat misleading because of the first and second generation of cases filed, settled, or processed during the early years of the ICSID. The ICSID Convention, also known as the Washington Convention, entered into force on October 14, 1966.[20]

Focus on the figures for a single year (2021) provides for a more immediate understanding of the *inefficiency*:

(b) For cases heard at the ICSID in calendar year 2021:
- 22%: proceeding discontinued at the request of both parties;
- 4%: proceeding discontinued at the request of one party;
- 1.5%: settlement agreement embodied in an award at the request of all parties.[21]

palatable, particularly when concerning capital-importing countries facing social exigencies, ranging from infant mortality arising from malnutrition and curable diseases, to unacceptable disparities between the poor and the affluent sectors of society. In the context of the human crises of this magnitude affecting life expectancy and caloric intake, diverting funds to settle a legal dispute are likely be received as politically unpresentable.

18 We need to keep in mind that *ad hoc* arbitrations represent a black box with respect to potentially helpful empirical data in both ICA and ISDS proceedings.

19 World Bank, at: https://icsid.worldbank.org/resources/publications/icsid-caseload-statistics (last accessed February 17, 2024).

20 World Bank, at: ICSID Convention.pdf (worldbank.org) (last accessed February 17, 2024).

21 *See* www.hkiac.org/about-us/statistics.

Applying the same rationale, the broadest and most generous construction favoring settlement based on these numbers would be 27.5 percent, closer to one-fourth of all cases for a single year. Again, we are assuming that all of the discontinued cases resulted in a settlement agreement. This assumption is untested and likely imprecise.

The ICA settlement rate is simply not acceptable. It certainly calls into question any claim to efficiency as a hallmark principle endemic to ICA.

The only analysis that can preserve ICA's claim to efficiency as a salient feature or fundamental pillar would be to argue that the process is conducted efficiently. Therefore, in ICA's current status, *efficiency* only concerns a process with the objective of yielding a binding and enforceable award. This understanding of efficiency as what we have been calling "*process efficiency*" is analytically suspect because it carves out of efficiency the highest and optimal resource allocation between the parties to a dispute, which can only be attained through settlement. In any event, however, even *process efficiency* is wanting in contemporary ICA proceedings (see Chapter 2 in this volume).

2.3 STATISTICAL ANALYSIS OF SETTLEMENTS IN US JUDICIAL PROCEEDINGS

In US federal and state courts, over 85 percent of all civil cases settle. This number is objectively verifiable and mathematically certain.[22]

22 In approaching the issue of settlement in the context of US federal and state court civil litigation, the general consensus seems to be that approximately 88 percent of all cases are terminated without a final adjudication, taking into account that as of the time of this writing (September 2024), only approximately 3 percent of all cases reach the end of all judicial labor pursuant to a jury trial, which has caused a reassessment of the US evidentiary tradition that is primarily based on condition of the type of evidence, irrespective of its relevance and materiality that can be proffered to a jury. See, e.g., John Sheldon & Peter Murray, "Rethinking the Rules of Evidentiary Admissibility in Non-jury Trials," 86 *Judicature* 227 (March–April 2003); Henry Zhuhao Wang, "The Fate of Evidence Law: Two Paths of Development," *E & P* 2020 24(3), 329–348 (2020). Citing Marc Galanter, "The Vanishing Trial: An Examination of Trials and Related Matters in Federal State Courts," 15 *Empirical Legal Stud.* 459 (2004), Henry Zhuhao Wang writes that:

> Marc Galanter famously stated, American jury trials are vanishing. Statistics indicate that the number of jury trials in the US federal and state courts in both civil and criminal cases has diminished for decades, in both absolute (i.e., total numbers) and relative terms (i.e., as a percentage of all case dispositives). [Citation omitted.] According to a recent study, the number of American trials has dropped so dramatically that "the jury trial is an exceptional rather than commonplace outcome" [citation omitted]. The percentage of federal civil cases decided by jury trial dropped from 5.5 percent in 1962 to 0.8 percent in 2013.

Henry Zhuhao Wang, "Rethinking Evidentiary Rules in an Age of Bench Trials," 13 *U.C. Irvine L. Rev.* 263, 302–303 (2022). Notwithstanding the surge in "bench," nonjury trials, bench trials are also declining.

Annual bench trial data of US federal district courts is extracted from the "Trials Completed" section of the corresponding year's "U.S. District Courts – Judicial Business" Report ("The U.S. Judicial Business Report" which is publicly available on the U.S. Courts website). For an example of bench

There are many, perhaps countless, reasons why judicial proceedings in the US settle. However, fourteen factors stand out the most:

(i) The *risk assessment* arising from the discovery (evidence-taking) system;
(ii) pleading practice requiring more than "notice pleading" or conclusory allegations merely alleging legal noncompliance;
(iii) motion practice that reconfigures the risk–reward ratios for all parties;
(iv) uncertainty arising from the jury system;

trial data of US federal district courts for the year 2020, the corresponding paragraph in the "U.S. Judicial Business Report 2020" states:

> Total civil trials declined 34 percent (down 1,314 trials) to 2,548. Seventy-six districts reported fewer civil trials. *Civil nonjury trials fell by 596 trials to 1,889*, with 65 districts reporting decreases. Civil jury trials dropped 52 percent (down 718 trials) to 659, with 78 districts reporting reductions.
>
> Total criminal trials decreased 28 percent to 5,433 (down 2,120 trials) as 79 district courts reported reductions in criminal trials. *Criminal nonjury trials dropped 24 percent to 4,329 (down 1,341 trials)*, with 73 district courts reporting lower numbers of these trials. Criminal jury trials decreased 41 percent to 1,104 (down 779 trials) as 73 district courts reported more trials of this type and totals in five district courts stayed the same. Article III judges accepted guilty pleas from 61,991 felony defendants, down 15 percent from 72,822 in 2019.

Citing "U.S. District Courts – Judicial Business 2020," U.S. Caseload Table of Statistics (CTS), www.uscourts.gov/statistics-reports/us-district-courts-judicial-business-2020 (https://perma.cc/3ZSX-G2GQ) (last accessed November 6, 2022) (original emphasis). For bench trial data of state courts, see Brian J. Ostrom, Shauna M. Strickland, & Paula L. Hannaford-Agor, "Examining Trial Trends in State Courts: 1976–2002," 1 *J. Empirical Legal Stud.* 755 (2004). However, there is a whole different school of scholarship claiming that bench trials are far less common than jury trials in the US, in both civil and criminal cases and at both the federal and state levels. See, e.g., Thomas A. Mauet, "Bench Trials," *LITIG.*, at 13 (Summer 2002) ("How often do bench trials occur? In criminal cases, about 10 to 15 percent of all trials are bench trials (the percentages can vary significantly among the state and federal jurisdictions). In civil cases, about 30 to 35 percent of all trials are bench trials."); Nora Freeman Engstrom, "The Diminished Trial," 86 *Fordham L. Rev.* 2131, 2137 (2018) ("[O]ver the years, we have seen a sharp rise in the proportion of jury trials as compared to bench trials: In 1983, the majority (56 percent) of federal civil trials were conducted without a jury; only a minority (44 percent) were jury trials. But by 2016, that had flipped: 71 percent of trials (1965 out of 2781) were jury trials; a mere 29 percent (816 out of 2781) weren't" (first citing Administrative Office of the U.S. CTS, Report of the Director, tbl.C-4 (1983))).

Wang, "Rethinking Evidentiary Rules," 263, 267–268, n. 14.

Irrespective of whether the trends and statistics establish that nonjury trials are more common than jury trials, the numbers reflect that both jury and nonjury trials are in sharp decline. The reason is that cases settled. And they settle because self-disclosure, discovery, and court-ordered mediation provide for the identification, quantification, and communication of risk.

For the sake of completeness, see Theodore Eisenberg & Charlotte Lanvers, "What Is the Settlement Rate and Why We Should Care?," 6 *J. Empir. Legal Stud.* 111, 112 (2009) (observing that the often cited proposition that "over ninety percent of all cases settle" is probably overstated). See also Kevin M. Clermont, "Litigation Realities Redux," 84 *Notre Dame L. Rev.* 1919, 1654–1655 (2009) (suggesting that of the 271,753 federal civil cases terminated in all federal districts during calendar year 2005, approximately 67.7 percent were quoted as settled in one way or another; approximately 20.7 were adjudicated at the pre-trial phase; approximately 1.3 percent were adjudicated at the trial phase; and the remaining 10.3 percent of cases "fell into a welter of other classification codes, predominantly remand or transfer to another court, whereby most would result as a matter of probability in an eventual settlement rather than a final adjudication").

(v) cost avoidance arising from the inevitability of protracted litigation, and a likely and equally protracted second instance appellate review process;
(vi) concerns arising from zero-sum-game determinations;
(vii) disruption to going concerns arising from expensive and often intrusive discovery (evidence taking), among other considerations;
(viii) the perception that a favorable prospective judgment can be reversed on appeal, or comparable uncertainty;
(ix) privacy and disclosure concerns that can be detrimental in a competitive market environment, or pursuant to disclosure requirements pertaining to publicly traded companies;
(x) mandatory mediations;
(xi) a culture of settlement that is supported and promoted by judges;
(xii) a culture of settlement that has been embraced by consumers of litigation services, that is to say, all stakeholders;
(xiii) motion practice serves as a means through which judges, either implicitly or explicitly, signal to the stakeholders the court's provisional views on the merits; and
(xiv) the procedural settlement benefits of an offer-of-judgment Rule.[23]

In the context of ICA, however, the offer-of-judgment approach would not have the same effect in favor of encouraging settlements as it does within the framework of US litigation because arbitrators enjoy the inherent authority to award attorneys' fees and costs to the prevailing party absent an agreement by the parties to preclude such award. This precept notwithstanding, an approach similar to that of an offer-of-judgment may still lead to settlement in the arbitral context because arbitrators' inherent authority to award attorneys' fees and costs is discretionary. Therefore, the offer-of-judgment approach would infuse this aspect of the proceeding with greater predictive value.

Certainly, most of these elements are not shared with ICA. Second instance review, discovery, and the jury system (very particular *unquantifiable risk*) are three such notable features. Also, it is impossible to discern how many factors contribute to the conclusion of litigation by settlement, whether all, some, or single. In this analysis, a syllogism governing settlement has been adopted that is very much related to evidence taking and *risk assessment*:

Major premise: (a) Risk assessment is necessary for settlement.
Minor premise: (b) Risk assessment is only possible pursuant to the taking and disclosure of evidence.

[23] In general terms, such rule provides that if a party to the litigation rejects a written and duly articulated and quantified offer-of-judgment, which is then followed by issuance of a final judgment less favorable than the offer-of-judgment that was rejected, the judge may award the offering party the attorney's fees and costs incurred as of the time that the offer-of-judgment was tendered and/or rejected. Thus, litigants are provided with an incentive to reach as comprehensive as possible an understanding of the value of the case, i.e., to quantify risk recovery as early as possible in the process.

Conclusion: (c) Therefore settlement is not possible absent the taking and disclosure of evidence.

It is for this reason that ICA rules governing the taking and presentation of evidence need to be revisited and meaningfully revised. The assumption made here is that a very significant and material reason why US civil cases mostly settle is attributable to the *risk assessment* made possible by the discovery and self-disclosure process. While it is also assumed that no single premise of the twelve stated is responsible for settlement, the *working assumption* is that none of the factors listed outweighs *risk assessment* arising from the discovery (evidence-taking) process.

The US civil litigation settlement rate is referenced only because of two structural features that it shares with arbitration for purposes of exploring *optimal efficiency*. First, it is noteworthy that US civil litigation is based on an *adversarial* system, in contrast with the civil law's long-enshrined inquisitorial rubric.

The *adversarial* system mirrors the arbitral principle of *party-autonomy*. For this reason, the structural overlap suggests that propositions conducive to settlement by a party, and not a judge-driven civil litigation framework, may better comport and be consonant with a nonjudicial dispute-resolution methodology, which at least theoretically, is premised on *party-autonomy*.[24] This proposition is subject to considerable qualification because of the many limitations to *party-autonomy*.[25] Not the least of these limitations is the "default" workings triggering exercise of *arbitrator discretion* (inherent powers of arbitrators) (see Section 1.1.1).

Second, in both the US common law adversarial system and ICA's *party-autonomy* galvanized proceedings, the parties are accorded the initiative with respect to (i) the taking and (ii) presentation of evidence.[26]

The empirical studies available do not all share a common methodology and in large measure are adversely affected because of fragmented rules of judicial

24 See Chapter 6, discussing the civil law inquisitorial system in the context of the Prague Rules on the Efficient Conduct of Arbitration Proceedings 2018 ("Prague Rules").

25 *See* Chapter 6, n. 43.

26 By design, this analysis only focuses on the US as the single judicial jurisdiction offering a settlement rate and rules of civil procedure that conceptually and didactically best illustrates the connection between evidence, evidence taking, and the use of evidence to quantify risk. A commentator exploring below-settlement rate in international arbitration has noted that the inquisitorial system in Switzerland has yielded high judicial settlement rates comparable to the judicial settlement rates in the US arising from an adversarial system. He observes that the inquisitorial approach in Switzerland has been successful in generating meaningful settlement rates because

> there has been a long-standing tradition of settlement facilitation through mandatory pretrial conciliation, requiring the parties to appear personally in formalized settlement hearings. Conciliation as practiced by Swiss courts is a *sui generis* method of settlement facilitation, but often draws on concepts and tools developed in mediation. Due to the high settlement rates, pretrial conciliation has been widely heralded as a key pillar of success of the Swiss civil justice system. Culturally, in line with the concept of judging, prevalent in the inquisitorial system more generally, the judge's mission is understood broadly and also encompasses settlement facilitation. (See Alleman, "Mind the Settlement Gap.")

administration in both the state and federal systems across the US. Also, many cases are adjudicated on the merits but not pursuant to a trial.[27]

2.4 JUDICIAL SETTLEMENT BASED UPON EMPIRICAL EVIDENCE

As a point of departure in analyzing data regarding judicial settlement in US courts, it is important to note that the vast majority of civil cases are filed in state and not federal courts.[28]

By way of example, in calendar year 2013, litigants filed approximately 16.9 million civil cases in state court as compared to 259,489 civil cases filed in US federal district courts.[29] This data is based on the findings of the National Center for State Courts (NCSC), memorialized in a study titled *The Landscape of Civil Litigation in State Courts* ("the Study" or "the Landscape Study").[30]

The purpose of the Study was to document case characteristics and outcomes in civil cases disposed that were adjudicated in state courts throughout the US. These findings were earmarked to inform the Conference of Chief Justices who convened the Civil Justice Improvements Committee (the *Landscape Study*) to make recommendations concerning best practices for state courts.

The *Landscape Study*'s dataset consisted of all non-domestic civil cases disposed between July 1, 2012 and June 30, 2013 in exactly 152 courts with civil jurisdiction in ten urban counties.[31] The 925,344 cases actually studied comprised approximately 5 percent of state civil caseloads nationally throughout the US during the relevant timeframe.[32]

Quite notably, *only* 4 percent of cases were disposed by bench trial, jury trial, summary judgment, or binding arbitration.[33] The Study reflects that of this 4 percent that were actually adjudicated, approximately 97 percent were bench trials, and 46 percent of these bench trials took place "in small claims or other civil cases." The statistics further establish that "three-quarters of judgments entered in contract cases following a bench trial were less than half of those in small claims cases ($1,785 versus $3,900)."[34] These findings provide a sound factual basis for two revealing conclusions.

First, these numbers expressly conflict with the unfounded perception that the majority of bench trials do not involve high-stakes complex litigation. According to this study, parties to complex sophisticated disputes opt for bench trials in order to

27 See, e.g., Federal Rules of Civil Procedure (FRCP), Fed. R. Civ. P. 12, 56.

28 Civil Justice Initiative, *The Landscape of Civil Litigation in State Courts* (November 11, 2015) at 6.

29 *Id.*

30 *Id.*

31 *Id.* at (iii).

32 *Id.*

33 *Id.* at (iv).

34 *Id.*

obviate the perceived uncertainty "inherent" in the jury system. Bench trials have a metaphorical relation to arbitration adjudications.

Second, it underscores that cases with large damages quantum at some point tend to be settled. This point of inflection leading to settlement, it is here contended, results from *risk assessment* that is only possible after the parties have engaged in fulsome and robust self-disclosure and discovery.

Most cases were disposed through an administrative process. In 46 percent of the cases, a judgment was entered but most of these judgments were likely default judgments. The *Landscape Study* reflects that while 10 percent of the cases were *explicitly* recorded as settlements, about one third of all cases were dismissed. And those dismissals were believed to have followed settlements.

Table 2.1 illustrates under the heading "All Courts" in the "Adjudicated Disposition" category that only 4 percent of cases were adjudicated.[35]

Under the heading "All Courts" in Table 2.1, there is a 35 percent figure reflecting dismissals, most of which are by joint stipulation of the parties pursuant to a settlement. Similarly, the unspecified judgments at 26 percent likely are consent judgments. Therefore, they are tantamount to settlements. We know for sure they are not a form of adjudication either through a jury trial, bench trial, or summary judgment.

This review brings us to summary judgment adjudications, which again are only 1 percent, further bolstering the likelihood that the majority of cases are disposed of pursuant to the common agreement of the parties in a settlement context.[36]

Table 2.2 contains the identical data as in Table 2.1, but now broken down into disposition by the type of case. The column under the heading "Contract" most likely would resemble the more common ICA cases, that is to say, a general contract dispute.

TABLE 2.1 *Percentage of case dispositions by court type*

	Single tier	General jurisdiction	Limited jurisdiction	All courts
Dismissed	31	36	37	35
Judgment (unspecified)	50	15	16	26
Default judgment	3	18	32	20
Settlement	13	12	6	10
Adjudicated disposition	1	4	5	4
Unknown	0	13	2	4
Summary judgment	0	1	1	1
Other disposition	1	2	1	1

35 *Id.* at 21.

36 *Id.* at 22.

TABLE 2.2 *Proportion of case dispositions by case type*

	Contract	Tort	Real property	Small claim	Other	All cases
Dismissed	33	39	37	47	31	35
Judgment (unspecified)	31	11	23	10	25	26
Default judgment	21	4	13	32	7	20
Settlement	7	32	12	2	19	10
Unknown	3	8	5	0	11	4
Adjudicated disposition	3	3	6	7	6	4
Other disposition	1	3	2	1	1	1
Summary judgment	1	1	3	0	0	1

Only 3 percent of cases adjudicated proceeded to a merits determination. Equally revealing, only 1 percent represent a merits determination pursuant to summary judgment.

The findings are clear. The data in Table 2.2 establishes that 95 percent of contract cases are concluded pursuant to agreement by the parties in some context, and not in a zero-sum-game scenario by virtue of the exercise of a third party's judgment.

Prior to the *Landscape Study*, the most recent large-scale national study of civil caseloads was the 1992 Civil Justice Survey of State Courts (the *Civil Justice Survey*).[37] That effort consisted of a periodic study of civil litigation funded by the U.S. Department of Justice, Bureau of Justice Statistics (BJS). These statistics concern cases filed in state courts based on filings in a sample of the seventy-five most populous counties.[38]

Approximately 750,000 civil case dispositions were analyzed in these seventy-five highly populated counties. Approximately half (48%) consisted of contract claims. The remaining half (49%) were based on tort allegations.[39]

According to the *Civil Justice Survey*, explicit settlement constituted the solitary most common outcome for civil cases at 62 percent, particularly when compared to 14 percent default judgments, 10 percent dismissals for failure to prosecute, 4 percent transfers to another court, 4 percent summary judgment, and only 3 percent judgments following a bench or jury trial.

Again, what is critical for present purposes are all of the non-trial (jury or bench) findings, which account for just slightly less than 97 percent of all dispositions.

These figures, pertaining to an adversarial system that is party-driven (i.e., that is foundationally based on *party-autonomy*),[40] stands in sharp contrast to the approximately 68–79 percent final hearing merits adjudications that characterize ICA.

37 U.S. Department of Justice, Office of Justice Programs, BJS, *Civil Justice Survey of State Courts, 1992*, Inter-university Consortium for Political and Social Research (distributor), November 11, 2011, doi .org/10.3886/ICPSR06587.v5.

38 *Id.*

39 *Id.*

40 *Id.*

It will be suggested that ICA *party-autonomy* driven evidence taking would benefit from enhancing the operational workings of *evidence taking* and *presenting* rules so as to render *risk assessment* viable early in the process. These rules should include encouraging arbitrators to discuss settlement with the parties, in part, by securing the parties' consent to the arbitrator commenting on the evidence.[41]

Transparency and predictive value need to be enhanced by allowing parties at the very commencement of an arbitral proceeding, and throughout the process to gauge with reasonable certainty the admissibility, relevance, materiality, and weight of evidence at the evidence taking phase. The presentation of evidence phase of a prospective final hearing would need to be governed by more rigorous, and therefore transparent, evidentiary rules. Such rules will temper *arbitrator discretion* while increasing *party-autonomy* and corresponding *risk assessment*.

[41] Arbitrator involvement in a mediation process, or related but distinct, in a role as a settlement facilitator, has been thoughtfully addressed in a handful of articles, see, e.g., Klaus Peter Berger, "The Direct Involvement of the Arbitrator in the Amicable Settlement of the Dispute: Offering Preliminary Views, Discussing Settlement Options, Suggesting Solutions, Caucusing," 35 *J. Int. Arb.* 5, 501–516 (2018), at: https://shorturl.at/Ee4uG (last accessed September 20, 2023); Klaus Peter Berger & J. Ole Jensen, "The Arbitrator's Mandate to Facilitate Settlement," 40 *Fordham Int'l L.J.* 3, 887 (2017), https://ssrn.com/abstract=3460136; Stutzer Hansjörg, "Settlement Facilitation: Does the Arbitrator Have a Role? The 'Referentenaudienz' – the 'Zurich-Way' of Settling the Case," 35 ASA *Bulletin* 3, 589–608 (2017), https://kluwerlawonline.com/journalarticle/ASA+Bulletin/35.3/ASAB2017052 (last accessed September 20, 2023); Thomas Stipanowich & Zachary Ulrich, "Commercial Arbitration and Settlement: Empirical Insights into the Roles Arbitrators Play," 6 *Penn State Yearbook on Arb. Mediat.* 1 (2014), Pepperdine University Legal Studies Research Paper, No. 2014/20, https://ssrn.com/abstract=2461839; Stefanie Pfisterer, "The Arbitrator as Settlement Facilitator" (2013), 24 *Am. Ren. Int'l Arb.* 649; Lucy Greenwood, "A Window of Opportunity? Building a Short Period of Time into Arbitral Rules in Order for Parties to Explore Settlement,"27 *Arb. Int.* 2, 199–210 (2011); and Gabrielle Kaufmann-Kohler, "Beyond Gadgetry: Substantive New Concepts to Improve Arbitral Efficiency," 5 *J. World Inv. Trade* 69–72 (2004).

This quantitatively modest body of work principally addresses five propositions. First, the need to distinguish between facilitating settlement and engaging in mediation such that arbitration is not transformed into a hybrid mediation/arbitration process. An arbitration proceeding is an arbitration proceeding and not a mediation. Second, many mediation techniques can be applied in an arbitral context without jeopardizing the integrity of foundational arbitration principles. Third, there no longer is any debate as to whether arbitrators should participate in settlement facilitation. The contemporary view on this matter is that arbitrator participation in facilitating settlement translates into a more efficient arbitral proceeding. Fourth, arbitrators' mandate to settle disputes is not limited to merits adjudication. Settlement is encompassed within such a mandate. Therefore, it is not a question of "whether" but rather of "how" arbitrators are to participate in facilitating settlement. Fifth and finally, the general consensus is that arbitrators should not privately caucus with the parties as part of the facilitation or qualified mediation process.

These very helpful writings, however, do not consider that risk assessment and quantification arising from the parties' evaluation of the evidence within the applicable procedural (admissibility, relevance, materiality, and weight) and substantive law framework is an indispensable necessity to a settlement that is equivalent to *optimal efficiency*. The application of sanitized mediation techniques to arbitral proceedings cannot yield meaningful settlements, particularly in the context of complex and high-stake commercial cases. The "bet-the-company" case will settle only after extensive consideration and evaluation of mathematical damages and liability models. See, Alleman, "Mind the Settlement Gap."

3

Engaging in a Thought Experiment

International Commercial Arbitrations Do Not Settle and Maximize Inefficiencies

3.1 THE MAJOR INSTITUTIONAL ARBITRAL RULES DO NOT PROVIDE FOR GUIDANCE IN EVIDENCE TAKING OR THE PRESENTATION OF EVIDENCE THAT WOULD BE CONDUCIVE TO THE REQUISITE TRANSPARENCY PROVIDING FOR THE APPROPRIATE *RISK ASSESSMENT* NECESSARY AS A CONDITION PRECEDENT TO SETTLEMENT

Perhaps second only to the process of empaneling an arbitral tribunal, evidence taking is the most consequential undertaking forming part of an arbitral proceeding. The very value and strength of a party's affirmative claims and defenses only is fully known and susceptible to quantification and *risk assessment* depending on the efficiencies of the evidence-taking process.

The standard for evidence-taking disclosure requirements and the criterion determining the admissibility, relevance, and materiality of evidence for purposes of presenting and admitting evidence at a hearing is absolutely no different from the rules that control the evidence-taking phase of an arbitral proceeding. This singular approach to two very different processes raises concerns.

The single factor that an arbitral tribunal will consider in assessing evidence not forming part of the extent to which evidence must be disclosed as part of the evidence-taking process, pertains to the *weight* to be accorded to evidence. Consideration of this factor (weight), however, is triggered only after admissibility, relevance, and materiality presumably have been determined.[1]

[1] Effective evidence gathering presumably would lead to influencing the *weight* to be accorded to evidence *presented* because it would affect the *quality* of the evidence. The ability to secure witnesses with direct and actual knowledge of material and relevant facts logically would make for more compelling testimony than an account based on second or third-hand hearsay. The same principle would apply to concerns such as witness credibility, and "best evidence" considerations with respect to any particular evidential proposition proffered.

Mnookin and Kornhauser, in an iconic law review article,[2] coined the phrase "bargaining in the shadow of the law."[3] This metaphor illustratively suggests that settlement negotiations occur in a context that is created by the extent to which procedural and substantive rules provide the parties with predictive value arising from the stakeholder's understanding of the extent to which the governing evidence provides for predictive value within this legal framework. Stated even more simply, settlement negotiations are governed by the parties' degree of certainty regarding the consequential effects of the application of law to fact. Evidential equipoise between the parties arising from access to available relevant documents objectively and subjectively enhances predictive value. This predictive value, in turn, can be expressed in terms of risk assessment.

Mnookin and Kornhauser developed the "bargaining in the shadow of the law" metaphor in the context of negotiations between divorcing parents and the legal rubric allocating custodial rights, alimony, child support and visitation:

> Divorcing parents do not bargain over the division of family wealth and custodial prerogatives in a vacuum; *they bargain in the shadow of the law.* The legal rules governing alimony, child support, marital property, and custody give each parent certain claims based on what each would get *if the case went to trial.* In other words, the outcome that the law will impose if no agreement is reached gives each parent certain bargaining chips – an endowment of sorts.
>
> A simplified example may be illustrative. Assume that in disputed custody cases the law flatly provided that all mothers have the right to custody of minor children and that all fathers only have the right to visitation two weekends a month. Absent some contrary agreement acceptable to both parents, a court would order this arrangement. Assuming further that the legal rules relating to marital property, alimony, and child support gave the mother some determinate share of the family's economic resources. In negotiations under this regime, neither spouse would ever consent to a divorce that left him or her worse off than if he or she insisted on going to court. The range of negotiated outcomes would be limited to those

2 *See* Chapter 1, n. 86; Mnookin & Kornhauser, "Bargaining in the Shadow of the Law," 968–969.

3 In a very insightful and thoughtful article, Alleman, "Mind the Settlement Gap," the author notes that the asymmetries in knowledge between and among litigants prevents settlement until such procedural juncture as the litigation unfolds, where "the informational asymmetries progressively decline as a result of the various pretrial and discovery procedures [ ], thus generating a set of previously unavailable bargaining tokens. Consequently, one can often expect parties' beliefs about the litigation outcome to converge well ahead of the judgment statement stage which frees the way for a mutually beneficial settlement." *Id.*, at 5 of 14, *citing to* Steven Shavell, *Foundations of Economic Analysis of Law* (2024), 412; and J. J. Prescott & Kathryn E. Spier, "A Comprehensive Theory of Civil Settlement," 91 *NYU L. Rev.* 59, 77 (2016).

This convergence of knowledge is the stage at which risk assessment ripens into an attainable state of affairs. In ICA, such convergence is not a product of consequence of rules rendering parity between the parties on evidentiary matters that can generate predictive value. The author, however, swerves from general risk assessment based upon evidential analyses and a recalibration of arbitral discretion and *party-autonomy*, to judicial mediation practices.

> that leave both parents as well off as they would be in the absence of a bargain.[4] (Emphasis added)

This example deliberately identifies pristine rules and wrests from the paradigm any uncertainty in presenting a circumstance where the parties have absolute predictive value as to what the outcome of the dispute would be. Legal rules governing most ICA proceedings are rarely so clear. Moreover, as already referenced (Section 1.2.2), *arbitrator discretion* looms large as an element of inherent uncertainty challenging predictive value. Even so, (i) timely and (ii) robust self-disclosure and evidence-taking rules, (iii) together with reasonable certainty governing relevance, materiality, and weight, would bolster risk assessment. Under such a framework the parties would be in a state of near informational equipoise. No party would be the beneficiary of knowledge of relevant and material evidence.

Having reached a stage near equipoise where the difference of evidential knowledge between the parties is statistically insignificant, the parties' negotiations over entitlements/tokens accorded to each by an understanding of enforceable rights, will create a scenario of cognizable risk assessment for all parties. While *arbitrator discretion* will continue to contribute uncertainty to the negotiation process, this inherent risk is one that applies equally to all stakeholders.

In a fair number of instances, a prevailing party determination yielding an arbitral award that fully compensates a claimant as a matter of law, may still prove to be unsatisfactory. Often enough, an arbitral tribunal lacks authority to grant injunctive relief or other forms of special damages that would best serve a stakeholder. In these instances, the need for rules that minimize uncertainty become all the more critical. The negotiating posture of the party in need of the special damages requires that stakeholder to prevail in communicating the highest possible quantum of risk to the opposing party in order to leverage a settlement that would yield the special damages that ICA cannot award.

General institutional laws purporting in form only to be primarily based on *party-autonomy*, but in fact enshrining *arbitrator discretion* in the context of *process efficiency* are now existential to ICA.

3.2 ICC RULES ON THE TAKING OF EVIDENCE (2021)

Notwithstanding the paramount importance of the taking of evidence in ICA, the major institutional rules provide little, if any, *procedural* or *substantive* guidance.[5] The 2021 iteration of the ICC Arbitration Rules are illustrative in this regard. These rules are not particularly scant. Instead, they mirror the "arbitration culture" pervading institutional rules on the issue of *evidence* generally.

4 *See* Mnookin & Kornhauser, "Bargaining in the Shadow of the Law," 968–969.

5 International Chamber of Commerce Arbitration Rules, 2021.

The ICC Rules contain forty-three Articles. No *single* Article, however, is dedicated to the *taking of evidence*. Indeed, the very word "evidence" appears only once throughout the entirety of the forty-three Articles. It does so in Art. 27 (Closing of the Proceedings and Date for Submission of Draft Awards), and only to assert that: "[a]fter the proceedings are closed, no further submission or argument may be made or *evidence* produced, with respect to the matters to be decided in the award, unless requested or authorized by the arbitral tribunal." (Emphasis added.)

This reference to "evidence," a term that is nowhere defined within the ICC Rules, is of no moment except to state generally the unremarkable proposition that only pursuant to the arbitral tribunal's explicit instructions can additional submissions of any type be made.

Terms such as "evidence gathering," "the taking of evidence," "document request," and "document production," are nowhere to be found, let alone articulated in the context of governing rules, standards, or principles. Self-disclosure requirements, as more fully described in what follows, are too attenuated even to be described as such.

Articles 4 and 5 of the ICC Rules are somewhat telling in this regard. Article 4, subsection 4.3(e) provides that a Request for Arbitration "shall contain the following information: e) Any relevant agreements and, in particular, the arbitration agreement(s)." While it certainly is appreciated that this requirement is in the mandatory "shall," it hardly educates the Tribunal or the parties as to the evidentiary, and therefore the actual, configuration of the case. Quite certainly, it does not and cannot allow the stakeholders, perhaps even the very claimant itself, an opportunity to engage in even rudimentary *risk assessment*. Instead, it contributes to process uncertainty and, therefore, *unquantifiable risk*.

A stricture requiring "any relevant agreements and, in particular, the arbitration agreement(s)," is little more than a perfunctory and very limited admissibility and scope disclosure requirement as to jurisdiction. A process concerned with educating the parties at the earliest possible time regarding the nature, sustainability, and viability with respect to proof of a claim, including liability and damages, would require compelling the claimant to disclose in tandem with the request for arbitration, or immediately after its submission, all documents upon which it intends to rely in furtherance of the claims asserted.

Article 5 (Answer to the Request; Counterclaims) is marginally more comprehensive. The final paragraph of Art. 5.1 provides that "[t]he respondent *may* submit such other documents or information with the Answer as it considers appropriate or as may contribute to the efficient resolution of the dispute." (Emphasis added.) Even though this language references "other documents" Art. 5.1 only articulates the word "document" in this final sentence and nowhere else in that section's preceding subsections.

Moreover, the respondent is invited (using the permissive "may") and not compelled to "submit such other documents." Thus, the "self-disclosure language" is in no way probative of the facts, defenses, or affirmative defenses asserted in the Answer. As with the Art. 4 self-disclosure stricture, it in no way allows the stakeholders, including the arbitral tribunal, to test the legal or factual sufficiency of the matters asserted.

Article 5.5 mirrors in every regard, but in the context of *counterclaims*, the disclosure suggestions that pertain to the Answer, and limits the mandatory only to "any relevant agreements and, in particular, the arbitration agreement(s)."

The Art. 22 (Conduct of the Arbitration) provision in Section 1 requires the arbitral tribunal and the parties to make "every effort to conduct the arbitration in an *expeditious* and *cost-effective* manner, having regard to the complexity and value of the dispute." (Emphasis added.) The taking of evidence certainly is not identified at all, let alone as a means for furthering the principle of efficiency that this subsection underscores within the framework of *party-autonomy* and *arbitrator discretion*.

Article 22.2 also is bereft of any plain or ordinary textual language concerning the taking of evidence. It does, however, state that the arbitral tribunal in adopting appropriate procedural measures that are not contrary to any agreement, "may include one or more of the case management techniques described in Appendix IV."

Here again the language is in the permissive "may" and not mandatory.

Appendix IV, titled "Case Management Techniques," does have helpful language regarding settlement and document production, albeit within a permissive framework. Subsection d) titled "*Production of documentary evidence*," reads:

(i) Requiring the parties to produce with their submissions the documents on which they rely;
(ii) Avoiding requests for document production when appropriate in order to control time and costs;
(iii) In those cases where requests for document production are considered appropriate, limiting such requests to documents or categories of documents that are relevant and material to the outcome of the case;
(iv) Establishing reasonable time limits for the production of documents;
(v) Using a schedule of document production to facilitate the resolution of issues in relation to the production of documents.

These case management techniques are all helpful in promoting efficiency generally. They are of no moment, however, with respect to fostering transparency and the production of documents that would allow parties to assess the sustainability of liability, damages, and credibility issues. Conspicuously absent from the document production management techniques is any reference to documents that would cause the parties to discuss settlement and that the parties considered to be most helpful in proving their respective cases.

While the document production case management techniques reference "establishing reasonable time limits for the production of documents," it does not specify that the production of such production must be prioritized and produced within thirty days or less from the date that an answer is due. Moreover, the provision needs to be crafted so that there is meaningful accountability in cases of willful or negligent noncompliance.

Efficiency is not inimical to transparency. Case management techniques addressing document production must foster both efficiency and transparency, so that *risk assessment* is possible and arbitration can redeem its promise to be efficient. To the extent that parties are unable to evaluate risk because of the absence of transparency arising from a less than fulsome and robust evidence-taking and presenting process, issues concerning arbitration process legitimacy will arise.

Subsection h) of the *Case Management Techniques* in Appendix 4 purports to address settlement. Here as well the rubric is the same permissive *may*, and hardly is there any substantive narrative that arbitrators are expected to articulate in connection with the possible settlement of disputes. It provides:

h) *Settlement of Disputes*:

(i) Encouraging the parties to consider settlement of all or part of the dispute either by negotiation or through any form of amicable dispute resolution methods such as, for example, mediation under the ICC Mediation Rules;
(ii) Where agreed between the parties and the arbitral tribunal, the arbitral tribunal may take steps to facilitate settlement of the dispute, provided that every effort is made to ensure that any subsequent award is enforceable at law.

This provision is a helpful example of seeing the trees but not the forest. The arbitral panel would be well served by being *required* and not *encouraged* to promote settlement by sharing with the parties foundational propositions that are endemic to arbitration proceedings. Consider sensitizing the parties to the following premises:

(i) The average ICC arbitration will take approximately two years. During that time you will be paying fees and costs to lawyers and to the arbitration panel;
(ii) There is no second instance merits review. Thus, prioritizing finality over precision in adjudication. The arbitral tribunal can be wrong in its interpretation of the governing law and most likely the award will stand.[6] Similarly, the arbitral tribunal can be wrong in its assessment of the operative facts, notwithstanding a clear record to the contrary, and most likely the award will still stand.[7] The arbitral tribunal can be wrong in its application of law to fact, and here again the award will survive;[8]

6 *Whites Springs Agric. Chems. Inc. v. Glawson Invs. Corp.*, 660 F. 3d 1277, 1280 (11th Cir. 2011) (stating that "courts generally are prohibited from vacating an arbitration award on the basis of errors of law or interpretation"); *Wilko v. Swan*, 346 U.S. 427, 436–437, 74 S. Ct. 182, 187, 98 L. Ed. 168 (1953) (observing that an arbitrator's erroneous interpretations or applications of law are not reversible), and *Raiford v. Merrill Lynch, Pierce, Fenner Smith*, 903 F. 2d 1410, 1423 (11th Cir. 1990) ("when the parties agreed to submit to arbitration, they also agreed to accept whatever reasonable uncertainties might arise from the process").

7 *Gherardi v. Citigroup Global Markets Inc.*, 975 F. 3d 1232, 1238 (11th Cir. 2020) (noting that "[a]rbitrators do not exceed their powers when they make errors, even 'a serious' error,") (quoting *Stolt-Nielsen S.A. v. Animal Feed Int'l. Corp.*, 559 U.S. 662, 671 (2010)).

8 *AIG Baker Sterling Heights, LLC v. Am. Multi-Cinema, Inc.*, 508 F. 3d 995, 1001 (11th Cir. 2007) (quoting *Del Casal v. E. Airlines, Inc.*, 634 F. 2d 295, 298 (5th Cir. Unit B. Jan. 1981)) (observing that

(iii) The parties will be accorded attenuated due process rights, and will lose control over such fundamentals as order of proof, and party discretion in ascertaining the requisite quantum of proof, let alone evidentiary discretion as to such issues as proof pertaining to thematic concerns, and impeachment;

(iv) At the end of the process upon issuance of an award, there will be a zero-sum-game scenario pursuant to which one party shall prevail and the other will be a non-prevailing party, i.e., a non-prevailing party who will walk away with no gains, and likely new obligations;

(v) Confidentiality and privacy are prized over transparency;

(vi) The arbitral tribunal may award attorney's fees and costs to the prevailing party even in instances where the parties to the underlying agreement deliberately excluded a prevailing party attorney's fees provision in the dispute resolution clause and/or elsewhere in the operative documents;

(vii) Before proceeding with an arbitration until the end of all arbitral labor, parties must consider the possible global expense of the process in relation to the amount in controversy, and where relevant and applicable, payment of the adverse party's attorney's fees and costs. It is not uncommon for an arbitral proceeding to develop into a scenario where the amount in controversy would not reasonably/mathematically justify the expense in prosecuting and defending an arbitration through the finality of all arbitral labor;

(viii) The arbitral tribunal is vested with very expansive inherent powers that find normative foundations in rules that often qualify such inherent powers by reference to "subject to the parties' agreement" a stricture that mostly is inoperable because of the adversarial nature of the proceeding itself;

(ix) Documents that the parties are yet to see significantly undermine their respective *liability* expectations;

(x) Documents that the parties are yet to see significantly undermine their *damages* expectations;

(xi) Expert reports as to damages and/or technical issues that the parties are yet to see materially undermine their expectations on such issues;

(xii) Notwithstanding the laudable workings of the New York Convention, there are no guarantees that even an enforceable award can be successfully executed;

(xiii) The relative strength of the parties' respective witness position as to liability, damages, and thematic concerns needs to be evaluated as a predicate to comprehensive *risk assessment* and meaningful cost benefit analyses concerning the viability of the proceeding;

(xiv) The parties are encouraged to attempt to quantify to the extent possible the business interruption cost that would be attendant to a proceeding lasting two years; and finally

because arbitration is intended to be an alternative to litigation, judicial review of an arbitral award "is among the narrowest known to law").

(xv) Notwithstanding the "private" status of arbitral proceedings, and the parties' ability to petition for confidentiality, overriding disclosure requirements arising from mandatory laws and rules in many jurisdictions, particularly as concern publicly-traded companies, may compel partial or complete disclosure.

Even the most cursory analysis of these non-exhaustive premises highlights the importance of the taking of evidence and presentation of evidence processes. Consideration of these factors demonstrates the profound relationship between taking of evidence and settlement. It generally is impossible for a party to quantify risk and to understand fully and appreciate the value of its own case; a proposition that is materially different from the theoretical value of a claim in a frictionless environment until such time as significant evidence taking has occurred.

At some point, the concept of flexibility becomes a euphemism for unbridled arbitral discretion. A degree of generality primarily transferring *party-autonomy* to the arbitral tribunal in all instances where the parties fail to agree, which we can assume would be most material issues in light of a contested all or nothing dispute, only nurtures a process that can find resolution at the end of all arbitral labor at the conclusion of a final hearing.

The absence of any timely evidentiary disclosure requirements, the failure to articulate a governing standard, and the lack of guidance as to the scope, form, and content of document production demands, witness (fact and expert) timely disclosure requirements, all tear into the very fabric of (i) efficiency, (ii) transparency, and (iii) any meaningful likelihood of settlement.

The lack of specificity bolsters *arbitrator discretion*. The prevalence of *arbitrator discretion* in turn minimized *party-autonomy*, and the ability for the parties systematically (i) to identify and (ii) to quantify risk. Thus, practically eviscerating any likelihood of settlement. Unqualified flexibility ultimately will raise questions concerning process legitimacy.

3.3 THE SCC RULES (2023)

The Stockholm Chamber of Commerce Arbitration Rules (SCC Rules) 2023 provide greater particularity and direction than contained in the ICC Rules.[9] The SCC Rules set forth self-disclosure requirements and a succinct but separate article discussing evidence. Significantly, in the mandatory – *shall* – both claimants and respondents are charged with producing evidence on which they rely. Although lacking in textual language, the present progressive form of the verb "to rely" would suggest the mandatory requirement is continuous:

[9] The Stockholm Chamber of Commerce Arbitration Rules 2023 (SCC Rules).

ARTICLE 29 WRITTEN SUBMISSIONS

(i) Within the period determined by the Arbitral Tribunal, the claimant *shall* submit a statement of claim which *shall* include, unless previously submitted:
  (i) The specific relief sought;
  (ii) *The facts and other circumstances that claimant relies on; and*
  (iii) *Any evidence that claimant relies on.* (Emphasis added)

The symmetrical provision for respondent states:

(1) Within the period determined by the Arbitral Tribunal, the respondent *shall* submit a statement of defense which *shall* include, unless previously submitted:
  (i) any objections concerning the existence, validity or applicability of the arbitration agreement;
  (ii) a statement whether, and to what extent, the respondent admits or denies the relief sought by the claimant;
  (iii) the facts and other circumstances *the respondent relies on*;
  (iv) any counterclaim or set-off and the facts and other circumstances *on which it is based; and*
  (v) *any evidence the respondent relies on.* (Emphasis added)

Article 31 titled “Evidence” is significantly richer than what is contained in the ICC Rules with respect to evidence. It is notable, however, that Art. 31 of the SCC Rules relies on the principle of *arbitrator discretion* to do the heavy lifting at the expense of transparency in the form of objective rules and principles:

ARTICLE 31 EVIDENCE

(1) The admissibility, relevance, materiality, and weight of evidence shall be for the Arbitral Tribunal to determine.
(2) The Arbitral Tribunal may order a party to *identify the documentary evidence* it intends to rely on and specify the circumstances intended to be proved by such evidence.
(3) At the request of a party, or exceptionally on its own motion, the Arbitral Tribunal may order a party to produce any documents or other evidence that may be *relevant to the case and material to its outcome.* (Emphasis added)

Article 31 of the SCC Rules is a decisive step in the right direction. Even though the terms “admissibility,” “relevance,” and “materiality” are not defined, the very reference to the three terms as core elements on which *arbitrator discretion* is to be exercised does serve to some extent as an organizing principles, which provide some basic directionality.

The term “intends to rely” in Art. 31.2 is helpful but considerably diminished because the stricture is worded in the permissive “may.” A mandatory rule coupled with the already present specificity requirement concerning the matter to be established pursuant to particular documents, introduces some level of transparency. Absent is a necessary timeframe within the early procedural junctures of the proceeding.

Finally, Art. 31.3 incorporates the only existing standard governing (i) the taking and (ii) the presentation of evidence in ICA: *relevant to the case and material to its outcome*. This standard has its origins in the 2010 iteration of the IBA Rules on the Taking of Evidence in International Arbitration, and is repeated on no less than nine occasions throughout the 2020 exemplar of the IBA Rules on the Taking of Evidence in International Arbitration.[10]

The reference to the "*relevant to the case and material to its outcome*" standard in Art. 31.3 would suggest that in any presentation of evidence, the parties would assume the standard also would apply to the exercise of arbitral discretion regarding the elements of Art. 31.1: admissibility, relevance, and materiality. This subsection also mentions "the weight of the evidence" as a factor that the arbitral tribunal must determine. The Rules do not suggest what factors are to be considered in according weight to evidence.

Article 33 of the SCC Rules represents a parallel provision to documentary evidence, also in the permissive "may," grants the arbitral tribunal discretion to require the parties to engage in self-disclosure of witnesses "they intend to call" at some unspecified time "[i]n advance of any hearing":

ARTICLE 33 WITNESSES

(1) In advance of any hearing, the Arbitral Tribunal *may* order the parties to identify each witness or expert they intend to call and specify the circumstances intended to be proved by each testimony.
(2) The testimony of witnesses or party-appointed experts may be submitted in the form of signed statements.
(3) Any witness or expert, *on whose testimony a party seeks to rely, shall attend a hearing for examination, unless otherwise agreed by the parties*. (Emphasis added)

Article 33.3 reflects a commitment to transparency by requiring in the mandatory – *shall* – fact and expert witnesses to attend a hearing for purposes of testing the factual and legal sufficiency of written declarations if in fact a party is to rely on such testimony. This provision is foundational to *risk assessment* and to the legitimacy of the entire arbitral proceeding. In addition, it demonstrates concern for unqualified due process.

[10] On the incorporation of this standard, *see* Pedro J. Martínez-Fraga, "Good Faith, Bad Faith, but Not Losing Faith: A Commentary on the 2010 IBA Rules on the Taking of Evidence in International Arbitration," 43 *Geo. J. Int'l L.* 387 (2011–2012).

Notwithstanding the extremely helpful suggestions and requirements in Art. 33, the stakeholders, including the arbitral tribunal, would greatly benefit from a direct and explicit reference to "cross examination" and not just "examination." Moreover, the evidence-taking standard articulated in Art. 31.3 (relevant to the case and material to its outcome) should be incorporated into Arts. 29, more broadly in 31.1 and 31.2, as well as in Art. 33.

The absence of a standard explicitly referenced and incorporated into the Rules, particularly where it is mentioned in a subsection of an Article, creates unnecessary ambiguity. Similarly, the omission of an article setting forth at minimum rudimentary requirements of witness statements, and some direction on witness examination (direct, cross, re-direct, and possibly recross) sacrifices objectivity, process transparency, predictive value and *party-autonomy* in favor of *arbitrator discretion*.

The SCC Rules do have the suggestion of premises that can be further developed, which are altogether absent from the ICC Rules.

3.4 SIAC RULES (2016)

The Singapore International Arbitration Centre Rules (SIAC Rules) 2016 are among the most tempered in balancing *party-autonomy*, *arbitrator discretion*, and the management of evidence throughout the conduct of proceedings.[11] The SIAC Rules most comprehensively and principally address evidentiary issues in Rules 19 (**Conduct of the Proceedings**), 25 (**Witnesses**), and 27 (**Additional Powers of the Tribunal**).

SIAC Rules 19 in pertinent part reads:

19.2 The Tribunal shall determine the relevance, materiality and admissibility of all evidence. *The Tribunal is not required to apply the rules of evidence of any applicable law in making such determination.*

19.3 As soon as practicable after the constitution of the Tribunal, the Tribunal shall conduct a preliminary meeting with the parties, in person or by any other means, to discuss the procedures that will be most appropriate and efficient for the case.

19.4 The Tribunal may, in its discretion, direct the order of proceedings, bifurcate proceedings, exclude cumulative or irrelevant testimony or other evidence and direct the parties to focus their presentations on issues the decision of which could dispose of all or part of the case. (Emphasis added)

Quite significantly, even though Rule 19 subsection 19.2 somewhat orients the parties by identifying (i) relevance, materiality and (iii) admissibility, no standard at all is articulated. The determination is left to the Tribunal's unchecked discretion.

[11] Arbitration Rules of the Singapore International Arbitration Centre SIAC Rules 6th Edition, 1 August 2016.

Noticeably absent is any reference to the Tribunal assessing the *weight* of admitted evidence. How is *weight* to be assessed.

Subsection 19.2 clarifies that there is no requirement for the Tribunal to apply the rules of evidence incident to any applicable law. This qualification is helpful and somewhat unique in the context of arbitral institutional rules, because the provision has the effect of tempering expectations of such evidentiary rules were they to be applied.

Subsection 19.3 is certainly helpful in principle, but too general to maximize its potential effectiveness, particularly in light of varying levels of experience and training among different arbitral tribunals and tribunal members. Even though efficiency is the governing and organizing principle of subsection 19.3, this objective would be best served were it explicitly to reference the imperative to engage in the self-disclosure of documents the parties intend to rely on, and to clarify this obligation would be continuous up to a specified cut-off date early in the proceedings. The subsection also would benefit from explicitly referencing the manner and form of document demands, the use of and requirements pertaining to all types of evidence addressing liability, damages, and impeachment, as well as demonstrative exhibits.

Consonant with arbitral culture, the Rules clearly are fashioned in order to expedite the conduct of the proceeding, but not to inform the parties so that they may engage in comprehensive *risk assessment* early in the case and thereby possibly obviate the proceeding in its entirety.

There are untested assumptions in subsection 19.4 that have the effect of bolstering *arbitrator discretion* under the banner of efficiency at the expense of certainty, transparency, and the party's due process expectations. Subsection 19.4 does not reference any governing evidentiary standard or rule.

In a single sentence, however, subsection 19.4 vests the Tribunal with authority to exclude evidence that it subjectively, and at minimum, contrary to the proffering party's expectations, deems "cumulative or irrelevant testimony or other evidence." It does so without any definition of *cumulative evidence* or of relevance.

By way of example, testimony may be duplicative or cumulative as to final conclusions and inferences, but based on different factual predicates. In such instances, which are extremely common, evidence is susceptible to be viewed as cumulative but still have uniquely material probative value.

As to *relevance*, evidence *prima facie* may appear not to be related and probative to the determinative issues of law and fact, but still contribute, for example, to an assessment of credibility, legitimacy, and reliability. In any event, vesting the arbitral tribunal with such vast unqualified discretion, at the clear expense of *party-autonomy* to present a case as duly envisioned by a party from an evidentiary perspective, ultimately will lead to profound questions concerning process legitimacy. Under no analysis, however, is this allocation of authority to the arbitral tribunal at all conducive to settlement and, therefore, to the maximum expression of efficiency that can be attained in ICA.

SIAC Rule 25 addressing the management of witnesses is genuinely extraordinary and robust. The rule is progressive in many respects. Most importantly, it carves out a critical role for testimonial evidence and its presentation.

Five observations are in order regarding Rule 25.[12] First, the permissive "may" in subsection 25.1 should be in the mandatory "shall." Additionally, the timing is far too vague ("[b]efore any hearing") and thereby codifies in the form of a rule vagueness and what can lead to "attenuated due process" violations. The identity and subject matter of *all* prospective witnesses has to be identified with sufficient lead time to allow for due notice (and due process) so that parties may, if appropriate, challenge the testimony. This lead time analysis of witnesses is a keystone factor of *risk assessment*.

The proposition that such pivotal disclosure *may* be required at some time *before any hearing* is simply too vague and infused with an unnecessary degree of arbitrariness. The ability to assess and to challenge witnesses cannot be compromised.

Second, subsection 25.2 is a shrine to *arbitrator discretion*. That a tribunal may limit or altogether disallow the appearance of witnesses at a hearing to testify, is simply an unremarkable but concerning proposition. It raises serious trepidation because the assertion of the premise without qualifying language, that is to say, stating specific grounds upon which oral testimony can be curtailed or proscribed, does not even place *reason* as a boundary to the exercise of *arbitrator discretion* regarding an issue that goes to the heart of due process: a party's right to present its case through oral testimony. What, then, is the purpose of the subsection?

Third, the examination of witnesses in ICA needs to be developed and rendered predictable as to examination techniques and corresponding objections. Cross-examination is the most critical component of witness examination. The only objective in compelling a witness who has submitted a witness statement to appear at the hearing if the proffering party is to use the witness statement in its case-in-chief, is to test the factual sufficiency of the declaration pursuant to cross-examination.

[12] SIAC Rule 25 (**Witnesses**) in pertinent part provides:

> 25.1 Before any hearing, the Tribunal may require the parties to give notice of the identity of witnesses, including expert witnesses, whom the parties intend to produce, the subject matter of their testimony and its relevance to the issues.
>
> 25.2 The Tribunal may allow, refuse or limit the appearance of witnesses to give oral evidence at any hearing.
>
> 25.3 Any witness who gives oral evidence may be questioned by each of the parties, their representatives and the Tribunal in such manner as the Tribunal may determine.
>
> 25.4 The Tribunal may direct the testimony of witnesses to be presented in written form, either as signed statements or sworn affidavits or any other form of recording. Subject to Rule 25.2, any party may request that such a witness should attend for oral examination. *If the witness fails to attend for oral examination, the Tribunal may place such weight on the written testimony as it thinks fit, disregard such written testimony, or exclude such written testimony altogether.*
>
> 25.5 It shall be permissible for any party or its representatives to interview any witness or potential witness (that may be presented by that party) prior to his appearance to give oral evidence at any hearing. (Emphasis added)

Subsection 25.3, however, merely states that the parties may question any witness who is testifying orally, and that the manner of questioning is relegated to the arbitral tribunal's discretion. Consequently, both *party-autonomy* and transparency are compromised because of the many possibilities as to the manner in which the sufficiency of a witness statement or other written declaration can be tested.

Fourth, subsection 25.4 provides the arbitral tribunal with discretion to consider a witness statement even where after a party requests that such a witness attend the hearing for oral examination, the witness fails to be present at the hearing. This vast latitude of *arbitrator discretion* is problematic.

Parties must be allowed to confront adverse witnesses. There is no coherent rationale allowing for the theoretical possibility that one party may submit a witness statement and have the facts contained in the witness statement considered by the arbitral tribunal for the truth of the matters asserted, while simultaneously precluding the party against whom the testimony is offered from testing the factual sufficiency and credibility of the declarant.

Allowing for this scenario as a possibility, or even one where the arbitral tribunal is vested with the discretion to accord less weight to the written testimony, violates the fundamental due process right to be treated equally. One party is allowed to present testimony, but the other party is precluded from challenging the facts asserted and the declarant's credibility. It makes no sense.

Fifth and finally, subsection 25.5 brings clarity to a practice that is somewhat obscured because of different legal cultures and traditions. Process transparency, *party-autonomy*, and predictability are best served by allowing parties to interview witnesses for potential service as witnesses in the proceeding. Articulating the rule creates a level playing field that under no scenario can cause prejudice to stakeholders. Of course, this Rule is subject to qualification by virtue of possible mandatory laws and rules governing the arbitration.

One of the most effective institutional rules concerning evidentiary issues can be found in SIAC Rule 27 (**Additional Powers of the Tribunal**). This Rule is emblematic of a stricture that broadens and defines *arbitrator discretion*, but does so in ways that furthers process transparency and *risk assessment* by providing for access to evidence.[13] SIAC Rule 27 adopts, as does the counterpart SCC arbitration

[13] SIAC Rule 27 (**Additional Powers of the Tribunal**) in relevant part reads:

> Unless otherwise agreed by the parties, in addition to the other powers specified in these Rules, and except as prohibited by the mandatory rules of law applicable to the arbitration, the Tribunal shall have the power to:
>
> ***
>
> d. order the parties to make any property or item in their possession or control available for inspection;
>
> e. order the preservation, storage, sale or disposal of any property or item which is or forms part of the subject matter of the dispute;

rule, the standard for evidence taking and presentation already discussed,[14] first identified in the 2010 iteration of the IBA Rules on the Taking of Evidence in International Arbitration. This standard is articulated in connection with document production.

The "relevant to the case and material to its outcome" standard, however, governs (i) the taking and (ii) the presentation of evidence. Therefore, it also applies to the content of witness statements and to witness oral testimony. Even though SIAC Rule 27 is an excellent contributor to predictability, due process, and *risk assessment*, it would benefit from vesting the Tribunal not only with the authority ("power" to borrow from the Rule's actual text) but also the *obligation* to order the production of such documents and materials to the extent that they meet the standard.

The amendment would be simple. One proposal would be for the language to state that "the Tribunal shall have the power to order, and shall order the parties to allow for inspection and to supply copies of any documents in their possession, custody, or control that may be relevant to the case and material to its outcome." Comparable language would institutionalize within the Rules' rubric a self-disclosure obligation on the parties' behalf.

It would also compel the arbitral tribunal to exercise a *proactive* and not just *reactive* role that may or may not be triggered in every case. The objective would be to have the tribunal charged with the obligation of ordering the parties to produce such documents as soon as the tribunal has been made aware of the operative claims and corresponding defenses.

Moreover, vesting the tribunal with this mandate strikes an appropriate balance between *adversarial* and *inquisitorial* legal systems. Thus truly *internationalizing* the proceeding on the critical issue concerning document disclosures that necessarily will lead to *risk assessment* and thus further efficiencies and process legitimacy.

The current iteration of SIAC Rule 27 fails to institutionalize the disclosure of the documents and items constituting its subject matter by having textual language that only provides the tribunal with authority to order such disclosure rather than with the *obligation* and authority to order production of this evidence early in the proceeding. Additionally, the Rule needs to state clearly that all of its subsections are governed by the "relevant to the case and material to its outcome" standard.

f. order any party to produce to the Tribunal and to the other parties for inspection, and to supply copies of, any document in their possession or control which the Tribunal considers relevant to the case and material to its outcome;

***

h. direct any party or person to give evidence by affidavit or in any other form;

***

o. determine any claim of legal or other privilege.

[14] *Id.*

The version of proposed language that would maximize the efficiency of SIAC Rule 27 would compel the parties to produce evidence that *may* meet the "relevant to the case and material to its outcome," talisman.[15] The workings of the Rule would be such as to err in favor of over production of evidence that would be, if anything, inadmissible rather than the converse proposition. The objective is transparency. And the ability to engage in *risk assessment* as early in the process as possible. The conditions for *optimal efficiency* require maximum disclosure.

A salient and somewhat unique feature of the SIAC Rules generally, and Rule 27 in particular, is subsection e) providing the arbitral tribunal with authority to "order the preservation, storage, sale or disposal of any property or item which is or forms part of the subject matter of the dispute." This subsection vests the arbitral tribunal with authority to issue *prohibitory* and *mandatory* injunctive relief to preserve or to dispose of evidence identified as relevant in the subsection by the explicit reference to forming "part of the subject matter of the dispute."

The provisions of the ICC, SCC, and SIAC Institutional Rules reviewed are emblematic of the extent to which timely and comprehensive evidence taking and evidence presentation is addressed. With the exception to Appendix IV of the ICC Rules, rules creating the proper evidentiary conditions for settlement are not to be found. They simply do not exist.

Likewise, settlement itself is not contemplated but for the commercial offering of Mediation Rules and a mediation process that itself is devoid of any of the evidence taking and presentation strictures that would allow parties to identify, to quantify, to assess, and finally, to communicate risk so as to foster a settlement of the dispute that maximizes efficiencies and altogether avoids a zero-sum-game final scenario.

These Rules indeed are very general and provide no practical evidence-taking and evidence-presentation guidance. Not surprisingly, they also fail to guide tribunals on how best to evaluate evidence and accord weight to evidential proffers. Even the more comprehensive and progressive exemplars, such as the SIAC Arbitration Rules, do not uniformly and with particularity articulate a governing standard or rule for production of evidence or its actual *introduction into evidence* by the arbitral tribunal, let alone (as referenced) *indicia* of the factors that an arbitral tribunal must consider in allocating weight to evidence deemed admissible.

Most Rules lack timely, systematic, and comprehensive self-disclosure of evidence requirements. The parties are not provided with the appropriate information at any point in the proceeding, let alone in its initial phases, that would emphasize the need, or even benefits, of exploring a commercial solution to the dispute.

[15] Language that would maximize the efficiency of SIAC Rule 27 (**Additional Powers of the Tribunal**):

> the Tribunal shall have the power to order, and shall order the parties to allow for inspection of and to supply copies of any documents in their possession, custody, or control that may be relevant to the case and material to its outcome.

These Institutional Rules do not require parties to explain in detail (i) the methodology and accounting used to arrive at alleged compensatory damages and (ii) to produce any and all documents upon which such damages computations were based. In this same vein, parties must be *required*, and not merely *encouraged*, upon penalty of inadmissibility, to disclose any and all evidence, including witness testimony (fact and expert), on which they intend to rely for purposes of demonstrating liability and corresponding defenses to affirmative claims.

The institutional rules lack standards and provisions governing disclosure are silent as to the workings of burden of proof, do not define critical terms such as *evidence, relevance, materiality*, and altogether fail to inform the parties on the manner in which evidence taking is to be conducted. Most institutional rules simply abdicate even the most perfunctory guidance on the taking of evidence by minimizing *party-autonomy* and maximizing, to an unreasonable extent, *arbitrator discretion*. None of the Rules further process transparency and predictability by emphasizing comprehensive and timely disclosure of evidence susceptible to self-disclosure or compulsory production pursuant to a document demand.

The technical configuration of witness statements and requests for disclosure/production of documents are altogether overlooked, as is any form of *compulsory* and *substantive* mediation. Put simply, in their quest to produce *process efficiency*, most institutional rules concern themselves only with the inefficiency of a dispute resolution methodology that culminates in a zero-sum-game (all-or-nothing) scenario fraught with risk, and likely to fracture the parties' business undertakings on a going forward basis. Comparable provisions from the ICDR Rules,[16] the LCIA Rules,[17] and the DIS Arbitration Rules merit consideration.[18]

16 *See e.g.*, ICDR Art. 22 (**Conduct of Proceedings**) (4), (5), (7), and (8); Art. 24 (**Exchange of Information**) (1)–(4), (6)–(10); and Art. 26 (**Hearing**) (2), (4), and (5).

17 LCIA Art. 14 (**Conduct of Proceedings**) (1), (2), (6) (ii); Art. 15 (**Written Stages of the Arbitration**) (2), (5); Art. 20 (**Witnesses**) (1)–(2), (9); and Art. 22 (**Additional Powers**) (1)(v), (vi).

18 Article 26 (**Encouraging Amicable Settlements**), in its entirety states:

> Unless any party objects thereto, the arbitral tribunal *shall, at every stage of the arbitration*, seek to encourage an amicable settlement of the dispute or of individual disputed issues. (Emphasis added)

> Article 27 (**Efficient Conduct of the Proceedings**), in relevant part reads:
>
> 27.4
>
> During the case management conference, the arbitral tribunal shall discuss with the parties the procedural rules to be applied in the proceedings pursuant to Article 21, as well as the procedural timetable.
>
> With a view to increasing procedural efficiency, the arbitral tribunal shall specifically discuss the following with the parties:
>
> ***
>
> (iii) *the possibility of using mediation or any other method of amicable dispute resolution to seek the amicable settlement of the dispute or of individual disputed issues*. (Emphasis added)

3.5 SALIENT FEATURES OF THE ICDR ARBITRATION RULES (2021)

Article 22 (**Conduct of the Proceeding**) subsection 8 of the ICDR Arbitration Rules is noteworthy because it outright empowers the tribunal to "draw adverse inferences," but in the context of the avoidance of "unnecessary delay" and "to protect the efficiency and integrity of the arbitration."[19] The provision is somewhat unique because it shrouds with general language of efficiency the tribunal's explicit authority under the Rules to draw adverse inferences that textually are not limited to the failure of a witness to attend a hearing or of a party to produce documents.

Subsection 24.1 is helpful because it balances due process ("each party's opportunity to present its claims and defenses fairly") in the context also of "avoiding surprise[s]," with efficiency. The unvarnished juxtaposition of due process and efficiency sharpens the complex relationship of inverse proportionality between the two.

The avoidance of surprise is a temporal issue that needs to be addressed early in the arbitration and viewed from a systematic perspective going forward, rather than on the eve of a final hearing. Avoiding surprises should be tantamount to the timely assessment of risk conducive to maximizing efficiencies.

One of the more helpful institutional rules concerning document requests is found in subsection 24.4. The "reasonably believed to exist" standard, notwithstanding the conjunctive "and" in the language "and to be relevant and material to the outcome of the case," serves to introduce broad but constructive identification of documents that may meet the "relevant and material to the outcome of the case," standard.

This subsection (24.4) provides guidance as to specific language that a document request should contain.

Subsections 24.8, 24.9, and 24.10 do merit close attention:

8 In resolving any dispute about pre-hearing exchanges of information, the arbitrator *shall* require a requesting party to justify the time and expense that its request *may* involve and may condition granting such a request on the payment of part or all of the cost by the party seeking the information. *The tribunal may also allocate the costs of providing information among the parties, either in an interim order or in an award.*

9 In the event a party fails to comply with an order for information exchange, the arbitrator may draw adverse inferences and *may take such failure into account in allocating costs.*

10 Depositions, interrogatories, and requests to admit as developed for use in U.S. court procedures *generally* are not appropriate procedures for obtaining information in an arbitration under these Rules. (Emphasis added)

[19] International Centre for Dispute Resolution – International Dispute Resolution Procedures – International Arbitration Rules – Amended and Effective March, 2021.

Requiring a party to justify time and expense that corresponds with a document request that it propounded may entail allocating that economic cost to the requesting party, which is one way of reconciling efficiency with transparency and disclosure. This allocation is conducive to appropriate *risk assessment*.

Subsection 24.8 is somewhat singular in this regard, and particularly in identifying the requesting party's potential obligation as one that may only extend to *part* of the costs involved. Equally worth underscoring is actually articulating the tribunal's inherent powers under the ICDR Arbitration Rules to allocate the cost of evidence taking (textually "the costs of providing information") among the parties not just in an award, but also in an interim order.

The inherent power to award costs for failure to comply with evidence taking, and presumably also self-disclosure requirements, is coupled with the stated authority to draw "adverse inferences" from compliance deficits.

Subsection 24.10 is absolutely unique to the ICDR Rules. This subsection merits reading and rereading.

The single sentence states that (i) depositions, (ii) interrogatories, and (iii) requests to admit, as these methodologies for US style discovery are used in that context, "*generally*" are not appropriate under the ICDR Arbitration Rules. Two significant observations are in order.

First, studiously absent from the US discovery methodologies articulated is the Federal Rule of Civil Procedure 34, Request for Production of Documents.[20] While the omission of US-style document demand does not necessarily mean that its exclusion is to be construed as an explicit allowance or proscription. Nevertheless, consideration and weight needs to be ascribed to this omission.

Indeed, formally there is no *material* difference between the document demand set forth in subsection 24.4 of the ICDR Rules and the request for production of documents contained in Federal Rule of Civil Procedure 34 (b)(1)(A)–(C).[21] The second sentence of subsection 24.4 of the ICDR Rules provides that: "[r]equests for documents shall contain [1] a description of specific documents or [2] classes of documents, [3] along with an explanation of their relevance and [4] materiality to the outcome of the case."

The actual difference between subsection 24.4 and Fed. R. Civ. P. 34 (b)(1)(A)–(C) concerns the governing standard for document disclosure. Subsection 24.4 is governed by the "relevant to the case and material to its outcome" standard. Fed.

20 Fed. R. Civ. P. 34 (b)(1)(A)–(C).

21 (b) Procedure.

(1) Contents of the Request. The request:

(A) must describe with reasonable particularity each item or category of items to be inspected;

(B) must specify a reasonable time, place, and manner for the inspection and for performing the related acts; and

(C) may specify the form or forms in which electronically stored information is to be produced.

R. Civ. P. 34 subscribes to the broader but more tempered disclosure requirements contained in Fed. R. Civ. P. 26 (4)(b)(1), which reads:

> (1) ***Scope in General.*** Unless otherwise limited by court order, the scope of discovery is as follows: Parties may obtain discovery regarding any nonprivileged matter *that is [1] relevant to any party's claim or defense and [2] proportional to the needs of the case, [3] considering the importance of the issues at stake in the action, [4] the amount in controversy, [5] the parties' relative access to relevant information, [6] the parties' resources, [7] the importance of the discovery in resolving the issues, and [8] whether the burden or expense of the proposed discovery outweighs its likely benefit. Information within this scope of discovery need not be admissible in evidence to be discoverable.* (Emphasis added)

Federal Rule of Civil Procedure 26 (4)(b)(1) was amended in 2015 to provide for the qualifications and considerations referenced in brackets [1] through [8] of the cited language. This standard since its amendment governs all of US discovery, and not just documents responsive to a request for production.

Contrary to aprioristic assumptions that ignore any textual analysis of this standard, it is inarguable that the standard, based upon its ordinary and plain language, safeguards against economic waste and the use of the pretrial right to evidence as a means for exerting economic and other burdens on a party with limited resources. It also limits document demands, or document requests that bear no *proportionality* to the parties' resources, or that does not comport with the importance of the matters in dispute, or the actual amount in controversy, three cornerstone considerations that elude most institutional rules.

Finally on this point, the adverb "generally" asserted in subsection 24.10 of the ICDR Rules that underscores the inappropriateness of US-styled depositions, interrogatories, and requests to admit, seems to be deftly drafted to suggest that there may be situations, issues, and factual configurations that *may* warrant recourse to similar techniques in the context of evidence taking.

It is not beyond man's wit that certain parties may consent to some or all of these discovery methodologies. If such construction of the adverb "generally" is possible, then it is unclear whether in fact the arbitral "relevant to the case and material to its outcome" standard furthers efficiency, *party-autonomy*, transparency, and predictability beyond the Fed. R. Civ. P. 26 (4)(b)(1) standard.

This proposition may seem heretical, but it is imbued with intellectual integrity and the normativity of the plain and ordinary meaning of simple language.

A literal interpretation of the word "generally" as used in that provision does not mean that the ICDR Rules provide for the importation, let alone the wholesale and unqualified incorporation, of US-style discovery into the evidence-taking process. If international commercial arbitration in fact is to be *international*, then borrowing doctrine, particularly with respect to evidence taking, from different legal systems would appear to be in order. In addition, such expansive approach to evidence taking, where necessary and consonant with the parties' agreement and the operative arbitral rules, certainly finds resonance in ICA's central feature of being *flexible*, as well as to its aspiration to greater process transparency.

ICDR subsection 23.4, explicitly references that witnesses are to testify "in the form of written statements signed by them." Beyond this statement, however, there is no instruction as to the content of the witness statement, the use of rebuttal witness statements, and the extent to which the facts asserted in witness statements should be relevant to the case and material to its outcome.

Subsection 23.4 only in the *permissive*, much in keeping with the majority of institutional rules canvassed, is vested with discretion to qualify the weight to be accorded to a witness statement, or altogether to disregard it where a witness has been requested to appear at the hearing and fails to do so.[22] As discussed, the permissive nature of this stricture is problematic (see Section 3.1).

Lastly, the inability to assess risk on a timely basis with respect to evidence in the form of witness testimony is exemplified in subsection 26.5. It provides that: "[a]t least 15 days before the hearings" constitutes the disclosure timeframe for the parties to provide each other and the tribunal with notice of the identity and contact information of witnesses intended to testify, as well as the subject matter of prospective witness testimony.

Statistics demonstrate that it is not uncommon for a final hearing to take place far beyond one year after commencement of an arbitral proceeding.[23] It is very difficult for parties to engage in meaningful *risk assessment* where, as suggested in subsection 26.5, the disclosure of witnesses and corresponding subject matter is to occur only fifteen days *before* an actual hearing.

3.6 LCIA ARBITRATION RULES (2020)

The LCIA Rules make clear the arbitral tribunal's inherent powers with respect to the conduct of proceedings is near absolute from a functional perspective.[24] Subsection 14.2 of Article 14 (**Conduct of Proceedings**) in part states that "[t]he Arbitral Tribunal *shall have the widest discretion* to discharge these general duties, subject to the mandatory provisions of any applicable law or any rules of law the Arbitral Tribunal may decide to be applicable." (Emphasis added.) This qualifying language ("widest") is not found in the comparable provisions of most arbitral institutional rules.

22 The relevant language reads:

> The tribunal *may* require any witness to appear at a hearing. If a witness whose appearance has been requested fails to appear without a valid excuse as determined by the arbitral tribunal, the tribunal *may* disregard any written statement by that witness. (Emphasis added)

23 Civil Justice Initiative, *The Landscape of Civil Litigation in State Courts*, at 6.

24 The London Court of International Arbitration Rules 2020.

Subsection 14.2 is extraordinary, however, because it explicitly references a "good faith" requirement imposed on the parties with respect to the "efficient and expeditious" conduct of the proceeding. This good faith standard in the context of *procedural efficiency* generally and evidence taking in particular, was first raised in the 2010 iteration of the IBA Rules on the Taking of Evidence in International Arbitration. The requirement also is contained in the more recent 2020 version of the IBA Rules (Chapter 4 in this volume).

Understanding the extent to which evidence taking and *risk assessment* in the context of making a meaningful settlement possible are at all addressed within the framework of institutional rules, it is noteworthy that Art. 14 (**Conduct of Proceedings**) nowhere mentions the terms "document," "disclosure," "evidence," or "production," let alone "evidence taking," or "evidence gathering." The LCIA Rules do show promise for *risk assessment*.

The Rules identify a "written stage of the arbitration,"[25] with corresponding time-frames. In addition to identifying the number of permissible submissions (all set within twenty-eight days of each other), Art. 15 imposes upon the parties a requirement to submit with each pleading "all documents relied upon."[26]

If the arbitral tribunal properly administers the twenty-eight-day document disclosure deadline incident to each of the four permissible pleadings,[27] the parties at a reasonably early stage in the proceeding may be able to assess some risk that can appropriately support meaningful settlement discussions.

The LCIA Rules, to some extent, contemplate that at the closure of the last permissible pleading pursuant to subsection 15.6, the parties shall be in possession of all necessary documentary evidence. The assessment of witness statements is central to *risk assessment*.

Disclosure of such evidence, however, within the framework of the LCIA Rules is less timely and very discretionary. Subsection 20.2 merely provides that at some unspecified point "[b]efore any hearing" the tribunal "may" require the disclosure of the identity of each witness a party intends to call.

Witness statements fall within the purview of subsection 20.3, and, therefore, there is no reason to believe that earlier and more timely disclosure for purposes of *risk assessment* is to be expected. Indeed, subsection 20.3 provides "the testimony of a witness may be presented by a party in written form, either as a signed statement or like document."

[25] LCIA Art. 15 (**Written Stage of the Arbitration**).

[26] *Id.* The requirement is articulated in subsections 15.2 through 15.5.

[27] The four pleadings referenced concern: (i) Claimant's State of the Case, or election to have the Request for Arbitration treated as the Statement of the Case (15.2–15.3), (ii) Respondent's Statement of Defence or election to have its Response treated as its Statement of Defence (15.3), (iii) Respondent's Counterclaim (15.3), and (iv) Claimant's Statement Reply to Counterclaim, or Statement of Defence to Counterclaim (15.4–15.5).

As to timely disclosure, subsection 20.4 does not specify a disclosure deadline, and merely allocates the task to the arbitral tribunal's discretion.[28] The relationship between witness statements and documentary evidence should not be undermined. It is common for witness statements to elaborate on documents, address alleged vagueness or ambiguity concerns, and explain chain of custody issues. Often witness statements require the disclosure of documents that were not previously produced.

The LCIA Arbitration Rules' efficient and strategic delineation of a "written stage of the arbitration," does not comport with the manner in which the timing of witness disclosure and corresponding witness statements are managed. For example, Art. 22 (**Additional Powers**) provides the tribunal with authority to extend evidence taking and evidence disclosure beyond the subsection 15.6 closure of the written phase that also foresees a possibility for the arbitral tribunal to do so, and to engage in further evidence taking and disclosure pursuant only to a *relevance* standard.

Subsection 22.1(v), in part states that the arbitral tribunal may decide:

> [t]o order any party to produce to the Arbitral Tribunal and to other parties documents or copies of documents in their possession, custody or power which the Arbitral Tribunal decides to be relevant[.]

This flexibility is warranted. As structured within the LCIA Rules' framework, however, qualifications as to time and circumstances would be appreciated. Particularly because the exercise of such authority, whether initiated *sua sponte* on the part of the arbitral tribunal or pursuant to party initiative, should be circumscribed so that *risk assessment* pursuant to the evaluation of newly-disclosed documents, may take place as proximate in time as possible to the written phase of the arbitration and long before a merits hearing.

The unqualified "relevant" standard articulated in subsection 22.1(v) if it is to be understood literally and based on ordinary meaning, is much broader than the "relevant to the case and material to its outcome" standard that is most prevalent in ICA evidence taking and disclosure practice. If indeed the only factor to consider in evidence taking and disclosure is *relevance*, then under the LCIA Rules (i) evidence taking, (ii) evidence disclosure, and (iii) the presentation of evidence all are governed by a standard that is significantly broader than the evidentiary standard set forth in the IBA Rules on the Taking of Evidence in International Arbitration. The standard actually would be broader than the standard articulated by the majority of the arbitration rules of the major arbitral institutes, and even the scope set forth in Fed. R. Civ. P. 26 (4)(b)(1).

[28] LCIA Arbitration Rules subsection 20.4 reads:

> The Arbitral Tribunal may decide the time, manner, and form in which these written materials [witness statements or other witness declarations] shall be exchanged between the parties and presented to the Arbitral Tribunal; and it may allow, refuse or limit the written and oral testimony of witnesses.

In sharp contrast to the *relevant* only standard contained in subsection 22.1(v), the LCIA Rules are quite unique by implicitly distinguishing between standards governing (i) the taking and self-disclosure of evidence, and (ii) the actual presentation of evidence. The carving of this conceptual space is helpful.

As referenced (see Section 3.1), one of the intriguing features of ICA is that the same standard is applied to *evidence taking* and to the *presentation of evidence*. The single distinction between the two (evidence taking *and* presentation of evidence) is that in determining *admissibility*, *relevance*, and *materiality*, arbitrators understandably are asked to determine the weight that is to be accorded to evidence. Except for considerations pertaining to the *weight* of the evidence, the standard for the taking of evidence, and the presentation of evidence in ICA *generally* is the same.

Subsection 22.1(vi) of the LCIA Rules are unique in empowering the tribunal in its discretion:

> (vi) to decide whether or not *to apply any strict rules of evidence* [or any other rules] as to the admissibility, relevance or weight of any material tendered by a party on any issue of fact or expert opinion; and to decide the time, manner, and form in which such material should be exchanged between the parties and presented to the Arbitral Tribunal[.][29] (Emphasis added)

The term "strict rules of evidence (or any other rules)," is less than helpful. It is both vague and ambiguous. It is not clear whether the suggestion is that a substantive body of evidentiary rules either arising in connection with the substantive law governing the proceeding, or the evidentiary law of the seat of the arbitration, is meant. Perhaps the arbitral tribunal is invited to elect or to formulate its own governing evidentiary principles. The reference to "or any other rules" is quizzical but not new. Subsection 22.1(6) of the LCIA Rules finds its origins in subsection 34.2(f) of the English Arbitration Act of 1996.[30]

As used in subsection 22.1(vi), there are two entries defining the adjectival form of the word *strict* that would be applicable. First, strict may refer to "[r]igorously established or implemented; *stec.* (**a**) (of a law, ordinance, etc.) stringently framed or executed, allowing no refusal or evasion; (**b**) (of an inquiry, investigation, etc.) carried out with unremitting attention to detail, relentless; (**c**) (of authority, discipline, etc.)

[29] LCIA Art. 22 (**Additional Powers**), subsection 22.1(vi).

[30] Subsection 34.2(f) states:

> Procedural and evidential matters include –
>
> ***
>
> (f) whether to apply strict rules of evidence (or any other rules) as to the admissibility, relevance or weight of any material (oral, written or other) sought to be tendered on any matters of fact or opinion, and the time, manner, and form in which such material should be exchanged and presented[.]
>
> ***

admitting no leniency, severe; (**d**) (of custody, confinement, etc.) involving severe restriction of space or freedom of movement."[31]

Second, the *OED*'s seventh entry defines *strict* as: "[o]f a quality, condition, etc.: maintained without deviation or abatement; absolute, entire, complete; (of truth, accuracy, etc.) exactly answerable to fact or reality."[32] It is a challenge to the imagination to conceive of the application of any set of rules, if they are to be at all applied, not to be strict either qualitatively, or in their application.

The absence of a direct temporal connection for execution of any additional evidence taking beyond the "written stage of the arbitration" (subsections 15.6 and 15.10) is glaring. Finally, it is noteworthy that subsection 22.1(vi) does not use the word "evidence" when referring to the subject matter of a proffer tendered or exchanged. Instead, the term "material" is applied.[33] This terminology suggests that written submissions, and not just evidence, are contemplated. The rules is not pristine.

3.7 DIS ARBITRATION RULES (2018)

The DIS Arbitration Rules are the most sparse of all institutional arbitration rules on the issue of evidence taking, or for that matter, the presentation of evidence.[34] In the actual text of the DIS Rules the word "evidence" only appears on three occasions in three separate Articles.[35] Moreover, it is only in Art. 28 subsection 28.2 that evidence is at all referenced in any context that may be construed as possibly allowing for evidence assessment, as the two remaining references appear at the closing of the proceedings,[36] and in the context of an award by consent.[37]

Article 28, subsection 28.2 reads:

> For this purpose [presumably establishing the facts of the case], the arbitral tribunal may, *inter alia*, on its own initiative, appoint experts, examine fact witnesses other than those called by the parties, and order any party to produce or make available

31 "Strict," *Shorter Oxford English Dictionary*, 5th ed. (Oxford University Press 2002).

32 *Id.*

33 Subsection 22.1(vi) reads:

> 22.1 The Arbitral Tribunal shall have the power, upon the application of any party or (save for sub-paragraph (x) below) upon its own initiative, but in either case only after giving the parties a reasonable opportunity to state their views and upon such terms (as to costs and otherwise) as the Arbitral Tribunal may decide:
>
> (vi) to decide whether or not to apply any strict rules of evidence (or any other rules) as to the admissibility, relevance or weight of any *material* tendered by a party on any issue of fact or expert opinion; and to decide the time, manner, and form in which such material should be exchanged between the parties and presented to the Arbitral Tribunal[.] (Emphasis added)

34 DIS Arbitration Rules 2018 (Annex 2 effective as of 1 July 2021). The Rules were amended in March 2024 to address third-party practice in arbitration proceedings.

35 *See* Art. 28 (**Establishing the Facts, Tribunal-Appointed Expert**), subsection 28.2, Art. 31 (**Closing of Proceedings**), and Art. 41 (**Award by Consent**), subsection 41.1.

36 *See* Art. 31.

37 *See* Art. 41, subsection 41.1.

any documents or electronically stored data. The arbitral tribunal shall not be limited to admit only evidence offered by the parties.

There is no discussion concerning

(i) evidentiary self-disclosure, for example in the form of reliance documents;
(ii) evidence-taking on the part of the parties;
(iii) and instruction on the form and content of document requests;
(iv) a standard that would govern the disclosure and/or the taking of evidence;
(v) a standard that would govern the presentation of evidence;
(vi) the preparation of witness statements;
(vii) the use of witness statements and the participation of witnesses at interim and/or final hearings;
(viii) the questioning of witnesses as to manner and form;
(ix) inferences that the arbitral tribunal may draw concerning the failure of witnesses to attend a hearing as requested by a party; and
(x) viable objection to the taking or admissibility of evidence.

Instead, the Rules are but a recitation of the scope of *arbitrator discretion*, without any meaningful reference to *party-autonomy*, let alone the exercise of such autonomy in the context of an evidentiary proceeding.

The DIS Rules have, however, a fascinating dialectical tension in the Rules' internal workings. Certainly these Rules do not provide for evidentiary initiatives on the part of the arbitral tribunal or the parties that can be construed as conducive to timely *risk assessment*, and therefore, to a settlement that may obviate the ills of having no recourse but a merits adjudication. Yet, notwithstanding these evidentiary deficits the DIS Rules are singular in emphasizing settlement and thereby promoting the highest possible expression of efficiency in ICA.

DIS Art. 26 (**Encouraging Amicable Settlements**) is a single-sentence provision stating that: "[u]nless any party objects thereto, the arbitral tribunal shall, *at every stage* of the arbitration, seek to encourage an amicable settlement of the dispute or of individual disputed issues." (Emphasis added.) This Article's intent is laudable as a general principle. Its scant nature and corresponding framework, however, render it practically inoperable.

None of the major institutional rules have a comparable mandate.[38] The language uses the compulsory "shall," qualified only by the extent to which the parties may object. That qualification itself invites analysis.

A scenario where parties raise a standing or *ad hoc* objection to an arbitral tribunal's exhortation at different procedural junctures for the parties to consider settling the dispute, practically is inconceivable. The succinct mandate to *encourage* the parties to consider settlement at each stage of the arbitral proceeding is a compelling

[38] Jus Mundi, "ICC Facilitating Settlement in International Arbitration," at 4.

admission that settlement is more efficient than an all-or-nothing merits adjudication. Even post-hearing settlement, while not optimal, is advisable.

This Rule also implicitly establishes that facilitating settlement constitutes an obligation with which arbitrators *shall* comply. Encouraging a non-merits adjudicative settlement of the dispute rises to the level of an obligation mandating compliance. In this regard the Rule is progressive and embodies contemporary thinking on the scope of an arbitrator's mandate and corresponding obligations.

Regrettably, this "encouraging amicable settlements" Article is limited to a single sentence. Consequently, no instruction is provided on *how*, *when*, and under *what* circumstances the exhortation to settle the case is to be communicated. No protection extending to the tribunal in its efforts to promote settlement is offered. The seismic conceptual lead amplifying an arbitral tribunal's obligation to facilitate settlement, is not rendered effectively operational.

Likewise, the tribunal is not provided with *any* guidance on how best to invite the parties to engage in settlement discussions. Obviously, not only this provision, but the DIS Rules in their entirety, are painfully short on converting an aspirational exhortation to settle into an effective technique that may yield a settlement. Moreover, even an elaborate settlement provision would be inoperable absent robust evidence-taking rules conducive to timely *risk assessment*.

Perhaps not inadvertently, but in what can be construed as an unfortunate (almost ironic) and unintentional *sequence* of provisions, the Art. 26 (**Encouraging Amicable Settlements**) exhortation is followed by Art. 27 titled: **Efficient Conduct of the Proceedings**. If *optimal efficiency* cannot be attained, efficiency losses can be mitigated by lesser effective measures that focus on the Rules' actual intent; yielding a binding and enforceable award.

Article 27, subsection 27.4(iii) in the mandatory states that for purposes of maximizing efficiency, an arbitral tribunal specifically shall discuss with the parties, among other things, "the possibility of using mediation or any other method of amicable dispute resolution to seek the amicable settlement of the dispute or of individual disputed issues." Here as well, albeit in an abbreviated manner, the benefit of an amicable settlement is stressed. The command, however, is too general.

This mandate would realize its potential if mediation were to be rendered obligatory and procedurally developed so as to require parties to use and to identify *all* documents upon which they intend to rely in connection with affirmative claims and defenses. The mediation process, however, would need to be clearly distinguished as separate and distinct from the actual arbitral proceeding. The arbitral process is not to be in form or actual practice as a hybrid arbitration/mediation proceeding.

Their brevity notwithstanding, Arts. 26 and 27 of the DIS Rules are uniquely positive, and in some sense capture the efficiencies incident to an amicable settlement.

The Rules unmistakably are intended to maximize the likelihood of yielding a binding and enforceable arbitral award. In furtherance of this objective the rules of many, but certainly not all, arbitral institutions first provide the highest normative standing to *party-autonomy*. Absent *party-autonomy*, all nonmandatory rules default to the arbitral tribunal's exercise of its own discretion pursuant to the tribunal's inherent powers.

Adverse parties in an arbitration that may have at stake the economic viability of corporations and natural persons as well, generally cannot find a meeting of the minds and reach agreement on most material matters underlying the dispute. Hence, the arbitral tribunal's default mechanism turns into the primary guiding principle of the process where the default exception engulfs the rule.

The end result is simple. The Rules, mostly concerned with yielding a binding and enforceable award, do not and cannot create an environment that is propitious to settlement. The shifting of guiding principles from parties who cannot agree to any material proposition, to the arbitral tribunal, minimizes the ICA core pillar of *party-autonomy*. It further contributes to a scenario that is not conducive to the (i) identification, (ii) quantification, and (iii) communication of risk among parties.

Lastly, the absence of a doctrinally developed body of rules addressing the taking and presentation of evidence further bolsters *arbitrator discretion* (the default mechanism). Unable to assess risk, and even to appreciate fully the value of their respective claims and defenses, the parties are left without recourse but to focus on the preparation for a final hearing. At this junction, settlement is unlikely.

Institutional rules reflect that the current practical workings of ICA principally rest with *arbitrator discretion* and not *party-autonomy*. In the context of the taking and presentation of evidence, this phenomenon, the operational prevalence of *arbitrator discretion* over *party-autonomy*, of course is compounded and made worse by a void of evidentiary rules capable of fostering *risk assessment* on a timely basis propitious to settlement.

4

Defining Standards to Render Risk Assessment and Settlement Possible

The IBA Rules mark an extraordinary effort seeking to bridge the stark differences among various legal systems while promoting fairness and efficiency in the *taking* and *presentation* of evidence in international arbitration (both ISDS and ICA). Although the task is daunting, the IBA Rules represent a threshold inviting substantial doctrinal development so that their objective may be greater than yielding binding and enforceable awards. The aspiration to serve as a conduit for risk assessment conducive to settlement is existential to ICA.

Understandably, the Rules are fashioned with the objective of contributing to an arbitration framework that has as its principal objective the issuance of a binding and enforceable arbitration award. It follows that in the context of evidentiary rules conducive to settlement, the IBA Rules represent a nascent point of departure. Indeed, as more fully discussed (see Section 4.3), the Rules articulate only one standard that is to serve the need of determining *both* the standard for (i) evidence taking and (ii) the admissibility (presentation) and *weight* to be ascribed to evidence, the latter with no epistemic framework.

On December 17, 2020, the IBA by resolution of the IBA Council adopted a new edition of its Rules that aspires "to provide an efficient, economical and fair process for the taking of evidence in international arbitrations, *particularly those between Parties from different legal traditions*."[1] (Emphasis added.) This 2020 iteration of the Rules benefits from thirty-seven years of experience arising from the practice and commentaries concerning the IBA Supplementary Rules Governing the Presentation and Reception of Evidence in International Commercial Arbitration (May 28, 1983),[2] the IBA Rules on the Taking of Evidence in International Arbitration (June 1, 1999),[3] and the IBA Rules on the Taking of Evidence in International Arbitration (May 29, 2010).[4]

1 *See* IBA, IBA Rules on the Taking of Evidence in International Arbitration, Pmbl, ¶ 1 (2020).
2 IBA Supplementary Rules Governing the Presentation and Reception of Evidence in International Commercial Arbitration (1983).
3 IBA Rules on the Taking of Evidence in International Arbitration (1999).
4 IBA Rules on the Taking of Evidence in International Arbitration (2010); *see also* Pedro J. Martínez-Fraga, "Good Faith, Bad Faith, But Not Losing Faith," *see* Chapter 2, n. 39 in this volume.

The 2020 IBA Rules represent an important effort to synthesize fundamental common law and civil law concerns, as well as to further fairness, and predictability regarding the taking and presentation of evidence. The Rules are laudable and successful as supplemental rules that contribute to institutional rules for purposes of facilitating a process aspiring to generate binding and enforceable arbitration awards. They are also helpful to the crafting of the procedural anatomy of arbitration proceedings.

The Rules adhere to the basic structure of a Preamble, Definitions, and nine Articles each with relevant subparts. There are four narrow but technically significant provisions that first were incorporated as "amendments" or "changes" to the Rules' 2010 predecessor regime. These provisions set forth technical foundations that can be doctrinally developed to provide parties with the ability to attain maximum efficiency in the form of settlement. And to underscore process transparency, and therefore, the requisite predictive value that will render the prospect of settlement "institutional" in character.

Particular attention will be directed at Art. 2 of the Rules. The "standards" that pervade the Rules will be identified in connection with *party-autonomy* and the relation to the self-disclosure and transparency requirements that this fourth-generation of Rules embodies. Transparency is analyzed in connection with maximum efficiency.

Two features are paramount: (i) the talisman "relevant to the case and material to its outcome," standard[5] and (ii) "good faith" in the conduct of the taking of evidence requirement.[6] Third, it will be suggested that the principle of "transparency," as promulgated by the very Rules themselves in the Rules' treatment of document disclosure and grounds for non-production, expert witnesses and expert reports, and access to original exemplars of translated iterations, may prove to be a meaningful first approach toward arriving at substantive definitions of good faith, best efforts, relevance, materiality, as well as the development of mandatory rules within the existing framework that promote settlement pursuant to risk evaluation.

4.1 THE RULES' APPLICABILITY

The IBA Rules are intended "to supplement the legal provisions and the institutional, *ad hoc* or other Rules that apply to the conduct of the arbitration." Clearly they are not designed to replace any such rules. Also, the parties and the tribunal may adopt the Rules in whole or in part. If the parties agree to the Rules either in the arbitration agreement or at the commencement of the proceeding, their actual normative application will be determined by the institutional rules governing the arbitration.

5 *See, e.g.*, 2020 IBA Rules, Art. 2, ¶ 3(a); *id.* Art. 3, ¶¶ (b), 9(*i*), 11; *id.* Art. 4, ¶ 9; *id.* Art. 8, ¶ 6; *id.* Art. 9, ¶ 2(a).

6 *See, e.g.*, *id.*, Pmbl. ¶ 3; *id.* Art. 9 ¶ 8.

Two sets of rules granting different normative hierarchical status to agreements of the parties with respect to evidentiary issues have been discussed (see Chapters 4 and 5). In any event, if there is a conflict between the institutional rules and the IBA Rules, it is most likely that deference will be accorded to the parties' agreement on this point. Specific agreements are found to supersede more general propositions. Absent agreement on this issue, the institutional rules would govern.

The Rules are not intended to constrain the flexibility inherent in arbitral proceedings. Instead, they are intended to comport with this central arbitral pillar. In this connection, the Preamble states that "Parties and Arbitral Tribunals are free to adapt them to the particular circumstances of each arbitration."

The definitions set forth in the Rules are quite unique and limited by design. Only one observation is warranted in this regard. The definitions are *operational* and not substantive.[7] They define words such as "claimant," "party," "party-appointed expert," "respondent," and "witness statements." These definitions are *operationally* necessary.

What is lacking is a section defining *substantive* terms that form part of the Rules, and the definition of which inevitably shall contribute to greater risk assessment (settlement).

Critical terms such as (i) *evidence*, (ii) *relevance*, and (iii) *material*, are glaringly missing. The term "weight," as in the weight to be ascribed to evidence, is in no way qualified or referenced in regard to a standard that may provide context as to qualitative or quantitative assessments. Burden of Proof is nowhere mentioned, let alone shifting burden concerning evidentiary proffers. Similarly, concepts such as "good faith" and "best efforts," also central to the Rules' better workings, are not defined. The use of these terms are thus as *ad hoc* as the tribunals charged with applying them.

The word "settlement" appears only once. It is referenced in the very last article at Art. 9.4(b) in the context of protecting the confidentiality of documents created or oral communications allegedly stated during the course of settlement negotiations.[8]

The Rules are not designed to promote settlement or to place the parties in a position to assess risk early in the proceeding (and throughout at critical junctures

[7] These definitions command consultation for purposes of developing a comprehensive understanding of the interplay between the Rules and the concept of *optimal efficiency* as here developed. At some point, hopefully sooner rather than later, the Rules must include substantive definitions regarding such key terms as "relevance" and "materiality." The absence of substantively defined terms has the implicit and practical consequence of transforming *arbitrator discretion* into a default provision that consequentially is overtaxed.

[8] In considering issues of legal impediment or privilege under Art. 9.2(b), and insofar as permitted by any mandatory legal or ethical rules that are determined by it to be applicable, the arbitral tribunal may take into account:

> (b) any need to protect the confidentiality of a document created or statement or oral communication made in connection with and for the purpose of settlement negotiations.

for settlement), let alone to ascertain with any degree of reasonable certainty the *admissibility* and *weight* that will be accorded to evidence presented.[9]

While the Rules certainly aspire to early disclosure, they do so with the primary objective of only promoting *procedural efficiency*.

4.2 ARTICLE 2 OF THE RULES

Article 2 titled ***Consultation on Evidentiary Issues*** was first introduced in its entirety in the 2010 iteration of the IBA Rules (see Section 4.5 in this volume). Significantly, subsection 2.1 poses an obligation in the mandatory "*shall*" on the arbitral tribunal to assist in implementing *party-autonomy* so that the parties may "consult" and presumably agree on "an efficient, economical and fair process for the taking of evidence." In effect, the explicit command codifies the tacit practice of emphasizing both *agreement* and *efficiencies* in the taking of evidence through *party-autonomy*.

The article artfully strikes a balance between the very direct and immediate participation of tribunals in civil law judicial cultures and the *party-autonomy* initiatives endemic to common law adversarial systems. The "consultative" component certainly creates an opportunity for parties from different legal traditions to discuss competing expectations in the taking of evidence.

Additionally, the mandatory *shall* stands in very sharp relief with the permissive "*is encouraged*" norm in paragraph 3 of this very same Art. 2 in connection with any issues that the arbitral tribunal may regard as "relevant to the case and material to its outcome," or with respect to which a preliminary determination may be appropriate.

Subsection 2.2(a)–(f) identifies six non-exhaustive categories that should constitute the subject matter of the consultation on evidentiary issues. The items identified are essential technical concerns. And to a large extent underscore *party-autonomy* and a compromise between legal systems.

Article 2 subsection 2(b), for example, points to the influence of common law advocacy by referencing "the taking of testimony at any Evidentiary Hearing," and thus forcing the parties "at the earliest appropriate time in the proceedings" presumably to consider the use of direct, cross, and re-direct examination, issues that all too often may cause delay, controversy, and uncertainty.[10] Yet, these core terms forming an essential part of oral testimony and examination are not at all referenced in this Article.

Even though Art. 2 does not compel the taking of oral testimony, its suggestion as a discussion point in this subsection at minimum identifies it as a reasonable methodology that, if agreed to early in the proceeding, may facilitate the conduct of evidentiary hearings and the final hearing.

9 The issue of admissibility, except for privilege, confidentiality, trade secret, or burden, really is a non-issue because admissibility is determined by the identical standard applied to disclosure/production. Therefore, if *disclosable*, then it will be *admissible*. No technical exclusionary rule will apply.

10 The term "cross-examination" is not explicitly referenced. It appears nowhere. The absence bespeaks a cultural integration concern.

The paucity of references to direct examination (even the very word "examination"), let alone actual instruction as to manner and form, limited only to three occasions in Art. 8, certainly is not conducive to appropriate *risk assessment*, process transparency, or predictive value. In fact, there is no actual reference to "*direct examination*" or "*re-direct examination*," but rather to "direct testimony" and "re-direct testimony." The term "examination" itself is nowhere referenced. This distinction is important.

The reference to direct and re-direct testimony in Art. 8, subsection 8.3 is intriguing. The absence of "examination" and the use of "question" appears to be a distancing from the Anglo-American tradition of interrogating witnesses. This distancing is not helpful. And it does not find any conceptual justification. Moreover, subsection 8.3 in relevant part provides that "[q]uestions to a witness during direct and re-direct testimony may not be unreasonably leading." Three observations are important.

First, what can it possibly mean for direct or re-direct testimony (if in fact it is "examination") questions not to be "unreasonably leading"?

Second, the inescapable logical consequence is that according to Art. 8, subsection 8.3 questions on direct or re-direct examination can be reasonably leading. This proposition is odd and impracticable.

Contextualization by analogy is important. Most jurisdictions do not allow for leading questions on direct or re-direct examination unless the leading questions (i) pertain to uncontested background facts, or (ii) are used to help a minor testify or someone who is mentally impaired (challenged or incapacitated) and needs the assistance of leading questions. Otherwise, counsel in an ICA hearing would not elect to compromise her own witnesses' testimony by posing leading questions.[11]

Third and finally on this issue of "unreasonably leading questions" in direct or re-direct "questioning," one arrives at the most baffling aspect of the rule. In ICA final hearings, generally there is no such thing as direct questioning or direct examination. Orthodox direct examinations are rare.

The culture of ICA is one where tribunals engage in the legal fiction that by dint of having received witness statements it (the Tribunal) has in effect secured the witnesses' declaration on what would in fact have constituted direct examination. At that point, so the argument says, all that remains for direct examination is authenticating the witness statement.

The witness also may be asked to authenticate her signature at the end of the witness statement, and to correct any inaccuracies that she may have identified in the witness statement. Plain and simple, that rote authentication typically constitutes direct examination ("questioning") in ICA and in its ISDS counterpart as to fact (not expert) witnesses. Certainly, the rule concerning "unreasonably leading questions" cannot be addressing such scenario.

[11] *See* case law on leading questions, Chapter 2, n. 7.

While there is a paucity (just three instances) of references to direct and re-direct testimony, there is absolutely no *explicit* mention whatsoever of the most important kind of oral testimony that can be presented in an ICA hearing: *cross-examination*. And of course, the same holds true for *re-cross-examination*.

Cross-examination obviously is contemplated in Art. 8, subsection 8.4(b), which reads:

> (b) Following direct testimony, *any other party may question such witness*, in an order to be determined by the Arbitral Tribunal. The Party who initially presented the witness shall subsequently have the opportunity to ask additional questions on the matters raised in the other Parties' questioning [technically re-direct][.] (Emphasis added)

The reference to "any other party may question such witness," really should state that any party adverse to the witness should cross-examine the witness. The Rules, perhaps in an effort to appear formally as *international* as possible, use nomenclature that turns out to be inadequate because there are no technical rules that apply to a questioning of a witness after direct testimony by other parties "in an order to be determined by the Arbitral Tribunal."

This deliberate ambiguity further undermines risk assessment, transparency, and therefore, predictive value. It similarly diminishes the requisite process transparency for legitimate integration of different legal cultures.

The Rules would be well served, for example, by clearly providing for actual strictures that determine the manner in which (i) direct examination, (ii) cross-examination, (iii) re-direct examination, and (iv) re-cross-examination are to take place. Such tenets would explain the different forms of questions that can be asked depending on the type of examination that is being conducted, along with the corresponding scope.

Further process transparency, elements for risk assessment, and predictive value can be incorporated into the ICA hearing if the Rules on witness examination and testimony would explain corresponding objections, beyond those governing the "nominal" admissibility and assessment of evidence under Art. 9, which *mostly* (certainly not exclusively) pertain to documentary evidence.

ICA is yet to develop a doctrinal body of work addressing technical objections to witness testimony as to the *form* of questions posed, as well as the *admissibility* and *weight* of testimony.[12] This deficit is a byproduct of the lukewarm embrace of examination generally and cross-examination in particular.[13]

Article 2 does enhance the likelihood of agreement or stipulation on formal aspects of (i) witness statements, (ii) expert reports, (iii) procedures pertaining to the

[12] This point is discussed in detail in Section 8.9.

[13] Cross-examination is discussed Section 8.8.

production of documents, and (iv) confidentiality, by raising the possibility of discussing the scope, timing, and manner of the taking of such evidence.[14]

Standing in sharp contrast to paragraph 2 of this Article, paragraph 3 merely states the "Arbitral Tribunal is *encouraged* to identify to the Parties, as soon as it considers it to be appropriate," any issue that the Arbitral Tribunal "*may*" regard as "relevant to the case and material to its outcome," and/or "for which a preliminary determination may be appropriate."[15]

Significantly, the drafters here did not engraft upon the arbitral tribunal a normative obligation but rather a permissive, "encouraged," suggestive criteria.[16] It is unclear whether the underlying objective is to strike a compromise between common law and civil law traditions by rendering conceptually possible for the tribunal to assume a lead role in this effort consonant with a civil law inquisitorial approach, while also remaining faithful to *party-autonomy*.

It remains a question. Still it would be helpful were the tribunal to explain the relevance of settlement and to facilitate settlement discussion from a technical perspective that would protect the tribunal on a going forward basis should settlement fail to materialize.

The divergent roles ascribed to the arbitrators evinced in paragraphs 2 and 3, however, is less than clear. It is difficult to understand *how* or *why* the management of the consultation process on evidentiary issues would require a higher standard of obligation with respect to the arbitral tribunal's interdiction in the process than the identification of issues "relevant to the case and material to its outcome."[17] The quizzical nature of the asymmetry is further highlighted because the arbitral tribunal is encouraged to act unilaterally and not as part of a consultation process in tandem with the parties.[18]

4.3 THE RELEVANT TO THE CASE AND MATERIAL TO ITS OUTCOME

Perhaps the IBA Rules' most significant doctrinal contribution is the standard of "relevan[ce] to the case and material[ity] to its outcome." Significantly, this standard is mentioned seven times throughout the Rules.[19] Indeed, this language appears and reappears at critical "decision-making" junctures. It is first encountered in this Article (Art. 2) at ¶ 3(a), which reads:

The Arbitral Tribunal is ***encouraged*** to identify to the Parties, as soon as it considers it to be appropriate, any issues:

14 *See, id.* Art. 2, ¶ 2(a), (c), (d).
15 *Id.* Art. 2, ¶ 3.
16 *Id.*
17 *Id.*
18 *See id.*
19 Art. 2, ¶ 3(a), Art. 3 (b), Art. 3, ¶ 9, Art. 3, ¶ 11, Art. 4, ¶ 9, Art. 8, ¶ 6, Art. 9, ¶ 2(a).

(a) That the Arbitral Tribunal may regard as ***relevant to the case and material to its outcome***...[20] (Emphasis added)

Even though the arbitral tribunal is merely "encouraged" and not tasked with the normative imperative of causing the parties to act (as is the case in paragraph 1 of this same Article), this provision is paramount to the anatomy of an arbitration and to the possible doctrinal development that may lead to a rule that would render risk assessment and settlement viable at an early stage. The arbitral tribunal is *encouraged* to identify "any issue," thus suggesting *all issues* of both fact and law, that are "relevant to the case and material to its outcome."

In addition to containing the embryonic workings of a viable risk assessment-settlement rule, this subsection of Art. 2 may be reasonably construed as empowering the arbitral tribunal to serve as a facilitator for the crafting of "evidentiary terms of reference." This undertaking may assist the parties and the Tribunal by framing the contours of all evidentiary, legal, and factual issues endemic to the proceeding. The potential and the actual significance of this standard at the consultative phase of the arbitration cannot be underestimated.

One very significant instance in which the "relevant to the case and material to its outcome" standard appears is in the documentary and disclosure section of the Rules.[21] It forms part of a critical mandatory requirement. Article 3, paragraph 3(a)–(b) provides:

3. A Request to Produce shall contain:

(a) a description of each requested Document sufficient to identify it, or (ii) a description in sufficient detail (including subject matter) of a narrow and specific requested category of Documents that are reasonably believed to exist; in the case of Documents maintained in electronic form, the requesting Party may, or the Arbitral Tribunal may order that it shall be required to, identify specific files, search terms, individuals or other means of searching for such Documents in an efficient and economical manner;

(b) a statement as to how the Documents requested are *relevant to the case and material to its outcome*.[22] (Emphasis added)

The "relevant to the case and material to its outcome" standard constitutes the guidepost of the obligatory statement that a requesting party must include in a Request for Production. A statement, in turn, may either elicit objections from the adverse party or, even the arbitral tribunal, on either insufficiency as to *relevance* or *materiality*, and thus limit or foreclose production. The statement premised on the standard is dispositive of the *discloseability* and admissibility of evidence within the construct of the Rules.

[20] *Id.* at Art. ¶ 3(a).

[21] Art. 3.

[22] *Id.*, Art. 3 ¶ 7.

As referenced (Section 4.1), one of the challenges inherent in the very architecture of the Rules is that they simultaneously address *procedure* and *evidence*, that is to say, (i) evidence taking and (ii) the presentation of evidence (admissibility and assessment).[23] And subject to the *weight* the arbitral panel is to place on admissible evidence, the *taking* and *presentation* of evidence in ICA and the IBA Rules are one and the same. The Rules are both procedural and evidentiary or hybrid, as the case may be.

The "relevant to the case and material to its outcome" standard governs the sufficiency of an objection. The test is articulated in Art. 3, ¶ 7, which in relevant part suggests:

> [t]he Arbitral Tribunal may order the Party to whom such Request is addressed to produce any requested Document in its possession, custody or control as to which the Arbitral Tribunal determines that (i) the issues that the requesting Party wishes to prove are relevant to the case and material to its outcome; (ii) none of the reasons for objection set forth in Articles 9.2 or 9.3 applies; and (iii) the requirements of Article 3.3 have been satisfied.[24]

The gamut of objections as to admissibility is sparse.[25] The Art. 3 subsection 3.3. objections primarily are limited (except for privilege, confidentiality, and burden) to custody, control, and objections having to do with the standard. Objections based on the standard "relevant to the case and material to its outcome" are very narrow and subjective. The standard itself is without meaningful objective content, and therefore, its meaning and application vary depending on the reader's personal interpretation.[26]

A third category of possible objections (subsection 9.2(a)) merely concerns objections in connection with the standard, which in the subsection 9.2(a) version is in the disjunctive "or" as in "relevance to the case or materiality to its outcome." The remaining four objections are all based on "legal impediment or privilege." Therefore, it stands to reason that the standard, "relevant to the case and material to its outcome," necessarily will be doing most of the work.

It is conceptually sound foı the identical standard to apply to the statement eliciting production of documents, as well as to the viability of objections that the producing party may face.

In keeping with this symmetry the standard governs the self-disclosure provision of the Rules. Article 3, paragraph 11, provides the parties with latitude to:

23 The position that differentiates between the use of the terms "procedural" and "substantive" should not be drawn, is acknowledged but not shared as an unqualified universal principle to be categorically applied.

24 *Id.*

25 IBA Rules, Art. 3 ¶ 7.

26 The Art. 9, subsection 9.3 set of objections admittedly are more generous than the Art. 3, subsection 3.3 counterpart. Still, however, note that of the seven objections, two (Art. 9, subsection 9.2 (c) and (g)) concern efficiency issues.

> submit to the Arbitral Tribunal and to the other Parties any additional Documents on which they intend to rely ***or*** which they believe have become relevant to the case and material to its outcome as a consequence of the issues raised in Documents, Witness Statements or Expert Reports submitted or produced, or in other submissions of the Parties.[27] (Emphasis added)

The disjunctive "or" further emphasizes the importance of this standard in the self-disclosure and additional supplementation sections of the Rules.

If due process is to be observed, parties must be allowed to present evidence that addresses newly introduced issues or other evidentiary concerns arising during the course of the proceeding as part of the flexible and organic nature of the arbitration process. The disjunctive "or" suggests that the Rules provide the parties and the arbitral tribunal with both a subjective and objective standard for determining the propriety of such supplemental disclosure. Greater rigor is necessary if risk assessment is to be rendered viable.

Article 3, paragraph 11 amplifies the scope of the "relevant to the case and material to its outcome" standard by broadening its application far beyond the confines of the claims and defenses asserted in the operative pleadings. The explicit linkage between the standard and (i) documents, (ii) witness statements, (iii) expert reports, and (iv) issues raised in "other submissions of the parties," only serve to call attention to the need to flesh out the elements of the standard (i.e., most notably *relevance* and *materiality*).

Application to compel the attendance of a recalcitrant witness requires recourse to the standard. In both theory and practice the incorporation of this standard into arbitral compulsory practice should encourage compliance, and create a chilling effect with respect to recourse to local courts.

Generally, and certainly with respect to the US common law, the standard governing an application to compel production or attendance on the part of a witness is broader than the "relevant to the case and material to its outcome" talisman.[28] Also, in the context of the FAA, the workings of Section 7 are tantamount to providing the arbitral tribunal with subpoena power,[29] which, much like Fed. R. Civ. P. 45,[30]

[27] *Id.* Art. 3, ¶ 11.
[28] *See* Chapter 3, n. 26 in this volume.
[29] Chapter 5, n. 22 in this volume.
[30] Federal Rule of Civil Procedure 45 in relevant part states:

> **(c) Place of Compliance.**
>
> (1) ***For a Trial, Hearing, or Deposition***. A subpoena may command a person to attend a trial, hearing, or deposition only as follows:
> (A) within 100 miles of where the person resides, is employed, or regularly transacts business in person; or
> (B) within the state where the person resides, is employed, or regularly transacts business in person, if the person
> (i) is a party or a party's officer; or
> (ii) is commanded to attend a trial and would not incur substantial expense.

provides the tribunal with compulsory authority as to witnesses and documents. The compulsory powers the FAA vests arbitral tribunals with the right to hold a recalcitrant witness in contempt, no differently than if the witness had failed to comply with a court order.[31]

Therefore the practical workings of the FAA with respect to compulsory practice is to provide the arbitral tribunal with a Fed. R. Civ. P. 26 standard in relation to the tribunal's authority to compel testimony.[32]

The standard that was fashioned to apply to documents also governs witness evidential compulsory practice.[33] Under the Rules, parties seeking the appearance of an involuntary witness may pursue two avenues of relief. First, a party may seek leave from the arbitral tribunal to secure whatsoever measures may be legally available to compel attendance, typically by resorting to municipal courts. Second, a party may also do so by petitioning the arbitral tribunal to order attendance upon penalty of having an adverse inference drawn.[34]

(2) ***For Other Discovery***. A subpoena may command:
  (A) production of documents, electronically stored information, or tangible things at a place within 100 miles of where the person resides, is employed, or regularly transacts business in person; and
  (B) inspection of premises at the premises to be inspected.

31 FAA 9 USC § 7, in relevant part providing that: "if any person or persons so summoned to testify shall refuse or neglect to obey said summons, upon petition to the United States District Court for the district in which such arbitrators, or a majority of them, are sitting may compel the attendance of such person or persons before said arbitrator or arbitrators, or punish said person or persons for contempt in the same manner provided by law for securing the attendance of witnesses or their punishment for neglect or refusal to attend in the courts of the United States."

32 *See* Chapter 5, n. 22 in this volume.

33 IBA Rules (2020) Art. 4, subsection 4.9, by way of example, reads:

> 9. If a Party wishes to present evidence from a person who will not appear voluntarily at its request, the Party may, within the time ordered by the Arbitral Tribunal, ask it to take whatever steps are legally available to obtain the testimony of that person, or seek leave from the Arbitral Tribunal to take such steps itself. In the case of a request to the Arbitral Tribunal, the Party shall identify the intended witness, shall describe the subjects on which the witness's testimony is sought and shall state why such subjects are *relevant to the case and material to its outcome*. The Arbitral Tribunal shall decide on this request and shall take, authorize the requesting Party to take or order any other Party to take, such steps as the Arbitral Tribunal considers appropriate if, in its discretion, it determines that the testimony of that witness would be *relevant to the case and material to its outcome*. (Emphasis added)

The "relevant to the case and material to its outcome" standard governs every aspect of witness testimony.

34 *Id.* Art. 9, subsections 6 and 7 explicitly address adverse inferences:

> 6. If a Party fails without satisfactory explanation to produce any Document requested in a Request to Produce to which it has not objected in due time or fails to produce any Document ordered to be produced by the Arbitral Tribunal, the Arbitral Tribunal may infer that such document would be adverse to the interests of that Party.
>
> 7. If a Party fails without satisfactory explanation to make available any other relevant evidence, *including testimony*, sought by one Party to which the Party to whom the request was addressed has not objected in due time or fails to make available any evidence, *including testimony*, ordered by the Arbitral Tribunal to be produced, the Arbitral Tribunal may infer that such evidence would be adverse to the interests of that Party. (Emphasis added)

The standard is reiterated twice within the same paragraph of Art. 9. Consequently, in addition to constituting the dispositive criterion of review for (i) consultation,[35] (ii) self-disclosure, (iii) disclosure procedural junctions,[36] and (iv) admissibility, the standard also governs (v) compulsory practice. For instance, the arbitral tribunal may request that "any person [ ] give oral or written evidence on any issue that the arbitral tribunal considers to be *relevant to the case and material to its outcome*."[37]

The use of this same standard for both (i) the taking of evidence and (ii) for purposes of admissibility presents challenges to *risk assessment* (see Section 4.4). Evidence *taking* and *admissibility* require different standards, beyond just the weight accorded to admissible evidence, if comprehensive *risk assessment* is to be rendered viable. The quality (probative value) of the evidence needs to be assessed in connection with the *presentation of evidence*: not so in the context of evidence taking.

The elements of "relevancy" and "materiality" for purposes of admissibility as probative evidence should be narrower and considerably more stringent than at the taking of evidence stage of the proceeding. The category of "weight," is the only factor distinguishing the standards applicable to the taking of evidence, and that governs the presentation (admissibility and reliability) of evidence.[38]

Most notably, the elements of the standard are nowhere defined in the Rules. The terms "relevant" and "material" simply are not explained anywhere in this framework. Indeed, even the terms "evidence" or "expert" find no definition.

While the term "expert report" is defined as a "written statement by a Tribunal/appointed Expert or a Party-appointed Expert," within the terms of the Rules,[39] there is no proposition within the Rules' framework from which to infer the meaning of the term "expert." Qualification of a witness as an expert is relegated, if at all, to the arbitral tribunal's discretion.

Certainly an argument can be made that the Rules need not address the issue of qualifying an expert as an expert from an evidentiary perspective because Art. 9 subsection 9.1 vests the tribunal with the inherent powers to "determine the admissibility, relevance, materiality and weight of evidence" the importance of expert testimony in ICA, however, would suggest that qualification of an expert is a required predicate the arbitral tribunal must consider. Similarly, the term "evidentiary hearing" is defined as "any hearing, whether or not held on consecutive days, at which the Arbitral Tribunal, whether in person, by conference, by video conference

35 *See id.* at Art. 2 subsection 2.2(a).

36 *See id.* at Arts. 3 subsection 3.3(b), 3.9, 8 subsection 8.6, and 9 subsection 9.2 (a). Even though the self-disclosure rubric in Art. 3, subsection 3.1 is premised on the "available to it on which it relies" standard for initial self-disclosure, ultimately the sufficiency of that effort is subject to the compulsory practice and sustainability of objections that, in turn, is predicated on the "relevant to the case and material to its outcome" standard. *See, e.g., Id.* at Art. 9, subsection 9.2(a).

37 IBA Rules (2020) Art. 8, subsection 8.6 (concerning evidentiary hearings).

38 *See* IBA Rules Art. 9.1, Chapter 5, n. 21 in this volume.

39 *Id.* Art. 5 (defining "expert report"). *Id.* Art. 7 (defining "evidentiary hearing").

or other method, receives oral or other evidence."[40] The seminal term "evidence," however, simply is not defined. The absence of any definition of the terms "relevance" and "material" frustrate any aspiration of meaningful *risk assessment*.

This problem is compounded and multiplied because of the widely divergent interpretations arising from the different legal and cultural backgrounds of practitioners and arbitrators. It is far from inconceivable to posit the likelihood of an arbitral tribunal where each of the three members has a different understanding of what is meant by "relevant" or "material," based on her training. These concerns can be mitigated were the Rules to suggest that for purposes of considering issues of *relevance* or *materiality* the parties are encouraged to submit authority on these definitions from a number of reasonable potential sources.[41]

The IBA Rules functionally mitigates these definitional gaps by enhancing *party-autonomy* from a structural perspective.[42] Their emphasis on *party-autonomy* does further transparency and *risk assessment* because limiting *arbitrator discretion* pursuant to *party-autonomy* contributes to carving out of ICA lack of predictive value arising from *arbitrator discretion* regarding procedural and evidentiary matters that are best known to the parties themselves.

The shift in paradigm from *arbitrator discretion* to *party-autonomy*, however, does not render possible a level procedural transparency and *risk assessment* necessary for *optimal efficiency* absent *absolute* and not *relative* definitions of foundational evidentiary concepts. Parties to an ICA proceeding need to have a higher degree of certainty concerning the admissibility or inadmissibility of evidence, beyond the mere exercise of *arbitrator discretion*.

The enhancement of *party-autonomy* does not redress this deficit. Structural uncertainty still pervades. And it clouds risk assessment. There must be some basic expectation regarding the methodology and principles that arbitral tribunals will

40 *Id*. Art. 7 (defining "evidentiary hearing").

41 A rule requiring substantive analysis of technical terms, even where the substantive rules may originate from different jurisdictions, itself is a step closer to uniformity. The parties know with lead time that conceptually the terms will be defined by settled rules and definitions of *some* jurisdiction, and not by the improvisations of an Arbitral Tribunal.

42 *See, e.g.*, IBA Rules (2020) Arts. 2, subsections 2.1 and 2.2(a)–(f); 3, subsections 3.1, 3.2., and 3.3(a)–(c) (providing the parties with initiative to serve a *Request to Produce* to an opposing party, and providing parties with self-disclosure initiative); 4 subsection 4.1 (providing parties with initiative to submit witness statements), subsection 4.9 (providing parties with initiative to engage in compulsory practice); 5 subsection 5.1 (allowing parties initiative to appoint an expert as a means of evidence on specific issues); 6 subsection 6.6 (providing parties with initiative to have a Tribunal-Appointed Expert present at an Evidentiary Hearing); 7 (providing a party with initiative "to inspect or require the inspection by a Tribunal-Appointed Expert or a Party-Appointed Expert of any site, property, machinery or any other goods, samples, systems, processes, or Documents, as it deems appropriate"); 8 subsections 8.1 and 8.2 (providing a party with initiative on calling witnesses whose appearance for testimony at an Evidentiary Hearing a party may desire to examine, and granting parties initiative to request Evidentiary Hearings to be conducted remotely); and 9 subsections 9.3 and 9.4(a)–(e) (providing party with initiative to exclude evidence).

employ in assessing the reliability and quality of evidence.[43] Absent this transparency negotiating in the shadow of the law will not be possible.

4.4 *RISK ASSESSMENT* CONDUCIVE TO *OPTIMAL EFFICIENCY* REQUIRES DEFINITIONS FOR "RELEVANCE" AND "MATERIALITY"

If process transparency and *risk assessment* at all matter in the taking and presentation of evidence in ICA, then the use of the standard "*relevant to the case and material to its outcome*," requires greater rigor. The articulation of a general statement only for every evidentiary phase of the proceeding merely renders the decision-making a subjective exercise epistemically lacking in possible risk assessment and predictive value. The status quo is not enough. And it will serve to render *risk assessment* in the context of settlement only *aspirational.*

Equipoise between *party-autonomy* and *arbitrator discretion* is necessary. Such equipoise, however, is not possible without a clear understanding of critical terms such as *relevance, materiality*, and even the concept of *evidence* itself. A *Free Proof* approach,[44] unqualified and devoid of guiding principles cannot reasonably lead to *optimal efficiency*.

To some extent, the lack of substantive definitions finds explanation in the status of the Rules as a "supplement to the legal provisions in the institutional, *ad hoc* or other Rules that apply to the conduct of the arbitration."[45] To be sure, while Art. 1, titled "*Scope of Application*,"[46] does provide some guidance for the interaction

43 In the US, by way of example, the Federal Rules of Evidence ("FRE," "Fed. R. Evid.," or "F.R.E.") (as amended in 2015) define "*relevant evidence*" as "ha[ving] any tendency to make a fact more or less probable than it would be without the evidence" when the fact at issue is "of consequence in determining the action." While there are similar common law and civil law principles defining relevance, the disparity between them is significant. The concept of relevance used in isolation and merely as a barometer highlights that lacking a definition for so critical an operational principle unduly and unfairly asks *arbitrator discretion* to carry too heavy of a conceptual load.

See generally, Peter Nicolas, *Evidence: A Problem-Based and Comparative Approach* (Carolina Academic Press 2009), 3–50; Caroline E. Foster, *Signs and the Precautionary Principle in International Courts and Tribunals: Expert Evidence, Burden of Proof and Finality* (Cambridge University Press 2011); Chantal Joubert, *Judicial Control of Foreign Evidence in a Comparative and International Context* (Rozenberg Publishers 2005); and Mirjan R. Damaška, *Crime, Procedure and Evidence in a Comparative and International Context: Essays in Honour of Professor Mirjan Damaška* (John D. Jackson, Máximo Langer, and Peter Tillers, eds.) (Hart Publishing 2008).

44 *Free Proof* is here defined as the methodology pursuant to which fact-finders in adjudicating the quality, reliability, admissibility, and weight of evidence rely on personal intuition and conviction instead of applying a strict rules approach that also entails exclusionary categories of evidence, such as "hearsay." This approach is most prevalent in civil jurisdictions. Chapter 5, n. 27 in this volume.

45 IBA 2020 Rules, at Pmbl., ¶ 1.

46 The 2020 version of the IBA Rules carries forward the 2010 iteration's amendment replacing Art. 2 of the 1999 Rules with a new Article that is materially identical to the 1999 predecessor, but for the insertion of Article 2, which provides that, "[w]here the Parties have agreed to apply the IBA Rules of

between the Rules and the *General Rules*,[47] the "*Scope of Application*" of the Rules is of no moment in placing limitations on "relevance" or "materiality" (whatever these terms may mean within this particular framework). The "*Scope of Application*" also is devoid of any standard that may be of theoretical or practical value in (i) self-disclosure, (ii) disclosure, (iii) compulsory practice, or any other aspect of the "taking of evidence," as framed by Art. 2 or embodied by the standard "relevant to the case and material to its outcome."

The scant and non-substantive nature of the treatment accorded to the elements of the "relevant to the case and material to its outcome" standard perfectly comports with the drafting approach undertaken with respect to the *Definitions* section of the Rules.[48] This section only consists of thirteen definitions.[49] The definitions accorded to these terms are *formal* and not *substantive*. The definitions are *operational* and not tasked with introducing process transparency, consistency, and predictability pursuant to objective standards.

The definitional effort of the Rules is limited to rendering the reading of the Rules consistent. The intent is not to provide substantive content to any of the principles underlying the Rules. In this regard the Rules enshrine arbitral discretion to the detriment of *party-autonomy* and possible *risk assessment*, certainly as concerns the admissibility and evaluation of evidence.

The *Definitions* section aspires only to provide specific nouns with a consistent nomenclature. It does not aim to supply substantive content to doctrinal tenets. Similarly, it is silent on the manner, form and scope of foundational procedural rights concerning witness testimony (see Section 3.1.3). Thus, the very understanding of "probative evidence" remains shrouded in mystery under the rules *Definitions* (see Section 4.8.2).

This want of substantive definitions has the literal etymological effect of failing *to define*, that is to say, to render finite or place limits on terms. Thereby leading to the inevitable consequence of vesting the arbitral tribunal with *textually* unbridled parameters in the exercise of its discretion to vest such pivotal elements with meaning on an *ad hoc* basis, and lacking in any structural-uniform guidance.

The principles of *party-autonomy*, predictability (*risk assessment*), uniformity, and process transparency (objective rules and standards) are significantly undermined in paragraphs 4 and 5 of Art. 1. Paragraph 4 of Art. 1 of the Rules reads, "[i]n the event of any dispute regarding the meaning of the IBA Rules of Evidence, the Arbitral Tribunal shall interpret them according to their purpose and in the manner most

Evidence, they shall be deemed to have agreed, in the absence of a contrary indication to the version as current on the date of such agreement." *Compare* IBA 1999 Rules, at Art. 2, subsection 2.2, with IBA 2010 Rules, and 2020 Rules, at Art. 1 subsection 1.2.

47 The General Rules are defined as meaning "the institutional, *ad hoc*, other rules that apply to the conduct of the arbitration." *See* IBA 2020 Rules, at 8, defining "General Rules."

48 *See* IBA 2020 Rules, Definitions.

49 *Id.*

appropriate for the particular arbitration."[50] Instead of subscribing to an objective standard that the tribunal would apply, the paragraph merely delegates a resolution of this problem to the tribunal's *discretion*.

Arbitral tribunals in international arbitrations tend to comprise representatives from different legal traditions and cultures. The absence of a "known standard" or "substantive definition" to be applied in interpreting the meaning of the Rules wrests from the parties the ability to predict likely baseline rulings on fundamental evidential issues.[51] This same spirit of deference to the tribunal and bolstering of *arbitrator discretion* is very much present in paragraph 5 of Art. 1 of the Rules:

> [i]nsofar as the IBA Rules of Evidence and the General Rules are silent on any matter concerning the taking of evidence and the Parties have not agreed otherwise, the Arbitral Tribunal shall conduct *the taking of evidence as it deems appropriate, in accordance with the general principles of the IBA Rules of Evidence.*[52] (Emphasis added)

As a consequence of not defining the terms "relevance," "evidence," and "taking of evidence," and supplementing this standard with evidentiary rules and principles that concern the admissibility and weight to be ascribed to evidence, the Rules do not clearly establish what is meant by "conduct the taking of evidence." This problem is compounded because the tribunal should manage the process consisting in "conduct[ing] the taking of evidence" not "as it deems appropriate," but rather (i) consonant with the parties' expectations, (ii) in keeping with due process, (iii) in furtherance of a policy that promotes *process efficiency* (i.e., the likelihood of issuance of a binding and enforceable award), and (iv) *optimal efficiency*, maximizing the parties' ability to engage in *risk assessment* and thus to render settlement a meaningful and viable possibility.

The Rules do not materially improve on their predecessors (the 2010 IBA Rules) because they fail to enhance *sufficiently* the fundamental principles of *party-autonomy*, uniformity, predictive value, and unchecked transparency. Article 1 paragraph 5 of the Rules grants authority to the arbitral tribunal. Reposing the "conduct [of] in the taking of evidence as it deems appropriate" in the arbitral tribunal subordinates the parties' will and thus the principle of *party-autonomy*. It does so in

[50] *See* 2020 IBA Rules at Art. 1 subsection 1.4.

[51] By way of example, within the framework of the Federal Rules of Civil Procedure in the US, the meaning of specific and potentially dispositive terms may be gleaned from many sources, including: (i) jurisprudence governing the construction of terms of art and other legal principles, (ii) advisory notes drafted by the committee members charged with drafting and revising the FRCP, (iii) a well-developed body of jurisprudence interpreting the Rules, and (iv) scholastic materials authored by academics and practitioners that extensively comment on most of the salient and material elements of the FRE. To date, the 2020 IBA Rules, and its predecessors, lack the benefit of any single one of these sources, let alone the gains arising from having the ability to consult all or some in unison as to a specific conflict. The academic literature on the rules is largely descriptive and not prescriptive.

[52] IBA 2020 Rules at Art. 5 subsection 5.1 (concerning the Scope of Application).

furtherance of an inquisitorial approach that is distinctively a feature of civil law jurisdictions. The requisite equipoise between *party-autonomy*, and arbitral discretion is sacrificed.[53] This approach is in keeping with a civil law *Free Proof* methodology with respect to evidential assessments.

Paragraph 1 of Art. 1 to *some* extent grants limited yields to *party-autonomy*:

> Whenever the Parties have agreed or the Arbitral Tribunal has determined to apply the IBA Rules of Evidence, the Rules shall govern the taking of evidence, *except to the extent that any specific provision of them may be found to be in conflict with any mandatory provision of law determined to be applicable to the case by the Parties or by the Arbitral Tribunal.*[54] (Emphasis added)

The second part of the disjunctive places the parties in *pari materia* with a determination by the arbitral tribunal. This exception to the general applicability of the Rules represents a significant concession to *party-autonomy*.

The absence of a standard or definition for "materiality" further causes confusion when adjudicating an evidentiary dispute between parties from disparate legal systems as the concept of materiality may be subject to different interpretations. Three factors are essential in arriving at an understanding of the meaning of "documents" that may be deemed "evidence" within the Rules' ambit.[55] These factors may help in mitigating the gap caused by the subjectivity of the term "material" within the meaning of the Rules.

First, the self-disclosure production of documents pursuant to the Rules is based on a showing of "reliance."[56] Particularly with respect to Art. 3 paragraph 2, parties

[53] *Id.* This paragraph is identical to its predecessor. For completeness' sake, it must be emphasized that ¶ 5 does expressly reference a scenario where "the Parties have not agreed otherwise." This language notwithstanding, however, the absence of a reference to potentially dispositive norms or other criteria is glaring and disconcerting. In fact, the Rules are completely bereft of any section or appendix purporting to enunciate underlying or governing general principles. Thus, it necessarily must be inferred that whatsoever "general principles of the IBA Rules of Evidence" may be referenced should be somewhat extrapolated from the totality of the Rules themselves. This task certainly requires greater guidance and more comprehensive analysis so that it may be of significant practical assistance to stakeholders. *See* IBA Rules on the Taking of Evidence in International Arbitration (1999), at Art. 2 subsection 2.4.

[54] *See* IBA 2020 Rules, n. 39 in this chapter, at Art. 1.

[55] As the Rules introduce a broader definition of "*Document*," any production or disclosure ambiguity is multiplied and likely rendered more prejudicial. IBA 2020 Rules at 7–8 defining "*Document*" as: "'*Document*' means a writing, communication, picture, drawing, program or data of any kind, whether recorded or maintained on paper or by electronic, audio visual or any other means."

[56] *See id.* at Art. 3 subsections 3.1 and 3.2, which read:

> 1. Within the time ordered by the Arbitral Tribunal, each Party shall submit to the Arbitral Tribunal and to the other Parties all Documents available to it *on which it relies*, including public Documents and those in the public domain, except for any Documents that have already been submitted by another Party.
>
> 2. Within the time ordered by the Arbitral Tribunal, any Party may submit to the Arbitral Tribunal and to the other Parties a Request to Produce. (Emphasis added)

seeking the admissibility of documents must state the reason(s) why the documents disclosed and sought to be admitted are being relied upon.[57] Such reasons certainly will assist in determining the "materiality" of evidence.

As to a request to produce, the requesting party would have to articulate the premises establishing the reasons why the documents are "relevant to the case and material to its outcome."[58] The relevance narrative (reliance) requirement is susceptible to the critique of being unduly limiting and tactically prejudicial.

For example, in contrast with the Rules' relevance framework commanding a relationship to the claims and defenses, and detailing the meaning of "relevance,"[59] parties seeking to disclose or otherwise elicit production often need to assert mental impressions concerning the strategy of the case that presumably would be furthered were the documents disclosed admitted as "evidence."[60]

The Rules' failure to establish a conceptual link between "reliance" with the claims or defenses rendering the standard "objective" not only taints the process with uncertainty and lack of guidance, but also fosters the publication of counsel's strategic thinking at a juncture that may be less than ripe or otherwise both strategically and tactically unadvisable. The objective in risk assessment is factual equipoise between the parties. Attaining and presenting this symmetry is critical to the process.

Disclosure of the parties' work-product strategic impressions rarely promotes the equitable administration of justice. This outcome is particularly so when evidence

57 *See id.* at Arts. 3 subsections 3(i)–(iii), and 3.11. Art. 3 subsection 3.11 reads:

> 11. Within the time ordered by the Arbitral Tribunal, the Parties may submit to the Arbitral Tribunal and to the other Parties any additional Documents on which they intend to rely or which they believe have become relevant to the case and material to its outcome as a consequence of the issues raised in Documents, Witness Statements or Expert Reports submitted or produced, or in other submissions of the Parties.

58 *See id.* at Arts. 3 subsection 3.3(a)–(b), which state:

> 3. A Request to Produce shall contain:
> (a) (i) a description of each requested Document sufficient to identify it, or
> (ii) a description in sufficient detail (including subject matter) of a narrow and specific requested category of Documents that are reasonably believed to exist; in the case of Documents maintained in electronic form, the requesting Party may, or the Arbitral Tribunal may order that it shall be required to, identify specific files, search terms, individuals or other means of searching for such Documents in an *efficient and economical manner*;
> (b) a statement as to how the Documents requested are relevant to the case and material to its outcome. (Emphasis added)

59 *See id.* at Art. 3 subsection 3.11 ("within the time ordered by the Arbitral Tribunal, the Parties may submit to the Arbitral Tribunal and to the other Parties any additional Documents on *which they intend to rely or which they believe have become relevant to the case and material to its outcome as a consequence of the issues raised in the Documents, Witness Statements or Expert Reports submitted or produced, or in other submissions of the Parties*"). (Emphasis added)

60 *See id.* at Art. 3 subsection 3.3(b), providing that a Request to Produce shall contain "a statement as to how the Documents requested are relevant to the case and material to its outcome."

is sought for impeachment, credibility purposes, as well as for thematic considerations, two categories that are completely absent from the Rules' framework. Also, often evidence is necessary to challenge premises on which adverse expert witnesses are likely to rely on.

Divulging the manner in which material propositions are to be proven may disadvantage the moving party. Pursuant to this architecture parties now must engage in a predicate analysis before submitting a formal document request to determine whether the benefits arising from the documents requested outweigh the partial or complete disclosure of the parties' arbitration strategy. The net effect is a strike against *optimal efficiency*.

The same analysis holds true for initial self-disclosure pursuant to Art. 3, paragraph 1. The Rules seek to placate expectations arising from multiple and diverse legal cultures exclusively in the context of yielding a binding and enforceable award. Hence, the arbitral tribunal is provided with latitude to question and to interrogate witnesses and parties as would a judge presiding in a civil law jurisdiction. Consequently, a party engaged in this preliminary analysis must assume that disclosure of its work-product shall be broader than the premises that the party advances because of the high likelihood of questions from the arbitral tribunal.

The undefined terms lead to an ambiguity that results in bolstering *arbitrator discretion* and contributing to an absence or disruption of equipoise between *arbitrator discretion* and *party-autonomy*. Yet, only this equipoise is conducive to *optimal efficiency*.

The want of guidance, instead of providing greater opportunity for advocacy, wrests authority and normative standing from *party-autonomy* and transfers it to the arbitral tribunal. The Rules *implicitly* resort to *arbitrator discretion* as a "catch-all" category. Worse still, it is identified as a principal guidepost throughout all phases of the *taking* and the *presentation* of evidence in an arbitral proceeding.

The word "material," or any of its permutations, has been removed from the U.S. FRE.[61] The meaning of this term, however, can be discerned from three distinctive bodies of jurisprudence. The Third Circuit Court of Appeals in *Szubak v.*

[61] Fed. R. Evid. 807 does not preserve "materiality" as a standard in subsection (A), which states that a "statement not specifically covered by Rule 803 or 804 but having equivalent circumstantial guarantees of trustworthiness is not excluded by the hearsay rule, if the court determines that (a) the statement is offered by evidence of a material fact …" Fed. R. Evid. 807(A). The current iteration of F.R.E. 807(a) provides that "[u]nder the following conditions, a hearsay statement is not executed by the rule against hearsay, even if the statement is not admissible under a hearsay exception in Rule 803 or 804." The term "material" was also removed from F.R.E. 401(b), and substituted for "(b) the fact is of consequence in determining the action." Thus, under the current iteration of Rule 401 and federal evidential regime, the term "material" has been deleted and in its place the concept of the term's workings has been used. (Test for Relevant Evidence), reads: "Evidence is relevant if: (a) it has any tendency to make a fact more or less probable than it would be without the evidence, and (b) *the fact is of consequence in determining the action.*" (Emphasis added.) "Material" in the US common law tradition is conceptually tantamount to "important."

Secretary of Health & Human Services[62] in the context of regulations pertaining to the Social Security Act, 20 C.F.R. § 405(g) explained that new evidence under that provision is "material" if it is relevant and probative and there is "a reasonable possibility that the new evidence would change the outcome of the [Commissioner's] determination, ..."

In this context the "materiality" of evidence must have some "tendency to make a fact more or less probable than it would be without the evidence,"[63] have probative value, and provide for the *possibility* (not *probability*) that the evidence would change the outcome of the determination at issue.

The question in that case concerned the extent to which purportedly new evidence would change a denial of benefits to an under-aged claimant. The Court explained that: "[a]n implicit materiality requirement is that the new evidence relate to the time period for which benefits were denied, and that it not concern evidence of a later-acquired disability or of the subsequent deterioration of the previously non-disabling condition."[64]

The absence of any definition, methodology of construction, or authority clarifying the meaning of the terms (i) "evidence," (ii) "relevance," and (iii) "material," diminishes the primacy and pervasiveness of the principle of *party-autonomy* throughout the Rules generally and regarding Arts. 2, 3, 4, 8, and 9.[65] Equally important is the dearth of a rule or standard based consideration of the reliability of evidence.

Moreover, the contention that the Rules are supplemental in nature and only meant to buttress the "General Rules" does not begin to cure the fundamental issues that arise from simply not having these terms defined or otherwise subordinated to "General Rules" that do in fact define them.

In order for evidence to be material the evidence must relate to an element of the case. In *Szubak* that element of materiality concerned the relevant timeframe. The definition of "material evidence" was explored by the Court of Appeals for Veterans' Claims in *Shade v. Shinseki*,[66] a case involving an appeal from the Board of Veterans' Appeals decision denying, among other things, a claim to reopen a previously denied petition for service in connection with a skin disorder.[67]

62 *Szubak v. Secretary of Health & Human Services*, 744 F.2d 831, 833 (3rd Cir. 1984).

63 *See* F.R.E. Rule 401(a).

64 *Id.*

65 It is possible to engage in the fiction that distorts *party-autonomy* beyond any conceivable recognition by asserting that having subscribed to the Rules in their current form, which lack these definitions, is a clear example of the exercise of *party-autonomy*. This argument would go on to assert that the parties elected to repose vast latitude on *arbitrator discretion*. Thus, the arbitral tribunal, so says the assertion, is but a mimetic representation of the parties who otherwise only would enjoy a semiotic representation. This contention, however, is fraught with internal inconsistencies that ultimately render the premise unsustainable.

66 *Shade v. Shinseki*, 24 Vet. App. pp. 110 (2010).

67 *Id.*

Central to claimant's appeal was the "single assertion of error: that the Board failed to properly apply 38 C.F.R. § 3.156(a) to the evidence presented in his claim to reopen."[68] In this connection, the Court noted that "the appellant argues that the Board's application of § 3.156(a) did not comport with the requirements of 38 U.S.C. § 5108, the statute requiring VA to reopen a previously denied claim *when new and material evidence had been presented*."[69] (Emphasis added.)

In reversing the Board's denial of benefits, the Court premised its findings on a redefinition of "material" to mean "existing evidence that … relates to an unestablished fact necessary to substantiate the claim."[70] Moreover, the Court noted that "the reasonable possibility portion of 3.156(a) cannot impose a greater burden to reopening than imposed by Congress by that language in the VCAA."[71] It therefore follows that (i) if a fact can be of reasonable consequence in the determination of the action, and (ii) relates to an element of the claims or defenses asserted, (iii) then it will be deemed to be *material* from an evidential perspective.

A third line of authority defining *material evidence* can be found in the context of jurisprudence addressing the materiality of suppressed evidence on the part of prosecutors that defense counsel requested under a *Brady* analysis.[72] By way of example, the Supreme Court in *United States v. Bagley*,[73] in analyzing whether there was a constitutional error arising from the government's failure to assist the defense by disclosing information that might have been helpful in conducting cross-examination and such that the withholding of such evidence "is material in the sense that its suppression undermines confidence in the outcome of the trial,"[74] reviewed its analysis in *United States v. Valenzuela-Bernal*,[75] and *Strickland v. Washington*.[76]

In the first of these cases, *United States v. Valenzuela-Bernal*,[77] the Court held that due process is violated when testimony is made unavailable to the defense by government deportation of witnesses "only if there is a reasonable likelihood that the testimony could have affected the judgment of the trier of fact."[78] Similarly, in *Strickland v. Washington*,[79] the Court found that a new trial would be warranted because of the incompetence of counsel foreclosing the introduction of evidence

68 *Id.* at 112.
69 *Id.*
70 *Id.* at 118, *citing to* 66 Fed. Reg. at 45, 629 (Aug. 29, 2001).
71 *Id.*
72 In the seminal case *Brady v. Maryland*, 373 U.S. 83, 87, 83 S. Ct. 1194, 10 L. Ed.2d 215 (1963), the U.S. Supreme Court held that prosecutors are required to disclose evidence that is both (i) favorable to the accused and (ii) "material either to guilt or punishment."
73 *United States v. Bagley*, 473 U.S. 667, 105 S. Ct. 3375, 87 L. Ed. 481 (1985).
74 *Id.* at 678.
75 *United States v. Valenzuela-Bernal*, 458 U.S. 858, 102 S. Ct. 3440, 73 L. Ed.2d 1193 (1982).
76 *Strickland v. Washington*, 466 U.S. 668, 104 S. Ct. 2052, 80 L. Ed.2d 674 (1984).
77 *U.S. v. Valenzuela-Bernal*, 458 U.S. 858, 102 S. Ct. 3440, 73 L. Ed.2d 1193 (1982).
78 *U.S. v. Valenzuela-Bernal*, 458 U.S. at 874.
79 *Strickland v. Washington*, 466 U.S. 668, 104 S. Ct. 2052, 80 L. Ed.2d 674 (1984).

only if "there is a reasonable probability that, but for counsel's unprofessional errors, the result of the proceeding would have been different."[80] In both cases the likely *consequential effects* of the suppression of evidence was identified as a paramount metric.

In this connection, the Court noted that "[t]he *Strickland* Court defined a 'reasonable probability' as 'a probability sufficient to undermine confidence in the outcome.'"[81] And concluded that the *Strickland* formulation of the *Agurs*:[82]

> test for materiality sufficiently flexible to cover the "no request," "general request," and "specific request" cases of prosecutorial failure to disclose evidence favorable to the accused: the evidence is material only if there is a reason probability that, had the evidence been disclosed to the defense, the result of the proceeding would have been different. A "reasonable probability" is a probability sufficient to undermine confidence in the outcome.[83]

The Supreme Court in *Bagley* teaches that *materiality* is conceptually defined by a *consequential effects* test premised on "reasonable probability" and not a "likely probability." This test for or definition of *material evidence* or *materiality* is operationally flexible. It is so particularly when supplemented by the predicate that the reasonable probability concerns an element in the case that may be determinative as to liability or damages. Moreover, it hardly can be characterized as limiting, constraining, or otherwise placing shackles on an arbitral tribunal that would lead to procedural inefficiency.

Fourth and finally, in the context of Federal Rule of Criminal Procedure 16,[84] the Second Circuit Court of Appeals articulated a standard to determine the materiality of suppressed evidence:

80 *Strickland v. Washington*, 466 U.S. at 694.

81 *U.S. v. Bagley*, 473 U.S. 667, 105 S. Ct. 3375, 87 L. Ed. 481 (1985) (quoting *Strickland v. Washington*, 466 U.S. 688, 694).

82 *United States v. Agurs*, 427 U.S. 97, 104, 96 S. Ct. 2392, 49 L. Ed. 2d 342 (1976) (holding that "[a] fair analysis of the holding in *Brady* indicates that implicit in the requirement of materiality is a concern that the suppressed evidence might have affected the outcome of the trial").

83 *U.S. v. Bagley*, 473 U.S. 667, 105 S. Ct. 3375, 87 L. Ed. 481 (1985).

84 Specifically, Fed. R. Civ. Crim. P. 16(a)(1)(C) reads:

Rule 16. Discovery and Inspection

(a) **Government's Disclosure.**

(1) *Information Subject to Disclosure.*

(C) Organizational Defendant. Upon a defendant's request, if the defendant is an organization, the government must disclose to the defendant any statement described in Rule 16(a (1)(A) and (B) if the government contends that the person making the statement:

(i) was legally able to bind the defendant regarding the subject of the statement because of that person's position as the defendant's director, officer, employee, or agent; or

(ii) was personally involved in the alleged conduct constituting the offense and was legally able to bind the defendant regarding that conduct because of that person's position as the defendant's director, officer, employee, or agent.

> An appellate court, in assessing the materiality of withheld information, considers [i] not only the *logical relationship between the information and the issues in the case*, but also [ii] the importance of the information in light of the evidence as a whole. To warrant a new trial, "[t]here must be some indication that the pretrial disclosure of the disputed evidence would have enabled the defendant significantly to alter the quantum of proof in his favor." [Citations omitted]

The Court further restated the second prong by observing that "the government's withholding of evidence that should have been disclosed does not automatically entitle [appellant] to a new trial, *for a defendant must show that the failure to disclose caused him substantial prejudice*."[85] (Emphasis added.)

The quality of the evidence for purposes of determining materiality was scrutinized as to (i) its nature, (ii) the extent to which it was related to important issues in the case, (iii) the asserted grounds for non-production, and (iv) the strength of the Government's legitimate and untainted proof.[86]

Applying the two-prong standard in the context of the qualitative analysis of the evidence withheld, the Second Circuit concluded "that the non-disclosure [at issue] was not so prejudicial to entitle [appellant] to a new trial, for the record as a whole substantially belied his claim of duress."[87]

Contrary to what may generally be the visceral reaction to evidentiary rules as somehow stratifying, the US common law approach to materiality, including its reincarnation in F.R.E. 401(b) ("the fact is of consequence in determining the action"), reveals flexibility and wide latitude of approaches circumscribing two very specific precepts:[88] (i) the need for the evidence at issue to be related to an element

[85] *Id.* at 1181, *citing to United States v. McElroy*, 697 F. 2d 459, 465 (2nd Cir. 1982).

[86] *Id.* at 1181.

[87] *Id.*

[88] Professor Graham explains the term "material" in Section 401:1, Michael H. Graham, *Handbook of Federal Evidence*, 9th ed. (Thomson Reuters 2020–2023):

> The term "material," now "fact is of consequence," and "relevant" to a considerable extent were prior to the Federal Rules of Evidence used interchangeably. Evidence which was objected to as immaterial was likely also to be objected to as irrelevant and vice versa. Considerable clarification of analysis is gained by distinguishing between the propriety of the proposition to be established and the propriety of the proof to establish it "fact is of consequence" describes a proposition which is in the case, and "relevant" describes evidence which has a tendency to prove or disprove the proposition. Whether a fact is of consequence is determined by the substantive law within the framework of the pleadings. Under Rule 401 [F.R.E.], the objection "irrelevant" raises both concepts, i.e., the evidence does not tend to make more or less probable the fact it is offered to establish or the fact for which offered to establish is not itself of consequence in the litigation.
>
> The term "fact is of consequence in determining the action" includes three general categories of fact. First, it includes which comprise direct evidence of an element of a claim or defense. Elements of a claim or defense were referred at common law to as "material propositions." Second, "fact is of consequence" includes those facts from whose establishment may be inferred as facts amounting to elements of claims or defenses.

in the case and (ii) the extent to which that evidence is consequential, or "is of consequence in determining the action."[89] The current conceptual understanding and application of "material evidence" within the IBA Rules, or more broadly in the general context of ICA, is unrooted. Much can be learned and borrowed from domestic legal cultures that develop doctrine and jurisprudence regarding fundamental evidentiary principles of materiality and relevance.

Much like Shakespearian beauty, in ICA, both *relevance* and *materiality* are "in the eye of the beholder."[90] An alternative dispute resolution methodology promising efficiency deserves more than a subjective *ad hoc* approach to precepts so central to epistemic evidentiary analysis as *relevance* and *materiality*. Objective certainty is necessary.

4.5 EVIDENCE DISCLOSURE PARALLELS BETWEEN THE U.S. FRE AND ARTICLES 2 AND 3 OF THE IBA RULES

Articles 2 and 3 of the IBA Rules provide a viable framework for early *risk assessment* and settlement. Unseemly and heretical as it may appear, the underlying tenets of these two Articles bear remarkable similarities to the U.S. Fed. R. Civ. P. 26 governing self-disclosure.

There exist no drafts, or notes suggesting that the U.S. FRCP by design *at all* influenced the IBA Rules. Therefore, whether unwittingly or by design, Art. 2 shares features in common with Fed. R. Civ. P. 26 titled "Duty to Disclose; General Provisions Governing Discovery."[91] The Rule 26(f) framework combines both preliminary consultation at the commencement of an action and self-disclosure, which

[89] F.R.E. 401(b).

[90] William Shakespeare, *Love's Labour's Lost*, Act II, Scene I, "Beauty is bought by judgment of the eye, …"

[91] Fed. R. Civ. P. 26 in pertinent part reads:

> (f) Conference of the Parties; Planning for Discovery.
>
> (1) Conference Timing. Except in a proceeding exempted from initial disclosure under Rule 26(a)(1)(B) or when the court orders otherwise, the *parties must confer as soon as practicable* – and in any event at least 21 days *before a scheduling conference* is to be held or a scheduling order is due under Rule 16(b).
>
> (2) Conference Content; Parties' Responsibilities. In conferring, the parties must consider the nature and basis of their claims and defenses and the possibilities for promptly settling or resolving the case; *make or arrange for the disclosures required by Rule 26(a)(1); discuss any issues about preserving discoverable information; and develop a proposed discovery plan. The attorneys of record and all unrepresented parties that have appeared in the case are jointly responsible for arranging the conference, for attempting* ***in good faith*** *to agree on the proposed discovery plan,* and for submitting to the court within 14 days after the conference a written report outlining the plan. The court may order the parties or attorneys to attend the conference in person. (Emphasis added)

are conceptually and practically very close to the Art. 2 consultation requirement,[92] and the Art. 3, paragraph 1 self-disclosure mandate.[93]

The commentaries to Rule 26 reference five specific principles that are shared with the *consultation* and *self-disclosure* tenets of the IBA Rules. All five of these precepts comport with principles of *party-autonomy* and procedural transparency that in turn render *risk assessment* possible early in the proceeding. Moreover, these principles also are fundamental to international arbitration.[94]

First, and quite significantly, the committee notes to Rule 26(f) state that: "only a 'conference' of the parties, rather than a 'meeting,'" is required.[95] Although the committee notes observe that "[t]hough face-to-face are preferred, Rule 26(f) does not require them."

The parties may confer through other means, such as by video conference, particularly in the post-Covid era. However, the court may order the parties to meet in person.[96] It is clear that geographic configurations, in some instances, may exact costs that do not justify an in-person meeting. The use of the word "consultation" in Art. 2 of the Rules,[97] similarly suggests communication between the parties in

[92] *See* IBA 2020 Rules, at Art. 2 subsection 2.1.

[93] *See id.* at Art. 3 subsection 3.1 (compelling self-disclosure). Article 3 states:

> Documents
>
> 1. Within the time ordered by the Arbitral Tribunal, each Party shall submit to the Arbitral Tribunal and to the other Parties *all Documents available to it on which it relies*, including public Documents and those in the public domain, except for any Documents that have already been submitted by another Party. (Emphasis added)

The emphasis of this provision is to avoid surprises and provide all parties with evidentiary notice of the intended proof. Thus, even documents forming part of the public records are to be disclosed if in fact a party intends to rely on such documents. The emphasis is not on *access* to documents but rather on the *identification* of documents on which a party relies.

[94] *See* Fed. R. Civ. P. 26 advisory committee's note, under *Discovery Conference*, subsection *Purpose and Topics*:

> Rule 26(f) was overhauled in 1993 to make it an integral part of discovery planning. The discovery planning conference and ensuing report serve three purposes:
>
> (1) to force the parties to think about and discuss their discovery needs before discovery begins;
>
> (2) to try to anticipate potential discovery problems and resolve them before they occur and cause trouble; and
>
> (3) to place all of this information before the court *early in the case* so that judge can make informed choices about the discovery needs of the case and build them into the Rule 16 scheduling order. *The principal purpose of the Rule 26(f) conference is for the parties to discuss and develop a discovery plan.* In addition, Rule 16(f) prompts the parties to use the discovery ***planning conference to consider settlement*** and per the 2006 amendments to discuss issues relating to discoverable information. (Emphasis added)

The reference to "settlement" underscores the importance of discussing settlement in the context of evidentiary disclosure early in the proceeding.

[95] *Id.* at Fed. R. Civ. P. 26 advisory committee's note.

[96] *Id.*

[97] IBA 2020 Rules, IBA Rules 2020 referenced as comparison, Art. 2 subsection 2.1.

flexible formats that comports with the transnational constitution of most international arbitrations.

Second, Rule 26(f) contemplates that the consultation shall facilitate the management of privileged information that would not be discoverable or susceptible to self-disclosure, and information covered by the work-product doctrine.

Similarly, pursuant to the Art. 2 construct, the parties to the arbitration are to discuss "the level of confidentiality protection to be afforded to evidence in the arbitration."[98] Even though there is a substantive distinction between "confidentiality" and "privilege," the underlying common denominator is the principle of nondisclosure under Rule 26 as to the proceeding and under Art. 2 of the IBA Rules with respect to non-parties. In both sets of rules *party-autonomy* is used as the fulcrum for the management of the two types of nondisclosures.[99]

The principal operational difference between Art. 2 subsection 2.2 of the Rules, and Fed. R. Civ. P. 26(f), is that the Art. 2 framework *only* contemplates *procedural efficiency*. *Optimal efficiency*, that is to say, settlement, finds no resonance in the Art. 2 consultation on evidentiary issues rubric.[100]

[98] *Id.* at Art. 2 subsection 2.2(d) reads:

> 2. The consultation on evidentiary issues may address the scope, timing and manner of the taking of evidence, including, to the extent applicable:
> (d) the level of confidentiality protection to be afforded to evidence in the arbitration[.]

[99] The committee notes attendant to the 2015 amendments emphasize that:

> A good Rule 26(f) conference should include a frank discussion about *proportionality*. That does not mean the parties must agree about what type or amount of discovery would be proportional to the needs of the case, or even how to access the underlying factors. What is critical is that the parties begin ***thinking*** about proportionality in their early planning and ***communicate*** with each other to start to understand the respective views on the benefits of proposed discovery and anticipated burdens. The 2015 Committee Notes to the Rule 26(b) proportionality amendment specifically suggests that parties begin discussing proportionality ***and provide information about benefits and burdens*** at the Rule 26(f) planning conference. The same judges specifically instruct the parties to discuss proportionality at the Rule 26(f) conference and address proportionality in the Rule 26(f) report. (Emphasis added) (Bold italics in original)

Although obviously post-dating the 2010 IBA amendments, but predating the current 2020 IBA iteration of the Rules, the "new" proportionality qualification on discovery pervading Fed. R. Civ. P. 26 reflects the incorporation into domestic law the international proportionality doctrine concerns. The exhortation to the parties to engage in proportionality analyses at the Fed. R. Civ. P. 26(f) early stage of the proceeding is tantamount to asking the parties to participate in substantive *risk assessment*. A comparable theoretical and operational rule in international arbitration would be conducive to significant ***risk assessment*** and, therefore, to meaningful settlement discussions.

[100] Article 2 subsection 2.2 only contemplates *process efficiency*. And it does so without reference to objective metrics that at all may contribute to transparency, *risk assessment*, or settlement. Article 2 subsection 2.2. reads:

> 2. The consultation on evidentiary issues may address the scope, timing and manner of the taking of evidence, including, to the extent applicable:
> (a) the preparation and submission of Witness Statements and Expert Reports;
> (b) the taking of oral testimony at any Evidentiary Hearing;
> (c) the requirements, procedure and format applicable to the production of Documents;

Although unstated the IBA Art. 3 subsection 3.1 disclosure requirement theoretically should be informed by the Art. 2 consultation on evidentiary issues process. Article 2 subsection 1 consultation "shall" take place "at the earliest appropriate time in the proceedings."[101] Presumably the Art. 3 subsection 3.1 *self-disclosure requirement* is to take place *immediately* after the Art. 2 evidentiary consultation conference.

The Art. 3 subsection 3.1 temporal qualification "[w]ithin the time ordered by the Arbitral Tribunal," is somewhat at odds with the Art. 2 subsection 2.1 stricture providing that the evidentiary consultation is to take place (i) "at the earliest appropriate time in the proceedings," (ii) principally driven by *party-autonomy*.[102] Article 3 generally, and subsections 3.1 and 3.2 in particular, however, shift timing and initiative to the arbitral tribunal.

The want of temporal immediacy in Art. 3, along with exclusion of *party-autonomy* focused undertakings, speak to an underlying policy of *process efficiency* exclusively concerned with structuring the anatomy of a proceeding having as a singular objective issuance of a binding and enforceable award. *Optimal efficiency* would have explicitly emphasized the real need of engaging in *risk assessment* through the symmetrical parity of document exchange in the form of self-disclosures as early as possible in the proceeding. Such qualifying language need not detract from a desire to have the evidence disclosure and evidence taking process controlled by the principle of *arbitrator discretion*, if such is the intent.[103]

Creating a conceptual temporal link between Arts. 1 and 2 of the Rules is a necessary but not sufficient condition to maximizing *risk assessment* and *optimal efficiency*. The self-disclosure component of Art. 3 is minimized, and

(d) the level of confidentiality protection to be afforded to evidence in the arbitration;
(e) the treatment of any issues of cybersecurity and data protection; and
(f) the promotion of efficiency, economy and conservation of resources in connection with the taking of evidence.

For the sake of completeness, it is worth underscoring that the tribunal is encouraged but no obligated "to identify to the Parties, as soon as it considers it to be appropriate, any issues: (a) that the Arbitral Tribunal may regard relevant to the case and material to its outcome; and/or (b) for which a preliminary determination may be appropriate." (IBA Rule 3 subsection 3.3.)

101 *See* n. 109, that follows.

102 The Art. 2 subsection 2.1 consultation requirement is premised on the arbitral tribunal inviting the parties "to consult each other with a view to agreeing on an efficient, economical and fair process for the taking of evidence." The process thus is based on *party-autonomy*.

103 Language modifying Art. 3 subsection 3.1 to read:

> Immediately following the Art. 2 Consultation on Evidentiary Issues, the Arbitral Tribunal shall order each Party to submit to the Arbitral Tribunal and to the other Parties all Documents available to it on which it *may* rely, no later than 14 days after the Parties' Art. 2 (Consultation on Evidentiary Issues) conference all Documents available to it on which it *may* rely including public documents and those in the public domain, except for any documents that have already been submitted by another Party. (Emphasis added)

This amendment would, to some extent, explicitly harmonize Arts. 2 & 3, at least from a temporal perspective that would enhance the likelihood of *optimal efficiency*, i.e., settlement.

subordinated to evidence taking, which in turn is limited to (i) evidence in the form of documents,[104] and (ii) liability related issues. Indeed, the word "damages" appears only once in the totality of the fourteen paragraphs and eight subsections comprising Art. 3.[105]

Article 3 subsection 3.11 reflects concern with more comprehensive disclosure pertaining to factual issues contained in witness statements, expert reports, and documents produced:

> ***Within the time ordered by the Arbitral Tribunal****, the Parties* ***may submit*** *to the Arbitral Tribunal and to the other Parties any additional Documents on which they intend to rely or which they believe have become relevant to the case and material to its outcome as a consequence of the issues raised in Documents, Witness Statements or Expert Reports submitted or produced, or in other submissions of the Parties.* (Emphasis added)

The first subordinate clause of Art. 3 subsection 3.11 mirrors that of its self-disclosure counterpart within Art. 3 subsection 3.1 ("[w]ithin the time ordered by the Arbitral Tribunal"). It therefore replicates the same deficit of not creating an immediate disclosure deadline in connection with the Art. 2 consultation session. This provision (Art. 3 subsection 3.11), however, inexplicably positions the disclosure "requirement" in the permissive "may submit."

The permissive language in Art. 3 subsection 3.11 stands in sharp relief with the mandatory "shall" in the Art. 3 subsection 3.11 self-disclosure obligation. There is no policy or conceptual justification that would explain different standards or equally relevant and material factual information the nondisclosure of which likely would give rise to due process issues. The preferred practice would be for parties to disclose *evidence* that is *relevant to the case and material to its outcome* (i) as a continuous obligation, and (ii) on a mandatory basis. This practice would enhance both *process efficiency* and *optimal efficiency*.

[104] Fact witnesses are addressed in Art. 4.

[105] It cannot be sufficiently underscored that the term "damages" only appears on three occasions within the Rules' framework. In all three instances, however, it is not used in the context of *risk assessment* disclosure. By way of example, the reference to the Rule in Art. 3 subsection 3.14 states:

> 14. If the arbitration is organised into separate issues or phases (such as jurisdiction, preliminary determinations, liability or damages), the Arbitral Tribunal may, after consultation with the Parties, schedule the submission of Documents and Requests to Produce separately for each issue or phase.

The use of "damages" in this context clearly refers to *process efficiency* in the context of maximizing efficiencies pursuant to the possibility of separate hearings on specific issues for arbitral phases, i.e., the actual proceeding itself and not *optimal efficiency* (settlement).

Art. 4 subsection 4.4 similarly references "damages" in the context of possible bifurcation or trifurcation, and language identical to that of Art. 3 subsection 3.14 except that the term "[i]f the arbitration" is substituted for "[i]f Evidentiary Hearings." Finally, the language used in Art. 8 subsection 8.4(e) is identical in every regard to the text of Art. 3 subsection 3.14.

The Art. 3 subsection 3.11 self-disclosure provision retains the "intend to rely" language. This standard is too narrow and subjective.[106] The disjunctive qualifying term, "or which they believe have become relevant to the case and material to its outcome as a consequence of issues raised in Documents, Witness Statements or Expert Reports submitted or produced, or in other submissions of the Parties," merely exacerbates the uncertainty. Premising *continuous* and *comprehensive disclosure* on the parties' "belief" renders Art. 3 subsection 3.11 purely aspirational in nature.

The permissive "may submit" together with a standard based on the parties' "belief" to have become relevant remove Art. 3 subsection 3.11 from the likelihood that non-production would be found to violate the "*good faith*" imperative that the Rules impose.[107] The very critical inclusion of a good *faith* standard in the Rules is to bolster due process by vesting arbitrators with the right to sanction parties that have not conducted the taking of evidence in "good faith." The prospective exercise of this now explicitly stated arbitral authority is altogether eviscerated if continuous submissions arising from procedural evidentiary developments are *permissive*, and furthermore, based upon subjective standards, such as "intent to rely" or "believe have become relevant."[108]

Article 3 subsection 3.11 cannot be said to provide a vibrant and robust self-disclosure continuing obligation (*process efficiency*), let alone one that renders *risk assessment* viable at critical procedural junctures (*optimal efficiency*). The inevitable development of self-disclosure obligations necessary to meet even qualified *attenuated arbitral due process* requires more.

4.6 A CLOSER LOOK AT SELF-DISCLOSURE CROSS-POLLINATION: RATIOS AND PROPORTIONS

The IBA Rules Art. 2 consultation requirement is conceptually linked to the IBA Rules Art. 3 disclosure obligations in the same way that the Fed. R. Civ. P. 26(f) consultation imperative is related to the Fed. R. Civ. P. 26(a)(1)(A) disclosure mandate. Ratios and proportions are best suited for the conceptualization of the these

[106] *See* IBA Rules 240.

[107] The 2010 iteration of the IBA Rules included a major and transformative amendment in the form of a "good faith" standard that must be adhered to by the parties in the conduct of the taking of evidence. The 2020 version of the Rules sagely kept this amendment. In this same vein, Art. 9 subsection 9.8 reads:

> 8. If the Arbitral Tribunal determines that a Party has failed to conduct *itself in good faith in the taking of evidence*, the Arbitral Tribunal may, in addition to any other measures available under these Rules, take such failure into account in its assignment of the costs of the arbitration, including costs arising out of or in connection with the taking of evidence. (Emphasis added)

[108] Article 3 subsection 3.11.

relations. Accordingly, it is formally and substantively sound to express the relationship of these ratios in the following proportion:

IBA Rules Art. 2 : IBA Rules Art. 3 :: Fed. R. Civ. P. 26(f) : Fed. R. Civ. P. 26(a)(1)(A) (Consultation) (Self-Disclosure) (Consultation) (Self-Disclosure)

The statement of these relationships as a proportion facilitate an understanding of the extent to which the IBA ratio (Art. 2 : Art. 3) may benefit from the FRCP ratio (26(f): 26(a)(1)(A)) in the context of *risk assessment* and *optimal efficiency* (settlement). Eight propositions are particularly noteworthy.

First, Fed. R. Civ. P. 26(f) (Conference of the Parties; Planning for Discovery) conceptually and temporally is connected to Fed. R. Civ. P. 26(a)(1)(A) (Duty to Disclose; General Provisions Governing Discovery). The time governing initial self-disclosure pursuant to Fed. R. Civ. P. 26(a)(1)(A) must take place "at or within 14 days after the parties' Rule 26(f) conference," unless otherwise modified.[109]

Articulating reasonable but aggressive deadlines for self-disclosure *immediately* following the obligatory conference maximizes the likelihood for *risk assessment* early in time, and provides for transparency while maximizing party autonomy. This set time for disclosure contributes to objective uniformity that minimizes *arbitrator discretion*.

The relationship between the IBA Art. 2 subsection 2.1 consultation requirement and the IBA Art. 3 subsection 3.1 self-disclosure mandate would benefit from a temporal disclosure imperative mirroring the Fed. R. Civ. P. 26(a)(1)(C)(D) deadlines for initial discovery.

Second, the standard for initial self-disclosure pursuant to Fed. R. Civ. P. 26(a)(1)(A)(i)–(ii) is governed by what a "party may use to support its claims or defenses."[110] This standard is subjective but considerably broader than the IBA Art. 3

[109] Fed. R. Civ. P. 26(a)(1)(C) reads:

> (C) *Time for Initial Disclosures – In General.* A party must make the initial disclosures at or within 14 days after the parties' Rule 26(f) conference unless a different time is set by stipulation or court order, or unless a party objects during the conference that initial disclosures are not appropriate in this action and states the objection in the proposed discovery plan. In ruling on the objection, the court must determine what disclosures, if any, are to be made and must set the time for disclosure.

> It is important to note that Fed. R. Civ. P. 26(D) for initial disclosure regarding parties served or joined later provides that "[a] party that is first served or otherwise joined after the Rule 26(f) conference must make the initial disclosures within 30 days after being served or joined, unless a different time is set by stipulation or court order."

[110] Fed. R. Civ. P. 26(a)(1)(A)(i)–(ii) reads:

> (A) *In General.* Except as exempted by Rule 26(a)(1)(B) or as otherwise stipulated or ordered by the court, a party must, without awaiting a discovery request, provide to the other parties:
> (i) the name and, if known, the address and telephone number of *each individual likely to have discoverable information* – along with the subjects of that information – that the disclosing party *may use to support its claims or defenses*, unless the use would be solely for impeachment;

subsection 3.1 counterpart based upon the "on which it relies" standard.[111] Similarly, the "likely to have discoverable information" standard set forth in Fed. R. Civ. P. 26(a)(1)(A)(i) governing the disclosure of names, addresses, and telephone numbers of potential witnesses seeks to mitigate the strictly subjective exercise of judgment in identifying the realm of possible witnesses.

The "likely" and "may use" in contrast with "on which it relies," materially suggests broader disclosure and, therefore, greater transparency conducive to *risk assessment* early in the proceeding.[112]

Third, the self-disclosure requirement prescribed in Fed. R. Civ. P. 26(a)(1)(A) extends to witnesses. Significantly, the word "witness" does not appear in the subsection. Hence, the absence of the use of the word "witness" suggests the term "may use" is to be expansively construed.

In keeping with this interpretation of the subsection, persons consulted with respect to information pertaining to "claims or defenses" would be subject to disclosure. Indeed, the Committee Notes suggest as much stating that "'[u]se' includes any use at a pre-trial conference, to support a motion, or at trial. The disclosure obligation is also triggered by intended use in discovery, apart from use to respond to a

(ii) a copy – or a description by category and location – of all documents, electronically stored information, and tangible things that the disclosing party has in its possession, custody, or control and *may use to support its claims or defenses*, unless the use would be solely for impeachment[.] (Emphasis added)

[111] IBA 2020 Rules, Art. 3 subsection 3.1, *see* n. 99 in this chapter.

[112] Interestingly, the Committee Notes to the 2000 amendment to Fed. R. Civ. P. 26 providing for Rule 26(a)(1) initial disclosure reflect an effort (i) to provide uniformity to the discovery process, and (ii) to narrow the scope of self-disclosure obligations. The Committee Notes in pertinent part state:

Committee Notes on Rules – 2000 Amendment

Purposes of amendments. The Rule 26(a)(1) initial disclosure provisions are amended to establish a nationally *uniform practice*. *The scope of the disclosure obligation is* narrowed to cover only information that the disclosing party may use to support its position. In addition, the rule exempts specified categories of proceedings from initial disclosure, and permits a party who contends that disclosure is not appropriate in the circumstances of the case to present its objections to the court, which must then determine whether disclosure should be made. *Related changes* are made in Rules 26(d) and (f). (Emphasis added)

* * *

These amendments restore *national uniformity to disclosure practice*. Uniformity is also restored to other aspects of discovery by deleting most of the provisions authorizing local rules that vary the number of permitted discovery events or the length of depositions. Local rule options are also deleted from Rules 26(d) and (f).

* * *

The disclosure obligation applies to "claims and defenses," and therefore requires a party to disclose information it may use to support its denial or rebuttal of the allegations, claim, or defense of another party. It thereby bolsters the requirements of Rule 11(b)(4), which authorizes denials "warranted on the evidence," and disclosure should include the identity of any witness or document that the disclosing party may use to support such denials. (Emphasis added)

discovery request; use of a document to question a witness during a deposition is a common example."[113] Similarly, the use of an individual, not necessarily a "witness," to disclose a document secured during self-disclosure or discovery also would trigger disclosure under the Rule.

The IBA Rules provide for the self-disclosure of witnesses in Art. 4 (**Witnesses of Fact**).[114] As stated, it does so pursuant to an "intends to rely" standard.[115] As with its Art. 3 subsection 3.1 counterpart, however, Art. 4 subsection 4.1. lacks any textual temporal disclosure imperative connecting self-disclosure to the Art. 2 consultation requirement that is to take place "at the earliest appropriate time in the proceedings."[116] Article 4 subsection 4.1 similarly provides for the self-disclosure of "witnesses" to take place "[w]ithin the time ordered by the Arbitral Tribunal."[117]

In the context of Art. 4 linking the witness disclosure requirement to Art. 2 becomes more of a conceptual stretch because in practice the arbitral tribunal may not be inclined to order parties to disclose witnesses on whose testimony the parties "intend to rely" on until such time as witness statements are to be submitted. Typically parties are not asked to exchange witness statements *before* the conclusion of the evidence gathering phase. In any event, however, it would be unorthodox to expect witness statements to be prepared and exchanged anytime close to the Art. 2 consultation between the parties.[118]

Notwithstanding the pragmatic customary practice of causing self-disclosure of witnesses in an arbitral proceeding within the context of the preparation of witness statements, the Art. 4 subsection 4.1 self-disclosure of witnesses requirement is formulated in the mandatory "shall," and for this reason there is more than just a slim reed on which to construe Art. 4 subsection 4.1 as temporally governed by the Art. 2 subsection 2.1 "at the earliest appropriate time" imperative.

As with its document self-disclosure counterpart (Art. 3 subsection 3.1), Art. 4 subsection 4.1 is but a single-sentence provision in a ten-paragraph Article with seven

[113] *See* Chapter 3, n. 1 in this volume.
[114] IBA Rule Art. 4 (**Witnesses of Fact**) subsections 1–10.
[115] IBA Rule Art. 4 subsection 4.1.
[116] IBA Rule Art. 2 subsection 2.1.
[117] IBA Rule Art. 4 subsection 4.1.
[118] The submission and exchange of witness statements is not set forth pursuant to any objective timeframe. Instead, it is relegated to the arbitral tribunal's discretion and couched in the permissive "may." The provisions relevant to witness statements in Art. 4 in pertinent part read:

> 4. The Arbitral Tribunal may order each Party to submit within a specified time to the Arbitral Tribunal and to the other Parties Witness Statements by each witness *on whose testimony it intends to rely*, except for those witnesses whose testimony is sought pursuant to Articles 4.9 or 4.10. If Evidentiary Hearings are organised into separate issues or phases (such as jurisdiction, preliminary determinations, liability or damages), the Arbitral Tribunal or the Parties by agreement may schedule the submission of Witness Statements separately for each issue or phase.

subsections.[119] The Art. 4 subsection 4.1 witness disclosure requirement is bereft of any particulars pertaining to the witnesses disclosed beyond "identity" and "subject matter of [the prospective] testimony."

Nowhere does the Article provide foundational predicates for timely identification, quantification, and communication of risk. For this reason its purpose and design cannot contribute to *optimal efficiency* in the form of settlement.[120]

Fourth, the Fed. R. Civ. P. 26(a)(1)(A) disclosure requirement addresses the foundational issue of damages. Moreover, it does so from evidentiary and mathematical perspectives that are conducive to risk assessment.

The parties are compelled to disclose (i) each category of damages, (ii) the damages must be computed, and (iii) the evidentiary bases for the computation(s) ("documents or other evidentiary materials, unless privileged or protected from disclosure").[121] The level of transparency is significant and conducive to *risk assessment*. These requirements make sense. They are not aberrant or idiosyncratic features of a distinct legal system. To the contrary, they are fundamental requirements that should form part of any damages claim made in good faith.

Damages disclosure is fundamental to maximizing the likelihood of obtaining *optimal efficiency*. It is conceptually impossible for parties to assess risk if they are procedurally foreclosed from the opportunity of submitting to strict and sustained scrutiny the opposing party's evidentiary damages predicates and the methodology giving rise to the damages averred.

Likewise, parties seeking to maximize the likelihood of *optimal efficiency* only can obtain a clear understanding of their own case when an opposing party is accorded the opportunity to dissect the propositions on which damages are

119 Article 4 subsection 4.1 in its totality provides that "[w]ithin the time ordered by the Arbitral Tribunal, each Party shall identify the witnesses whose testimony it intends to rely and the subject matter of that testimony."

Article 4 subsection 4.4 reads:

> The Arbitral Tribunal may order each Party to submit within a specified time to the Arbitral Tribunal and to the other Parties Witness Statements by each witness on whose testimony it intends to rely, except for those witnesses whose testimony is sought pursuant to Articles 4.9 or 4.10. If Evidentiary Hearings are organised into separate issues or phases (such as jurisdiction, preliminary determinations, liability or damages), the Arbitral Tribunal or the Parties by agreement may schedule the submission of Witness Statements separately for each issue or phase.

120 *See, e.g.*, Art. 3 subsection 3.3(a)–(c) detailing the substantive requirements of a "Request to Produce," production obligations (Art. 3 subsection 3.4), and the management of objections concerning document production during the course of the proceeding (Art. 3 subsection 3.5–3.8).

121 Fed. R. Civ. P. 26(a)(1)(A)(iii) states:

> A computation of each category of damages claimed by the disclosing party – who must also make available for inspection and copying as under Rule 34 the documents or other evidentiary material, unless privileged or protected from disclosure, on which each computation is based, including materials bearing on the nature and extent of injuries suffered[.]

premised. This symmetrical access to relevant categorical facts is a necessary condition to attaining *optimal efficiency* and needs to be a central feature of ICA institutional rules.

The IBA Rules do not provide for similar damages disclosure imperatives in the context of either *process efficiency* or *optimal efficiency* (see Section 4.1). Moreover, the evidentiary rubric regarding the presentation of evidence lacks a structure providing for a rule-based reliability testing approach to evidential assessment, which generally is the subject matter of expert report and testimony.

Fifth, the Fed. R. Civ. P. 26 self-disclosure rubric forecloses parties from attempting to circumvent the disclosure obligation pursuant to non-meritorious defenses. There is no such effort, let alone comparable language, in the IBA Rules, or in institutional rules.

The disclosure imperative is grounded on a *reasonableness* standard. The parties are obligated to disclose "information then reasonably available to [them]."[122] An opposing party's breach of a disclosure obligation, in whole or in part, does not discharge the nonbreaching party's obligation to disclose.[123] Also, the disclosing party's inability to have fully investigated the case similarly does not excuse it from its duty to disclose.

The articulation of "unacceptable excuses" underscores the commitment to disclosure *before* any discovery takes place. A similar framework in the context of ICA identifying unacceptable defenses commonly raised in the context of self-disclosure prior to the taking of evidence, that is to say, the formal filing of a Request to Produce documents pursuant to Art. 3 subsection 3.3(a)–(c), would emphasize the importance of pre-evidence taking information and document exchange. More importantly, identifying formal and recurring objections to self-disclosure in the context of ICA as well serves (i) to create a better defined pre-evidence taking procedural juncture, (ii) to educate arbitrators on how best to manage self-disclosure, and (iii) to vest self-disclosure with the procedural dignity and importance that it must have if it is to serve as part of the foundation for *optimal efficiency*.

The identification of viable or inviable objections at the self-disclosure stage already is somewhat in keeping with the architecture of the IBA Rules. By way of example, Art. 3 subsection 3.5–3.8 identify possible objections in the context of

[122] Fed. R. Civ. P. 26(a)(1)(E):

> (E) ***Basis for Initial Disclosure; Unacceptable Excuses***. A party must make its initial disclosures based on the information then reasonably available to it. A party is not excused from making its disclosures because it has not fully investigated the case or because it challenges the sufficiency of another party's disclosures or because another party has not made its disclosures.

[123] *Id.*

evidence taking,[124] and also instructs the arbitral tribunal on how best to manage the evidentiary-objection process.[125]

Engrafting on the self-disclosure requirements concerning documents (Art. 3 subsection 3.1), and fact witnesses (Art. 4 subsection 4.1) instructions as to viable and inviable objections would contribute to robust *risk assessment* within a formal and procedural format that comports with existing architecture in furtherance of *process efficiency*. Such amendments merely would constitute providing the self-disclosure stage with the identical architecture already present in Arts. 3, 4, 8, and 9.[126] The amendment hardly would be seismic.

Sixth, the Fed. R. Civ. P. self-disclosure strictures place considerable emphasis on the disclosure of expert testimony, even though this self-disclosure obligation does not technically or formally fall under "Initial Disclosures" that are to take place "without awaiting a discovery request."[127] The expert testimony self-disclosure requirement is contained in Fed. R. Civ. P. 26(a)(1)(A)(2).

Understandably, this evidence (expert testimony) cannot form part of initial discovery (or evidence taking), because of its very nature. Emphasis, however, is placed

[124] IBA Rule Art. 3 subsection 3.5 reads:

> If the Party to whom the Request to Produce is addressed has an objection to some or all of the Documents requested, it shall state the objection in writing to the Arbitral Tribunal and the other Parties within the time ordered by the Arbitral Tribunal. The reasons for such objection shall be any of those set forth in Articles 9.2 or 9.3, or a failure to satisfy any of the requirements of Article 3.3. If so directed by the Arbitral Tribunal, and within the time so ordered, the requesting party may respond to the objection.
>
> Article 9 subsections 9.2 and 9.3 in turn provide:
>
> 2. The Arbitral Tribunal shall, at the request of a Party or on its own motion, exclude from evidence or production any Document, statement, oral testimony or inspection, in whole or in part, for any of the following reasons:
>   (a) lack of sufficient relevance to the case or materiality to its outcome;
>   (b) legal impediment or privilege under the legal or ethical rules determined by the Arbitral Tribunal to be applicable [citation omitted];
>   (c) unreasonable burden to produce the requested evidence;
>   (d) loss or destruction of the Document that has been shown with reasonable likelihood to have occurred;
>   (e) grounds of commercial or technical confidentiality that the Arbitral Tribunal determines to be compelling;
>   (f) grounds of special political or institutional sensitivity (including evidence that has been classified as secret by a government or a public international institution) that the Arbitral Tribunal determines to be compelling; or
>   (g) considerations of procedural economy, proportionality, fairness or equality of the Parties that the Arbitral Tribunal determines to be compelling.
> 3. The Arbitral Tribunal may, at the request of a Party or on its own motion, exclude evidence obtained illegally.

[125] *See, e.g.*, IBA Rule Art. 3 subsection 3.6–3.7.

[126] *See* Section 4.4. *See also* Art. 8 subsections 8.3 and 8.6.

[127] *See* Fed. R. Civ. P. 26(a)(1)(A).

on its timeliness, which must be "*at least* ninety days before the date set for trial or for the case to be ready for trial."[128]

The timing of expert witness disclosure remains flexible. In the context of complex litigation, by way of example, it is foreseeable that the specific configuration and needs of a case may prompt the court to modify expert witness self-disclosure deadlines.[129]

Moreover, with some regularity, it is likely that a Fed. R. Civ. P. 16 Scheduling Order may interfere with the expert witness self-disclosure requirement. In this regard, a court is granted unbridled discretion and may cause self-disclosure requirements to be altered, without limitation, for reasons such as "improving the quality of the trial through more thorough preparation."[130]

The expert witness self-disclosure requirement that the Fed. R Civ. P. 26(2)(A)–(E) contemplates, in addition to vesting the court with authority to modify the disclosure timetable to meet the needs of a specific case, also is intended to promote settlement because Fed. R. Civ. P. 26(a)(2) cannot be construed as independent of the settlement precepts contained in Fed. R. Civ. P 16(a)(1)–(5)[131] and Fed. R. Civ. P. 16(c)(1).[132] Comparable revisions to the IBA and institutional rules would meaningfully contribute to *optimal efficiency*.

[128] Fed. R. Civ. P. 26(a)(2)(D)(i). Impeachment or rebuttal evidence "on the same subject matter identified by another party under Rule 26(a)(2)(D) or (C), [must be disclosed] within thirty days after the other party's disclosure." *See* Fed. R. Civ. P. 26(a)(2)(D)(ii).

[129] 6 *Moore's Federal Practice*-Civil Section 26.23, *citing to* Manual for Complex Litigation Section 11.481 (4th Ed. 2004).

[130] Fed. R. Civ. P. 16(a)(4).

Fed. R. Civ. P. 16(a) (Pre-Trial Conferences; Scheduling; Management) in pertinent part reads:

> (a) **Purposes of a Pretrial Conference**. In any action, the court may order the attorneys and any unrepresented parties to appear for one or more pretrial conferences for such purposes as:
> (1) expediting disposition of the action;
> (2) establishing early and continuing control so that the case will not be protracted because of lack of management;
> (3) discouraging wasteful pretrial activities;
> (4) improving the quality of the trial through more thorough preparation; and
> (5) *facilitating settlement*. (Emphasis added)

[131] *See id.* underscoring "*facilitating settlement*."

[132] Fed. R. Civ. P. 16(c)(1) reads:

> (c) Attendance and Matters for Consideration at a Pretrial Conference.
> (1) ***Attendance***. A represented party must authorize at least one of its attorneys to make stipulations and admissions about all matters that can reasonably be anticipated for discussion at a pretrial conference. If appropriate, the court may require that a party or its representative be present or reasonably available by other means to consider possible settlement. (Emphasis added)

5

Revisiting Rules and Principles of Evidence in ICA

5.1 THE NORMATIVE FRAMEWORK OF RULES ADDRESSING THE TAKING AND PRESENTATION OF EVIDENCE

Often the merits of an arbitral dispute turns on the facts established and not necessarily the legal analysis. Put simply, the facts matter. Indeed, they are dispositive. If this proposition is true, why is there so vast a doctrinal void in the taking and presentation of evidence in ICA? Would not so pivotal a feature of disputes adjudication command, at minimum, a corresponding level of doctrinal development? This hiatus between the consequential importance of evidence to a merits determination and the underdevelopment of the ICA evidential framework helps explain why ICA proceedings typically do not settle.

And even if such doctrinal strictures somehow have not been generated, why not import into ICA *some* of the evidentiary precepts applied by national courts in most jurisdictions? Rules of evidence promote transparency and predictive value. If in fact they do not form part of ICA, why is such the case? In this regard, is ICA too Eurocentric? Are there evidential principles universally accepted and forming part of ICA that guide arbitrations in according *weight* to evidence? Is the *status quo ante* in this regard acceptable?

Even a superficial analysis of domestic laws of evidence suggests a rich Petri dish of choices from which ICA stakeholders may borrow precepts that lead to transparency and efficiency without creating cumbersome frameworks. Four of these sources are particularly salient.

First, the law of evidence *incident to the substantive law* that parties choose to apply to the arbitral proceeding seems to be logical source from which to borrow evidentiary principles. It certainly is consonant with *party-autonomy*. The application of these precepts would comport with the underlying liability and damages policy of the substantive law that most stakeholders freely elected, presumably at arm's-length.

A second and most notable option would be to apply the *evidence law of the seat of the arbitration*. Here again, the suggestion is not without a rational relationship to the regulatory workings of the arbitral proceeding in question. The *lex arbitri* of the seat of the arbitration, at least theoretically, represents a source for applicable procedural law.

It also would follow that application of such evidentiary rubric would harmonize with *party-autonomy*. In a properly drafted arbitration clause the parties would have agreed on the arbitral seat. There is more than just aesthetic symmetry in having the rules of evidence of the geopolitical subdivision representing the single jurisdiction where any challenge to set aside, annul, or vacate an award can take place.

Third, the evidentiary framework of the *place where enforcement likely would be sought* also stands out as a potentially viable candidate. Typically, such jurisdictions are quite familiar to the parties and particularly to a respondent/prospective defendant against whom an adverse award may issue. Of course, this model becomes more complex in the context of counterclaims. And admittedly it is less likely to yield consent.

Fourth and lastly, *the arbitral venue, the physical place where the arbitration hearing is to take place*, in instances where arbitral seat and venue do not coincide may serve as a point of connectivity. It is commonplace for the parties to agree to hold physical hearings and the final hearing at a venue other than the seat of the arbitration. Such venue presumably would be more likely to secure the parties' consent regarding governing evidentiary principles. Procedural neutrality, in this sense, matters.[1]

These considerations are driven by efficiencies in logistics that accommodate tribunal members, the parties, and third-party witnesses (fact and expert). Although at first glance it may not appear that applying legal evidentiary principles from such a jurisdiction would be theoretically as comprehensive as the first three alternatives, the possibility is still a reasonable one that may serve principles of expediency and transparency (predictive value), and as referenced, neutrality.

Why, then, are principles of evidence completely wanting from ICA doctrine? What reason or reasons cause the culture of arbitration to sacrifice process

[1] *See, e.g.*, Born, "Procedures in International Arbitration," chapter 15, 1, identifying the centrality of procedural neutrality:

> §15.01 [A] Objectives of International Arbitral Procedures
>
> The international arbitral process seeks to achieve a number of related objectives. The most significant of these are procedural neutrality, fairness, efficiency, expertise, and flexibility permitting the tailoring of procedures to specific disputes and parties.
>
> One of the fundamental objectives of most international commercial arbitrations is procedural neutrality. [Citation omitted.] International disputes almost inevitably involve parties from different jurisdictions (e.g., a Kuwaiti company, with procedural experience and expectations rooted in Islamic law and culture, contracting with a French company, whose procedural experience and expectations will be based upon contemporary European civil law procedures.) One of the fundamental objectives of international arbitration is to ensure that, unless the parties agree otherwise, disputes will not be resolved in accordance with the procedures of one party's – and not the other party's – home jurisdiction, [citation omitted] which may favor, explicitly or implicitly, one party over the other.

transparency, predictive value, and party autonomy by causing the principle of *arbitrator discretion* to serve as the single fulcrum on which evidentiary rulings, without more, are to be premised? Guardrails for the qualitative analysis of evidence (weight to be ascribed) are necessary.

5.2 THERE ARE NO INTERNATIONAL LAW RULES OF EVIDENCE: TESTING UNTESTED ASSUMPTIONS

International conflicts are not free from factual disputes. And factual contentions are merits determinative. Yet, it is not an exaggeration to state that there is no single set of rules that properly and descriptively can be identified as "international law rules of evidence."

There are no learned writings that address this issue beyond just regurgitating the "*what*" and not the "*why*." The phenomenon is described but its cause is not articulated, let alone explained.[2]

[2] Charles N. Brower, "Evidence Before International Tribunals: The Need for Some Standard Rules," 28 *Int.'l L.* 47 (1984) (Judge Brower observes that "[i]nternational tribunals inherently are poorly equipped for the fact-finding task." He adds that for "a variety of reasons, not the least of which is lack of standard rules of evidence to govern submission and the evaluation of evidence in international proceedings, international tribunals frequently find it extremely difficult to establish facts." In the context of international arbitration, he notes that such proceedings

> are subject to no "single international rules of evidence" that in any manner resemble the technical rules often followed in proceedings before domestic courts – in particular, courts of the Anglo-American tradition. Indeed, the view of one commentator the *ad hoc* character of most international tribunals has contributed to the slow development of a definite body of rules relating to evidence, to the extent that "[e]ach tribunal tends to be a law onto itself, the rules adopted and applied for the occasion being to a considerable degree determined by the legal background of the members of the tribunal.")

Michael Z. Green, "No Strict Evidence Rules in Labor and Employment Arbitration," 15 *Tex. Wesleyan L. Rev.* 533 (2009) (the author notes that evidentiary rules can be straight-jackets foisted onto a proceeding but argues, "[h]owever, [that] arbitrators should not just allow anything to be admitted into evidence for what it is worth because this approach confuses the advocates and adds unnecessary costs and delays to the arbitration process. Instead, arbitrators need to strike an appropriate balance between letting everything in and strict application of the rules." He adds that

> "[a]rbitrators in labor and employment arbitration can provide consistency by using the underlying principles behind the rules of evidence as a tool to inform the parties at the hearing whether evidence offered is not only going to be admitted but what weight the arbitrator will give it. Then the parties will have the guidance they need to take advantage of the benefits of the arbitration process without being subjected to unwieldly evidence expectations and uncertainty by being informed that the arbitrator will only take it for whatever it is worth. While not strictly applying the rules of evidence, the arbitrator will still be able to benefit by offering a framework to achieve better fact-finding and evaluation of the evidence presented through an efficient hearing.")

Susan L. Karamanian, "Overstating the 'Americanization' of International Arbitration: Lessons from ICSID," 19 *Ohio St. J. on Disp. Resol.* 5, 27 (2003):

The jurisprudence on the subject is bereft of any acceptable conceptual narrative beyond the *what*. The U.S. Supreme Court in *Bernhardt v. Polygraphic Co.*, 350 US 198, 203–04 n. 4 (1956) observed that an "arbitrator is not bound to hear all of the

> Like many rules of international arbitrations, the ICSID rules lack detailed evidentiary standards. The guiding principle is as follows: "the tribunal shall be the judge of the admissibility of any evidence adduced and of its probative value." [citation omitted] This rule is being tested, because many witnesses are now appearing at the oral hearing, in which they are being cross-examined, and there is a growing likelihood that a party will have access to other party's relevant documents.

Mary Ellen O'Connell, "Rules of Evidence for the Use of Force in International Law's New Era," 100 *Am. Soc'y Int'l L. Proc.* 44 (2006):

> Plainly international law does not currently have a well-developed body of evidentiary rules on the use of force. According to Lobel: "Questions involving the standards and mechanisms for assessing complicated factual inquiries are generally not accorded the same treatment given by the legal academy to the more abstract issues involved in defining relevant international law standards. Unfortunately, international incidents generally involve disputed issues of fact, and in the absence of an international judicial or other centralized fact-finding mechanism, the *ad hoc* manner in which nations evaluate factual claims is often decisive." [Citation omitted.] The International Court of Justice has made statements regarding what is credible evidence, evidence to be given "weight" in international cases. It has not, to date, made any straightforward, express statement of the standard of proof expected.

and Paul Radvany, "The Importance of the Federal Rules of Evidence in Arbitration," 36 *Rev. Litig.* 469, 511–12 (2016):

> It is broadly true that most evidence proffered is likely to be accepted in arbitration. However, it is still important for counsel and arbitrators to appreciate evidence-based arguments in the context of arbitration for a number of reasons. Evidence and discovery function in different and inverted ways in civil litigation versus arbitration for reasons of efficiency, cost, and ease of dispute resolution. This does not, however, eliminate the underlying rationale of evidence law: to promote the resolution of disputes upon more, rather than less, reliable evidence … Failure to consider these principles can lead to situations where arbitrators lend greater weight to questionable or unreliable evidence by not taking the time to consciously "weigh" evidence properly. Use of evidence law during arbitration by counsel would serve to force arbitrators to do so.

c.f., e.g., Born, "Procedures in International Arbitration," chapter 15, §15.09(b) *Differences between Arbitral and Judicial Procedures*,

> Particular attention is devoted to issues of procedural fairness in international arbitration because international arbitration conventions, national arbitration legislation and institutional arbitration rules guarantee the parties' rights to due process and procedural regularity, and in part because arbitral tribunals normally take these guarantees seriously. [Citation omitted.] *Equally, the "rules of evidence" used in international arbitration are material improvements in complex commercial disputes when compared with technical, often archaic, evidentiary codes generally employed in many domestic legal systems*. [Citation omitted] (Emphasis added)

and *Parker v. United Mexican States*, Award in U.S. & Mexico General Claims Commission of 31 March 1926, IV R.I.A.A. 35, 39 (1952) ("As an international tribunal, the Commission denies the existence in international procedure of rules governing the burden of proof borrowed from municipal procedure."), and at ¶ 5:

> [H]owever appropriate may be the technical rules of evidence obtaining in the jurisdiction of either the United States or Mexico as applied to the conduct of trials in their municipal courts,

evidence tendered by the parties.... [H]e must give each of the parties to the dispute an adequate opportunity to present its evidence and arguments." In that note, the court further cites authority for the proposition that "[a]rbitrators are not bound by the rules of evidence." [Citations omitted.]

The scant treatment accorded to the use of rules of evidence and consideration of evidentiary issues rests on a very simplistic and primitive view of arbitration. Consider the following language from the *Bernhardt* opinion:

> The nature of the tribunal where suits are tried is an important part of the parcel of rights behind a cause of action. The change from a court of law to an arbitration panel may make a radical difference in ultimate result. Arbitration carries no right to trial by jury that is guaranteed by the Seventh Amendment ... Arbitrators do not have the benefit of judicial instruction on the law; they need not give reasons for their results; the record of their proceedings is not as complete as it is in a court trial; and judicial review of an award is more limited than judicial review of a trial...[3]

The view that arbitration concerns itself with technical legal issues that somehow do not require the acumen of a judge, and that arbitral tribunals rely on abbreviated records that are not susceptible to second instance review, and thus are not bound, and should not be constrained by rules of evidence, at best is anachronistic. It makes little sense. If at one time it was relevant, it no longer is.

More modern authority, however, is not much better. It hardly goes beyond a mere description of the *what*. The Seventh Circuit Court of Appeals' analysis in *Generica Ltd. v. Pharmaceutical Basics*, 125 F.3d 1123 (7th Cir. 1997) is illustrative.

In the context of affirming a judgment entered confirming entry of an arbitral award and denying a motion to vacate, the Seventh Circuit, in part, reviewed whether the arbitral tribunal's refusal to reopen cross-examination of a witness violated respondent's due process rights and, therefore, supported set-aside ("vacatur" under the U.S. Federal Arbitration Act) of the underlying arbitral award entered

> they have no place in regulating the admissibility of and in the weighing of evidence before this international tribunal. There are many reasons why such technical rules have no application here, among them being that this Commission is without power to summon witnesses or issue processes for the taking of depositions with which municipal tribunals are usually clothed. The Commission expressly decides that municipal restrictive rules of adjective law or of evidence cannot be here introduced and given effect by clothing them in such phrases as "universal principles of law," or "the general theory of law," and the like. On the contrary, the greatest liberality will obtain in the admission of evidence before this Commission with the view of discovering the whole truth with respect to each claim submitted.

See also, Mary Ellen O'Connell, "Lawful Self-Defense to Terrorism," 63 *U. Pitt. L. Rev.* 889, 895–96 (2002) (articulating and amply documenting the following two propositions: (i) "[i]nternational law has no generally-accepted law of evidence[,]" and (ii) "The International Court of Justice (ICJ) has no established rules of evidence."); David Caron & Lee M. Caplan, *The UNCITRAL Arbitration Rules: A Commentary*, 2nd ed. (Oxford University Press 2013), 573 ("There is, in principle, no prohibition or what is known in common law as 'hearsay.'").

3 *Bernhardt* at 203.

against respondent and in favor of claimant. After tracing the contours of cases articulating the informal and expeditious nature of arbitral proceedings, the Court cited to the First Circuit observing:

> An arbitrator enjoys wide latitude in conducting an arbitration hearing. Arbitration proceedings are not constrained by formal rules or *procedure* or *evidence*; the arbitrator's rule is to resolve disputes, based on his consideration of all relevant evidence, once the parties to the dispute have had a full opportunity to present their cases. (Citing *Hoteles Condado Beach*, 763 F.2d 34, 38 (1st Cir. 1985)) (Emphasis added)

Furthermore, it reiterated its own pronouncement on arbitral attenuated due process:

> As Judge Cudahy recently wrote for our court, a party's choice to accept arbitration entails a trade-off. A party can gain a quicker, less structured way of resolving disputes; and it may also gain the benefit of submitting its quarrels to a specialized arbiter … Parties lose something, too: the right to seek redress from the courts for all but the most exceptional errors at arbitration.[4]

Consequently, the Court first adopted three precepts from the First Circuit: (i) a "party's choice to accept arbitration entails a trade-off," this trade-off leads to a (ii) quicker, "less structured" dispute settlement, at the price of (iii) losing "the right to seek redress from the courts for all but the most exceptional errors at arbitration." This flexibility and agility, the Court reasoned, dispenses with the need to apply state court rules of evidence.[5]

It noted that an "arbitrator enjoys wide latitude in conducting an arbitration hearing," and, therefore, "[a]rbitration proceedings are not constrained by formal rules or procedure or evidence; the arbitrator's rule is to resolve disputes, based on his consideration of all relevant evidence, once the parties to the dispute have had a full opportunity to present their cases."[6]

4 *Generica Ltd.* at 1130.

5 In *Generica Ltd.*, "the parties agreed, in the Terms of Reference, that the 'arbitrator,' in his discretion, [shall] decide what evidence to admit and in what form evidence is to be tendered, 'and also the weight to be given to any particular evidence shall be a matter for the judgment of the Arbitrator.'" *Id.* at 1129.

6 *Id.* at 1130. *See also United Paperworks Int'l Union v. Miso Inc.*, 484 U.S. 29, 37–38 (1987) ("Courts thus do not sit to hear claims of factual or legal error by an arbitrator as an appellate court does in reviewing decisions of lower courts."); *Bernhardt v. Polygraphic Co.*, 350 U.S. 198, 203 n. 4 (1956) (holding that "arbitrators are not bound by the rules of evidence"); *Major League Baseball Players' Ass'n. v. Garvey*, 532 U.S. 504, 509 (2001) (holding that "[c]ourts are not authorized to review [an] arbitrator's decision on the merits despite allegations that the decision rests on factual errors or misinterprets the parties' agreement"); *Bartlit Beck LLP v. Okada*, 25 F.4th 519, 522 (7th Cir. 2022) (observing that "[a]lthough they are entitled to fair proceedings, 'parties that have chosen to remedy their dispute through arbitration rather than litigation should not expect the same procedures they would find in the judicial arena'"); and *Slaney v. Int'l Amateur Athletic Federation*, 244 F.3d 580, 590 (7th Cir. 2001) (same).

It has been ruled as a matter of law that: (i) arbitrators have "great flexibility and the courts should not review the legal adequacy of [ ] evidentiary rulings,"[7] (ii) arbitrators may accept "hearsay evidence from both parties, as they are entitled to do,"[8] and (iii) "in making evidentiary determinations arbitrators need not follow all the niceties observed by federal courts."[9]

5.3 THE HYBRID NATURE OF ICA AND THE DUALITY OF EVIDENTIARY RULES: TWO REASONS CONDUCIVE TO UNCERTAINTY AND INEFFICIENCY

In trying to arrive at the "why" rules of evidence do not apply in arbitration, the actual original normative jurisprudence on the subject virtually is silent. Certainly, one may be able to tease no more than two sparse sentences suggesting that somehow principles of efficiency and flexibility, together with the parties' decision to pursue nonjudicial dispute resolution, serve as some sort of explanation. They do not.

In fact, however, the jurisprudence serving as authority for the proposition that rules of evidence do not apply to arbitral proceedings are silent on explaining *why such is the case*. They are equally mute on the similarly seductive inquiry on *why* it is not necessarily the case that rules of evidence do not apply to arbitral proceedings.

Not surprisingly, the underlying reason is nowhere to be found. As is suggested, part of the answer is related to the incorporation into arbitration of a "*Free Proof*" approach to evidence that is adopted by virtually all civil law jurisdictions. Another part of the responsive premise concerns ICA's evolving identity: its reflexive self (see Chapter 8).

Indeed, a number of major arbitral institutional rules suggest that tribunals are at liberty to apply rules of evidence, such as SIAC Rule 19.2,[10] LCIA Art. 34.2(f),[11] and ICDR Art. 22.1(vi).[12] There is no authority that even purports to explain *why* rules of evidence are excluded from ICA proceedings. Oddly enough, the authority on which arbitration counsel, commentators, and arbitrators rely on for the proposition that rules of evidence do not apply to arbitral proceedings not only are short on any reasoning or narrative in support of this premise, but also conflict with authoritative

7 *Amalgamated Meat C.B. v. Neuhoff Bros.*, 481 F.2d 817, 820 (5th Cir. 1972).

8 *Petroleum Separating Co. v. Interamerican Refining Corp.*, 296 F.2d 124 (2nd Cir. 1961); *see Barker v. Gov't Emps. Ins. Co.*, 339 F. Supp. 1064, 1067 (D.D.C. 1972).

9 *White v. Four Seasons Hotel and Resorts*, 244 F. Supp. 3d 1, 4 (D.D.C. 2017).

10 SIAC Rule 19.2:

> The Tribunal shall determine the relevance, materiality and admissibility of all evidence. The Tribunal is not required to apply the rules of evidence of any applicable law in making such determination.

11 *See* LCIA Art. 34.2(f).

12 *See* ICDR Art. 22.1(vi).

sources suggesting that evidentiary rules indeed *may* and *should* be applied.[13] Why, then, this glaring void that seemingly defies explanation of any kind?

The general explanation advanced in the jurisprudence is wholly inadequate, and foundationally unsustainable. ICA's emphasis on efficiency, flexibility, and the qualified benefits of not having second instance merits review, simply cannot account for the phenomenon.

Consider the following question. How would adopting a "Hearsay-Rule" undermine flexibility or efficiency? Also, in what manner would rules precluding the admissibility of documents that cannot be authenticated disavow cornerstone principles of expediency, efficiency, and flexibility? And are not privileges, such as the attorney–client privilege, the accountant–client privilege, and other actual rules of evidence having exclusionary effects, applied in ICA with unquestioned and unvarnished success?[14]

Rules of evidence requiring for the declarant to testify on personal knowledge, or documents to be authenticated or capable of self-authentication, and for privileged communications to remain so, all further efficiency and flexibility if appropriately administered. This is even when applied within a rubric that defers to a qualified *Free Proof* methodology pursuant to which deference is accorded to *arbitrator discretion* when exercised in the context of evidentiary principles. More so, they render possible predictive value, process transparency, and legitimacy. All of which enhance the likelihood of *optimal efficiency*.

Process legitimacy suffers when merits rulings are premised on testimony or documents that never should have been admissible, let alone outcome determinative. Aprioristically foreclosing the application of evidential rules is not conceptually sustainable on the grounds that the existing *culture* on the subject would seem to suggest as much.

5.4 FOUR NON-EXHAUSTIVE REASONS EXPLAINING THE SEEMINGLY IRRATIONAL

It is necessary to challenge the untested and irrational assumption that rules and principles of evidence are inimical to the efficiency pillar of ICA. They are not.

Four reasons stand out on why arbitrators reluctantly, if at all, apply rules of evidence. First, arbitration is yet to define itself fully. Today it is besieged by polarized and uncompromising views concerning ICA's very nature. While these views only may have marginal practical consequences, much like St. Thomas Aquinas'

[13] *See* LCIA Art. 21(vi).

[14] For a thoughtful and comprehensive analysis of the challenges posed by the attorney–client privilege in international arbitration where in effect Tribunals are provided with cases "in a legal vacuum [having] similarities to those navigating the unsettled territory of the 'wild west,'" *see* Susan D. Franck, International Arbitration and Attorne–Client Privilege – a Conflict of Law Approach, 51 *Ariz. St. L.* 3, 935 (2019).

position on the number of angels able to dance on a pin's head, a less than defined construct occasionally may influence the contextual fabric with respect to which judgment is exercised.

One extreme position asserts that arbitration, much like the platonic forms (the *eidos*), is "de-localized."[15] These proponents with great verve maintain that ICA is detached or removed from any and all geopolitical subdivisions. It is a dispute resolution methodology private in nature and thus divorced from the workings of the State. Therefore, so the argument says, it is not in the very constitution of arbitration (in its nature) to avail itself of legal frameworks such as rules of procedure or evidence that are used by courts. These localized judicial tribunals, so it is said, that represent arbitration's conceptual and doctrinal antithesis.[16]

Indeed, this approach hides behind a semi-atomistic construct and asks that arbitration in this context be viewed without reference to the need to seek from State courts for (i) compulsory witness practice, (ii) recognition and enforcement, and (iii) set-aside challenges, and to focus only on the extent to which an arbitral award should be construed as independent from the *lex arbitri* of the State where the award issued.[17] The approach is arbitrarily coarse, that is to say, does not consider the process as a whole, but only in random parts so that the proposition can be rational.

On the other extreme, the premise is advanced that even though ICA is a creature of contract,[18] it is subject to and dependent on national and international regulatory

[15] *See, e.g.*, Plato's *Republic* BKVI, (5090-513E) (addressing the divided lane, the second half of which illustrates the proposition asserted).

[16] In a short article published in January 1983 (a veritable relic in the space-time continuum of scholarship), Paulsson stated (it is unclear from the article the extent that the proposition was developed sufficiently without relying on analogies to constitute an "argument") as follows:

> Those who reject the delocalization process seem to mistake the purpose of the permitting parties to unbind arbitrations from the law of the *situs* of proceedings. They wrongly conclude that what is sought is an "escape" from national jurisdictions.
>
> To seek completely to avoid national jurisdictions would be misguided. Indeed, the international arbitral system would ultimately breakdown if no national jurisdictions could be called upon to recognize and enforce awards.
>
> The question is rather whether in certain situations international arbitration may be liberated from local peculiarities of a place of arbitration chosen either fortuitously or for reasons of neutrality having nothing to do with the parties' attachment to local rules of arbitration. Jan Paulsson, "Delocalisation of International Commercial Arbitration: When and Why It Matters,"32 Int'l and Comp. L.Q. 1, 53–61 (January 1983).

The term "peculiarities of the place of arbitration," and the use of words such as "*liberal*," "unbind," and "free," only serve to detract from whatsoever theoretical force the proposition may have. For a contrasting and preferable view devoid of theoretical "spicing," *see, e.g.*, William W. Park, "The *Lex Loci Arbitri* and International Commercial Arbitration," 32 *J.C.L.Q.* 22, 25 (1983), to which Paulsson was addressing.

[17] *Id.*

[18] *Parsons & Whittemore Overseas Co. v. Societe Generale de L'Industrie du Papier (RAKTA)*, 508 F.2d 969 (2nd Cir. 1974).

regimes without which it cannot exist. The argument further asserts that ICA's most important pillar and unique element is enforceability.

Ultimately an award must be recognized and enforced pursuant to national courts. Such recognition and enforcement in turn relies on the New York Convention and the national legislation and jurisprudence of the enforcing State.[19]

This view of ICA also is buttressed on the premise that other than the discretionary *weight* the arbitral tribunal may accord to evidence,[20] and adverse inferences to be drawn from noncompliance with an arbitral tribunal's evidentiary rulings,[21] arbitrators lack compulsory powers.[22] Thus, even for purposes of compelling witness attendance recourse to national courts is indispensable.

Having this perspective of ICA is one that, while acknowledging that it is a private creature of contract, views ICA as existentially operating within national[23] and international regulatory regimes.[24] For this reason, it can hardly be characterized as a self-sustaining system that is detached from any geopolitical judicial, legislative, or international system. ICA is not "delocalized," that is to say, freed from the limitations of locality.

The proponents of this understanding of ICA's core elements and nature to some extent understand ICA also as an inevitable part of a State's (albeit qualified) exercise of sovereignty much as States exercise sovereignty through judicial systems. ICA existentially relies on the State's law governing arbitration, as much as it relies on the workings of the New York Convention: organic positive law and treaty law.

The hybrid nature of arbitration itself, which straddles the borders between (i) private and public, (ii) *disposition* and *resolution*, as well as (iii) vacillating to and from a commercial dispute and adjudicating merits based upon the rigorous application of law to fact, has contributed to doctrinal underdevelopment regarding the *taking* and *presentation* of evidence in ICA. Lacking ontological identity only serves to nurture the untested and flawed assumption that a select and specific limited number of rules of procedure and evidence only are to find resonance in the workings of national courts. Nothing could be farther from the truth.

19 *Id.*

20 IBA Rules Art. 9.1 reads:

> 1. The Arbitral Tribunal shall determine the admissibility, relevance, materiality and weight of evidence.

21 IBA Rules Art. 9.7 provides:

> 7. If a Party fails without satisfactory explanation to make available any other relevant evidence, including testimony, sought by one Party to which the Party to whom the request was addressed has not objected in due time or fails to make available any evidence, including testimony, ordered by the Arbitral Tribunal to be produced, the Arbitral Tribunal may infer that such evidence would be adverse to the interests of that Party.

22 FAA, 9 U.S.C. §§ 1–16 at § 7, Federal Arbitration Act (FAA) (9 U.S.C. §§ 1–307).

23 *Lex Arbitri* is central to ICA's perfect workings; hence the proliferation of the UNCITRAL Model Law and its multiple iterations. It is not even theoretically viable to posit ICA absent the context of a sovereign State.

24 Chapter 1, n. 9 in this volume.

The second proposition that helps to explain why evidentiary principles are practically, if not theoretically, non-existing in the context of ICA concerns the very nature of rules of evidence themselves. Here, more is warranted.[25]

[25] *See, e.g., Tidd v. Walmart Stores Inc.*, 757 F. Supp. 1322, 1323 n. 1 (N.D. Ala. 1991) ("The Federal Rules of evidence are procedural in nature, not substantive." 56 F.R.D. 183 (1972)); *D'Orio v. West Jersey Health Systems*, 797 F. Supp. 371, 375 (D.N.J. 1992) (sitting in diversity and observing that *Erie* doctrine inapplicable because after canvassing cases where state evidence rules conflict with the FRE, "[w]hile the rationale of these cases vary, it is most often grounded either [i] in the notion that evidence rules are 'procedural' rather than 'substantive' or [ii] on the paramountcy of the Federal Rules of Evidence by virtue of their effectiveness having been dependent on the approval of Congress."); In *Re Air Crash Disaster Near Chicago, Ill.* On May 25, 1979, American Airlines and McDonnell Douglas Corp., 701 F. 2d 1189, 1193 (7th Cir. 1983) (holding that "the Federal Rules of Evidence apply and that as a consequence the district court may not categorically exclude certain kinds of evidence relevant to the determination of damages"); *Rabon v. Automatic Fasteners Inc.*, 672 F. 2d 1231, 1238 (5th Cir. 1982) (holding that "[i]n this diversity case, federal law governs procedural matters, [citation omitted] including admissibility of evidence"); *Ostroski v. United States*, 2007 WL 9701868 *3 (S.D. Fla. August 23, 2007) (holding that "matters of evidence are procedural in nature, not substantive requiring the application of Federal Rules of Evidence"); *Reid v. BMW of North America*, 464 F. Supp.2d 1267, 1271 (N.D. Ga. 2006) (holding that "Federal law and the Federal Rules of Evidence govern the admissibility in diversity action because the admissibility of evidence is a procedural matter"); and *c.f.* In re Rules of Evidence for United States Courts and Magistrates 56 F.R.D. 183 (1972) regarding Federal Rules Decisions, effective July 1, 1973, Justice Douglas (Dissenting). Relevant sections of the dissent and corresponding analysis are set forth as follows:

> There are those who think that fashioning of rules of evidence is a task for the legislature, not for the judiciary. Wigmore thought the task was essentially a judicial one. 1 Wigmore on Evidence, pp. 251 at ***et seq***. (30 ed. 1939); and I share that view, leaving the problem for case-to-case development by the courts or by Congress.
>
> But my concern with these Rules of Evidence is two-fold. First, I doubt if rules of evidence are within the purview of the statute under which we are authorized to submit proposed Rules to Congress. The Act provides the Supreme Court shall have the power "to prescribe by general rules, the forms of process, writs, pleadings and motions, *and the practice and procedure* of the district courts and courts of appeals of the United States in civil actions, including admiralty and maritime cases, and appeals therein, *and the practice and procedure in proceedings* for the review by the courts of appeals of decisions of the Tax Court of the United States and for the judicial review or enforcement of orders of administrative agencies, boards, commissions, and officers." 28 U.S.C. § 2072.
>
> I can find no legislative history that rules of evidence were to be included in "practice and procedure" as used in § 2072. The Committee Reports on the original Act throw no light on the question. H.R. Rep. No. 1829, 73rd Cong., 2d Sess.; S. Rep. No. 1049, 73rd Cong., 2d Sess. The words "practice and procedure" in the setting of the Act seem to me to exclude rules of evidence. They seem to me to be words of art that describe *pretrial procedures*, pleadings, and *procedures* for preserving objections and taking appeals.
>
> Second, this Court does not write the Rules, nor supervise their writing, nor appraise them on their merits, weighing the pros and cons. The Court concededly is a mere conduit. Those who write the Rules are members of a Committee named by the Judicial Conference. The members are eminent; but they are the sole judges of the merits of the proposed Rules, our approval being merely perfunctory. In other words, we are merely the conduit to Congress. Yet the public assumes that our imprimatur is on the Rules, as of course it is.
>
> We are so far removed from the trial arena that we have no special insight, no meaningful oversight to contribute. The Rules of Evidence – if there are to be some – should be channeled

Rules of evidence are generally *classified* as *procedural*.[26] This classification, however, leaves much to be desired because evidence rules, depending on the rule and the test applied, can be legitimately and conceptually categorized as (i) procedural, (ii) substantive, or (iii) both (a hybrid of substantive and procedural rules).[27]

through the Judicial Conference whose members are much more qualified than we to appraise their merits when applied in actual practice. (Emphasis added)

It is Justice Douglas' first of two grounds that are particularly important for present purposes. While he does not state that the Rules of Evidence are not *procedural* in nature, Justice Douglas does go far enough to say that they certainly (in his opinion) do not fall under the umbrella "practice and procedure" within the scope of § 2072. This much he reiterates on three occasions throughout the course of the brief dissent.

In turn, 28 U.S.C. § 2072 (Rules of Procedure and Evidence; Power to Prescribe) in pertinent part reads:

(a) The Supreme Court shall have the power to prescribe general rules of practice and procedure and rules of evidence for cases in the United States district courts (including proceedings before magistrate judges thereof) and courts of appeals.
(b) Such rules shall not abridge, enlarge or modify *any substantive right*. All laws in conflict with such rules shall be of no further force or effect after such rules have taken effect. (Emphasis added)

Certainly, § 2072 distinguishes between "rules of procedure and evidence," but it is not by any means asserting that rules of evidence are not procedural in nature, even though they do not pertain to rules of civil procedure, which do not speak to the presentation of evidence, but rather *discovery*.

This reading of 28 U.S.C. § 2072 seems to be buttressed by subsection (b), in part stating that: "[s]uch rules shall not abridge, enlarge, or modify any *substantive right*." (Emphasis added.) Therefore, it is plain that the Act limits itself to *procedural rules* and not just *rules of procedure*. These procedural rules, according to the majority of the Supreme Court in 1972, include Rules of Evidence that are procedural in nature, i.e., the application of which do not "not abridge, enlarge, or modify any substantive right[s]."

In Federal Rules Decisions, 56 F.R.D. 183 (1973), the ordinary and plain language of paragraphs 1 and 2 concern rules that are procedural in nature and character:

1. The Rules hereafter set forth at pages 194–353, to be known as the Federal Rules of Evidence, be, and they thereby are, prescribed pursuant to Sections 3402, 3771, and 3772, Title 18, United States Code, and Sections 2072 and 2075, Title 28, United States Code, *to govern procedure* in the proceedings and to the extent set forth therein, in the United States courts of appeals, the United States district courts, the District Court for the District of the Canal Zone and the district courts of Guam and the Virgin Islands, and before United States Magistrates.
2. That the aforementioned Federal Rules of Evidence shall take effect on July 1, 1973, and shall be applicable to actions and proceedings brought thereafter and also *to further procedure* in actions and proceedings then pending, except to the extent that in the opinion of the court their application and particular action or proceeding then pending would not be feasible or would work injustice in which event the former *procedure* applies. (Emphasis added)

The very enabling order of the FRE, particularly in the context of Justice Douglas' dissent, points to the hybrid and non-static character of evidentiary rules.

26 The rules of evidence in Spain, Italy, France, Germany, and Portugal, for example, are all found in their respective codes of *civil procedure*, *see* Chapter 7, n. 2 in this volume.

27 *Hottle v. Beech Aircraft Corporation*, 47 F.3d 106 (4th Cir. 1995); *Erie R.R. v. Tompkins*, 304 U.S. 64, 58 S. Ct. 817, 82 L. Ed. 1188 (1938). The Fourth Circuit Court of Appeals provided a comprehensive analysis arising from the interplay between state court rules of evidence and FRE in the context of an *Erie* analysis that brings into very high relief the hybrid nature of Rules of Evidence:

Much depends on the particular rule at issue and more banal issues of classification as "practice and procedure."

In addition, the rule or standard applied for determining whether a principle is procedural or substantive is yet to be conclusively developed.[28] There is no single rule or framework for classification. And rules of evidence themselves are sufficiently varied so as to qualify, depending on the rule, as procedural, substantive, or both, thus meeting the entire gamut of rules and standards for the determination of substantive and procedural.[29]

In *Erie R.R. v. Tompkins* [citation omitted], the Supreme Court held that because Congress had no power to declare substantive rules of common law application in a state, federal courts sitting in diversity must apply substantive law, decisional as well as statutory, in the adjudication of state-created rights. Thus, began the general rule that a federal court is to apply state substantive law and federal procedural law in diversity cases. [*Citing to Stonehocker v. General Motors Corp.*, 587 F.2d 151, 154 (4th Cir. 1978)]. However, the Supreme Court also has noted that where a state's procedural rule is bound up with substantive policy, a federal court is to apply the state rule. [*Byrd v. Blue Ridge Rural Elec. Co-op., Inc.* 356 U.S. 525, 535, 78 S. Ct. 893, 899, 2 L.Ed. 2d 953 (1958)]. Yet, in a later case involving a conflict between Federal Rule of Civil Procedure 4(d)(1) and a state service of process rule, the Court rejected the substantive-procedural test in that context and found the federal rule controlling under the authority of the rules Enabling Act. [*Hanna v. Plumer*, 380 U.S. 460, 469–73, 85 S. Ct. 1136, 1143–45, 14 L. Ed. 2d 8 (1965)]. The Court explained that "*Erie* and its offspring cast no doubt on the long-recognized power of Congress to prescribe housekeeping rules for federal courts even though some of those rules differ from comparable state rules." Accordingly, we [4th Circuit] along with other courts of appeals, *have held that the Federal Rules of Evidence, as validly enacted procedural rules, govern in diversity cases.*

However, there is no uniformity among circuits as to whether federal rules control when a state evidentiary rule either embodies or is closely tied to a state substantive policy. In such a situation, application of the Federal Rules of Evidence, *although beyond argument procedural*, may encroach upon a state's substantive law. This circuit [4th Circuit], along with the First, Third, Fifth, Seventh, Eighth, and Tenth have held that although the Federal Rules of Evidence *typically govern in diversity cases*, "there are circumstances in which a question of admissibility of evidence is so intertwined with a state substantive rule that the state rule … will be followed in order to give full effect to the state's substantive policy." (Emphasis added), *Hottle*, 47 F.3d 109–10.

28 Using the *Erie* legal imperative as context, and upon noting that "[g]enerally, rules of evidence are procedural, but 'some state evidentiary rules have substantive aspects, thereby define the substance – procedure distinction in creating a potential *Erie* conflict[,]' [citation omitted] [i]n such cases, courts should decide whether the provision at issue 'either creates rights and obligations or is so bound with [state-created] rights and obligations that it must be considered substantive.'" *Crossley v. Minnesota Life Insurance Co.*, 217 WL 5653603 *2 (E.D. Mich. Apr. 19, 2017) (*citing to Shropshire v. Laidlaw Transit, Inc.*, 550 F.3d 570, 575 (6th Cir. 2008)) (quoting *Byrd v. Blue Ridge Rural Elec. Co-op., Inc.* 356 U.S. 525, 535 (1958). *See also Monarch Insurance Company of Ohio v. Spach*, 281 F.2d 401, 404–405 (5th Cir. 1960) (observing:

The fact that rules of evidence are ordinarily thought of as procedural or, for that matter, are covered a least in part by specific FRCP does not really solve the problem. For we are taught that while the lines are shadowy and we may but dimly see the path, the *Erie* [citation omitted] adjustment which our constitutional federalism imposes on a federal court hearing a diversity cases is not satisfied by a talismanic label of "procedural" or "substantive." But this is not, as some have occasionally felt or uttered, to say that in diversity cases substance and procedure are now one and the same thing or that, as one dissenting Justice characterized it, the Supreme "Court riddled the distinction between 'substantive' and 'procedural.'")

29 By way of example, there are evidentiary rules that include: (i) the parole evidence rule, (ii) presumptions, (iii) privileges, and (iv) witness competency rules that have been construed as substantive and

The third premise explaining the evidentiary void concerns turning a blind eye to the *efficiencies* that would result from applying *personal knowledge*, *hearsay*, *expert opinion admissibility*, and *authentication* evidentiary principles to ICA. Evidentiary principles that necessarily would curtail the proliferation of documents, as well as factual witness statements, expert reports, and incident oral testimony, can constitute a premise from which a reasonable person may infer that such principles would be paradigmatically efficient.

The status quo is such that there is a complete disconnect between admissibility and reliability of evidence. Absent privilege, confidentiality, or excessive burden, all evidence is admissible to the extent that it is disclosable.[30] This state of affairs cannot be seriously characterized as efficient. Arbitral panels are (i) inundated with evidence that must be construed as "admissible," but (ii) left without guardrails as to both admissibility and the weight to be accorded to such evidence.

Fourth and lastly, although kept silent, it also is assumed that if arbitration panels were to be held accountable for the proper application of evidentiary principles governing admissibility, somehow arbitration would be left vulnerable to second instance merits review. This proposition is also flawed. Allowing stricter and better defined rules regarding the (i) *taking* and (ii) *presentation* of evidence would help better define very narrow aspects of *arbitrator discretion* and in no way cause a fissure allowing challenge to arbitral finality.

Arbitral awards would still be subject to Arts. III and IV of the New York Convention.[31] The existing ratio with respect to *arbitrator discretion* and *party-autonomy*, and therefore, *attenuated arbitral due process*, would remain intact (see Section 4.6).

5.5 ICA'S NORMATIVE FRAMEWORK: A REMAKE IN FURTHERANCE OF *OPTIMAL EFFICIENCY*

The incorporation of select rules or principles of evidence mostly governing personal knowledge, hearsay, and authentication, would not alter the existing normative framework establishing the hierarchy of rules that govern the *taking* and *presentation* of evidence in ICA. That normative framework can be gleaned from

not procedural. *See e.g.*, *Legg v. Chopra*, 286 F.3d 286, 290 (6th Cir. 2002). These rules concern the meaning of contracts, the competency of witnesses, and tend to establish the elements of substantive rights or remedies. *See also American Legion Post No. 57 v. Leahey*, 681 So.2d 1337, 1343 (Ala. 1996), *overruled on other grounds* by *Marsh v. Green*, 782 So.2d 223 (Ala. 2000) (holding that the collateral-source rule "as a whole is a rule of substantive law," but one that contains a procedural component. (Emphasis omitted.))

30 "[T]o the extent that it is disclosable," means if "relevant to the case and material to its outcome." *See* Section 4.3.

31 As of the time of this writing (September 2024), there are 172 state parties to the New York Convention. The UN currently has 193 Member States. Hence, 89 percent of all states recognized by the UN are signatories to the New York Convention.

a number of authoritative sources. Perhaps the more notable are (i) the English Arbitration Act, (ii) the UNCITRAL Model Law (UNCITRAL Model Law or Model Law),[32] and (iii) the major institutional rules.[33] The English Arbitration Act provides a descriptive paradigm of the hierarchy of rules that govern evidentiary issues.

5.5.1 *The English Arbitration Act*

The English Arbitration Act, Section 4 (**Mandatory and non-mandatory provisions**) in part states:

(i) The mandatory provisions of this Part are listed in schedule 1 *and have effect notwithstanding any agreement to the contrary.*
(ii) The other provisions of this Part (the "non-mandatory provisions") allow the parties to make their own arrangements by agreement but provide rules which apply in the absence of such agreement.
(iii) The parties may make such agreements by agreeing to the application of institutional rules or providing any other means by which a matter may be decided. (Emphasis added)

The English Arbitration Act is transparent and unique in that it sets forth in schedule 1, the mandatory provisions that take precedent in any arbitration governed by this law.[34] The very nature of the subject matter of each of these sections manifests why these laws are mandatory in nature.

[32] UNCITRAL Model Law in International Commercial Arbitration of 1985 with amendments adopted in 2006.

[33] For a comprehensive discussion of the normative framework governing the taking of evidence in international arbitration generally, see Stefan Kröll, "The Normative Framework on the Taking of Evidence," in *Handbook of Evidence in International Commercial Arbitration: Key Issues and Concepts* (Franco Ferrari & Friedrich Rosenfeld eds.) (Wolters Kluwer 2022), 23–39.

[34] Schedule 1 Mandatory Provisions of Part I, provides:

sections 9 to 11 (stay of legal proceedings);
section 12 (power of court to extend agreed time limits);
section 13 (application of Limitation Acts);
section 24 (power of court to remove arbitrator);
section 26(1) (effect of death of arbitrator);
section 28 (liability of parties for fees and expenses of arbitrators);
section 29 (immunity of arbitrator);
section 31 (objection to substantive jurisdiction of tribunal);
section 32 (determination of preliminary point of jurisdiction);
section 33 (general duty of tribunal);
section 37(2) (items to be treated as expenses of arbitrators);
section 40 (general duty of parties);
section 43 (securing the attendance of witnesses);
section 56 (power to withhold award in case of non-payment);
section 60 (effectiveness of agreement for payment of costs in any event);
section 66 (enforcement of award);

Section 34 (**Procedural and Evidential Matters**) demonstrates that while the highest and first order of normative standing is ascribed to the Arbitration Act's mandatory provisions, "[i]t shall be for the Tribunal to decide all procedural and evidential matters, subject to the right of the parties to agree on any matter." Hence, mandatory norms are *followed* by the agreement of the parties as second in the pecking order.

The third and penultimate normative standing pertains to institutional rules and non-mandatory provisions of the law governing an arbitration. Fourth and lastly, are the decisions of the arbitral tribunal.[35]

This formal expression of the hierarchy of rules governing evidentiary issues is somewhat misleading. In both theory and practice, the agreement of the parties (second ranking), and non-mandatory provisions contained in institutional arbitration rules, and the law governing the arbitration (third rank) often constitute the subject matter of *arbitrator discretion*. The inherent powers of the tribunal play a leading protagonistic role in the second and third orders of rank.

Such is particularly the case because non-mandatory trigger or default provisions are qualified as bestowing the arbitral tribunal authority, *subject to the parties' agreement*. Depending on the applicable rules, the arbitral tribunal is the final authoritative source preempting the agreement of the parties on a number of issues.[36]

sections 67 and 68 (challenging the award: substantive jurisdiction and serious irregularity), and sections 70 and 71 (supplementary provisions; effect of order of court) so far as relating to those sections;
section 72 (saving for rights of person who takes no part in proceedings);
section 73 (loss of right to object);
section 74 (immunity of arbitral institutions, &c.);
section 75 (charge to secure payment of solicitors' costs).

35 In effect, however, the pronouncements of the Arbitral Tribunal take the place of the parties' agreements because parties only agree in exceptional circumstances. Moreover, there are circumstances where the Arbitral Tribunal may override the parties' agreement if doing so would facilitate, for example, the conduct of a hearing.

36 *See* Luca Radicati di Brozolo, "International Commercial Arbitration and Private International Law," in *Cambridge Compendium of Commercial and* Investment *Arbitration* 441 (F. Ferrari, S. Kroll & A. Bjorklund eds.) 464 (Cambridge University Press 2020), observing that "[i]t is now generally acknowledged that, in deciding the merits, arbitrators must apply overriding mandatory rules (competition law, anti-corruption, embargoes, sanctions, protection of financial markets and natural heritage, and so on) since arbitration cannot be a means to circumvent such rules"; there is agreement that *party-autonomy* is not unlimited and that arbitral tribunals are generally bound by certain mandatory rules, Marcus Commandeur & Sebastian Gößling, "The Determination of Mandatory Rules of Law in International Arbitration – An Attempt to Set Out Criteria," 1 *SchiedsVZ* 12, 12 (2014). There is ample authority holding that the failure to apply the institutional arbitral rules agreed to by the parties will not be deemed sufficient, absent a showing of prejudice, to defeat enforcement pursuant to a New York Convention Art. V(1)(d) defense, absent an evidentiary showing of prejudice. *See, e.g., Calbex Mineral Ltd. v. ACC Resources Co.*, 90 F. Supp. 3d 442, 465 (W.D. Pa. 2015) (holding that "[t]he undisputed evidence of record shows the Beijing panel did not forward the documents it obtained from [party seeking enforcement] to [party opposing enforcement]. Under these circumstances, the Beijing panel did not follow the CIETAC Arbitration Rules, and, therefore, its procedure violated the agreement of the parties, i.e., the 2010 contract."); *Reasuransi Umum Indonesia v. Evanston Ins. Co.*, 1992 WL 400733 at *1 (S.D.N.Y. Dec. 23, 1992) (finding that:

Section 34.2 (**Procedural and Evidential Matters**) provides a non-exhaustive list of non-mandatory provisions that can constitute the subject matter of the parties' agreement and/or *arbitrator discretion* where the parties do not agree.[37] As to the procedural and evidentiary matters that the parties' agreement *would govern* over *arbitrator discretion*, four observations are absolutely imperative.

First, notwithstanding the parties' right to agree on any of the issues set forth in Section 34.2(a)–(h), or on any of the propositions set forth in the institutional rules of an administering arbitral body, one practical premise commands consideration. The parties *are* in arbitration. Therefore, it is unlikely that they will agree on *anything*, that is to say, (i) the time of day, (ii) the day of the week, or even (iii) the number of hours in one day. The disputing parties *disagree* on practically any premise susceptible to disagreement.

Therefore, subsection 34.1 providing that the tribunal may decide any of the issues before it (set forth in Section 34.2(a)–(f)), but subject of course to the right of the parties to agree on any of these matters, should be construed as the tail wagging the dog. Typically, the default scenario contemplating issues to be decided pursuant to *arbitrator discretion* where the parties do not agree actually turns out to be the *rule* rather than the *exception*. This proposition matters.

It reflects the practical workings of ICA principally rest with *arbitrator discretion* (inherent powers) and not *party autonomy*. In the context of the *taking* and *presentation* of evidence this phenomenon, the operational prevalence of *arbitrator discretion* over *party-autonomy*, of course is made worse by the void of evidentiary rules and corresponding doctrinal development. In this domain, there is no uniformity or arbitral practice beyond a *Free Proof* atomistic (not holistic) approach to evidential determinations.

Second, in a substantive sense the procedural hierarchical formulation stated in Section 34.1, subordinating arbitral discretion to agreement of the parties, can be viewed as aspirational from an operational perspective. The primacy of *arbitrator*

> [i]t is clear that certain of the AAA's procedure rules were not followed. The proceedings were not filed with the AAA, the required fees were not paid, and proper notice and acknowledgement by the AAA were not given to PTR … There is no dispute that PTR received timely notice of the demand to arbitrate the selection of respondents' arbitrator. Applying the standard disputed above, the award should not be vacated based on a procedural irregularity because PTR was not "substantially prejudiced" by respondents' failure to comply with the AAA's procedural rules for commencing an arbitration proceeding.

Purus Plastics GmBH v. Echo-Terr Distributing Inc., 2018 WL 3064817 at *7 (W.D. Wash. June 21, 2018) (reiterating that even where the procedural rules contemplated by the parties' agreement was not followed, the party challenging enforcement pursuant to the New York Convention Art. V(1)(d) must establish that the alleged procedural violation "were substantial prejudice to the complaining party"). *See also Karaha Bodas Co., L.L.C. v. Perusahaan Pertambangan Minyak Dan Gas Bumi Negara*, 190 F. Supp. 2d 936, 945 (S.D. Tex. 2001) (*quoting Compagnie des Bauxites de Guinee v. Hammermills*, 1992 WL 122712 at *5 (D.D.C. May 29, 1992)), *aff'd.*, *Karaha Bodas Co., L.L.C. v. Perusahaan Pertambangan Minyak Dan Gas Bumi Negara*, 364 F. 3d 274 (5th Cir. 2004).

[37] Section 34.2 (**Procedural and Evidential Matters**), (1), (2) *(a)–(h)*, (3).

discretion, however, if properly honed may constitute a compelling force in favor of *optimal efficiency*. As to evidentiary and procedural matters, *arbitrator discretion* will prevail even with respect to issues where the parties have an explicit meeting of the minds.

In instances where the arbitral tribunal expressly and explicitly overrides the agreement of the parties, the arbitral tribunal's decision to do so is limited only by ICA's attenuated principle of due process. Consequently, only in the most extreme and egregious of circumstances can and will a tribunal be held accountable for overriding the parties' agreement on a procedural or evidentiary issue.[38]

Third, Section 34.2(f) providing that "[p]rocedural and evidential matters include whether to apply strict rules of evidence (or any other rules) as to the admissibility, relevance or weight of any material (oral, written or other) sought to be tendered on any matters of fact or opinion, and the time, manner and form in which such material should be exchanged and presented." This language comports verbatim with LCIA Art. 22, subsection 22.1(vi). Section 34.2(f) served as the LCIA's inspiration with respect to subsection 22.1(vi).[39]

Fourth and finally, it is worth noting that Section 34 is titled: "**Procedural and Evidential Matters**." At first glance, the *chapeaux* may seem innocuous. After all, what is there to be gleaned from so simple a title to a section in a legislative act?

When words are to be construed textually, however, in their ordinary and plain meaning, it seems evident the drafters may not exactly deem evidential matters to be procedural, at least not in whole. The use of the word "and" should not be dismissed. The *chapeaux* suggests that evidentiary matters are treated *together* with procedural issues in Section 34. It distinguishes between *procedural* and *evidentiary* matters.

This distinction is important because we have said that principles of evidence, depending on the principle (rule), and the test applied presumably to determine whether a proposition is procedural or substantive, will inevitably lead to the conclusion that rules of evidence are hybrid. And perhaps even more complex than just dualistic in nature. In fact, the proposition was asserted that this very duality, together with ICA's own dialectical process of defining itself in relation to the State as an abstract principle, in large measure may be responsible for the fragmented and inefficient status quo pursuant to which evidentiary pronouncements are based not on the application of doctrine, but rather the subjectivity of *ad hoc* tribunals.[40]

The English Arbitration Act's Section 4 providing a narrative of the hierarchy of rules that govern the *taking* and *presentation* of evidence in ICA is mirrored by the

38 *See* Chapter 4, n. 37.

39 LCIA Art. 22 (**Additional Powers**), subsection 22.1(vi).1.

40 The *standard* argument is that somehow *flexibility* would be compromised if strict evidentiary principles and exclusionary evidence approach formed part of ICA evidence presentation. This proposition, however, does not resist sustained analysis. Evidentiary rigor of some kind can only serve to temper submissions and to enhance procedural fairness.

UNCITRAL Model Law. The Model Law, in one iteration or another, is the most universally adopted arbitration law in the international community.[41]

5.5.2 *The UNCITRAL Model Law*

The two most relevant articles on the hierarchy of rules governing procedural and evidentiary issues actually are set forth in the Model Law's Chapter 5 (**CONDUCT OF ARBITRAL PROCEEDINGS**) in order of importance. Article 18 (*Equal Treatment of Parties*) states:

The parties shall be treated with equality and each party shall be given a full opportunity of presenting his case.

Immediately following Art. 19 (*Determination of Rules of Procedure*) states:

(1) Subject to the provisions of this Law, the parties are free to agree on the procedure to be followed by the Arbitral Tribunal in conducting the proceedings.
(2) Failing such agreement, the Arbitral Tribunal may, subject to the provisions of this law, conduct the arbitration in such a manner as it considers appropriate. The power conferred upon the Arbitral Tribunal includes the power to determine the admissibility, relevance, materiality, and weight of any evidence.

The norm or rule of highest normative standing is the due process right articulated in Art. 18. Accordingly, the Art. 19.1 reference to "provisions of this Law," as (i) *superseding* and *circumscribing party-autonomy* (agreement of the parties), and (ii) *arbitrator discretion*, principally refers to mandatory norms such as due process and only a handful of conceptually related provisions such as those contained in Art. 24.[42] A similar provision that preempts *party-autonomy* and arbitral tribunal, for example, also is found in Art. 31 (Form and Contents of Award).

What follows the mandatory provisions in order of rank are (i) *party-autonomy* (agreement of the parties) and (ii) *arbitrator discretion*. Hence, theoretically as a matter of formal normative hierarchy, while Art. 19.2 makes clear that the arbitral tribunal, among other things, is vested with "[the] power to determine the admissibility, relevance, materiality and weight of any evidence," the parties by agreement may set forth the framework and applicable standard and procedural mechanisms that would govern the taking and presentation of evidence throughout the entirety of the proceeding.

It is conceptually possible for the parties to formulate a rubric that would include the exchange of material evidence likely to be relied upon by the parties with respect

[41] See Section 5.1, UNCITRAL Model Law on International Commercial Arbitration 1985, with amendments as adopted in 2006.

[42] *See e.g.*, ICDR Art. 22 (**Conduct of Proceedings**) (4), (5), (7), and (8); Art. 24 (**Exchange of Information**) (1)–(4), (6)–(10); and Art. 26 (**Hearing**) (2), (4), and (5).

to both liability and damages early in the proceeding and thus create an appropriate settlement environment. The parties may agree to authorize the tribunal to share the tribunal's views of the merits with the parties at any time during the course of the proceeding.

The arbitration rules of the major arbitral institutes comport with the normative framework articulated in the Model Law and the English Arbitration Act. The institutional rules of the principal arbitral institutes, however, do divert on the primacy accorded to *party-autonomy* and arbitral discretion from both the English Arbitration Act and the Model Law. Illustrative is LCIA Rule Art. 14. Subsection 14.2 places *arbitrator discretion before party-autonomy* regarding the conduct of the proceedings:

> 14.2 The Arbitral Tribunal shall have the widest discretion to discharge these general duties [the conduct of the proceedings], [i] subject to the mandatory provisions of any applicable law or [ii] any rules of law the Arbitral Tribunal may decide to be applicable; and at all times the parties shall do everything necessary in good faith for the fair, *efficient* and expeditious conduct of the arbitration, including the Arbitral Tribunal's discharge of its general duty.[43] (Emphasis added)

The SCC Arbitration Rules are illustrative of institutional norms that formally place *party-autonomy* before, and therefore higher in the hierarchy of governing rules, than *arbitrator discretion*. Subsection 23.1 provides that "[t]he Arbitral Tribunal

[43] *See also* Art. 13, subsection 13.1 of the *Hong Kong International Arbitration Centre (HKIAC) Arbitration Rules* 2018:

> 13.1 Subject to these rules, the arbitral tribunal shall adopt suitable procedures for the conduct of the arbitration in order to avoid unnecessary delay or expense, having regard to the complexity of the issues, the amount in dispute and the effective use of technology, and provided that such procedures ensure equal treatment of the parties and afford the parties a reasonable opportunity to present their case[;]
>
> Rule 19, *Singapore International Arbitration Centre (SIAC) Arbitration Rules*:
>
> 19.1 The Tribunal shall conduct the arbitration in such manner as it considers appropriate, after consulting with the parties, to ensure the fair, expeditious, economical and final resolution of the dispute.
>
> 19.2 The Tribunal shall determine the relevance, materiality and admissibility of all evidence. The Tribunal is not required to apply the rules of evidence of any applicable law in making such determine[;] *International Centre for Dispute Resolution (ICDR) Arbitration Rules* (Rules effective March 1, 2021) Art. 22, subsection 22.1 reads:
>
> 1. Subject to these Rules, the arbitral tribunal may conduct the arbitration in whatever manner it considers appropriate, provided that the parties are treated with equality and that each party has the right to be heard and is given a fair opportunity to present its case[;] and *International Court of Arbitration of the International Chamber of Commerce (ICC) Arbitration Rules* (in force as of January 1, 2021) Art. 19 (Rules Governing the Proceeding) states:

The proceedings before the arbitral tribunal shall be governed by the [i] Rules and, [ii] where the Rules are silent, by [iii] any rules which the parties or, failing them, the arbitral tribunal may settle on, [iv] whether or not reference is thereby made to the rules of procedure of a national law to be applied to the arbitration.

shall conduct the arbitration in such a manner as it considers appropriate, subject to the Arbitration Rules *and any agreement between the parties.*"[44] (Emphasis added.) This drafting, however, is susceptible to the critique that operationally it places primacy on tribunal discretion because of the unlikely party agreement on substantive issues.

It is within the context of this normative rubric that the parties may apply the IBA Rules, the Prague Rules, or any set of institutional rules addressing the taking and presentation of evidence in ICA. It is clear that this existing normative framework is sufficiently flexible to allow for significant contributions that may facilitate settlement and contribute process transparency and process legitimacy to ICA proceedings. The cultural and academic consciousness that settlement equals absolute efficiency, however, is a necessary predicate. Of course, at this stage, the predicate remains aspirational.

[44] Arbitration Rules Stockholm Chamber of Commerce (SCC) Arbitration Institute (in force January 1, 2023). *See also*, Deutsche Institution für Schiedsgerichtsbarkeit (DIS) Arbitration Rules (March 2018) Art. 21 (Rules of Procedure) provides:

> 21.1 The parties shall be treated equally. Each party shall have a right to be heard.
>
> 21.2 The Rules shall apply to the proceedings before the arbitral tribunal *except to the extent that the parties have agreed otherwise*.
>
> 21.3 When the Rules are silent as to the procedure to be applied in the proceedings before the arbitral tribunal, *such procedure shall be determined by agreement of the parties, in the absence of which the arbitral tribunal in its discretion shall decide upon the procedure*, after consultation with the parties.
>
> 21.4 *The arbitral tribunal shall apply all mandatory provisions of the arbitration law applicable at the seat of the pending arbitration.* (Emphasis added)

6

The "Prague Rules" and Moving beyond Formal Concerns with Evidence Taking and Closer to Maximizing the Likelihood of Settlement

The Prague Rules represent an ideal paradigm for an analysis of *optimal efficiency*. These Rules purport to have arbitration efficiency as their stated goal. They further assert that the IBA Rules, while deserving merit for attempting to bridge the civil and common law cultural divide, are wanting because the IBA Rules (in the words of the Prague Rules' drafters) favor a common law approach to evidence taking and the conduct of arbitral proceedings.

Having these two premises as organizing principles, the Prague Rules purport to temper – diminish – *party-autonomy* in favor of enhancing *arbitrator discretion*. This experiment is helpful because sustained analysis of the Prague Rules demonstrates that the vaunted civil law adjustments do not yield any greater efficiency than the *process efficiency* that is present in the IBA Rules. Therefore, by attempting to create efficiencies within a framework of *process efficiency* that only pays inconsequential lip service to *optimal efficiency*, the drafters of the Prague Rules unwittingly demonstrate that absent an evidential rules regime providing for timely risk analysis conducive to *optimal efficiency*, *process efficiency* cannot redeem arbitration's longstanding promise to be efficient.

Indeed, irrespective of the extent to which a procedural rules framework favors legacy *party-autonomy* or the exercise of *arbitrator discretion*, more is necessary. Neither approach enhances the requisite risk assessment/predictive value concerned with *optimal efficiency*.

Likewise, a more expansive definition of *party-autonomy* supporting a non-zero-sum settlement of proceedings requires an evidential regime yielding considerable predictive value. The Prague Rules, therefore, are eloquent in helping to establish the proposition that no iteration of *process efficiency* will help ICA shed the moniker that settlement in ICA proceedings simply is not a probability. In this sense, the Prague Rules' epistemic contribution is invaluable.

On September 1, 2018, a "*draft*" of a document titled "Rules on the Efficient Conduct of Proceedings in International Arbitration" (the Prague Rules) was made public and circulated. The Note from the Working Group of the draft iteration of the Prague Rules advised that the draft was to be approved in "December 2018."

That ratification ensued. The final iteration of the Prague Rules bears very close textual resemblance to the September 1, 2018 iteration. Substantively, however, the foundational premises and underlying principles contained in the draft exemplar of the Prague Rules manifestly are embodied in the final iteration that was ratified and approved on December 14, 2018.

Structurally, the Draft Prague Rules and the approved ratified Prague Rules are materially identical.[1] The Prague Rules, true to its draft predecessor, comprise twelve Articles, a Note from the Working Group, and a Preamble. Three of the four paragraphs constituting the Preamble are identical. Only a parenthetical clause contained in the first paragraph of the final iteration differs from its predecessor. This single sentence invites close attention.

The first sentence of the Preamble of the Draft Prague Rules provides:

> The Rules on the Efficient Conduct of Proceedings in International Arbitration ("the **Rules**") are intended to provide a framework and/or guidance for Arbitral Tribunals and Parties *for the efficient conduct of arbitration proceedings by using a traditional inquisitorial approach*. (Emphasis added)

The Prague Rules substitute the language highlighted in the referenced citation (*for the efficient conduct of arbitration proceedings by using a traditional inquisitorial approach*) for the qualifying clause, "on how to increase efficiency of arbitration by encouraging a more active role for Arbitral Tribunals in managing proceedings."

This difference in language represents more than just a mere restated qualification. The term contained in the actual Prague Rules, "a more active role for Arbitral Tribunals in managing proceedings," omits communicating the drafters' intent to engraft "a traditional inquisitorial approach" on the Prague Rules. Several observations are compelled.

The revised iteration of the Preamble, that logically presumably gives rise to insight into the drafters' intent. It notably is more "politically correct" because it does not give rise to a clash of juridical cultures by emphasizing a penchant for any particular legal tradition over another. Yet, it is much less eloquent than its draft predecessor in demonstrating the drafters' objective to provide the *international* arbitration community with rules that find greater conceptual affinity with a particular and very specific judicial tradition ("a traditional inquisitorial approach").

Irrespective of the judicial cultural mantle the Prague Rules may use to cloak its normative foundations, the normativity at issue is in furtherance of "how to increase [the] efficiency of arbitration..." Leaving to one side any possible cultural clash leading the Prague Rules' drafters to opine that an inquisitorially managed proceeding

[1] There are only two modifications as to nomenclature to the title of two Articles: Draft Prague Rules Article 1 reads: "Application of the Prague Rules," while Prague Rules Article 1 is titled: "Application of the Prague Rules." Article 12 of the Draft Prague Rules is titled: "Award," while Article 12 of the Prague Rules reads: "Deliberations."

will be more efficient than one premised on common law principles,[2] it is efficiency and the need to redeem arbitration's promise in this regard that constitutes the only objective justification ostensibly underlying the Prague Rules.

Indeed, the Prague Rules rely on the principle of efficiency as the foremost organizing precept and aspiration, albeit, at least from the drafters' perspective. The drafters opine this objective can best be attained pursuant to an inquisitorially managed process. In this regard, the Prague Rules do not purport to represent a hybrid formulation aiming to establish equipoise between "competing" legal traditions. The Rules do not aspire to have arrived at a golden mean that would establish equipoise between *arbitrator discretion* and party autonomy: a ratio that is conducive to *optimal efficiency*.

Similar insights into the (i) drafters' intent, (ii) policies, and (iii) objectives can be gleaned from the considerable propositions candidly contained in the Rules' Note from the Working Group. Many of the central premises, however, studiously were omitted from the more tempered and neutral-sounding final iteration.

The Note from the Working Group does assert, as it must, that in the drafters' view, "[o]ne of the ways to increase the efficiency of arbitral proceedings is to encourage Tribunals to take a more active role in managing the proceedings [*as is traditionally done in many civil law countries*]."[3] Indeed, in the very next sentence the drafters make clear that "[w]ith this in mind a Working Group was formed with representatives from thirty, *mainly civil law* countries."[4]

The Prague Rules' Note from the Working Group, notably, does not reflect the comprehensive gamut of assumptions upon which the Rules are based. A number of these premises, however, can be reasonably inferred from the totality of that effort's framework. Accordingly, the limited aspirational goal of this section merely is to analyze the Prague Rules' core root premises and the extent to which they may lead to *optimal efficiency*, that is to say, settlement, beyond just procedural efficiencies designed to conclude in a *zero-sum* outcome embodied in an award that is binding and enforceable.

It will be advanced that the drafters of the Prague Rules largely concern themselves with just *process efficiency* by identifying common law procedural practices that improperly managed may contribute to procedural inefficiencies. The drafters of the Prague Rules undertook this crusade under the banner of "efficiencies" while omitting to consider that: (i) settlement constitutes *optimal efficiency*, notwithstanding Art. 9 of the Rules (**Assistance in Amicable Settlement**), (ii) the connection between centralized process management and settlement is not of necessity directly proportional, and (iii) only fulsome and robust evidence gathering is conducive to the desired economic settlement that does not lead to a zero-result. These deficits do

[2] The right to present fact witnesses and to engage in cross-examination come to mind as paradigmatic in this regard.

[3] Draft Prague Rules, Note from the Working Group, at 2.

[4] *Id.* (Emphasis added.)

not necessarily lead to the conclusion that the Prague Rules are fundamentally flawed if measured by the metric of the extent to which they do or can lead to settlements.

As shall be discussed, it does raise the specter of the need to compromise, and, therefore, for universality. A visceral reaction against evidence taking in the name of efficiency certainly has a superficial seductive appeal. Deeper and more sustained analysis, however, suggests that only the plenary disclosure of evidence on the part of the parties can lead to *optimal efficiency* in the form of settlement.

The structure and governing principles organizing the Prague Rules cry for further development of conceptual doctrines that are conducive to meaningful *risk assessment* in the form of the identification and quantification of potential exposure. Their anatomy commands closer scrutiny.

6.1 TITLE AND STRUCTURE

The title of the Prague Rules appears to be something of an incomplete misnomer when read in the context of the Working Papers: Rules on the Efficient Conduct of Proceedings in International Arbitration (Prague Rules). The second and third paragraphs of the Draft Prague Rules', Note from the Working Group, explicitly suggest that the Prague Rules represent a belated countermeasure to or effort to replace, the IBA Rules. This specific language is helpful:

> The drafts of the IBA Rules on the Taking of Evidence in International Arbitration (**IBA Rules**) bridged a gap between the common law and civil law traditions taking of evidence. The IBA Rules were very successful in developing a nearly standardized procedure in international arbitration, at least for proceedings involving Parties from different legal traditions and those having significant amounts at stake.
>
> However, from a civil law perspective, the IBA Rules are still closer to common law traditions, as they follow a more adversarial approach regarding document production, fact witnesses and party-appointed experts. In addition, the Parties' entitlement to cross-examine witnesses is almost being taken for granted.

The Prague Rules' relationship, albeit ostensibly a reactionary one[5] to the IBA Rules, demonstrates that the Prague Rules' prevalent subject matter concerns the taking of evidence in international arbitration. Indeed, the very formal structure of the Prague Rules, including the single substantive standard these Rules enunciate,[6]

5 As shall be discussed, with respect to critical propositions governing the taking or admissibility (presentation) of evidence, the Prague Rules are in fact substantively, despite formal differences, closer to the IBA Rules than both the drafters of the IBA Rules and the Prague Rules, respectively, would care to admit.

6 The "relevant and material to the outcome of the case" standard first set forth in Art. 4.5.A of the Prague Rules cannot help but bring to mind the IBA Rules' "relevant to the case and material to its outcome" talisman for (i) self-disclosure, (ii) disclosure and production, and (iii) admissibility. *See* n. 62 in this chapter.

TABLE 6.1 *A comparison between the IBA and Prague Rules*

IBA	Prague
(i) Scope of application	(i) Application of Prague Rules
(ii) Consultation on evidence issues	(ii) Proactive role of the arbitral tribunal
(iii) Documents	(iii) Fact-finding
(iv) Witnesses of fact	(iv) Documentary evidence
(v) Party-appointed experts	(v) Fact witnesses
(vi) Tribunal-appointed experts	(vi) Experts
(vii) Inspections	(vii) *Iura Novit Curia*
(viii) Evidentiary hearing	(viii) Hearing
(ix) Admissibility and assessment of evidence	(ix) Assistance in amicable settlement
–	(x) Adverse inference
–	(xi) Allocation of costs
–	(xii) Deliberations

mirrors that of the IBA Rules. Table 6.1 is a comparison of IBA and Prague Rules. Thus, the absence of reference to the "taking of evidence" in the Prague Rules' title certainly is intriguing.

As a matter of practical nomenclature and transparency, reference to the explicit principal subject matter of the Prague Rules would have been welcomed. From a strictly structural perspective the Prague Rules, despite closely adhering to the IBA Rules' formal anatomy, omit the IBA Rules' Art. 5 party-appointed experts provision. This omission represents a feature that the drafters of the Prague Rules have taken great care to emphasize.

The Draft Prague Rules' Note from the Working Group identifies the IBA Rules' pronouncement on party-appointed experts as one of the features that in the drafters' view merit describing in the IBA Rules as "still closer to common law traditions, as they follow a more adversarial approach regarding … fact witnesses."[7] The omission of an Article addressing party-appointed expert witnesses, however, is much more cosmetic than substantive.

While Art. 6 of the Prague Rules, titled "Experts," primarily transfers to the arbitral tribunal the management of the appointment of experts, it does not do so without carving out significant space for the parties' suggestion of experts to be appointed. In this regard, Art. 6.2.A in part states that in cases in which the arbitral tribunal has decided to appoint an expert the tribunal "shall":

> a. *Seek suggestions from the parties as to who should be appointed as an expert.* For these purposes, the arbitral tribunal may establish the requirements for potential experts, such as qualification, availability, costs, and communicate to the parties. The arbitral tribunal shall not be bound by the candidates proposed by either party… (Emphasis added)

7 Draft Prague Rules, Note from the Working Group, at 2.

In addition to significant, albeit nonbinding, input from the parties as to the arbitral tribunal's expert appointment process, two qualifying observations are in order.

First, a party may demand examination of the arbitral tribunal's appointed expert at the final hearing.[8] This provision is somewhat remarkable within the Prague Rules' framework because the Prague Rules ostensibly minimize the importance of oral advocacy in the arbitration process.[9] This limitation on examination can be construed as a procedural measure that limits the exposure of the party proffering the evidence. Therefore, it minimizes risk that in fact could, and actually should, be conducive to constituting part of elements to be considered part of risk quantification and settlement.

Second, despite the absence of a free-standing Article addressing party-appointed expert witnesses, the practical workings of the Prague Rules' Art. 6 is not meaningfully far afield from the IBA Rules' Art. 5 (party-appointed experts). Specifically, Art. 6.5. states:

> The appointment of any expert by the Arbitral Tribunal does not preclude a Party from submitting an expert report by any expert appointed by that Party. At the request of any other party or on the Arbitral Tribunal's own initiative, such Party-appointed expert *shall be called for examination* during the hearing.[10] (Emphasis added)

Consequently, pursuant to Art. 6 of the Prague Rules, parties may submit expert reports and engage in examination of *any* expert, whether appointed by the tribunal or a party. Significantly, Art. 6.5 only references the right of a party to conduct an "examination during the hearing" of such an expert.[11] The type

8 *Id.* at Art. 6.4 providing that "[a]t the request of a party or on the arbitral tribunal's own initiative, the expert *shall* be called for examination at the hearing." (Emphasis added.)

9 By way of example, Art. 8 (Hearing) reads:

> 8.1. In order to promote cost-efficiency and to the extent appropriate for a particular case, the arbitral tribunal and the parties should seek to resolve the dispute on a documents-only basis.
> 8.2. If one of the parties requests a hearing or the arbitral tribunal itself finds it appropriate, the parties and the arbitral tribunal shall seek to organize the hearing in the most cost-efficient manner possible, *including by limiting the duration of the hearing* and using video, electronic or telephone communication to avoid unnecessary travel costs for arbitrators, parties and other participants. (Emphasis added)

Quite notably, this final iteration of Art. 8 is much more comprehensive in limiting, or altogether removing oral advocacy from a final hearing, if in fact there is to be one, than the predecessor draft Art. 8 of the Prague Rules, which merely contained the more universally adopted language providing that "[i]f one of the Parties insists on holding a hearing or the Arbitral Tribunal finds it appropriate on its own initiative, the hearing should be conducted in a cost-effective manner, including by means of electronic communication."

10 Prague Rules, at Art. 6.5.

11 The very reference to "examination" is remarkable. As noted, the IBA Rules do not mention the term "examination" in addressing the subject of questions posed by parties to witnesses.

IBA Rules Art. 8.4(a) provides for direct examination, and does so by referencing "oral testimony at an Evidentiary Hearing." Subsection (a) specifically provides that "the Claimant shall ordinarily first present the testimony of its witnesses, followed by the Respondent presenting the testimony of its

of examination, whether direct, cross, re-direct, or re-cross is not specified.[12] Article 6 of the Prague Rules as concerns party-appointed experts may be operationally no different in general terms from the IBA Rules' counterpart Art. 5.

witnesses[.]" In subsection (b), the term "direct testimony" is ascribed to this exercise. Hence, it necessarily follows that the direct testimony is in response to a direct examination.

IBA Rules 8.4(b), in part provides that "[t]he Party who initially presented the witness shall subsequently have the opportunity to ask additional questions on the matters raised in the other Parties' questioning[.]" The asking of questions by the party initially propounding the witness is a reference to redirect examination.

Notably, Art. 8.3 explicitly references "direct" and "re-direct" testimony, and therefore the corresponding form of examination that elicits such testimony, direct and re-direct examination.

The IBA Rules' studious omission of the terms "direct examination," "cross-examination," and "re-direct examination," is suggestive of an effort to avoid including procedural legal terms or "terms of art" pertaining to a particular legal system or legal culture. The context and use, however, of nomenclature such as "direct testimony" and "re-direct" testimony, however, is very clear in identifying the functional equivalent to "direct examination" and "re-direct examination." Such is conceptually and contextually more self-evident because these terms appear within a framework that explicitly references "oral testimony."

The term "oral testimony" appears nowhere in the Prague Rules.

12 A deficit shared with the IBA Rules that clouds critical evidence presentation issues. The IBA Rules Art. 8.3 prescribes that "[q]uestions to a witness during direct and re-direct testimony may not be *unreasonably leading*." (Emphasis added.) This provision very succinctly acknowledges the legitimate use of leading questions within the framework of the IBA Rules.

The US is perhaps the common law jurisdiction with the most fully developed jurisprudence on the proposition that generally leading questions are proscribed on direct examination save for specific carve-outs. *See, e.g.*, Fed. R. Evid. Rule 611 (Mode and Order of Examining Witnesses and Presenting Evidence) in relevant part reads:

(c) **Leading Questions.** Leading questions *should* not be used on direct examination except as necessary to develop the witness's testimony. Ordinarily, the court should allow leading questions:
  (1) on cross-examination; and
  (2) when a party calls a hostile witness, an adverse party, or a witness identified with an adverse party. (Emphasis added)

The Notes of Advisory Committee on Proposed Rules as to *Subdivision (c)* explains:

The rule continues the traditional view that the suggestive powers of the leading question are as a general proposition undesirable. Within this tradition, however, numerous exceptions have achieved recognition: The [i] witness who is hostile, unwilling, or biased; [ii] the child witness or [iii] the adult with communication problems; [iv] the witness whose recollection is exhausted; and [v] undisputed preliminary matters. 3 Wigmore §§ 774–778. An almost total unwillingness to reverse for infractions has been manifested by appellate courts. [Citations omitted.] The matter clearly falls within the area of control by the judge over the mode and order of interrogation and presentation and accordingly is phrased in words of suggestion rather than command.

The rule also conforms to tradition in making the use of leading questions on cross-examination a matter of right. The purpose of the qualification "ordinarily" is to furnish a basis for denying the use of leading questions when the cross-examination is cross-examination in form only and not in fact, as for example the "cross-examination" of a party by his own counsel after being called by the opponent (savoring more of re-direct) or of an insured defendant who proves to be friendly to the plaintiff.

The final sentence deals with categories of witnesses automatically regarded and treated as hostile. Rule 43(b) of the FRCP has included only "an adverse party or an officer, director, or

From a risk analysis, and therefore the extent to which Prague Rules Art. 6 is conducive to *optimal efficiency*, it falls short of its IBA Rules Art. 5.2(a)–(i) counterpart's strictures, which are conducive to *risk assessment* and at a *timely*

managing agent of a public or private corporation or of a partnership or association which is an adverse party." This limitation virtually to persons whose statements would stand as admissions is believed to be an unduly narrow concept of those who may safely be regarded as hostile without further demonstration. *See*, for example, *Maryland Casualty Co. v. Kador*, 225 F.2d 120 (5th Cir. 1955), and *Degelos v. Fidelity and Casualty Co.*, 313 F.2d 809 (5th Cir. 1963), holding despite the language of Rule 43(b) that an insured fell within it, though not a party in an action under the Louisiana direct action statute. The phrase of the rule, "witness identified with" an adverse party, is designed to enlarge the category of persons thus callable.

Major jurisdictions have mostly or *verbatim* adopted Federal Rule of Evidence 611(c) in their respective evidence code. *See, e.g.*, (Florida) **Fla. Stat. § 90.612 Mode and Order of Interrogation and Presentation. –**

(3) Leading questions should not be used on the direct examination of a witness except as may be necessary to develop the witness's testimony. Ordinarily, leading questions should be permitted on cross-examination. When a party calls a hostile witness, an adverse party, or a witness identified with an adverse party, interrogation may be by leading questions.

The judge shall take special care to protect a witness under age 14 from questions that are in a form that cannot reasonably be understood by a person of the age and understanding of the witness, and shall take special care to restrict the unnecessary repetition of questions.

The majority of state court pronouncements assert the view that leading questions on direct examination is inappropriate except for noted exceptions. *See, e.g.*, *Anderson v. State*, 517 P.3d 538, 594 (Wyo. 2022) (reiterating that "'[l]eading questions should not be used on the direct examination of a witness except as may be necessary to develop his testimony'"); *State of Montana v. Sayler*, *State v. Sayler*, 384 Mont. 497, 380 P.3d 743, 2016 MT 226 (Mont. 2016) (observing that "[t]he well-established exception to using leading questions is within M.R. Evid. 611(c). This exception recognizes the use of leading questions on direct examination with a 'child witness or an adult with communication problems.'"); *State of New Jersey v. Bueso*, 137 A.3d 516, 524 (N.J. 2016) (same); *State of Connecticut v. Saliman*, 949 A.2d 1092, 1127–28 (Conn. 2008) (observing that "[l]eading questions generally are inappropriate on direct or re-direct examination of a witness, although the court has discretion to allow them under certain circumstances [citation omitted], … the court may permit leading questions when they are 'necessary to develop a witness' testimony ….' The commentary [citation omitted] explains that, under that exception, the court 'may allow the calling party to put leading questions to a young witness who is apprehensive or reticent' or 'to a witness who has trouble communicating, by virtue of either a disability or language deficiency ….' [citation omitted]"); and *State of Ohio v. Drummond*, 854 N.E.2d 1038, 1065 (Ohio 2006) (stating that "[a] leading question is 'one that suggests to the witness the answer desired by the examiner.' [citation omitted] '[L]eading questions should not be used on the direct examination of a witness except as may be necessary to develop his testimony.' However, the trial court has discretion to allow leading questions on direct examination.").

Therefore, IBA Rules Art. 8.3 proscribing only "unreasonably" leading questions in the context of direct and re-direct testimony is actually conceptually broader than the codification contained in the U.S. Federal Rules of Evidence (Rule 611(c)), as well as the majority view on the issue throughout the 50 U.S. state jurisprudence.

The IBA Rules Art. 3 pronouncement on the use of leading questions and direct and re-direct examination also provides a compelling predicate from which it may be inferred that the Rules contemplate the exercise of leading questions on cross-examination, or in the vernacular of the IBA Rules, the questioning by "any other party" of a witness "following [the] direct testimony [of that witness]." (IBA Rules Art. 8.4(b).)

procedural juncture.[13] The party-appointed expert disclosure requirements embodied in IBA Art. 5.2(a)–(i) are indispensable predicates to the ability of an opposing party to assess the likely effectiveness of a party-appointed expert.

Aside from disclosure of such determinative information such as (i) the particular instructions with respect to which the expert is providing opinions and conclusions,[14] (ii) disclosure of facts upon which expert opinions and conclusions are premised,[15] (iii) disclosure of actual opinions and conclusions, together with methodology applied and evidence and other data relied upon that are yet to be disclosed,[16] Art. 5 commands party-appointed experts to disclose /information that may lead to impeachment and even disqualification. The counterpart Prague Rules, Arts. 5 and 6, are bereft of any comparable requirement.

By way of example, IBA Rules Art. 5 compels party-appointed experts to disclose (i) present and past relationships, to the extent they exist, with any of the stakeholders to the proceeding, including the arbitral tribunal,[17] (ii) the expert witness' independence from all stakeholders to the proceeding, including the arbitral tribunal and legal counsel,[18] and (iii) an affirmation of the expert's genuine belief regarding the correctness of the opinions expressed in the report.[19] Also in this connection, Art. 5.2(i) compels disclosure of authorship attribution to the extent that an expert report is signed by more than one expert.

[13] IBA Rules Art. 5.2 provides:

> 2. The Expert Report shall contain:
> (a) The full name and address of the Party-Appointed expert, a statement regarding his or her present and past relationship (if any) with any of the Parties, their legal advisors and the Arbitral Tribunal, and a description of his or her background, qualifications, training and experience;
> (b) A description of the instructions pursuant to which he or she is providing his or her opinions and conditions;
> (c) A statement of his or her independence from the Parties, their legal advisors and the Arbitral Tribunal;
> (d) A statement of the facts on which he or she is basing his or her expert opinions and conclusions;
> (e) His or her expert opinions and conclusions, including a description of the methods, evidence and information used in arriving at the conclusions. Documents on which the Party-Appointed Expert relies that have not already been submitted shall be provided;
> (F) if the Expert Report has been translated, a statement as to the language in which it was originally prepared, and the language in which the Party-Appointed Expert anticipates giving testimony at the Evidentiary Hearing;
> (g) an affirmation of his or her genuine belief in the opinions expressed in the Expert Report;
> (h) the signature of the Party-Appointed Expert and its date and place; and
> (i) if the Expert Report has been signed by more than one person, an attribution of the entirety or specific parts of the Expert Report to each author.

[14] *Id*. Art. 5.2(b).

[15] *Id*. Art. 5.2 (d).

[16] *Id*. Art. 5.2 (e).

[17] *Id*. Art. 5.2 (a).

[18] *Id*. Art. 5.2 (c).

[19] *Id*. Art. 5.2 (g).

Although at first blush these requirements appear to be but a formal disclosure of a perfunctory nature only, they actually can be essential for purposes of (i) evaluating the substantive integrity of the report (i.e., its quality and reliability), and (ii) cross-examination. The absence of these disclosure requirements is generally problematic, but all the more disconcerting in the context of settlement analysis.

The conduct of a case dispositive hearing, that is to say, an evidentiary hearing on jurisdiction or merits, under Prague Rules Art. 8,[20] is reduced to three single-sentence paragraphs. These scant "instructions" do not (i) inform any of the stakeholders to the arbitration on the order of presentation of proof, (ii) the type of questions as to form or substance that can be posed to a witness, (iii) the order in which a witness may be questioned by a party adverse to the party proffering the witness, or (iv) the extent to which objections to questions posed can be raised, (v) let alone the form and substantive content of any such objections.[21]

The lack of guidance in Prague Rules Art. 8 (Hearing) can hardly be deemed to maximize cost-efficiency. To the contrary, Prague Rules Art. 8 sets forth a *black box* that fails to assert any organizing principle beyond general references to "cost-efficiency" and "cost-efficient manner possible," without further guidance beyond suggesting the limitation on the duration of the hearing.

It is an untested assumption, and less than a clear one, that focusing on what purports to be only *process efficiency*, and even then in a manner that excludes any reference to the structure of the evidentiary hearing and the order of proof, can at all contribute to *process efficiency*, let alone *optimal efficiency* in the form of settlement. The absence of a structured architecture within which the arbitral tribunal would exercise its inherent powers constitutes an extremist position with respect to *process efficiency*, and even legitimacy, that engrafts uncertainty to the proceeding as a whole.

Parties are left with no recourse but to speculate concerning the (i) general structure of a final hearing, (ii) order of proof, (iii) if and how witnesses are to be examined, (iv) formal and substantive evidentiary objections, (v) extent to which witness statements, if at all, are predicates to testimony, or even (vi) scope of examinations to the extent that there are any, are hardly in a position to identify, quantify, and

[20] *See* n. 22 that follows.

[21] Prague Rules Art. 8 (Hearing) stands in high relief to its IBA Art. 8 (Evidentiary Hearing) counterpart. This latter Article provides transparency and predictive value by setting forth a comprehensive structure for the evidentiary hearing, while still preserving "complete control over the evidentiary hearing" for the Arbitral Tribunal. IBA Art. 8 (Evidentiary Hearing) in relevant part reads:

> 3. The Arbitral Tribunal shall at all times have complete control over the Evidentiary Hearing. The Arbitral Tribunal may limit or exclude any question to, answer by or appearance of a witness, if it considers such question, answer or appearance to be irrelevant, immaterial, unreasonably burdensome, duplicative or otherwise covered by a reason for objection set forth in Articles 9.2 or 9.3. Questions to a witness during direct and re-direct testimony may not be unreasonably leading.

communicate evidentiary risk with sufficient certainty so as to contribute to meaningful settlement analyses.

The Prague Rules' wresting of *party-autonomy* from the arbitral procedure, and emphasis on an inquisitorial approach on the part of the arbitral tribunal, simply cannot constitute a reasonable factual premise from which it could be inferred that (i) procedural efficiencies and (ii) *optimal efficiency* (settlement) are maximized. To the contrary, this transformation of the procedural governing arbitral proceedings from a dynamic of tension between *party-autonomy* and *arbitrator discretion* (inherent powers of arbitrators) in furtherance of a delicate but necessary equipoise, into a strictly tribunal-driven process lacking evidentiary and procedural predictive value, only can lead to uncertainty and inefficiencies.

The extent to which fact and expert witnesses would be able to sustain spirited cross-examination can be, and typically is, a material element of risk analysis. Like its IBA Rules counterpart,[22] the Prague Rules do not mention the term "cross-examination."[23]

Despite the Prague Rules' formal discouragement of cross-examination,[24] and of orality generally as part of the arbitral process,[25] they in fact provide sufficient conceptual latitude so as to accord parties with a reasonable expectation that posing questions to a witness tendered by an adverse party is *not* textually foreclosed, and, to the contrary, finds reasonable support in the ordinary and plain language in Art. 5, subsection 5.9. This provision states:

> At the hearing, the examination of any *fact witness* shall be conducted under the direction and control of the arbitral tribunal. The arbitral tribunal can reject a question posed to the witness if the arbitral tribunal considers it to be irrelevant, redundant, not material to the outcome of the case or for other reasons. After having heard the parties, the arbitral tribunal may also impose other restrictions, including setting the order of examination of the witnesses, time limits for examination or types of questions to be allowed or hold witness conferences, as it deems appropriate. (Emphasis added)

[22] *United States of America, Appellee, v. David Stevens, Defendant-appellant*, 985 F.2d 1175 (2nd Cir. 1993); and *see id. at* 1181, *citing to United States v. McElroy*, 697 F. 2d 459, 465 (2nd Cir. 1982).

[23] The closest *suggestion* to cross-examination within the Prague Rules is found in Art. 5.7, which reads: "However, if a party insists on calling a witness whose witness statement has been submitted by the other party, as a general rule, the arbitral tribunal should call the witness to testify at the hearing, unless there are good reasons not to do so." This provision textually concerns the oral examination of an adverse witness, which is tantamount to cross-examination, to some extent. *See* nn. 12 and 13 in this chapter.

[24] As previously referenced in this chapter, the Prague Rules' draft Note from the Working Group distances the Prague Rules by noting that pursuant to the IBA Rules, "the party's entitlement to cross-examined witnesses is almost being taken for granted." The draft Preamble underscores that the Prague Rules "are intended to provide a framework and/or guidance for Arbitral Tribunals and Parties for the efficient conduct of arbitration proceedings by using a traditional inquisitorial approach." Such "traditional inquisitorial approach" does not contemplate cross-examination.

[25] See n. 10 in this chapter.

The reference to "a question posed to the witness" by a party with respect to which the arbitral tribunal will consider whether such question is "irrelevant, redundant, [and/or] not material to the outcome of the case," states the textual case for the oral interrogation of witnesses in the context of both direct and cross-examination. The text, however, is devoid of any reference to the manner and circumstances pursuant to which questions are posed to a *fact witness* during an "examination" at the hearing. This literal narrative, together with the Note from the Working Group, are enough to alert the parties to the very reasonable likelihood that the proceeding may be conducted without according parties the right to cross-examine witnesses.

This procedural uncertainty is inimical to *risk assessment* with respect to the effectiveness of areas where parties may seek cross-examination vulnerabilities in their own case, as well as concerning adverse witnesses (fact and expert).[26] Technically, the inherent powers of an arbitral tribunal grant the arbitral tribunal authority to control every aspect of the manner in which an evidentiary or final hearing is conducted, particularly in light of the command on the part of most institutional arbitral rules directed at arbitrators to manage proceedings expeditiously and efficiently.[27]

The Prague Rules add five Articles that are not contained in the IBA Rules counterparts.[28] Three of these five Articles, although not set forth as individual Articles in the IBA Rules, substantively form part of them.[29]

[26] Prague Rules subsection 5.9, in part, states that "the arbitral tribunal may also impose other restrictions [on the examination of witnesses], *including setting the order of examination of the witnesses*, time limits for examination or *types of questions to be allowed* or hold witness conferences, as it deems appropriate." (Emphasis added.)

[27] *See* Chapter 2, n. 12 in this volume. "The due process cornerstone right to be heard and to present a case has overshadowed, if not altogether eviscerated, its twin principle in the form of 'a right of how to present a case.' In fact, this right has not been cognizable at law." Pedro J. Martínez-Fraga, "Developing Equipoise Between Party-Autonomy and the Inherent Power of Arbitrator Discretion in the Gathering of Evidence in International Arbitration," in *Inherent Powers of Arbitrators* (Franco Ferrari & Friedrich Rosenfeld eds.) (JurisNet, 2019), chapter 8, 209.

[28] The Prague Rules contain the following five Articles that have no counterpart in the IBA Rules:

(i) Article 7 (*Iura Novit Curia*),
(ii) Article 9 (Assistance in Amicable Settlement),
(iii) Article 10 (Adverse Inference),
(iv) Article 11 (Allocation of Costs), and
(v) Article 12 (Deliberations).

See Prague Rules in Table 6.1.

[29] *Id.*, at Art. 10 (Adverse Inference) substantively and identically is set forth in IBA Rules Art. 9.6, which asserts:

> If a Party fails without satisfactory explanation to produce any Document requested in a Request to Produce which it has not objected in due time or fails to produce any Document ordered to be produced by the Arbitral Tribunal, the Arbitral Tribunal *may infer that such document would be adverse to the interests of that Party*. (Emphasis added)

As with the different formatting and editorial techniques addressing the treatment of party-appointed experts in the Prague Rules, the adverse inference stricture set forth in Art. 10 of those Rules is substantively and functionally indistinguishable from its IBA counterpart. Both sets of Rules provide for the possible application of an adverse inference arising from party noncompliance.

Article 11 (Allocation of Costs) of the Prague Rules of course provides that "[w]hen deciding on the allocation of costs in an award, the Arbitral Tribunal may take into the account the Parties' conduct during the arbitral proceedings, including their cooperation and assistance (or the lack thereof) in conducting the proceedings in a cost-efficient and expeditious manner." From a broad and very general policy perspective, this Article substantively is *similar* to Art. 9.8 of the IBA Rules.[30]

The operational principle of the two Rules is identical. The only difference rests in the IBA Rules' reliance on "good faith" whereas conceptually the Prague Rules use a pragmatic litmus test: namely, "cost-efficient and expeditious manner."[31] Certainly the argument can be made that the Prague Rules in this regard provide a more objective test.

Hence, the two sets of Rules, as to this issue as well, have considerable points of intersection and commonality than would first appear to be the case if focus only is limited to underscoring the extent to which the Prague Rules operate on the assumption that diminishing *party-autonomy*, deemphasizing document production (without eviscerating it and referring it to *arbitrator discretion*), and deemphasizing all aspects of oral advocacy, is conducive to maximum *process efficiency*. The IBA and the Prague Rules are fundamentally concerned with different approaches to *process efficiency* only. Oddly, more unites the two sets of rules than separates them.

The Prague Rules do, however, set forth two very novel and remarkable sections, Art. 7 (*Iura Novit Curia*)[32] and Art. 9 (Assistance in Amicable Settlements). Both provisions compel discussion. Only Art. 9 (Assistance in Amicable Settlement) can lead to *optimal efficiency*, but only when fully and appropriately integrated into the structure of relevant provisions. This integration, as discussed later, is absent.

30 *See* IBA Rules (2020), *see* Chapter 8, n. 68 in this volume, at Art. 9.8, Prague Rules at Art. 11.

31 Prague Rules, Art. 11.

32 Article 7 (*Iura Novit Curia*) reads:

> 7.1. A Party bears the burden of proof with respect to the legal position on which it relies.
>
> 7.2. However, the Arbitral Tribunal may apply legal provisions not pleaded by the Parties if it finds it necessary, including, but not limited to, public policy Rules. In such cases, the Arbitral Tribunal shall seek the Parties' views on the legal provisions it intends to apply. The Arbitral Tribunal may also rely on legal authorities even if not submitted by the Parties if they relate to legal provisions pleaded by the Parties and provided that the Parties have been given an opportunity to express their views in relation to such legal authorities.

Prague Rules, Art. 7.

6.2 *IURA NOVIT CURIA*

Iura Novit Curia is far removed from being a construct conducive to *optimal efficiency*. Certainly, the relative merits of the application of *Iura Novit Curia* in international arbitration have been amply chronicled.[33] Commentators, arbitrators, arbitration counsel, and sophisticated consumers of arbitration services dispute the extent to which central features unique to arbitration as a dispute resolution methodology are structurally and substantively compatible with this doctrine.[34] Certainly, it is contrary to *risk assessment* and, therefore, to *optimal efficiency*.

[33] *See generally* Giuditta Cordero-Moss, "General Report on *Jura Novit* Arbiter," in Iura Novit Cura *in International Arbitration* (Franco Ferrari & Giuditta Cordero-Moss eds.) 477 (Juris Publishing 2018).

[34] Rosenfeld, for example, assumes a position of compromise and conceptual reconciliation pursuant to which he used *Iura Novit Curia* as sufficiently pliant or inapposite to international arbitration depending on the application of either a "party-centric" or a "poly-centric" paradigm of where an international adjudication is at stake. In turn, the applicability of either paradigm is based on multiple factors that, among others, include: (i) the authority, resources and legal expertise of the adjudicator, (ii) the legal expertise and relative strength of the parties as well as (iii) the interests of the international community may affect the assessment of which of the two paradigms prevail. Freidrich Rosenfeld, "*Iura Novit Curia* International Law," in Jura Novit Curia *in International Arbitration* 461 (Franco Ferrari & Freidrich Rosenfeld eds.) (Juris Publishing 2018). Although comprehensive and boasting the seductive powers of seeming to reconcile all objections through a "case-by-case" and dual-shifting paradigms, Rosenfeld's helpful approach raises more queries that it could ever hope to address satisfactorily. Not the least of which is the requirement for civil traditions to yield to "a totality of circumstances" approach that is unlikely to find resonance in such quarters.

See, e.g., (A) *In favor of the principle*: (i) Bing Cheng, *General Principles of Law as Applied by International Courts to Tribunals* (Stevens & Sons 1953), 299–301 ("questions of law, as distinct from questions of fact, need not be raised by the parties themselves but the Court can and should examine them *propio motu*." *Citing PCJ International Commission of the River Oder Case* (1929)); (ii) Graham Cook, A *Digest WTO Jurisprudence on Public International Law Concepts and Principles* ¶ 725 (Cambridge University Press 2015) ("It being the duty of the court itself to ascertain and apply the relevant law in the given circumstances of the case, the burden of establishing or proving rules of international law cannot be imposed upon any of the parties, for the law lies within the judicial knowledge of the Court." *Citing* ICJ Fisheries Jurisdiction Case (*United Kingdom of Great Britain and Northern Ireland v. Iceland*) Merits (1974)); (iii) Takne Sugiahra, "The Principle of *Jura Novit Curia* in the International Court of Justice: With Reference to Recent Decisions," 55 *Japanese Y. B. Int'l L.* 77, 109 (2012) (the article mentions that Judge Leuterpacht "emphasized the necessity of the maximum reinforcement of the operations for the improvement of the quality and authority of Court's decisions. At the same time, this reinforcement is bound to inspire *the Jura Novit Curia principle*.") (Emphasis added); (iv) Georges Abi-Saab, "The International Court as a World Court," in *Fifty Years of the International Court of Justice: Essays in Honor of Sir Robert Jennings* (Vaughan Lowe & Malgosia Fitzmaurice eds.) (Cambridge University Press 1996), 3–16; (v) James Hope, "Why Choose Stockholm: Reflections of an English Lawyer after Two Years Practicing International Arbitration in Sweden," 2 *Stockholm Int'l Arb. Rev.* 21–38 (2008) ("'In Swedish court practice, and in purely domestic arbitration, the principle of *Jura Novit Curia* applies' … however, the general view appears to be that the principle 'should be modified for international arbitration proceedings,' because '[i]t is simply not true that the arbitrator knows the law.'"); (vi) Swiss law generally holds in favor of the principle of *Iura Novit Curia*; **(A)** Federal Tribunal established that it is an obligation for the arbitrators to apply the law *ex officio* (Decision 4 P. 100/2003, 22 ASA Bulletin (2004) No. 22, at 574 ff. especially figure 5, at 579); **(B)** *Against the use of the principle*; *see, e.g.*, (i) Zdeněk Kühn, "The Authoritarian Legal Culture at Work: The Passivity of the Parties and the Interpretational Statements of Supreme Courts," 2 *CYELP*. 25, 25–26 (2006):

The notion that parties and an arbitral panel from diverse jurisdictions and legal cultures can somehow engraft on the panel the affirmative obligation "to know" the law and related issues that the parties have not identified or considered can in no way lead to procedural predictive value that is rendered all the less workable in the context of a genuine international dispute with a corresponding arbitral tribunal.

Even the Prague Rules' ostensible concern with *process efficiency* is belied by what appears to be the overriding objective of institutionalizing an inquisitorial procedural structure at the expense of arbitrator immunity. The likelihood of *optimal*

> Judges are the final authoritative interpreters not because they are omniscient and infallible, but because of their function and status within the legal system. The authority of the judge to decide the case "correctly" is ultimately tested by real-life cases. If understood from this perspective, abstract judicial interpretational statements are not only against the very core of authoritative legal discourse, they are also in conflict with the basic tenets of the separation of powers.

(ii) Emmanuel Gaillard & John Savage (eds.), *Fouchard, Gaillard, Goldman: On International Commercial Arbitration* (Kluwer Law International 1999) (authors find that the application of the principle *Iura Novit Curia* is "inadequate" for arbitration); (iii) Julian D. M. Lew, Loukas A. Mistelis & Stefan M. Kröll, *Comparative International Commercial Arbitration* 442 (2003) ("In contrast to courts, Tribunals may have to apply more often than not laws they are not necessarily familiar with," cited by Christian P. Alberti, "*Iura Novit Curia* in Commercial Arbitration: How Much Justice Do You Want?," in *International Arbitration and International Commercial Law: Synergy, Convergence and Evolution* 3 (S. Kröll et al. eds.) (Wolters Kluwer 2011)); (iv) John Chong & Michael J. Moser, *Hong Kong SAR Asia Arbitration Handbook* (2011), 189–98 ("[M]ost Hong Kong tribunals would hesitate to apply the maxim *Iura Novit Curia* ..."); (v) Gabrielle Kaufmann-Kohler, "*The Governing Law: Law Or Fact?*," in *Best Practices in International Arbitration: ASA Swiss Arbitration Association Conference*, January 27, 2006, Zürich, ASA Special Series (Markus Wirth ed.) (Association Suisse de L'Arbitrage 2006), 84 ("[A] hard and fast *Iura Novit Curia* rule would be inappropriate in international arbitration. This is due to the transnational legal environment involving participants from different legal cultures, and to the possible difficulties of accessing the applicable law, be it for reasons of language, availability, or reliability of the pertinent sources"); (vi) Yves Derains, "Observations-Cour d'App de Paris (1 re Ch. C) 13 Novembre 1997 – Lemeur v SAR Les Cités Invisible," 1998 *Rev. Arb.* 711 (1998) ("L'adag *jura novit curia* n'a pas sa palce en matière d´arbitrage [the *jura novit curia* has no place in arbitration]"); (vii) Rodrigo Jijón & Daniela Páez, "¿Cabe la aplicación del principio Iura Novit Curia en el arbitraje comercial?," 5 *Revista Ecuatoriana de Arbitraje*, 161 (2013) ("in conclusion, in international arbitration, the belief that arbitrators know the law is, to put it mildly, debatable." In the original Spanish language reads: "En conclusión, en el arbitraje internacional la creencia de que los árbitros conocen el derecho es, por decirlo en términos livianos, debatable."); (C) *Eclectic position*: (i) Nigel Blackaby & Ricardo Chirinos, "Consideraciones Sobre la Aplicación del Principio Iura Novit Curia en el Arbitraje Comercial Internacional," 6 *Anu. Colomb. Derecho Int.* 77, 88 (2013)

> *La forma más adecuada para abordar la aplicación del principio de Iura Novit Curia en arbitraje comercial internacional es a través de una postura intermedia que responda a la necesidad de poner todos los intereses en la balanza .... Por un lado, el tribunal debe analizar los argumentos de las partes ...." Al tiempo que "es natural y aconsejable que los miembros del tribunal, en caso de tener legítimas dudas sobre puntos concretos de derecho, puedan indagar por su propia cuenta para aclararlas....*

(ii) Joanna Jemielniak & Stefanie Phisteer, "Should Arbitrators Know the Law? The *Iura Novit Curia* Principle in International Commercial Arbitration," University of Copenhagen, Conference of Nov. 7, 2014 (2014) (*Iura Novit Curia* principle has a place in international arbitration. However, its application needs to take into account the interaction of the principle with other fundamental procedural precepts.)

efficiency (settlement) is maximized when *party-autonomy* and *arbitrator discretion* are at equipoise. The Prague Rules generally, and particularly with the inclusion of *Iura Novit Curia*, do not render this ratio at all viable.

Another seemingly universal tenet with respect to the relationship between *Iura Novit Curia* and international arbitration is that the doctrine does violence to *party-autonomy*. While it is beyond the scope of this writing to trace the contours of the many legal propositions and rulings from multiple jurisdictions that directly or implicitly grant weight to the proposition that *Iura Novit Curia* is contrary to international commercial arbitration because it adversely compromises the polestar principle of *party-autonomy*,[35] three salient premises require attention.[36]

First, the normative allocation of adjudicatory obligations pertaining to a party in a judicial proceeding and a judge differs from that of a party and an arbitral tribunal. Arbitrators are charged with applying the parties' choice of law and "*adjudicating*" the issue presented to them.[37] These narrow parameters do not apply to dispute

[35] Treaty-based arbitral awards are far from being unanimous as to the applicability of *Iura Novit Arbiter*. *See, e.g.*, favoring application of the doctrine: (i) *Jan Oostergetel and Theodora Laurentius v. The Slovac Republic*, UNCITRAL, Award ¶ 141 (April 23, 2012); (ii) *Metal-Tech Ltd. v. Republic of Uzbekistan*, ICSID Case No. ARB/10/3, Award ¶ 287 (October 4, 2013); (iii) *Daimler Financial Services A.G. v. Argentine Republic*, ICSID Case No. ARB/05-1, Decision on Annulment, ¶ 295 (January 7, 2015); (iv) *Quiborax S.A. and Non-Metallic Minerals S.A. v. Pluri National State of Bolivia*, ICSID Case No. ARB/06/2, Award ¶ 92 (September 16, 2015); (v) *Vestey Group Ltd. v. Bolivarian Republic of Venezuela*, ICSID Case No. ARB/06/4, Award ¶ 118 (April 25, 2016); (vi) *Churchill Mining PLC and Planet Mining Prty Ltd v. the Republic of Indonesia*, ICSID Case No. ARB/12/14, Award ¶ 72 (December 6, 2016); (vii) *Burlington Resources, Inc. v. Republic of Ecuador*, ICSID Case No. ARB/08/5, Decision on Reconsideration and Award, ¶¶ 45, 155 (February 7, 2017); (viii) *Jürgen Wirtgen v. Argentine Republic*, ICSID Case No. ARB/14/32, Decision on Jurisdiction ¶ 172 (June 29, 2018); (ix) *Werfen Austria GMbH v. Polar Electro Europe B.V.*, Finnish Supreme Court, Case No. 1517 of July 2, 2008.

Standing in contrast to this authority rejecting application of the doctrine *see, e.g.*, (i) *Klöckner Industrie-Anlagen Gmbh v. United Republic of Cameroon*, ICSID Case No. ARB/01/2, Ad Hoc Committee Decision on Annulment ¶ 91 (May 3, 1985); (ii) *Enron Corp. v. Argentine Republic*, ICSID Case No. ARB/01/3, Decision on the Application for Annulment of the Argentine Republic ¶ 375 (July 30, 2010); (iii) *Caratube Int'l Oil Co. LLP v. Republic of Kazakhstan*, ICSD Case No. ARB/08/12, December on the Annulment Application of Caratube Int'l Oil Co. LLP, ¶ 95 (February 21, 2014); (iv) Tribunal Fédéral (TF) (Federal Tribunal) September 30, 2003, 100/2003, ¶ 6.2 (Switz.); and (v) *Luis Dreyfus S.A. v. Holding Tusculum B.V.*, Quebec Superior Court, December 8, 2008, ¶¶ 106–108.

[36] National courts are divided on the applicability of the doctrine to international commercial arbitration disputes. *See generally* Cordero-Moss, "General Report on *Jura Novit* Arbiter," 477.

[37] *See* Piero Bernardini, "The Role of the International Arbitrator," 20 *Arb. Int'l.* 113 (2014); V. V. Veeder, *The Historical Keystone to International Arbitration: The Party-Appointed Arbitrator: From Miami to Geneva*, Proceedings of the ASIL Annual Meeting (Cambridge University Press 2013), 107: 387–40; Sundaresh Menon, "Adjudicator, Advocate, or Something in Between? Coming to Terms with the Role of the Party-Appointed Arbitrator," 34 *J. Int'l. Arb.* 348, 351–354 (2017); Andreas F. Lowenfeld, "The Party-Appointed Arbitrator in International Controversies: Some Reflections," 30 *Tex. Int'l L.J.* 59 (1995); and Yves Derains, "The Deliberations of the Arbitral Tribunal – 'Retour au délibéré arbitral'," in *The Resolution of the Dispute: From the Hearing to the Award, ASA Special Series* No. 29, chapter 2 (Markus Wirth ed.) (Association Suisse de L'Arbitrage 2007).

resolution in a judicial context pursuant to which a judge represents a State's exercise of sovereignty through the judicial system.

Second, *Iura Novit Curia*, if applied to an international arbitration proceeding, would transfer to the arbitral tribunal a normative authority that both broadens and deepens all of the already considerable inherent powers of *arbitrator discretion* vested in the tribunal,[38] while tearing deeply into the fabric of *party-autonomy*; namely, the specific set of party expectations arising from the election of the applicable substantive law

Absent explicit reference to *Iura Novit Curia* in an arbitration clause, or its indirect incorporation by citing to sponsoring institutional arbitral rules that include the doctrine,[39] the parties' choice of law cannot contemplate the doctrine's application. This paradox is not susceptible to reconciliation.

[38] *See* Pedro J. Martínez-Fraga, *The American Influence on International Commercial Arbitration: Doctrinal Developments and Discovery Methods*, 2nd ed. (Cambridge University Press 2019), 54–55, discussing the inherent powers of arbitrators in the context of evidence gathering in comparison with a judge, observes:

> The adjudicative role of arbitrators differs from that of judges with respect to the pivotal element of discretion. Arbitrator discretion is virtually boundless. Moses observes that the International Law Association issued a report in April 2014 that defines as the "discretionary powers" of an arbitrator those powers "which are the broad powers generally provided for but not specifically enumerated in the arbitration rules or governing law." [Citation omitted]
>
> This broad power inherent to arbitrators that appears in the form of arbitrator discretion has a distinctive nature that defies tidy classification schemes. Its only check and balance are the mechanical, almost visceral, fall-back catch-all category of "procedural due process." With respect to the gathering of evidence, for example, this discretion is qualified only by the general standard "relevant to the case and material to its outcome." [Citation omitted] Therefore, the scope of, weight attributed to, an admissibility of evidence are all governed by this single general standard. [citation omitted] Indeed, the institutional rules of all major arbitral institutions represent a normative basis for the exercise of the broadest arbitral discretion with respect to all procedural phases of an arbitration, including the conduct of hearings. [Citation omitted]

See also, Chang Seung Wha, "Inherent Powers of the Arbitral Tribunal to Investigate Its Own Jurisdiction," 29 *J. Int'l. Arb.* 171 (2012); Sam Luttrell & Isuru Devendra, "Inherent Jurisdiction and Implied Power to Stay Proceedings in Aid of Arbitration: A Nice Question," 32 *J. Int'l. Arb.* 493 (2015); Alejandro E. Leañez, "The Future of the Anti-suit Injunctions: The Power of the Arbitral Tribunal to Issue Anti-suit Injunctions," 14 *Vindobona J. Int'l & Comm. L. & Arb.* 33 (2010); Chester Brown, "The Inherent Powers of International Courts and Tribunals," 76 *Brit. Y. B. Int'l. L.* 195 (2006); Robert Peitrowski, "Evidence in International Arbitration," 22 *Arb. Int'l.* 373, 379 (2006) (observing the tribunals "inherent power to determine the probative value of all of the evidence."); Janet A. Rosen, "Arbitration under Private International Law: The Doctrines of Separability and Compétenz de la Compétenz," 17 *Fordham Int'l. J.* 599, 610 (1993) ("it is widely accepted that the arbitral tribunal's power to investigate its own jurisdiction (*compétenz de la compétenz*) is a power inherent in the appointment of the tribunal"); Alan Redfern, "The Jurisdiction of International Commercial Arbitrator," 3 *J. Int'l. Arb.* 19, 27 (1986) ("It is generally accepted that an arbitral tribunal has power to investigate its own jurisdiction."); Margaret L. Moses, "Inherent Power of Arbitrators to Deal with Ethical Issues," *Loyola Univ. Chicago School of Law, Public Law Research Paper*, No. 2014-016.

[39] Most sponsoring arbitral institutions have not crafted a *Iura Novit Curia* default rule. The LCIA (2020) represents a notable exception: under Art. 22 (Additional Powers), subsection 22.1(iii) reads:

Arbitration aspires to be as self-standing as possible notwithstanding necessary reliance on the State and on an international law regime. National-State rules of civil procedure are of limited application.[40] Such rules would only apply to compulsory practice directed at parties and non-parties, and contingent on the qualifications of the applicable national arbitration law addressing set-aside only in the enforcement phase. By way of example, the U.S. Supreme Court has made clear that procedural rules forming part of arbitration agreements shall not be displaced by the procedural frameworks pertaining to the choice of law provision of the jurisdiction selected.[41]

It is thus from a procedural law perspective conceptually impossible to reconcile *Iura Novit Curia* with the principle of *party-autonomy* because application of the doctrine would fall beyond the ken of the party's choice of law.

Third, although the principle of *party-autonomy* is far from absolute and its prominence often overstated in the context of international commercial arbitration,[42]

22.1 The Arbitral Tribunal shall have the power, upon the application of any party or (save for sub-paragraph (x) below) upon its own initiative, but in either case only after giving the parties a reasonable opportunity to state their views and upon such terms (as to costs and otherwise) as the Arbitral Tribunal may decide:

***

(iii) to conduct such enquiries as may appear to the Arbitral Tribunal to be necessary or expedient, including whether and to what extent the Arbitral Tribunal should itself take the initiative in identifying relevant issues and ascertaining relevant facts and the law(s) or rules of law applicable to the Arbitration Agreement, the arbitration and the merits of the parties' dispute[.]

The ICDR, ICC, and SCC do not reference the principle or otherwise incorporate the doctrine. It is critical to note, however, that there is authority under Swedish law providing that within the framework of procedural guidance so as to preserve due process and avert unforeseen arguments, arbitrators are empowered to raise legal provisions that have not been asserted. *See* Government Bill 1998/99: 35 at 120 and 146; *see also* City Sakerhet (i) Stockholm AB, Reg. No. 556747-2138 The Safe Team I Sverig A B, Reg. No. 556336-1681, Herkulesgatan (i) 417 01 Gothenburg, Matter: Challenge of Arbitration Award tendered in Stockholm on Dec. 11, 2015 SVA COURT OF APPEAL, Department 02, Division 020106.

The DIS Rules *border* in adopting *Iura Novit Curia*, Art. 28 (Establishing the Facts, Tribunal-Appointed Expert), in relevant part, is particularly intriguing on this point:

2.82 For this purpose, the arbitral tribunal may, *inter alia* on its own initiative, appoint experts, examine witnesses other than those called by the parties, and order any party to product or make available any document or electronically stored data. *The arbitral tribunal shall not be limited to admit only evidence offered by the parties*. (Emphasis added.)

40 *See* Gordon Blanke, "The Use of National Civil Procedure Rules in International Arbitration," 9 *ERA Forum*, 283, 283–290 (2008).

41 *Preston v. Ferrer*, 128 S. Ct. 978, 81 (2008). The Supreme Court identified the issue before it as whether "the FAA overrides not only state statutes that refer certain state law controversies initially to a judicial forum, but also state statutes that refer certain disputes initially to an administrative agency?" The query was answered in the affirmative, holding "that when parties agree to arbitrate all questions arising under a contract, state laws logging primary jurisdiction in another forum, whether judicial or administrative, are superseded by the FAA." *Id.*

42 The competence of a party as a consequence of age or health (to cite only two factors) represents a limit to *party-autonomy* that affects arbitrability. Similarly, the ability of the parties to an arbitration

still few would contend that it is not existential to an agreement to arbitrate.[43] The minimalist expression of *party-autonomy* in this context is that in international arbitration proceedings parties would have standing to determine under what

to expand the grounds for judicial review to confirm, set aside, or modify arbitral awards represents a limit to *party-autonomy* that translates directly into a qualification on arbitrability.

For an analysis concerning limits to *party-autonomy* placing constraints on arbitrability, *see* Cordero-Moss, "General Report on *Jura Novit* Arbiter," 477 (comparing scholarly commentaries outlining the powers of arbitral tribunals across fifteen national jurisdictions and public international law, and identifying common limitations on *party-autonomy* concerning the applicability of

> rules against corruption or money-laundering, competition law, regulations of import or expert. In these areas, States usually issue overriding mandatory rules, or *lois de police*, and the underlying principles are often considered to be fundamental (public policy, *ordre* public). Other areas where *party-autonomy* is restricted for the sake of third-party rights and certainly of the legal system are company law, as well as the law regulating insolvency and encumbrances).

See also Rachel Engle, "Party-Autonomy in International Arbitration: Where Uniformity Gives Way to Predictability," 15 *Transant. L.* 323 (2002).

Currently, many countries recognize *party-autonomy* by statute or through case law, but not without limitations. First, courts generally do not uphold a party's choice of law if the purpose of the choice is to avoid provisions of the law that would apply absent the choice. Second, national laws or legal principles may limit the express choice of the parties. For example, in European civil law countries, while the trend is to respect the parties' choice of law, some countries have held that the parties' choice of law applies only when it is consistent with the conflict of laws rules of the forum or those of the site of the arbitration. *See* Diego P. Fernández-Arroyo, "Arbitrators' Procedural Powers: The Last Frontier of Party-Autonomy?," in *Limits to Party-Autonomy in International Commercial Arbitration* (Franco Ferrari ed.) (Juris 2016), 202, 202–206 (summarizing the public mandatory rules and private mandatory rules that set forth "clear limits" to *party-autonomy*); Inka Hanefeld, "Limits to Party-Autonomy Imposed by European Mandatory Law," in *Limits to Party-Autonomy* (Ferrari ed.), 402, 402–413 (identifying three categories of limits to substantive aspects of *party-autonomy*, namely: (i) European competition law, (ii) the European agency directive, and (iii) the law of sanctions); Restatement (Second) of Conflicts of Laws § 187 (1971), *see also id.* at cmt. on subsection (2) at 11–14:

> (1) The law of the state chosen by the parties to govern their contractual rights and duties will be applied if the particular issue is one which the parties could have resolved by an explicit provision in their agreement directed to the issue.
>
> (2) The law of the state chosen by the parties to govern their contractual rights and duties will be applied, even if the particular issue is one which the parties could not have resolved by an explicit provision in their agreement directed to that issue, *unless either (a) the chosen state has no substantial relationship to the parties or the transaction and there is no other reasonable basis for the parties' choice, or (b) application of the law of the chosen state would be contrary to a fundamental policy of a state which has a materially greater interest than the chosen state in the determination of the particular issue in which, under the rule of § 188, would be the state of the applicable law in the absence of an effective choice of law by the parties.* (Emphasis added)

43 As commentators habitually state, often viscerally so and without reflecting on the external constraints to *party-autonomy*, there is no negating that the most foundational element of ICA is *consent* between the parties, and, therefore, *party-autonomy*. *See, e.g.*, Michael Mcilwrath & John Savage, *International Arbitration and Mediation: A Practical Guide*, 13 (Wolters Kluwer 2010) ("Arbitration is a creature of contract. An arbitration agreement, or agreement to arbitrate, is itself the contract in which parties agree to resolve disputes between them through arbitration."); W. Michael Reisman, *The Systems of Control in International Adjudication and Arbitration: Breakdown and Repair* (Duke University Press 1992), 5 ("Arbitral jurisdiction is entirely consensual. As in Roman law and the system influenced by it, arbitration is a creature of contract. The arbitrator's powers are derived from the

conditions and pursuant to which particular methodologies a private dispute resolution system, separate and distinct from the State's exercise of judicial sovereignty, would apply to the settlement of a specific dispute arising from an agreement, without resorting to appellate recourse.

Once this premise is accepted as a descriptive account of *party-autonomy*, it simply cannot follow that an arbitral tribunal can decide which theories of liability and damages *not raised* by the parties are to be pursued. This lack of symmetry points to more than an aesthetic shortcoming generally, and particularly in the context of *risk assessment* conducive to settlement.

The introduction of *Iura Novit Curia* to ICA proceedings foundationally is contrary to *optimal efficiency* because it creates *nonquantifiable risk*. Uncertainty that cannot be in any way assessed and lacking in absolute terms of any predictive value only can serve to disrupt the pursuit of *optimal efficiency*. The workings of *optimal efficiency* are premised on a transparency arising from two very distinct but related propositions.

First, there must be evidentiary disclosure between the parties in the form of self-disclosure and process-driven compulsory disclosure. The ability to engage in objective risk analysis is directly proportional to the comprehensiveness of fact and expert evidence disclosure. The norm-centered model of risk assessment that here has been assumed as necessary for risk assessment conducive to *optimal efficiency* relies on a meaningful degree of evidential certainty.

Second, process or procedural certainty conducive to procedural predictive value also is a predicate to *risk assessment* conducive to *optimal efficiency*. Such process certainty at minimum would require timely disclosure of the following eleven factors:

(i) Documents available to parties on which they *may be* intent to rely;
(ii) Documents disclosed by the parties that are relevant to the case and material to its outcome;
(iii) A pristine understanding of the elements that a request for production must contain, such as a description of each document requested with sufficient particularity so as to identify the document, as well as equally narrowly tailored descriptions of document categories and the manner in which such documents are relevant to the case and material to its outcome;
(iv) Documents responsive to the parties' Request to Produce;

contract."); Donald L. Carper, John A. McKinsey, & Bill W. West, *Understanding the Law* (Cengage South-Western 2002), 187 ("Since arbitration is the creature of contract, parties to arbitration are free to devise arbitration process in a way they see fit."); *United Steelworkers of Am. v. Am. Mfg. Co.*, 363 U.S. 564, 570–71 (1960) ("To be sure, since arbitration is a creature of contract, a court must always inquire, when a party seeks to invoke its aid to force a reluctant party to the arbitration table, whether the parties have agreed to arbitrate the particular dispute."); *Bell v. Cendant Corp.*, 293 F.3d 563, 566 (2d Cir. 2000) ("[a]rbitration is a creature of contract, and the person may only be compelled to arbitrate a dispute to the extent that he has agreed to do so.").

(v) A delineated and limited set of objections that may have a bearing on the parties' obligations to engage in fulsome self-disclosure or disclosure in response to a request for production of documents;

(vi) The manner in which documents are to be produced, i.e., copies conforming to the original and an original available for inspection if necessary or otherwise requested, electronically stored data to be produced in a manner that is cost-efficient and economically viable for all parties, and (non-exhaustively) the extent to which translations and original language are to be managed;

(vii) The identification of *all* prospective witnesses, including witnesses who *may* have information relevant to the case and material to its outcome;

(viii) A specific standard for the content of witness statements, their use, and the evidentiary weight to be accorded depending on the extent to which witnesses elect not to appear at a hearing contrary to a party's request;

(ix) A disclosure regime for party and or tribunal-appointed experts;

(x) The order of proof at all evidentiary hearings; and

(xi) Clear rules governing direct, cross, re-direct, and re-cross-examination, including viable formal and substantive objections.

The principle of *Iura Novit Curia* militates against the transparency and certainty endemic to any regime concerned with these fundamental features that would render possible *risk assessment* and quantification in furtherance of *optimal efficiency*. As noted later in this chapter, an Article on settlement, that is to say, *optimal efficiency*, within the framework of a particular set of rules on evidence gathering and the conduct of an arbitral proceeding is of no moment absent the requisite evidentiary transparency rendering *risk assessment* possible.

Settlement cannot be premised on risk that by nature is unquantifiable. Such would be the case with a rules regime that is impervious to fulsome transparency with respect to the disclosure, taking, presentation, assessment, and challenge to evidence of any kind. The principle of *Iura Novit Curia* cannot be reconciled with *risk assessment* conducive to *optimal efficiency*.

6.3 THE PRAGUE RULES' SETTLEMENT PROVISION

The Prague Rules' Art. 9 (Assistance in Amicable Settlement) represents a meaningful step in the recognition of the need for settlement to constitute an integral part of ICA's essential fiber, and ability to redeem its efficiency promise. The inclusion of a complete and self-standing Article on settlement is laudable and promising. This amicable settlement provision reads:

> 9.1. Unless one of the parties objects, the Arbitral Tribunal *may* assist the parties in reaching an amicable settlement of the dispute *at any stage* of the arbitration.

9.2. Upon the prior written consent of all parties, any member of the Arbitral Tribunal may also act as a mediator to assist in the amicable settlement of the case.

9.3. If the mediation does not result in a settlement within an agreed period of time, the member of the Tribunal who has acted as mediator:

a. may continue to act as an arbitrator in the arbitration proceedings after obtaining written consent from all parties at the end of the mediation; or

b. shall terminate his/her mandate in accordance with the applicable arbitration rules if such written consent is obtained. (Emphasis added)

Subsection 9.1 represents a significantly less effective iteration of its draft predecessor. The subsection 9.1 (draft) imposed on the arbitral tribunal an obligation to assist the parties with respect to "reaching an amicable settlement of the dispute." This draft provision included the imperative "*shall*" in connection with the assistance to explore amicable settlement.[44]

The current and final version of subsection 9.1 contains the permissive "may." Thus vesting the arbitral tribunal with discretion on whether it elects to facilitate, or at all render possible settlement discussions within an institutional rules and proceedings framework. Moreover, the draft iteration of subsection 9.1 provides that the arbitral tribunal's *obligation* to assist the parties with respect to settlement is to be exercised "[a]t all stages of the proceedings."[45] Here as well, the final version of subsection 9.1 further dilutes the primacy of *optimal efficiency* by extending *arbitrator discretion* with respect to settlement to "any stage of the arbitration," rather than prescribing an obligation to assist parties to explore and to develop amicable settlement possibilities "[a]t all stages of the proceedings."[46]

Subsection 9.2 of the final version of the Prague Rules similarly represents a distancing from *optimal efficiency* when compared to the predecessor draft subsection 9.2. Again, relying on the permissive "may," subsection 9.2 enhances *arbitrator discretion* at the expense of *party-autonomy* and, therefore, to the detriment of equipoise between the two concepts, as well as the diminution of *optimal efficiency*. The final version of subsection 9.2 does little more than state that any member of the arbitral tribunal "*may*" serve as a mediator. The predecessor draft subsection 9.2, standing in sharp relief, presents a fulsome framework for settlement. It reads:

9.2. To the extent permissible under *lex arbitri*, in order to assist in an amicable settlement of the dispute, the Arbitral Tribunal, upon obtaining consent from

44 The draft version of subsection 9.1. states: "*At all stages* of the proceedings, the Arbitral Tribunal *shall* assist the Parties in reaching an amicable settlement of the dispute." (Emphasis added)

45 *Id.*

46 *See* Prague Rules Draft subsection 9.1, n. 46 in this chapter.

all of the Parties, *shall* be entitled to express its preliminary views with regards to the Parties' respective positions. The expression of such preliminary views should not be considered as pre-judgment or serve as a ground for disqualification of any member of the Arbitral Tribunal. (Emphasis added)

This draft subsection 9.2 expresses a thoughtful and unqualified commitment to *optimal efficiency*. Learning the tribunal's "*preliminary*" views as a matter of right, so long as the consent of the parties is duly-secured, in most instances likely shall galvanize settlement discussions. It is significant that this draft subsection speaks in terms of the *arbitral tribunal's* "preliminary" views, and not the views or opinions of individual members.

Moreover, the effect of publishing these views to the parties is well tempered by the exhortation that "preliminary views should not be considered as pre-judgment or serve as a ground for disqualification of any member of the Arbitral Tribunal." Preserving the fluidity of the preliminary views aired (particularly in the context of the procedural phase when such views are expressed) infuses sufficient uncertainty to foster arms-length structured settlement discussions.

This draft subsection would have benefitted from having been further tailored by containing references to particular procedural junctures at which time the parties would be best served to petition the arbitral tribunal for such views. Both *process transparency* and *risk assessment* would have been substantially furthered had the subsection 9.2 draft survived the scrutiny that led merely to the possibility of having a tribunal member serve as a mediator so long as the predicate consent of the parties is tendered.

This final iteration of subsection 9.2 underscores the difference between the metaphorical vector force attaching to having actual pristine access to the views of the tribunal as a whole on the merits of the case versus a single tribunal member's effectiveness as an arbitrator. In this second scenario contemplated by the final iteration of subsection 9.2, parties are likely to select the tribunal President. Even under this scenario, however, in the role of mediator it is not to be expected for the tribunal president serving as mediator to express a particular or collective view of the merits of the case.[47]

The current version of subsection 9.3 contemplates that after serving as mediator, the tribunal member "may" only continue to serve as an arbitrator in the proceedings "after obtaining written consent from all parties at the end of the mediation[.]"[48]

47 The selection of a tribunal member to serve as mediator can be a high-risk situation that may lead to the arbitrator's disqualification and removal. The efficiency consequences of such removal, particularly where the mediating arbitrator is the Tribunal President, are bound to be quite negative in terms of delays and additional expenses. The "preliminary views" approach also is far more promising in this regard: in terms of both process *and optimal efficiency*.

48 Prague Rules Subsection 9.3, *The Prague Rules' Settlement Provision*.

In the alternative, subsection 9.3.b contemplates that absent consent, the arbitrator's mandate shall be terminated consonant with applicable rules.[49]

The draft counterpart subsection 9.3 of the Prague Rules, in part, seeks to obviate the inefficiencies of having to reconstitute the arbitral tribunal, most likely at the critical arbitrator President level, by providing that the participation of the arbitral tribunal or any of its members as a mediator in a proceedings that does not reach settlement, "shall not disqualify the members of the Arbitral Tribunal from continuing to act as arbitrators in the arbitration proceedings if the mediation does not result in settlement." Here, too, the draft iteration would have been amply more effective from both process and *optimal efficiency* perspectives.[50]

Certainly Art. 9 (Assistance in Amicable Settlement) of the Prague Rules is a helpful and important measure in the direction of promoting *optimal efficiency*, notwithstanding that its predecessor draft iteration presented a more compelling and effective contribution to settlement. The placement of this Article in the latter part of the twelve-Article structure of the Prague Rules is emblematic of the standing that *optimal efficiency* has within the Prague Rules' rubric.

The lack of a mandatory imperative to assist in settlement, and the equally meaningful deficit of not emphasizing *optimal efficiency* as an imperative at *all* stages of the arbitration proceeding, also bespeaks to the standing of settlement within the rules as merely perfunctory, and certainly not a priority. *Optimal efficiency* practically is ignored, Art. 9 notwithstanding.

Emphasizing settlement at an early stage of the proceedings at the Case Management Conference certainly would comport with the policy and strictures already present in Prague Rules Art. 2 (Proactive Role of the Arbitral Tribunal).[51] The Case Management Conference presents a timely occasion for discussing mediation. Article 2.4, in pertinent part, provides that the arbitral tribunal may elect to communicate to the parties "its preliminary views on: (i) the allocation of the burden of proof between the parties; (ii) the relief sought; (iii) the disputed issues; and (iv) the weight and relevance of evidence submitted by the parties." This provision

[49] *Id.*

[50] The draft Art. 9 (Assistance in Amicable Settlement) iteration of the Prague Rules reads:

> 9.1. At all stages of the proceedings, the Arbitral Tribunal shall assist the parties in reaching an amicable settlement of the dispute.
>
> 9.2. To the extent permissible under *lex arbitri*, in order to assist in an amicable settlement of the dispute, the Arbitral Tribunal, upon obtaining consent from all of the Parties, *shall* be entitled to express its preliminary views with regards to the Parties' respective positions. The expression of such preliminary views should not be considered as pre-judgment or serve as a ground for disqualification of any member of the Arbitral Tribunal.
>
> 9.3 To the extent permissible under *lex arbitri* and upon the written consent of all Parties, the Arbitral Tribunal or any of its members may also act as a mediator. This shall not disqualify the members of the Arbitral Tribunal from continuing to act as arbitrators in the arbitration proceedings if the mediation does not result in settlement.

[51] See Prague Rules, Art. 2.

can be construed as tantamount "to express[ing] its preliminary views with regard to the Parties' respective positions," set forth in Draft Prague Rules subsection 9.2.[52]

The "preliminary views" provision contained in Art. 2, subsection 2.4.e.i-iv, already provides the structural features that can galvanize and sustain a meaningful settlement effort early in the proceedings that, without prejudice, if unsuccessful can be revisited at a later procedural juncture.

By providing language in subsection 2.4.e cautioning that preliminary views are not to be construed as "lack of independence or impartiality and cannot constitute grounds for disqualification," on the part of the arbitral tribunal, the panel is provided with discretion to comment on the merits without the predicate need to secure the parties' consent.[53] Consequently, the incorporation of or reference to Art. 9 in subsection 2.4.e is conceptually consistent with the mechanics of Art. 2, and certainly would represent a major stricture in furtherance of *optimal efficiency* within the workings of the Prague Rules.

Construing the Art. 2 Case Management provision as textual ordinary and plain language supporting settlement discussions and protecting the arbitral tribunal from disqualification for doing so in the context of subsection 2.4.e mitigates to some extent the Rules' inability to foster *risk assessment* by enhancing *arbitrator discretion* while diminishing *party-autonomy*.

6.4 A LACK OF CAUSAL CONNECTION BETWEEN FOUNDATIONAL UNTESTED ASSUMPTIONS AND THE PRAGUE RULES OBJECTIVES

Between the time that the Draft Prague Rules issued (September 1, 2018) and the publication of the final iteration of the Prague Rules (December 2018), the most significant edits were those contained in the Draft Prague Rules' Note from the Working Group.[54] These edits, however, did not arise because of substantial changes to the text of the Draft Prague Rules as embodied in the actual Prague Rules' final exemplar.[55]

This point matters. The form, substance, and policies between these two sets of rules (draft and final version) remained the same. A more reasonable and plausible ground for the edits to the Note from the Working Group contained in the Draft Prague Rules concerns political expediency, political correctness, and the need to appear more content neutral, that is to say, less beholden to any single legal tradition.

If so, then the Note from the Working Group embodied in the Draft Prague Rules serves as an eloquent historical document from which the drafters' intent may be very accurately discerned.

52 *See* Chapter 4, n. 30.
53 *See* Prague Rules, Art. 2, subsection 2.4.e.
54 *See* Chapter VI of the Prague Rules.
55 *See id.*

6.5 DELAY, LACK OF EFFICIENCY, AND EXPENSE AS PROBLEMS PLAGUING INTERNATIONAL COMMERCIAL ARBITRATION

As discussed,[56] the very title of the Prague Rules suggests their scope is beyond the mere taking of evidence in international arbitration. These "evidentiary rules" do not even mention the words "taking" or "evidence." Instead, the subject of the title is the "Efficient Conduct of Proceedings in International Arbitration." This language cannot more forcefully express the extent to which *process efficiency* has been so enshrined as to altogether ignore *optimal efficiency*. The Prague Rules' principal ostensible objective is to provide the universe of consumers of arbitral services with a set of Rules that are conducive to the *efficient* and, therefore, less costly conduct of arbitration proceedings.

In support of the proposition that "[i]t has become almost commonplace these days that users of arbitration are dissatisfied with the time and cost involved in the proceedings," the Note from the Working Group contained in the Draft Prague Rules suggests the Rules, which "initially [were] intended to be used in disputes between companies from civil countries,"[57] are premised on four foundational but *untested* assumptions.

First, the Note from the Working Group teaches the drafters opined that the current state of evidence taking in international arbitration is in part to blame for the excessive time and expenses characterizing contemporary international arbitration proceedings.[58] The drafters, however, fail to account for the manner in which the taking of evidence causes delays and inefficiency. Absent is reference to *any* empirical study suggesting as much.

The Draft Prague Rules and the Prague Rules themselves did not advance any comparative analysis between, by way of example, purported delays arising from the taking of evidence versus delays attributable (i) to arbitral tribunals failing to rule quickly and efficiently, (ii) the cost and delays attributable to bifurcation, and often the trifurcation of proceedings, (iii) post-evidentiary hearing memorials, or (iv) memorial writing, to name just a few of the most salient causes for delay and excessive costs.

It would be somewhat enigmatic (if not altogether contrafactual) to assert that the conduct of cross-examination or participation of party-appointed experts somehow rose to the level of any of the four immediately referenced delay fault lines, let alone all four of them. Likewise, it is equally quizzical to posit that the institutionalization on the part of the Prague Rules of an inquisitorial system, to the detriment of *party-autonomy*, would generate efficiencies and process oriented predictive value.

56 *Id.*

57 Prague Rules, Note from the Working Group, n. 1 in this chapter.

58 *Id.*

These assumptions are not conducive to *process efficiency* or *optimal efficiency*. Indeed, even the contribution of the more limited final iteration of Art. 9 (Assistance in Amicable Settlement) is of limited utility if the Rules themselves do not provide for the necessary evidence taking and process transparency to render possible the *identification*, *quantification*, and subsequent *communication* of risk bilaterally between adverse parties. The Prague Rules in this regard are sorely wanting.

Second, the Note from the Working Group of the Prague Rules emphasizes "document production" as the most problematic phase of evidence taking in international arbitration, purportedly responsible for delays and increase in costs. As with evidence taking generally, the drafters do not specify *what* aspect of document production they opine to be responsible for such inefficiencies. Glaring is the absence of *any* empirical data.

By way of illustration, the self-disclosure phase of document production under the IBA Rules and the Prague Rules are substantively, albeit not formally, very similar from an operational perspective.[59]

Similarly, despite the incongruous assertion in Art. 4.2 (Document Evidence) of the Prague Rules asserting that "[g]enerally, the Arbitral Tribunal and the parties are encouraged to avoid any form of document production, including e-discovery," the balance of Art. 4 is materially, from a performance/tactical perspective, functionally almost identical to Art. 3 of the IBA Rules.

Both Art. 4 (Prague Rules) and Art. 3 (IBA Rules) base document production on the identical standard: IBA Rules, "relevant to the case and material to its outcome" (Art. 3.10); Prague Rules, "relevant and material to the outcome of the case" (Art. 4.5.a). Indeed, both sets of Rules rely on self-disclosure based upon *relevance* and *materiality*, as well as the "upon which [the party] intends to rely in support of its case" standards.[60] The similarities between each of the respective regimes

59 *See* n. 6 in this chapter

60 *See, e.g.*, Prague Rules, at Art. 4.1 providing that "[e]ach party shall submit documentary evidence *upon which it intends to rely in support of its case as early as possible in the proceedings*." (Emphasis added.) *Compare* to IBA 2020 Rules, at Art. 3.1, which reads:

> Within the time ordered by the Arbitral Tribunal each Party shall submit to the Arbitral Tribunal and to the other Parties, all Documents available to it *on which it relies*, including public Documents and those in the public domain, except for any documents that have already been submitted by another Party. (Emphasis added)

A close reading of the two Articles (IBA Rules Art. 3 and Prague Rules Art. 4) actually establishes that IBA Rules Art. 3 places greater constraints on the party requesting production. This fact is uncontroverted and merits underscoring. Quite notably, as part of a detailed imperative addressing the content of a Request to Produce, the requesting party in part must set descriptive narratives with considerable particularity.

The Prague Rules are devoid of any comparable requirements. The closest imperative is contained in Art. 4.3:

> However, if a party believes that it would need to request certain documents from the other party, it should indicate this to the Arbitral Tribunal at the Case Management Conference and

concerning the basic provisions governing self-disclosure and document demands further invite skepticism over the Prague Rules' untested assumption that evidence taking, as concerns document production, is responsible for delays that have given rise to dissatisfaction among consumers of arbitral services at a global level.

Third, the Prague Rules' drafters identify "multiple fact and expert witnesses and their cross-examination at lengthy hearings" as fundamental premises giving rise to the undue delays and prohibitive costs that dismay ICA stakeholders. The drafters point to no empirical evidence. This proposition merely is asserted and expected to be embraced much as another self-evident premise. The assumption, when submitted to even basic analysis, makes clear that it does not support the conclusion for which it is relied upon.

It is not within this writing's purview to set forth exhaustively all propositions establishing beyond cavil that the number of fact and expert witnesses generally used in arbitral proceedings *are not* grounds for international arbitrations' increase in costs and delays, particularly with respect to treaty-based arbitrations that on average exceed three years' time from the filing of a request for arbitration until the end of all arbitral labor. To the contrary, disclosure of prospective fact and expert witnesses contributes to *risk assessments* and, therefore, potentially to realizing *optimal efficiency*.

Even *arguendo*, for purposes of ascribing to the Prague Rules the benefit of any doubt that somehow ICA is plagued with too many fact and expert witnesses that when submitted to cross-examination final hearings are lengthier than they otherwise would be, the *average* merits hearing likely does not exceed two weeks' time. Consequently, even assuming that such hearings would be reduced by 50 percent of their current duration by excluding a greater number of expert and fact witnesses, as well as curtailing cross-examination, reducing the entire length of the arbitral proceeding by one week would hardly cure the efficiency deficits that currently are being experienced. Moreover, such abbreviation would come at the cost of due process and process transparency-*risk assessment* concerns.

Additionally, were cross-examination to be eliminated, the time used to cross-examine a witness by a party representative only would be transferred from the party to the arbitral tribunal who then presumably would pose the relevant questions. This transposition of responsibilities, however, is contrary to the relevant efficiency externalities because arbitral tribunals lack resources comparable to those of the parties for purposes of testing the factual assertions and assumptions of both fact and expert witnesses. Therefore, in addition to preserving greater "inefficiencies" in the

explain the reasons why the document production may be needed in this particular case. If the Arbitral Tribunal is satisfied that the document production *may be needed*, it should decide on a procedure for document production and make an appropriate provision for it in the procedural timetable. (Emphasis added)

Prague Rules, Art. 4.3.

form of truth-seeking by way of witness examination, the quality of such examinations and the integrity of the entire proceeding both would be compromised.

Fourth, the Prague Rules' drafters acknowledge that "[t]he drafters of the IBA Rules on the Taking of Evidence in International Arbitration … bridged a gap between the common law and civil law traditions of taking evidence," and further observe that "[t]he IBA Rules were very successful in developing a nearly standardized procedure in international arbitration."[61] These premises notwithstanding, they note that, because in their opinion the IBA Rules "are still closer to the common law tradition,"[62] they conclude that the IBA Rules, bridging different legal cultures, but nonetheless still closer to the common law tradition, represent a major reason why inefficiencies pervade international arbitration.

Two untested assumptions underlie this statement. At the outset, it is less than clear that the IBA Rules favor a common law culture. As referenced earlier in this writing (Section 4.3), the IBA Rules do not limit the inherent power of *arbitrator discretion*. Emblematic of the IBA Rules' regime in this regard is the centralization of authority vested in the arbitral tribunal that is reiterated throughout the Rules, but most notably contained in Art. 8.3 (Evidentiary Hearing), which reads:

> 3. The Arbitral Tribunal *shall at all times have complete control over the Evidentiary Hearing*. The Arbitral Tribunal may limit or exclude any question to, answer by or appearance of a witness, if it considers such question, answer or appearance to be irrelevant, immaterial, unreasonably burdensome, duplicative or otherwise covered by a reason for objection set forth in Articles 9.2 or 9.3. Questions to a witness during direct and re-direct testimony may not be unreasonably leading. (Emphasis added)

The workings of the IBA Rules, but particularly the structure and imperative of Art. 8 governing the conduct of the Evidentiary Hearing, strikes a balance between the expectations of practitioners and common law and civil law traditions. Certainly, the IBA Rules wrest from the parties adversarial control of the proceedings by providing the arbitral tribunal with an unqualified panoply of civil law jurisdiction inquisitorial mandates.

A second assumption shared by the drafters of the Prague Rules' characterization of the IBA Rules as contributing to inefficiencies because of the IBA Rules' purported affinity with the common law legal tradition, merely begs the question; what evidence suggests that the common law is conducive to inefficiencies that will lead the consumers of arbitral services to question the very extent to which international arbitration is preferable to its judicial counterpart?

The drafters of the Prague Rules simply are silent on this query. Empirical surveying or modeling would have been welcomed. Moreover, it would have been a

61 Draft Prague Rules, Note from the Working Group, *see* n. 1 in this chapter.
62 *Id.*

necessary exercise as a condition precedent to fashioning a set of rules that assert the aspiration of curing inefficiencies: a goal that the proposed framework simply cannot meaningfully address, let alone redeem.[63]

6.6 THE UNTESTED PREMISE IN SUPPORT OF EFFICIENCY

The Note from the Working Group contained in the final published iteration of the Prague Rules sets forth a premise expressed in a politically palatable, neutral to tepid tone. It (the premise) is assumed as the cure for inefficiencies purportedly driving the increased costs of international arbitration. There is no substitute for the original language:

> It has become almost commonplace these days for users of arbitration to be dissatisfied with the time and cost involved in arbitral proceedings.
>
> One of the ways to increase the efficiency of arbitral proceedings is to encourage tribunals to take a more active role in managing the proceedings (as is traditionally done in many civil law countries).[64]

This pronouncement commands attention. The entire focus of efficiency is placed on "managing the proceedings." Embedded in that term is a more eloquent iteration of the same proposition, namely, "*managing the proceedings until the end of all arbitral labor.*" The only focus is on *process efficiency*.

Efficiencies in the context of the overarching objective, a *non-zero-sum* resolution of a dispute completely are ignored. Efficiency is circumscribed and limited only to the aspirational reduction of costs, fees, and expenditure of time in furtherance of a process that will yield presumably a binding and enforceable award. That award most likely (i) will have to be submitted to domestic courts for recognition and enforcement, (ii) defended as to scope and enforcement throughout the execution process, and (iii) defended in the context of possible a set-aside proceeding. The sole focus on *process efficiency* misses the point, and places the cart before the horse.

[63] In the Note from the Working Group contained in the Draft Prague Rules, the drafters regrettably are somewhat sparse on the issue of academic and scholastic sources. This omission is most notable when citing to sources in generic terms wanting in all particularity and therefore unidentifiable. Instead, the tone of these citations assumes that the proposition asserted is simply intuitively true. The following is an eloquent case in point:

> These factors contribute greatly to the costs of arbitration, while their efficiencies sometimes rather questionable. *For example, most commentators admit that it is very rare, if ever, that document production brings a smoking gun to light. Likewise, many commentators express doubts as to the usefulness of fact witnesses and the impartiality of Party-appointed experts.* Many of these procedural features are not known or used to the same extent in non-common law jurisdictions, such as continental Europe, Latin America, Middle East, and Asia. (Emphasis added)

Draft Prague Rules, Note from the Working Group, *see* n. 1 in this chapter.

[64] *Id.*

Presumably, the procedural-structural remedy for the ill of inefficiency in the form of empowering the arbitral tribunal "to take a more active role in managing the proceedings," much as is "done in many civil law judicial tribunals," purports to be a solution that resulted from what the drafters described to have been an empirical study. The Prague Rules assert that working groups drawing on "representatives from around thirty, *mainly civil law countries*,"[65] were constituted.

The groups' constituent members purportedly undertook an empirical study, each with respect to her specific national jurisdiction, in the form of "a survey on procedural traditions in international arbitration in their respective countries."[66] It was presumably "[o]n the basis of this research [that] the *Working Group* prepared the first draft of the Rules."[67]

The Note from the Working Group of the Draft Prague Rules, which was issued just slightly over two months before the final iteration was published, provides an account that is politically less neutral, amply and ostensibly partial to one single legal tradition, and lacking in *any* reference to purported empirical analyses undertaken throughout thirty countries and exhaustively debated over time. This prior version of the Note from the Working Group reveals more of a *culturally* and not a *scientifically* based analysis for the drafting of a set of rules that deliberately seeks to expand the inherent power of *arbitrator discretion* at the explicit expense of *party-autonomy*. Only perfunctory reference to settlement is contained as a clear second-tier byproduct of the process. And not even as an objective found to be in *pari materia* with *process efficiency*.

This exemplar of the drafters' working papers does not mince words. A cultural juridical approach is held out to be tantamount to constituting a more efficient methodology, notwithstanding any empirical foundation for the proposition, while altogether turning a blind eye to *optimal efficiency*.

After detailing the many ills associated with what is identified as a common law based taking of evidence framework in international arbitration, the drafters share with the international arbitration community that "[i]n light of all of this, the drafters of the Prague Rules believe that developing the Rules *on Taking Evidence* which are *based on the inquisitorial model of procedure and would enhance more active role of the arbitral tribunals* would contribute to increasing efficiency in international arbitration."[68] (Emphasis added.) The drafters further affirm that "[b]y adopting a more inquisitorial approach of the Arbitral Tribunal, the new Rules will help the Parties and Arbitral Tribunals reduce the duration and costs of arbitrations."[69]

65 *Id.*
66 *Id.*
67 *Id.*
68 *Id.*
69 *Id.*

As suggested (Table 6.1), with the exception of Arts. 7 (*Iura Novit Curia*) and 9 (Assistance in Amicable Settlement), when stripped of adjectives and adverbs, the *actual* workings and practical consequences of the application of the Prague Rules only are marginally dissimilar to those of the IBA Rules. They do not warrant the proposition that the Prague Rules substantively represent an extreme reactionary pendulum swing away from the IBA Rules. It is so only in *form* and certainly not *substance*.

To the extent the intent of the drafters of the Prague Rules can be gleaned from the Note from the Working Group, it becomes all the more compelling that the Prague Rules are but a civil law cultural expression of the IBA Rules. Indeed, both sets of Rules suffer from the same or related deficits. The principal shortcoming of both IBA and Prague Rules' framework is the insistence on *process efficiency* and unqualified disregard for *optimal efficiency*. Neither set of Rules redeems ICA's cornerstone promise to be efficient.

It is similarly evident that there is no empirical, theoretical, or conceptual support for the proposition that "adopting a more inquisitorial approach of the arbitral tribunal" shall "reduce the duration and costs of arbitration."[70]

What an ordinary and plain meaning analysis of the Prague Rules' textual language demonstrates is that the net effect of these Rules is to provide the arbitral tribunal, that is to say, the inherent authority of *arbitrator discretion*, with greater *initiative*, but no more *authority* than supplied to the arbitral tribunal by IBA Rules Art. 8.3.[71] There is a difference between substantively enhancing the ambit of *arbitrator discretion* in the form of specific additional authority over identifiable procedural or substantive principles, and contributing to the inherent power of *arbitrator discretion* by vesting it with more *initiative*. This distinction matters.

A transfer of authority to the arbitral tribunal represents a substantive conveyance of rights. Transferring to the arbitral tribunal, however, an *initiative* that historically or otherwise parties held, and that may be subject to additional caveats, such as "subject to the parties' agreement" or a right transferred to the arbitral tribunal in the permissive is not a material conveyance of great consequence.[72]

This distinction further calls into question whether under any reasonable hypothesis of fact, logic, law, or equity follows that (i) vestiges of common law evidence taking in the IBA Rules lead to the delays and excessive costs of arbitral proceedings and (ii) "adopting a more inquisitorial approach of the Tribunal" would cause a

70 *See* n. 66 in this chapter.

71 IBA 2020 Rules, n. 13 in this chapter at Art. 8.3.

72 As previously noted, Chapter VI, A – Prague Rules, Art. 6 seemingly at first glance appears to vest the arbitral tribunal with absolute control over the appointment of experts in a proceeding. Closer scrutiny, however, demonstrates that the parties may submit their own expert report (Art. 6.5), may examine the tribunal-appointed expert (6.4), and may equally examine a party-appointed expert (6.5). Thus, when appropriately scrutinized, Art. 6 is operationally very close to IBA Rules Art. 6 (Tribunal-Appointed Experts).

reduction in "the duration and costs of arbitration." All of these concerns, however, are but considerations attaching merely to *procedural efficiency*. *Risk assessment* and, therefore, settlement remain marginalized, if not altogether excluded.

Whether it is the substantive *transfer of rights* from the parties to the arbitral tribunal or the conveyance of *initiative*, it does not follow that either measure or both in tandem shall mitigate or eviscerate delays and excessive costs. Both propositions (i) and (ii) lack normativity and relation to the conclusion that the drafters of the Prague Rules reached.

More importantly, in addition to using a simplistic paradigm focused on tribunal initiative to assert somehow that *procedural efficiency* is maximized, the Prague Rules (i) ignore *optimal efficiency*, (ii) do not address the consequences and economic externalities attaching to a *zero-sum* result, (iii) turn a blind eye to the inefficiencies inherent in recognition and enforcement, and (iv) similarly ignore the risks and inefficiencies incident to set-aside proceedings. The Prague Rules in discouraging comprehensive evidence taking, create a dispute environment that renders *risk assessment* opaque, if not altogether impossible.

The Rules maximize *optimal inefficiency* and further compromise procedural predictive value. The absence of a structure for summary disposition additionally multiples the already considerable inefficiencies forming part of a framework that only purportedly concerns itself with reducing minimal costs and time in furtherance of the issuance of what is hoped to be a binding and enforceable award.

The Prague Rules exist. Their existence alone argues in favor of an underlying driving *necessity*, perceived or real, it matters not. The extent of such necessity, however, beyond a cultural drive to seek parity with a perceived common law oriented framework, only will ripen and render itself known to the international arbitration community with the passage of time. The literal interpretation and workings of the Prague Rules' text, however, do not suggest a doctrinal contribution to efficiency in ICA such that the promise to resolve disputes in a manner potentially conducive to a *non-zero-sum* outcome minimizing costs in the process for all stakeholders, will be furthered by the Rules' application.

Similarly, the Prague Rules' settlement provision (Art. 9 (Assistance in Amicable Settlement)) appears as an unworkable provision that is out of context within the Rules' rubric. This provision is dysfunctional because the Rules themselves do not provide for *risk assessment* of any kind. Indeed, *process efficiency* and *optimal efficiency* appear to have been sacrificed at the altar of cultural parochialism.

7

Toward a Qualitative Evidentiary Approach and Not Rigid Categorical Exclusionary Rules of Evidence

7.1 THE APPLICABILITY OR NON-APPLICABILITY OF FRE IN NONJURY BENCH TRIALS: PERHAPS A HELPFUL ANALOGY TO ARBITRAL TRIBUNAL FACT-FINDERS

The absence of a developed technical framework of qualitative (reliability) and exclusionary evidentiary rules in ICA, a practice that ICA inherited from international tribunals more generally,[1] can be provided with still greater and more useful context. All European countries having a civil-law-based legal system that lack a rule-based reliability and exclusionary rules approach to the law of evidence in the form of a code or other statutory rubric.[2] This fact seems to bolster the epistemic

[1] *See* Chapter 5, n. 2 in this volume.

[2] *See* German Code of Civil Procedure, full text, at: www.gesetze-im-internet.de/englisch_zpo/englisch_zpo.html (last accessed September 6, 2023). The German Code of Civil Procedure lacks provisions akin to hearsay, non-hearsay, opinion evidence, or the effects of prior acts or prior convictions. It also lacks any provision purporting to qualify an expert witness or to test the quality and reliability of expert reports proffered as evidence. Several observations are in order. Section 395 (instruction of a witness to tell the truth; personal information of the witness) in part reads:

> (1) Prior to the examination, the witness shall be instructed to tell the truth; his attention shall be drawn to the fact that, in the cases provided for by law and under certain circumstances, he may have to swear an oath regarding his testimony.

The instructions do not circumscribe or otherwise qualify the testimony by limiting it to *personal knowledge*.

Section 396 (Examination regarding the dispute) reads:

> (1) The witness is to be induced to tell the court in context *whatever facts are known to him* regarding the subject matter of his examination.
>
> (2) By way of ensuring the clarity and *completeness of the testimony*, while also investigating *the basis on which the knowledge of the witness is based*, the court is to ask further questions where necessary. (Emphasis added)

There is no provision concerning hearsay, personal knowledge, or otherwise providing for the application of exclusionary rules of evidence, or even the manner of examination.

Section 397 (Right of the parties to ask questions) provides:

possibility that a strict rule-based exclusionary methodology for determining the admissibility and weight to be accorded to evidence may have its origins in the

> (1) The parties are entitled to have those questions put to the witness that they believe expedient for clearing up the matter, or for establishing the circumstances of the witness.
>
> (2) The presiding judge may permit the parties to directly address questions to the witness, and is to grant this permission to their counsel upon the latter's request.
>
> (3) In case of doubt, the court shall rule on whether or not a *question* is admissible (permissible). (Emphasis added)

This Section seems to suggest in the broadest of terms and without the use of adjectives or adverbs, that certain *questions* may not be *admissible* or *posed*. It is silent, however, on whether certain types of *answers* are inadmissible.

Title 9 (Evidence Provided by Records and Documents) certainly delves into some basic issues concerning authenticity, mostly in the form of self-authentication, but certainly proves to be extremely liberal (in the sense of *Free Proof* concerning the admissibility of public records and private documents). By way of example, Section 439 (Declaration as to the authenticity of private records) and documents states:

> (1) Pursuant to the stipulations of section 138, the opponent of the party tendering evidence is to react in substance as regards the authenticity of a private record or document.
>
> (2) Insofar as the record or document is signed by a name, the said declaration is to address the authenticity of the signature.
>
> (3) Where this declaration is not made, the record or document shall be deemed to have been acknowledged as authentic unless the other declarations made by the party indicate that it intends to dispute the record's or the document's authenticity.

The workings of Section 439 suggest an initial rebuttable presumption of authenticity. Only subsection (2) requires the declarant to take one affirmative step to authenticate the signature. Moreover, subsection (3) functionally, operationally is such that a document is deemed authentic, and therefore admissible, absent a specific challenge. This proposition is corroborated by subsection 440.1, which provides that "[e]vidence is to be provided of the authenticity of a private record or document *that has not been acknowledged authentic*." (Emphasis added.)

See also French Code of Civil Procedure, allow, at: https://allowb.org/acts_pdfs/CPC.pdf (materially the same as the German Code of Civil Procedure with respect to evidentiary issues). The French Code of Civil Procedure on evidentiary matters has no exclusionary rules based upon hearsay, generally personal knowledge, or qualifications to opinion testimony, testimony on character, the reliability of expert testimony, the qualification of an expert, the use of prior convictions, prior bad acts, or the qualifications of expert testimony. Similarly, Arts. 189–196, addressing the testimony of parties does not qualify the scope of the question, or the scope and foundation of testimony. Article 199 (Statements of Third Parties) does, however, provide that "[w]here testimonial evidence is admissible, the judge will receive from third parties statements that will clarify the dispute and facts about which they have *personal knowledge*. These statements will be made in writing or brought by means of an inquiry, depending on whether they are written or oral." (Emphasis added.) There is no provision addressing the opportunity of a party against whom such written evidence is brought to test the factual sufficiency of the written declaration, such as by cross-examining the declarant.

Chapter 4, Section 1 of the Civil Code addressing affidavit testimony, has no personal knowledge qualification in Arts. 200–203. Furthermore, Art. 211 governing the administration of oaths provided to witnesses, does not limit or qualify the witness' testimony on any basis. To the contrary, as to such matter and scope, Art. 213 asserts that "[t]he judge may hear or examine the witnesses *on all facts whose evidence is legally admissible, even where these facts are not stated in the decision ordering the investigation*." (Emphasis added.)

perceived need to screen from the jury the consideration of facts that can be more misleading than probative and reliable.

See Spanish Code of Civil Procedure, www.diputados.gob.mx/ (Evidence, Chapter 1 (General Rules)) Art. 93 of the Spanish Code of Civil Procedure provides that "as a matter of law the following shall constitute evidence:

(i) An admission;
(ii) Public documents;
(iii) Private documents;
(iv) Expert reports;
(v) Judicial notice or judicial conclusions resulting from inspection;
(vi) Witnesses;
(vii) Photographs, writings, notes and transcriptions, and in general, all factual propositions and discoveries supported by science; and
(viii) All presumptions."

Articles 109–110 governing witness answers to examinations merely state that a witness shall answer questions posed "in the affirmative or negative, but shall be free to explain the witnesses' answer should it deem appropriate, or if the tribunal so requires." These provisions, however, do not contain any exclusionary rules of evidence or restrictions on actual testimony. They also are short on principles designed to evaluate reliability and quality. Moreover, while Arts. 136–142 focus on the authenticity of documents, mostly in the context of signatures, operationally except for a claim that a document has been furtively and fraudulently confected or a signature similarly forged, the code would liberally admit documents as evidence without regard to any level of hearsay.

Quite notably, Art. 305 (Method of Responding to Examination) merely provides that "the party being interrogated will respond to questions without reference to notes, but shall be allowed to consult, contemporaneous with the effort to respond, documents, or notes, where the tribunal deems that such consultation would refresh recollection." Moreover, Art. 305.2 provides that answers shall be stated "in the affirmative or the negative, and to the extent that such answer is not possible in light of the specific question posed, the response must be precise and to the point. The declarant indeed may explain the answer, but the explanation also must comport with the question posed." There is no limitation as to personal knowledge, or hearsay. Indeed, Art. 308 provides that where the declarant does not have personal knowledge of facts forming part of the declarant's response, in responding to the question posed the declarant

> shall respond according to the declarant's knowledge, always providing the basis for this knowledge, and in fact the declarant also may assert that a third party is better placed to respond to the particular question(s) posed because of the third party's connection to the subject matter of the question. In such instances the declarant will accept whatsoever consequences may arise from such declaration.

Spain's Code of Civil Procedure bears no resemblance to the exclusionary and evidence rules forming part of the U.S. Federal Code of Evidence. Indeed, it materially is the same on evidentiary issues as its German and French counterparts.

The Italian Civil Code, approved by Royal decree no. 262 of 16 March 1942 (amended up to Decree No. 291 of December 7, 2016), under Title III evidentiary issues are addressed. This code is materially and operationally akin to its German, French, and Spanish counterparts. For example, a private writing, i.e., a document that is not of public record, pursuant to Section 2, subsection 2702, is deemed admissible as a matter of law unless its authenticity is expressly and affirmatively challenged. It does not constitute hearsay, notwithstanding its inherent generic status as an out-of-court statement that would be offered to prove the truth of the matter asserted. Subsection 2708 (Notation at foot, on margin, or on back of document) is equally illustrative. This subsection provides that "[a] notation made by a creditor at the foot, on the margin, or on the back of a document left in his possession *has evidentiary value*, if it tends to show release of the debtor, *even if the notation is not signed by such creditor*." (Emphasis added.)

The orthodox understanding of Anglo-American evidence law is that it is that the law of evidence is the offspring of the jury system.[3] Hence, a rich discussion has arisen from the suggestion that "the rules of evidence applicable to jury trials should not prevail where the judge is also the trier of the facts" (see Section 7.1).

Substituting the judge for the jury, so the argument says, obviates the need for strict rules of evidence based on an exclusionary approach to the question of *admissibility*. The reasoning is that, because, among other things, a judge as fact-finder is vested with considerable discretion that necessarily would obviate many of the workings of the evidence law rubric comprising the U.S. FRE.

Such result, it is argued, would minimize evidence-based objections, and likely diminish appeals on evidentiary questions because of the difficulty in meeting an appellate abuse of discretion standard.[4] It is further asserted that strict laws of evidence based on an exclusionary approach altogether are destined to disappear in favor of a *Free Proof* approach.

It also is advanced that "it is often psychologically impossible for a judge effectively to apply rules of evidences [herself]; [because] [she] must frequently listen to testimony in order to determine its admissibility, [she] may be unable to eradicate its influence in a later decision on the facts."[5] On this point, where a judge presiding

The Italian Civil Code is bereft of any provisions addressing admissibility of expert opinion, character evidence, impeachment, inference or conclusions arising from prior acts, or any personal knowledge requirement.

See also Mirjan Damaška, "Free Proof and Its Detractors," 43 *Am. J. Comp. L.* 343, 344–346 (1995) (asserting that in the continental system there is no evidentiary rubric comparable to that found in common law jurisdictions, and emphasizing that the fact-finder's personal experience, and logic serve "to guide the trial judge in demonstrating that his belief states – no matter how causally formed – enjoy firm support in the canons of valid reasoning"); H. N. Aragaki, "Applicability of Rules of Evidence Where the Judge Is the Trier of Facts in an Action at Law," 42 *Harv. L. Rev.* 258 (1928); Kenneth Culp Davis, "An Approach to the Rules of Evidence for Nonjury Cases," 50 *A.B.A.J.* 723, 726 (1964) (exhorting common law countries to follow the European civil law tradition that materially disavows strict rule-based and exclusionary approach to evidence in deciding *admissibility* and *weight*); Karl H. Kunert, "Some Observations on the Origins and Structure of Evidence under the Common Law System and the Civil Law System of 'Free Proof' in the German Code of Civil Procedure," 16 *Buff. L. Rev.* 122, 141–143 (1966); and John H. Langbein, "The German Advantage in Civil Procedure," 52 *U. Chi. L. Rev.* 823, 829 (1985) (underscoring that the German Code of Civil Procedure has no analog to common law evidence law providing for strict rules and exclusionary approach).

3 *See id.* 42 *Harv. L. Rev.* 258–59, n. 1, *citing to* John Henry Wigmore, A *Treatise on the Anglo-American System of Evidence in Trials at Common Law*, 2nd ed. (Little, Brown & Co. 1923) § 4b; James Bradley Thayer, A *Preliminary Treaties on Evidence at the Common Law* 180, 266, 534 (Little, Brown & Co. 1898); Henry Summer Maine, *Village-Communities in the East and West*, 7th ed. (John Murray 1895), 302. *See also* Mirjan Damaška, *Evidence Law Adrift* (Yale University Press 1997), 2; Mirjan Damaška, "Evaluation of Evidence," in *Evaluation of Evidence: Pre-modern and Modern Approaches*, ASCL Studies in Comparative Law (Cambridge University Press 2019).

4 *Id.*

5 *Id.*; *see also* Wigmore, A *Treatise on the Anglo-American System of Evidence*, § 8a, at 621 ("The Rules of evidence are mainly aimed at guarding the jury from the overweening effect of certain kinds of evidence. The whole fabric is kept together by that purpose, and the rules are supposed to enshrine that purpose."). *See* Laird C. Kirkpatrick, "Evidence Law in the Next Millennium," 49 *Hastings L.J.*

in a nonjury trial excludes evidence opining that as a matter of evidence law the proffered evidence should not be considered in the general evaluation of the factual record, it cannot be realistically inferred with apodictic certainty that the fact-finder in this scenario would not fall prey to the same misleading features that the purportedly inadmissible evidence would have had on jurors in a jury trial. Here Professor Jennifer L. Mnookin provides a helpful illustration:

> [T]he evidentiary value of the excluded piece of evidence is probably not zero. Even if [the evidence] is excluded, the judge's assessment of the prior odds of guilt or liability might have shifted, thanks to the evidence's [very] existence. Even if she tries to not let the excluded item of evidence affect her subjective belief about the overall odds of guilt or liability, the judge may tend to value other items of evidence differently because of the non-zero probative weight of the excluded evidence.[6]

Hence, the single judge presiding in a bench trial as fact-finder as well as adjudicator of (i) admissible and inadmissible evidence and (ii) the weight or value to

11, 363, (1998) (*citing to* Thayer, A *Preliminary Treaties* for the proposition that the common law's incorporation of strict rules of evidence of admissibility are foundationally related to the rise of the jury system, and offering a contrasting view of the origin of exclusionary rules of evidence, John J. Langbein, "Historical Foundations of the Law of Evidence: A View From the Ryder Sources," 96 *Colum. L. Rev.* 1168 (1996) (attributing rise of evidence law to adversarial criminal trials and not to the need to edit a jury's exposure to evidence)).

It is also noted that U.S. Federal Rules of Evidence based upon strict rules and featuring an exclusionary approach by carving out categories such as (i) hearsay, (ii) character evidence, and (iii) opinion testimony,

> were rules of the common law, and not of equity, because equity had no juries and needed no similar concept of admissibility. Somehow, when law and equity were joined in the United States, the rules of admissibility became integrated into the equity practice as well. As a result, in most state and federal trial courts across the country those rules now control proof presented to judges as well as to juries, on equitable issues as well as legal ones.

Sheldon & Murray, "Rethinking the Rules," 227.

6 Jennifer L. Mnookin, "Bifurcation and the Law of Evidence," 155 *U. Pa. L. Rev. Penn. Umbra.* 134, 136 (2006), (Professor Mnookin in her article supplies a very specific example of a person's diary as constituting inadmissible hearsay in order to explain further this critical proposition:

> The diary is excluded. The judge knows she shouldn't consider it. She may well genuinely try not to consider it. And yet, isn't it possible – perhaps even likely, that the existence of the diary entry will color her evaluation of the two witnesses who claim to have seen Samantha at the bar? The Federal Rules of Evidence, which tend to evaluate evidence in an item-by-item, atomistic fashion, may require exclusion; *but certainly as a matter of logic, the existence of the diary entry makes the claims of the other two witnesses more credible than they would be without it* … Or, to put it differently, she may even think that she *is* ignoring it; and yet, her evaluation of the credibility of the two other bar witnesses might be different than it would have been if she didn't know of the diary entry. *She just might find one or both of them especially believable, for reasons that she can't quite express.* (Emphasis added) (*Id.* at 137))

See Wang, "Rethinking Evidentiary," 302–303 (analyzing this very issue *citing to* the passages here referenced in Professor Mnookin's article and contributing to its incorporation into this writing).

be ascribed to such evidence, may suffer from the same epistemological-cognitive impressions that would doubtless also cause jurors exposed to such evidence to experience in evaluating other evidence of record or in evaluating the extent to which actual facts may meet standards of proof or the elements of a cause of action.

The question of whether the FRE should apply to nonjury trials is all the more enticing, in addition to the reasons stated, because FRE, Rule 1101 states that: "[t]hese rules apply to proceedings in United States courts." Moreover, FRE, Rule 1101 governing the applicability of the Rules do not exempt nonjury trials.[7]

Other structural features of the FRE, however, seem to comport with the proposition that the exclusionary (admissibility) Rules should not be binding on judges because this evidentiary framework is designed to keep jurors from being exposed to what might be very relevant evidence that laypersons are somehow considered to be incapable of evaluating, but which evidence *presumably* a judge is able to process without prejudice to the equitable administration of justice.

By way of example, in this regard, FRE, Rule 403 (Excluding Relevant Evidence for Prejudice, Confusion, Waste of Time, or Other Reasons) states that: "[t]he court may exclude relevant evidence if its probative value is substantially outweighed by a danger of one or more of the following: unfair prejudice, confusing the issues, *misleading the jury*, undue delay, wasting time, or needlessly presenting cumulative evidence." (Emphasis added.) This Rule textually establishes that its core purpose is to keep *relevant* evidence from the jury's consideration.

Can it be asserted with any degree of certainty that the same rule serves no practical purpose when applied to judges? An answer in the affirmative would be laced with dispositive untested assumptions.

To add yet another layer of complexity to this consideration, notwithstanding the command contained in FRE, Rule 101 concerning the applicability of the FRE "to proceedings in United States courts," the applicability of exclusionary rules of evidence to judges presiding over a nonjury trial is rendered all the more deliciously intricate because (i) even though the FRE apply to nonjury proceedings, courts[8]

7 *See* Fed. R. Evid. Rule 1101.

8 *Fields Engineering Equip., Inc. v. Cargill, Inc.*, 651 F. 2d 589, 593 (8th Cir. 1981) (*citing to Montgomery Ward & Co. v. Steele*, 352 F. 2d 822, 830 (8th Cir. 1965)) (underscoring the Eighth Circuit "has held that '[i]n the trial of a case to the court without a jury, the presumption is that the trial court considered only competent evidence and disregarded all evidence which was incompetent'"); *Builders Steel Co. v. Commissioner of Internal Revenue*, 179 F. 2d 377, 379 (8th Cir. 1950) (observing that:

> a trial judge who, in the trial of a non-jury case, attempts to make a strict ruling on admissibility of evidence, can easily get his decision reversed by excluding evidence which is objected to, but which, on review, the appellate court believes should have been admitted … [w]e think that experience has demonstrated that in a trial or hearing where no jury is present, more time is ordinarily lost in listening to arguments as to the admissibility of evidence and in considering offers of proof than would be consumed in taking the evidence proffered and then, even if the

and commentators[9] opine that in nonjury cases, the FRE are not applicable *in the same way* as they are in jury trials largely because the judge is not serving also in the role of "gatekeeper." Thus, a number of exclusionary rules are altogether carved out of the process.

> trier of facts, by making close rulings upon the admissibility of evidence, does not save himself some time, that saving will be more than offset by the time consumed by the reviewing court in considering propriety of his rulings and by the consequence delay in the final determination of the controversy.)

The Eighth Circuit in *Builders Steel* went on to clarify that "[o]ne who is capable of ruling accurately upon the admissibility of evidence is equally capable of sifting it accurately after it has been received, and, since he will base his findings upon the evidence which he regards as competent, material and convincing, he cannot be injured by the presence in the record of testimony which he does not consider competent or material." *Id.*

Schultz v. Butcher, 24 F. 3d 626, 632 (4th Cir. 1994) (observing that "[f]or a bench trial, we are confident that the district court can hear relevant evidence, weighs its probative value and reject any improper inferences"); *Podraza v. Comm'r of Internal Revenue*, T.C. Summ. Op. 2015-67, 2015 WL 7423525 *2 (T.C. Nov. 19, 2015) (stating that:

> [g]enerally, to resolve evidentiary objections, the Court applies the Federal Rules of Evidence applicable in nonjury trials in the U.S. District Court for the District of Columbia. [Citation omitted] Rule 174(b) and §§ 7453 and 7463(a), however, carve out an exception for trials of small tax cases. Under this exception, the Court conducts small tax cases as informally as possible consistent with orderly procedure and "any evidence deemed by the Court to have probative value shall be admissible." [*Citing to Schwartz v. Commissioner*, 128 T.C. 6, 7 (2007)])

The tension between the clear applicability of the FRE in all federal actions, for example, and a majority practice among federal courts to diminish the role of exclusionary rules of evidence in favor of erring on the side of admissibility galvanized the Seventh Circuit Court of Appeals to note that "[t]he Federal Rules of Evidence are statutes, and district judges may not disregard statutes no matter how inconvenient or cumbersome they believe the rules to be." In re: Oil Spill by the Amoco Cadiz Off the Coast of France on March 16, 1978, 954 F. 2d 1279, 1305 (7th Cir. 1992).

9 9 A. *Fed. Prac. and Proc. Civ.* § 2411 (Wright & Miller) (3d ed.) (observes under the hearing § 2411 Practice Under Original Rule 43 – Evidence in Nonjury Cases:

> The exclusionary rules were of less importance in nonjury cases for two reasons. First, as originally promulgated, Federal Rule 43(c) called on the district judge to hear and report in a nonjury case even evidence to which an objection had been sustained except when privilege was claimed or when "t clearly appears that the evidence is not admissible on any ground." [Citation omitted.] Second, the erroneous admission of evidence often would not be a sufficient ground for reversal, since the appellate courts indulged the gracious presumption that the trial judge relied only on the evidence that properly was admitted during the trial. [Citation omitted.]
>
> Taken together, these two factors suggested that in a nonjury case the court should be slow to exclude evidence challenged under one of the exclusionary rules. The court so held [citation omitted] the governing attitude was stated strongly by Judge B. Sanborn of the Eighth Circuit:
>
> In the trial of a nonjury case, it is virtually impossible for a trial judge to commit reversible error by receiving incompetent evidence, whether objected to or not. An appellate court will not reverse a judgment in a nonjury case because of the admission of incompetent evidence, unless all of the competent evidence is insufficient to support the judgment or unless it affirmatively appears that the incompetent evidence induced the court to make an essential finding which would not otherwise have been made. *** On the other hand, a trial judge who, in the trial of a nonjury case, attempts to make strict rulings on the admissibility of evidence, can easily get his decision reversed by excluding evidence which is objected to, but which, on review, the appellate court believes should have been admitted. [Citation omitted.]

The tension between and among

(i) an unregulated practice of *Free Proof* (disavowance of formal and technical application of the FRE on the part of trial judges presiding over nonjury trials) and the federal statutory imperative that the FRE are to be applied in all court proceedings,

> *In theory, the Federal Rules of Evidence apply equally in court trials and jury trials.* [Citation omitted.] In a court trial, however, the trier-of-facts cannot be separated, let alone immunized, from the process of admission and exclusion of evidence. As a result, district judges often cannot avoid seeing the evidence that they subsequently decide to exclude. The federal civil justice system simply relies on judges' professional training to enable them to filter out information that has been proffered by one of the parties and then excluded it. (Emphasis added)

See also Wang, "Rethinking Evidentiary Rules," 302–303 (noting that a steep statistical decline in jury trials with an increase in nonjury trials requires rethinking of a binary approach to the application of the FRE to nonjury trials. While Professor Wang acknowledges that technically the FRE apply to both jury and nonjury trials, in practice, trial judges only loosely apply exclusionary rules of evidence when presiding without a jury. Professor Wang compellingly suggests that the current *Free Proof* approach that trial judges sitting without a jury apply has operational deficits that warrant the application of customized rules for nonjury trials.); Frederick Schauer, "On the Supposed Jury-Dependence of Evidence Law," 155 *U. Pa. L. Rev.* 165 (2006) (stating that:

> [a]t the moment, it is sufficient to conclude that it is hardly self-evident that the practices of so many trial judges in assuming that the rules of evidence are for other and lesser people is as beyond reproach and beyond remedy as is currently believed. More broadly, it is far from clear that the increasing academic and judicial momentum in favor of some form of *Free Proof* rests on solid empirical or conceptual foundations. Factual inquiry no less than normative legal prescription is usefully assisted by rules that are taken seriously, appoint systematically neglected by the *Free Proof* tradition. That tradition, in the large as well as in some of its ambitious manifestations, thus stands exposed of failing to explain why rules are important for law but not for facts, and of continuously clinging to a romantic image of the trial judge as a figure largely free of the cognitive failings we see and appreciate in lay jurors. Until the *Free Proof* tradition can meet the burden of explaining why these two significant omissions of justification do not substantially undercut the whole *Free Proof* idea, there will remain a significant place in the law of evidence for the real rules that impose real constraints on real judges. In law this should come as little surprise.);

Kenneth Culp Davis, "Hearsay in Nonjury Cases," 83 *Harv. L. Rev.* 1362 (1970) (writing five years *before* the FRE were enacted, Professor Davis forcefully asserted that the framers of the proposed FRE appear to codify existing hearsay rules in ways that fail to distinguish the applicability of these rules to jury and nonjury trials. The need for this distinction, so argued Professor Davis, is all the more compelling because at the time (1970) (and even more so today) nonjury trials are more numerous than jury trials in federal district courts, and constitute less than 7 percent of trials in all federal tribunals (judicial and administrative). The need for different rules is also all the more exigent, according to Professor Davis, because the most significant issue regarding hearsay in nonjury trials is not the question of *admissibility* but rather *evaluation*. Hence, he concluded that the proposed Rules of Evidence should govern both admissibility of hearsay, and also the common practice of admitting hearsay evidence that is technically inadmissible, such that proposed rules should address whether and when findings may be premised on inadmissible hearsay.); and A. Leo Levin & Harold K. Cohen, "Exclusionary Rules in Nonjury Criminal Cases," 119 *U. Pa. L. Rev.* 905, 908 (1971) (arguing for recognition of the informal but ubiquitous practice of disavowing exclusionary rules of evidence in nonjury cases)

(ii) the proposition that judges as professionally educated fact-finders are immune from the cognitive and epistemic deficits thought to mislead jurors were the latter to consider relevant but inadmissible hearsay evidence, and the heuristically and empirically sounder proposition that a trial judge presiding over a nonjury trial is susceptible to the same deficits and cognitive shortcomings as jurors, and

(iii) processing nonjury trials in a manner that is flexible and informal, and at the same time engaging in a reasonable standard or rule guided *qualitative* analysis of evidence compensating for expansive admissibility, all point to the conclusion that the principle of efficiency cannot be asked to shoulder the impossible task of justifying unbridled *Free Proof* in nonjury cases.

Free Proof, notwithstanding its claims to flexibility, and positive informality, does not aprioristically lead to greater efficiency. It simply lacks *ex ante* normativity.

7.2 APPLICATION OF THE NONJURY TRIAL JUDGE ANALOGY: THE ARBITRAL TRIBUNAL AND THE FOIBLES OF *FREE PROOF*

Notwithstanding the deficits inherent in all arguments based upon analogy, the *similarities* between a judge presiding over a nonjury trial and an ICA arbitral tribunal when processing proffered evidence by disputing parties constitutes a rich Petri dish for analysis in determining whether a system based on *Free Proof* is most conducive to the *optimal efficiency* of settlement.[10] The unbridled flooding

[10] The tension between application of the FRE with rigor and in their entirety in the context of bench trials with no jury where the finder of fact is not serving as a gatekeeper role, also extends to the role of Administrative Law Judges (ALJ) presiding over disputes before federal administrative agencies. In such proceedings ALJs in most instances engage in the ad hoc cherry-picking of evidentiary rules and concepts, but generally ignore exclusionary rules. To be sure, hearings before an ALJ, for example, in the context of an administrative agency such as the Social Security Administration (SSA) very closely resemble a judicial proceeding. The ALJ (i) receives evidence and (ii) examines witnesses regarding disputed factual issues in a case (§§ 405(b)(1), 1383 (c)(1)(A)). Indeed, those hearings, as described in the SSA, 49 Stat. 620, as amended, 42 U.S.C. § 301 *et. seq*., "are recognizably adjudicative in nature." *See, e.g., Biestek v. Berryhill*, 587 U.S. 97, 99, 139 S. C.t 1148, 203 L. Ed. 504 (2019) examining the duties performed by an ALJ, the Supreme Court noted:

> There can be little doubt that in the role of the modern federal hearing examiner or administrative law judge … is "functionally comparable" to that of a judge. [Her] powers are often, if not generally, comparable to those of a trial judge: [she] may issue subpoenas, rule on proffers of evidence, regulate the course of the hearing, and make or recommend decisions. More importantly, the due process of agency adjudication is currently structured so as to assure that the hearing examiner exercises [her] independent judgment on the evidence before [her], free from pressures by the parties or other officials within the agency.

Butz v. Economou, 438 U.S. 478, 513, 98 S. Ct. 2894, 57 L. Ed. 895. The Court in *Butz* concluded that ALJs were "entitled to absolute immunity from damages liability for their judicial acts." *Id.* at 514, 98 S. Ct. 2894.

Moreover, discovery, by way of example in *Federal Maritime Commission* administrative adjudications, generally are no different from discovery in federal civil litigation (*see* 46 U.S.C. App. § 1711(a)(1) (1994 ed.) (instructing that in FMC adjudicatory proceedings "discovery procedures…, to the extent practicable, shall be in conformity with the rules applicable in civil proceedings in the district courts of the United States"). In both types of proceedings, parties may conduct depositions, *see, e.g.*, 46 C.F.R. § 502.202 (2001); Fed. R. Civ. P. 28, which are governed by similar requirements. *Cf.* §§ 502.202, 502.203), and 502.204), with F.R.E. 28, 29, 30, and 31. "Parties may also discover evidence by: (1) serving written interrogatories, *see* § 502.205); Rule 33; (2) requesting that another party either produce documents, *see* § 502.206) (a)(1); Rule 34 (a)(1), or allow entry on that party's property for the purpose of inspecting the property or designated objects thereon, § 502.206(a)(2); Rule 34(a)(2); and (3) submitting requests for admissions, § 502.207; Rule 36 and a party failing to obey discovery orders in either type of proceeding subject to a variety of sanctions, including the entry of default judgment *see* § 502.210) (a); Rule 37 (b)(2)." *Federal Maritime Commission v. South Carolina State Port's Authority*, 553 U.S. 743, 758, 122 S Ct. 1864, 152 L. Ed. 962 (2002).

In fact, "[n]ot only are discovery procedures virtually indistinguishable, but the role of the ALJ, the impartial officer designated to hear a case, *see* § 502.147), is similar to that of an Article III judge. An ALJ has the authority to 'arrange and give notice of hearing.'" [Citation omitted.] *Id.*

Notwithstanding these similarities, ALJs *also* flout a rigorous rule approach to evidence. *See, e.g.*, *Bridges v. Wixon*, 326 U.S. 135, 155, 65 S. Ct. 1443, 89 L. Ed. 2103 (1945) (observing in the context of Immigration and Naturalization Service that "it has long been settled that the technical rules for the exclusion of evidence applicable in jury trials do not apply to proceedings before federal administrative agencies in the absence of statutory requirement that such rules are to be observed"); *Securities and Exchange Commission v. Jarkesy Jr*, 144 S. Ct. 2117, 2125–26 (2024) (observing in the context of the Security and Exchange Commission that in those "proceedings, the Commission or its delegee decides discovery disputes [citation omitted] and the SEC's Rules of Practice govern [citation omitted]. The Commission or its delegee also determines the scope and form of permissible evidence *and may admit hearsay and other testimony that would be inadmissible in federal court* [citation omitted]." (Emphasis added.)); *Interstate Commerce Commission v. Baird*, 194 U.S. 25, 44, 24 S. Ct. 563, 48 L. Ed 860 (1904) (in the context of the Interstate Commerce Commission, citing to authority here omitted, notes that,

> [t]he inquiry of a board of the character of the Interstate Commerce Commission should not be too narrowly constrained by technical rules as to the admissibility of proof. Its function is largely one of investigation, and it should not be hampered in making inquiry pertaining to interstate commerce by those narrow rules which prevail in trials at common law, where a strict correspondence is required between allegation and proof.);

Spiller v. Atchinson, 253 U.S. 117, 126, 40 S. Ct. 466, 64 L. Ed. 810 (1920) (noting in the context of the Interstate Commerce Commission's authority to investigate matters that such "provisions allow a large degree of latitude in the investigation of claims for reparation, and the resulting findings and order of the Commission may not be rejected as evidence because of any errors in its procedure not amounting to a denial of the right to a fair hearing, so long as the essential facts are based upon substantial evidence"); and *United States v. Abilene & S.RY. Co.*, 265 U.S. 274, 287–88, 44 S. Ct. 565, 68 L. Ed. 1016 (1924) (reiterating that:

> [t]he contention of the Commission is that, because its able examiner gave notice that "no doubt it will be necessary to refer to the annual reports of all these carriers," its Rules of Practice permitted matter into the reports to be used as freely as if the data had been formally introduced in evidence. *The mere admission by an administrative tribunal of matter which under the rules of evidence applicable to judicial proceedings would be deemed incompetent does not invalidate its order.* (Emphasis added))

Quite remarkably, whether by *de facto* or *de jure*, the Supreme Court in *Hopp Cotton Mills, Inc. v. Administrator of Wage and Hour Division of Department of Labor*, 312 U.S. 126, 155, 61 S. Ct. 524,

of an ICA arbitral tribunal with documents that presumably are screened by the same body of rules and principles,[11] as are used in evidence gathering cannot lead to uniformity, process transparency, or predictive value. Having the same rules governing the taking of evidence also determine admissibility of evidence is tantamount to unbridled *Free Proof*. This rubric is conducive to *unquantifiable risk*. It does not work.

The absolute absence of *any* rules governing admissibility or serving as a guide to the *weight* to be ascribed to evidence is much more problematic in the ICA-arbitral tribunal context than where a trial judge is presiding over a nonjury trial. The happenstance and fragmented approach to evidentiary proffers in an ICA scenario is made worse because the arbitrators comprising an arbitral panel typically are from different judicial systems and cultures.[12] In fact, even the tried-and-true "relevant to the case and material to its outcome" IBA Rules and Prague Rules standard used for both evidence gathering *and* admissibility-weight, is susceptible to conflicting applications and interpretations for this very reason.

Much like the trial judge presiding over a nonjury proceeding, the arbitral panel will be flooded with documents that were produced pursuant to a single standard (*relevant to the case and material to its outcome*) during the

(i) self-disclosure phase,
(ii) memorial writing juncture of the proceeding as documents on which counsel intends to rely upon; and
(iii) as part of the evidence gathering process. Likewise, the arbitral tribunal will be exposed to expert reports that in turn will rely on assumptions and/or facts supplied to the expert by a party or counsel that presumably has been disclosed at an appropriate procedural stage in the arbitration.

Optimal efficiency would require the stakeholders to have some reasonable understanding, preferably before the commencement of the arbitration, but certainly by the time that the initial Case Management Conference takes place, of the *likely* limits on admissible evidence. And *some notion* of the weight to be accorded to such evidence.

When compared to the predicament of the trial judge presiding over a nonjury trial in terms of yielding a more transparent *risk assessment* scenario with respect to evidentiary rulings, the ICA current status quo pales. As referenced (see Section 7.1), the trial court judge is charged applying the FRE. And indeed, she does so but loosely under the theory that the "gatekeeper" role is of no moment.

85 L. Ed. 624 (1941), made it clear that it is the exclusionary technical rules of evidence "applicable in jury trials" that "do not apply to proceedings before federal administrative agencies…" The Court refrained from referencing exclusionary rules of evidence applicable in federal trials; meaning, jury and nonjury trials alike. *Id.*

11 Such as the IBA Rules that in fact are permissible guidelines and not mandatory rules or standards.

12 Assuming a three-person panel.

Instead of applying the hard and fast admissibility rules, most notably hearsay, its exceptions and distinguishing non-hearsay, but certainly not exclusively, the trial judge still applies evidentiary rules beyond mere *relevancy*. She tests the quality and reliability of evidence. Applying the FRE even "*loosely*," the trial judge still is managing evidence within the context of a body of fixed rules.

Authentication of evidence takes place and often hearsay within hearsay is teased out by granting a party the right to cross-examine the out-of-court declarant. Yet, not even the semblance of such approach is present in ICA. At some point, the argument that rigorous rules of evidence and an exclusionary approach are but the offshoot of the jury system, and for this reason inapplicable to nonjury fact-finders, must be revisited. Indeed, while certainly the majority of the literature points to the system of evidence based upon strict rules and an exclusionary approach as having its origins in the jury system,[13] there is also a school of thought that understands this approach to evidence as rooted in the adversarial system.[14]

The arbitral tribunal itself will have ad hoc independent thinking with respect to each of its members. And then again, the arbitral tribunal will be layered with another mantle of non-systematic reasoning arising from the barebones standard to be applied both (i) to *evidence gathering* and (ii) the assessment of evidence, that is to say, *evidence weighing*. Both *evidence gathering* and evidence *weighing*, although profoundly related, are very much different conceptual undertakings each requiring a tailored approach.

It is necessary to mention the inverse proportionality rule applying to a US nonjury trial conducted under the FRE and the FRCP, and the workings of the inverse proportionality rule in the context of ICA. This issue has to be examined, if ever so fleetingly, in order to address the objection that the workings of the inverse proportionality rule may somehow justify the current evidentiary state of affairs in ICA, despite obvious inefficiencies and its black-box effect lacking predictability.

[13] *See* n. 6 in this chapter.

[14] *See, e.g.*, Damaška, *Evidence Law Adrift*, 2, who succinctly explains:

> Why is it that Anglo-American fact-finding is so peculiar? Despite the great variety of answers advanced, most reflection on the matter has circled around two competing theories. According to the first, older theory, the principal reason for the common law's distinctive character is the employment of lay people as judges of the facts. As was famously stated by James Thayer, the common law's fact-finding arrangements are first and foremost "the child of the jury system." [Citations omitted.] According to the second, more recent theory, these arrangements are primarily the result of the prominent role partisan counsel play in gathering evidentiary material and presenting it to the court. On this second view, then, common law evidence is first and foremost the child of the adversarial system.

Citing in support of this proposition:

An early proponent of this theory was Edmund Morgan, "The Jury and the Exclusionary Rules of Evidence," 4 *U. Chi. L. Rev.* 247 (1937). Its thoughtful contemporary expositor is Dale Nance, "The Evidence Principle," 73 *Iowa L. Rev.* 227, 229 *passim* (1988). Of course, the two theories mentioned in the text need not be mutually exclusive; in fact, they are often used in combination. *See, e.g.*, Colin Tapper, *Cross and Tapper on Evidence*, 6th ed., ed. Colin Tapper (Oxford University Press 1985).

7.3 THE DEFICITS OF HAVING THE SAME STANDARD APPLY TO EVIDENCE GATHERING AND TO THE ADMISSIBILITY OF EVIDENCE

In the context of a US judicial proceeding at the close of discovery, the critical path of evidence flow has been bilaterally exhausted. The case then may be ready for partial of complete summary adjudication.[15] At that point, all discoverable evidence under the Fed. R. Civ. P. 26 discovery standard has been secured.

The quantity of discoverable evidence reaches apogee. For this reason, the parties are best placed to learn whether summary judgment disposition viable. Of equal importance, however, the parties are now ideally placed to identify, to quantify, and to communicate risk bilaterally. Evidential symmetry has been achieved.

One strategic methodology for communicating risk is to show the strength of evidence in the form of a motion for summary judgment even though the movant may understand that it is highly unlikely that summary judgment would be secured or if granted sustained on appeal. The moving papers, however, would identify *quantifiable risk* to the opposing party, thus creating appropriate atmospherics for settlement discussion.[16]

While at this stage in a judicial proceeding the quantum of evidence is at apogee, application of the inverse proportionality rule would suggest that moving forward, that is to say, past the close of discovery, in a jury trial where the FRE are strictly enforced, the exclusionary rules of the FRE would materially diminish the quantum of admissible evidence or evidence. Therefore, evidence multiplies and reaches maximum quantity prior to trial (the equivalent of an arbitral final hearing), and evidence diminishes and reaches perigee because of the application of the FRE's exclusionary rubric and exacting rules for assessing reliability at the time of trial (the counterpart to an arbitral proceeding's final hearing). *Risk assessment* is amply feasible at this juncture.

The converse inverse proportionality rule governs ICA. During the evidence-gathering phase in an ICA proceeding it generally can be stated that the *relevant to the case and material to its outcome* standard will be applied. Even an expansive application of this standard, however, likely would require the parties seeking documents to have to demonstrate at some level (there is no applicable rule, principle, or standard) that the document(s) sought are *necessary* for purposes of meeting an element of a claim, to prove damages sought, or to establish a defense. Evidence gathering in ICA represents perigee in terms of evidence quantum. At this point not much is necessarily known. It stands in contrast to its US litigation counterpart.

In the context of ICA, because the same standard applies to evidence gathering and to the determination of admissibility, relevance, and materiality of evidence,

[15] Fed. R. Civ. P. 56 (**Summary Judgment**).

[16] The specter of summary judgment likely can be counted on appearing again at the directed verdict stage if the case proceeds to trial. The risk is recurring with even greater likelihood of success.

the actual merits-evidential record is constituted and evaluated *throughout* the entire arbitral process. Much like a civil law jurisdiction trial, the evaluation of evidence coincides with the very commencement of the proceeding. To a great extent, from the perspective of evidential assessment on the part of the decision-makers, the final hearing begins once the first document request is lodged.

At the time of the final hearing in ICA, however, evidentiary perigee becomes apogee. In addition to documents secured pursuant to the evidence taking *discovery* counterpart, at the final hearing the arbitral tribunal is presented with the universe of all documents the parties independently deemed to be relevant, and therefore, admissible. It would be contrafactual at this point to assume that the respective parties would pare down documents by engaging in a corresponding "materiality" analysis beyond that which already took place in securing the responsive documents in the first instance.[17]

To the contrary, the respective parties in anticipation of the hearing will submit those documents that they *subjectively* determine will be relied upon in proving affirmative claims or defenses. No consideration will be accorded to issues concerning admissibility, such as authentication reliability or quality of the evidence. Certainly, no thought would be extended to any form of hearsay considerations. Attenuated due process would quell any such concerns.

In the context of an ICA, proceeding evidentiary quantum reaches apogee at this point, standing in sharp relief to its judicial action counterpart (the actual trial). Ostensibly, premises then would be sufficiently ripe for concluding that somehow because the arbitral tribunal "only" would be receiving documents already meeting the *relevant to the case and material to its outcome* standard (the evidence-taking documents) merely supplemented by documents "upon which the parties intend to rely," the tribunal would be poised to engage in a qualitative evidentiary analysis. Such assessment would determine the *weight* to be ascribed to *all* documents forming part of the evidence taking process in addition to those documents upon which the parties intend to rely.

This document-critical flow viewed from the perspective of the inverse proportionality rule in the context of ICA has the effect of flooding the tribunal with three general categories of documents.

7.3.1 *Documents Voluntarily Exchanged during Evidence Taking*

The first such category is comprised by documents the parties voluntarily exchanged during the evidence taking process. These documents could have been responsive

[17] As there is no definition of "materiality," and certainly the parties would seek to introduce as many documents as possible so long as in their minds such "evidence" would tend to prove any aspect of their claim or defense, it follows that documents secured through the evidence taking process would represent a floor and not a ceiling.

to a document request or part of the self-disclosure document production requirements. Typically, the documents comprising this set (First Set) will not be seen by the tribunal until the time of the hearing because of the voluntary nature of its production. Thus, the conclusion that they meet the standard is one that the responsive parties subjectively determined. It is not clear that they in fact do so, in part, because of the adversarial tactical thinking underlying the self-disclosure-production process.

Many of the documents produced may be, and often are, self-serving and only partially responsive, if at all. For this latter reason, it cannot be concluded that these documents have been in any way assessed other than through the prism of adversarial eyes.

7.3.2 *Documents Produced over Objections*

The second universe of documents to reach the final hearing's door are documents adversarially requested in a document demand that were withheld on the ground of one or more objections, but which the tribunal ordered the objecting party to produce. These documents (the Second Set) presumably have been fully vetted by the tribunal and ruled admissible, relevant, and material,[18] otherwise their production would not have been compelled.

It is reasonably safe to assume that from a very general perspective this set of documents is likely to constitute the most significant evidentiary body of work for purposes of the proceeding. It is unlikely that, with the exception of privilege or confidentiality-based objections, the documents sought, and initially withheld and objected to, were not produced because of the non-movant's concern for arbitral expediency and efficiency. The documents in the Second Set likely will have the greatest probative and/or impeachment value.

7.3.3 *Documents on Which the Parties Intend to Rely*

The third and final body of documents are those the parties subjectively have determined to be documents upon which they intend to rely. The extent to which parties may be compelled to disclose prior to the actual final hearing each document falling within this Third Set, and how they are to be used, constitutes less than a standard practice. This Third Set, much like the First Set, mostly will be comprised by documents having as their solitary evidentiary normativity the parties' subjective strategic and tactical best interest. This state of affairs is hardly a model for efficiency or *quantifiable risk assessment* conducive to settlement.

In fact, the documents comprising the Third Set typically will form part of the Statement of Facts and Statement of Defense. It follows that they will be made

[18] If documents are *material*, they will also be *relevant*.

available to the tribunal for substantive consideration at an early date. Practically, however, these documents will be assessed at the final hearing.

In the context of an investor-State arbitration, the documents will be submitted with the initial briefings (Memorial/Counter-Memorial/Reply/Joinder). In both instances, ICA and ISDS, the consequences are identical and plain. The arbitral tribunal will be inundated with documents and exposed to evidence and facts that certainly can serve to confuse, to mislead, and to cloud a lucid and analytical discernment of the case.

With respect to all three sets of documents referenced, the arbitral tribunal will have to assess the *weight* of the evidence. In doing so, not only does the tribunal lack any operative rules or standards to do so, but it is actually in most cases plagued by the evidential doctrines of different, and often conflicting, legal systems and traditions.

The conceptual category referred to as *weight* of the evidence in the context of ICA is wholly devoid of any content. Therefore, it is not analytically possible to assess risk at all with respect to this critical conceptual and doctrinal element.

An essential part of *risk assessment* concerns the ability to predict the likely importance, credibility, and probative value that a specific instrument or body of evidence may be accorded to an element of a claim or defense. Risk assessment like the negotiating process, concerns analysis "in the shadow of the law." The trial judge presiding over a nonjury trial herself will be exposed to inadmissible evidence, and in this regard certainly the psychological effects and the weight that such evidence may have on the trier of fact, simply cannot be addressed.

The parties' arguments, however, directed at the *quality* of such evidence at a very minimum will sensitize the trier of fact as to the weight that should be attributed to the evidence and the limits, if any, to be imposed on its probative value. These arguments, presumably based on evidentiary rules, will not circumscribe the trial judge's vast discretion, the exercise of which is virtually impervious to appellate review. They will, however, cause the fact-finder to test the reliability of the evidence. A predicate to such arguments is a definable set of evidentiary expectations that as of yet simply find no place in ICA.

As to the First Set (documents voluntarily exchanged) and the Third Sets (documents which the parties intend to rely), the tribunal would have to determine all four evidentiary elements: *admissibility*, *relevance*, *materiality*, and *weight*. The same deficits ascribed to *weight* are also shared by *admissibility*, *relevance*, and *materiality*. These terms are hollow in the context of ICA and therefore as ad hoc as are the very tribunals struggling to apply these principles yet to be defined.

The path forward does not consist in shackling arbitral tribunals with strict rules of evidence and an exclusionary approach. As a practical matter at this time legal-arbitral culture would not be receptive to any such suggestion, even if it were the best approach, *which it is not*.

7.4 A NONBINARY APPROACH TO AN INTERNATIONAL ANALYTICAL METHODOLOGY

The question, much like the title of one of Soren Kierkegaard's transformative works, *Either/Or*, simply is not binary. Contrary to the suggestions in some quarters, there is a middle ground.[19] Evidential approaches to ICA fact-finding and adjudication need not embrace a stratified and rigid evidentiary regime. Similarly, the current ad hoc and *laissez-faire* approach simply is not a viable option. It has led to a quantifiable decline in ICA, to a trend favoring judicial choice of court and choice of law provisions.[20]

Free Proof is dysfunctional. It does not work. Particularly if *risk assessment* and predictive value are to form part of ICA. Similarly, engrafting mandatory rules of evidence and an exclusionary approach, whether exogenously imported from common law systems, or endemic to international law resulting from a hybrid cross-pollination of doctrines from different legal traditions, simply would not work even if academics, arbitrators, and counsel were open to such an endeavor, which they are not at this historic moment.

It is clear that arbitration needs to find equipoise between (i) the flexibility and pliant dynamic between *party-autonomy* and arbitral discretion (inherent powers), (ii) the informality[21] inherent in a private (non-sovereign State-driven) methodology for

[19] "Applicability of Rules of Evidence Where the Judge Is the Trier of Facts in an Action at Law," 42 *Harv. L. Rev.* 258 (1928), Chapter 6, n. 1, discussing applicability of strict rules of evidence and an exclusionary approach to the issue of admissibility versus *Free Proof* in the context of a trial judge presiding over a nonjury trial, the author observes:

> The paramount reason, however, for the view that the exclusionary rules should not bind the judge is that such rules are designed to keep from the jurors relevant evidence which laymen are considered unable to evaluate, but which a judge is supposedly qualified to handle. Unquestionably, an experienced judge can appraise the probative value of evidence better than the average juror. But since jurors normally must act on all sorts of evidence in governing their daily affairs, and since the judges who preside in courts of first instance often lack the desired training and experience, it may be doubted whether the difference in fact-finding ability is great. Although there is apparently no middle course between applying the jury rules and giving the judge general discretion, *it is highly questionable whether the ordinary rules of evidence should be wholly abandoned where the judge is the sole trier of fact.* (Emphasis added)

In the context of ICA, arbitral tribunals are without even the blunt compass of loosely applying *known principles* for purposes of evaluating the quality of evidence.

[20] *See* Chapter 1, n. 7.

[21] The "informal" character of arbitration in many substantial ways already has dissipated. Arbitral disputes quite often are in the billions of dollars and often entail complex regulatory issues, intellectual property, sophisticated technological questions, and going concerns that have micro and macroeconomic consequences in addition to affecting entire global industries. The privatization of transnational disputes in the form of ICA has far outstripped disputes between small businesses over rudimentary contractual questions. Therefore, considerable "formalities" are observed, particularly with respect to the analyses and evaluation of expert reports and testimony.

dispute resolution, and (iii) the dire need to have some predictability and uniformity in the qualitative assessment of the reliability of all forms of evidence (documentary, testimonial, and expert opinion). This balance is delicate. It does not currently exist.

An ad hoc *Free Proof* "methodology" that pervades the practice of arbitral tribunal "adjudication" is inherently incapable of serving the primary objective of *optimal efficiency*. Therefore, the *status quo ante* cannot be embraced as an acceptable paradigm.

Consumers of arbitral services and counsel crave predictability and the ability to engage in *risk assessment* throughout the proceeding. Arbitrators cannot exercise unchecked discretion to accept *all* evidence tempered only by categories of relevance and materiality that are not even ill-defined because they are not at all defined.

Unchecked arbitral discretion in the context of *Free Proof* assumes that substantial percentages of all of the evidence will be admissible and, somehow, pursuant to standards, rules, and methodologies unknown to all stakeholders (*and often to the Arbitral Tribunal itself*). The belief is that all will be straightened out and lead to the best result consonant with the equitable application of law to fact, and the expectations of all shareholders. This mantra is a slim reed on which to rest the parties' fortunes, as well as the assessment of reliable evidence in the context of international commerce's preferred dispute resolution methodology.

The *status quo ante* necessarily leaves all stakeholders (with the exception of the arbitral tribunal that presumably exists in order *to assist parties in resolving disputes*) wondering how the qualitative analysis of evidence, if at all, has taken place. Arbitrators cannot just ignore the need to understand systematically and doctrinally that there is evidence falling into specific categories that plainly define the evidence as intrinsically unreliable, albeit subject to degrees depending on the particularly of the evidentiary factual matrix.

Is it reasonable to insist and persist in applying an ad hoc *Free Proof* approach to the concept of "*weight*" to be provided to evidence? Can a blind eye be turned to the need for a systematic qualitative analysis of evidence that is intrinsically unreliable but arguably admissible? The reasonable answers to these questions are clear.

8

A New Framework for a Modern Conception of ICA

The following ten listed Sections 8.1–8.10 as discussed in this chapter are non-exhaustive propositions that should form part of a framework that arbitrators must ensue. They are designed to suggest a point of departure for the conversation that needs to be had. At issue is more than just the extent to which procedural transparency and predictability may be cultivated regarding the *taking* and *presentation* if evidence. At the heart of risk assessment is the need to incorporate rules fostering objectivity that enhance ICA's ability to redeem its promise to be efficient. A promise that now appears anachronistic, if not altogether abandoned. A promise that appeared to have been intended to apply to early twentieth-century simple contractual disputes between stakeholders who rejected the proverbial delays of judicial tribunals and the ever-increasing expense of litigation, fifty years prior to the enactment and codification of the FRE.

8.1. The Current *Free Proof* Schema is an *ad hoc* Black-Box Paradigm of Unworkable Adjudication
8.2. Exclusionary Rules of Evidence Are Not Foreign to ICA
8.3. The Quality of Evidence Must Be Discussed with the Parties
8.4. Evidence Admissibility and Qualitative Assessment Must Be Based on Transcultural Principles in the Form of Rules and Not Standards
8.5. Evidentiary Principles (Rules) Must Hold Sacrosanct the Inherent Powers of Arbitrators and Corresponding Exercise of Arbitral Discretion
8.6. The Parties Must Be Exhorted to Use the *Best Evidence*
8.7. The Rule of Reliability and Due Process: Politically Correct Euphemisms for a Hearsay Rule to Test Reliability
8.8. Cross-Examination Has to Be Understood and Embraced as a Cross-Cultural Methodology Concerned with Persuasion through the Presentation of Evidence
8.9. Witness Examination Objections as to Form and the Need for a Corpus of Objections to Improper Examination Questions
8.10. *Free Proof* Is Particularly Unreliable When Evaluating the Quality of a Witness' Standing as an Expert and Expert Witness Evidence in the Form of Reports and Testimony.

Today, ICA is just as expensive as litigation, notwithstanding having sacrificed (i) fulsome and robust due process, (ii) second instance review, (iii) privacy and confidentiality over transparency, (iv) comprehensive rules of civil procedure, and (v) manifest disregard of the law and facts, to the altar of efficiency. International Commercial Arbitration now stands adorned by the rhetoric of its initial promise, still holding out to the universe of existing and prospective consumers of arbitral services the aspiration of being more flexible, expedient, and efficient than judicial tribunals, although the empirical data for such claims long vanished.[1] And what remains is the unparalleled success of the New York Convention, and little more.

The reaction from the corporate world has been stark.[2] A number of Fortune 500 companies have turned their backs on ICA, and even to its ISDS public international law counterpart,[3] instead opting for the certainty of appellate review, proven mandatory mediation regimes that lead to settlement, and the empirically established proposition that, at least in the US, the overwhelming majority of civil actions settle.[4] The zero-sum-game component that once created unquantifiable uncertainty has disappeared from civil litigation, in large measure because multiple reforms, and most recently the 2015 proportionality amendment to Fed. R. Civ. P. 26, have tamed discovery while rendering *risk assessment* all the more viable.[5]

Process, as in the ICA process, is a victim of the New York Convention's formidable success.[6] Yet, the certainty of the New York Convention's workings is no longer enough. The sheer size and complexity of cases that simply were not foreseeable during the first quarter of the twentieth century when ICA commenced its trek toward *Mitsubishi*,[7] and the doctrinal gains of standing in *pari materia* with the normativity of federal and state courts have not kept pace with the need for *optimal efficiency*. The contemporary development of ICA warrants reform conducive to certainty and, therefore, to *optimal efficiency* upon penalty of itself being lodged in the unglamorous museum of failed experiments subject to a standing no greater than that of Phlogiston and Ptolemaic epicycles.

8.1 THE CURRENT *FREE PROOF* SCHEMA IS AN *AD HOC* BLACK-BOX PARADIGM OF UNWORKABLE ADJUDICATION

To borrow from David D. Caron and Lee M. Caplan, "[t]he expectation of parties from different legal systems are never so likely to conflict as with questions of evidence; [q]uestions of evidence are among the most problematic aspects of any

1 *See ICC Commission Report Controlling Time and Costs in Arbitration*, p. 11.
2 *See* Chapter 2, n. 9 in this volume.
3 *See* Chapter 2.
4 *Id.*
5 *See* Chapter 4, n. 107.
6 *See* Chapter 1, n. 12.
7 Mentschikoff, "Commercial Arbitration," 850.

regulation of international arbitration."[8] The cultural and policy divide between common law and civil law approaches to evidence, and particularly to exclusionary rules, is longstanding and vast.

A thumbnail sketch would suggest that in the aftermath of the French Revolution, the doctrinal body of rules having their origin in Roman canon law was criticized and viewed as a cumbersome relic that interfered with a fact-finder's personal and direct assessment of evidence. The fact-finder's direct analysis of evidence was assumed to be the most fateful and pristine conceptualization that could lead to a truthful and fair determination of the probative value of the matter asserted. A rubric of evidentiary principles, so that argument went, that qualified the classes of evidence did little more than interfere with what otherwise would be unvarnished optics that shared a communion with the truth. Such is the nature of arguments based on historical legacy.

Damaška elegantly narrates that "[a]s a reaction to the ills of the Roman-Canon system-ills, by the way, that were greatly exaggerated by its critics – the principle was espoused that the law should refrain from regulating the probative effects of evidence, or the necessary quantum and quality of proof."[9] He further explains that the "validity of proof was to be left to the legally unconstrained judgement of the trier of fact – to his *conviction intime*. Rules of weight, including rules of corroboration, were thus gradually eliminated from evidence law."[10]

The tenets underlying this "modern approach" that would develop into *Free Proof*, that is to say, an approach to evidence assessment unshackled by evidentiary constraints that purportedly denaturalize the probative effect of evidence if left undistorted by the false prism of evidentiary rules, would be far greater, and therefore, much more in keeping with the truth. An aprioristic approach to evidentiary adjudication, so this *modern view* asserts, would disfigure evidence and frustrate its assessment by removing the evidence from the entirety of its context and in so doing extracting from the finder of fact the ability to judge correctly the quality and quantity of the evidence, as well as its contextual significance. Damaška explains,

> On the epistemic level, then, the embrace of Free Proof was an act of resignation, the choice of the second best. If it were possible to devise a reliable scheme for the measurement of probative value – as early Enlightenment philosophers believed to be the case – powerful arguments would have had to have been advanced in

[8] Caron & Caplan, *The UNCITRAL Arbitration Rules*, 555.

[9] Damaška, "Free Proof and Its Detractors," 344.

[10] *Id*. Damaška qualifies this statement as follows:

> There were exceptions, however. In Holland, for example, the rule survives to the present day that a conviction cannot be based on the statement of a single witness. As a reaction against the ancient view that the defendant's confession is "the queen of proof," several jurisdictions also require that a conviction cannot rest on the confession alone. But all these surviving corroboration rules are of little practical importance.

Id. at n. 3.

favor of converting this scheme into mandatory legal regulation. On the political plane, however, the embrace of Free Proof was more than a *faute de mieux* solution: removing "legal chains" from evidence processing was thought necessary to introduce desirable forums of lay participation in the administration of justice.[11]

In broad strokes, the civil law system developed an evidentiary legal culture pursuant to which the fact-finder's subjective experiences, knowledge, training, and "common sense"[12] were deemed to be the finest instruments and conceptual categories for the assessment of evidence and understanding of its probative effects. Aprioristic evidentiary categories and other evidence-based qualifying principles merely served to obscure and to derail the fact-finder's ability to establish a causal link between evidence and a factual proposition asserted in its connection.[13]

Certainly this subjectivity was an insufficient model. The role of discursive reasoning became an essential necessity for a verdict to survive appellate scrutiny. Put simply, "the judge's conviction had to be '*raisonné*.'"[14]

While certainly different views within the civil law *Free Proof* domain developed mostly in connection with the extent to which factual determinations could be made "intersubjectively acceptable" based upon the extent to which logic and experience should limit or qualify a fact-finder's evidentiary determinations, two principles remained as systemic polestars. First, aprioristic classification of evidence was to be shunned. Second, a fact-finder's decision, that is to say, personal conviction (*conviction intime*) would need to be removed from the domain of the subjective and thus objectified through rational discursive reasoning and experience, but *not* pursuant to qualifying evidentiary rules.

The common law approach to evidence could not be farther removed. The fact-finder's personal conviction or intuitive understanding of evidence plays no role. And, therefore, can hardly be identified as even an element of the decision-making process. The analytical approach does not purport to buttress intuitive perception and understanding with the scaffolding of reason and experience in order "*to objectify*" the finding. And thereby bestow normative standing.

The common law system, as will be briefly demonstrated in what follows, enshrines the objectification of evidence (see Section 8.7). Standards of proof underscore what purports to be an objective quantitative metric. Jury instructions are read to jurors so that their personal cognitive processing of evidence can be appropriately qualified for purposes of determining weight, and in some instances whether to ascribe

11 *Id.*

12 One cannot help but reflect on René de Cartes' tongue-in-cheek remark in the first sentence of his *Discourse on Method*, "Le bon sens est la chose au monde la mieux partagée."

13 The *Free Proof* approach relies on the fact-finder's personal experience, training, professional judgment, and personal intuition as the unfettered and unvarnished instruments that cannot be compromised or tainted by evidential principles.

14 Damaška, "Free Proof and Its Detractors," at 345, *citing to* Gerhard Walter, *Freie Beweiswürdigung* (Mohr 1979), 69–73 at n. 5.

any value to the evidence itself. Hence, their direct understanding of the evidence is meaningfully shaped by evidentiary rules. The common law approach views the evidentiary rubric as appropriately focusing the optics of the lens through which evidence need to be analyzed.

The contrast in the approach between the civil law and the commons law systems could not be more stark. Here again Damaška is pithily suggestive:

> We can now begin to see why the rhetoric of Free Proof resonates differently in continental and common law jurisdictions. In the former, free evaluation of evidence has been elevated to the rank of a regulative principle of considerable importance in legal argumentation against binding rules weight. In common law countries, on the other hand, Free Proof lacks normative status and is not even a term of art. The legal system openly aspires to guide triers of fact in their analysis of evidence. If despite all these features common law can still be assessed with Free Proof, it is mainly because unexplained jury verdicts are, in fact, largely immune from challenge. They can be final even when they lack support in canons of valid reasoning. In this descriptive sense, common law fact-finders are indeed eminently "free" in reaching their decision.[15]

These foundational different approaches to the law of evidence raise significant epistemological concerns that are beyond the analysis of settlement and *risk assessment* in ICA. By way of example, should probative evidence ever be deemed inadmissible in ICA assuming that its basis for inadmissibility does not concern a cognizable privilege? To what extent is a fact-finder's decisional freedom impaired or enlightened by the scientific transformation of factual inquiries? More broadly, is legal expertise a necessary predicate to factual determinations? Should probative evidence ever be inadmissible? And if so, what response should arbitrators have when they encounter unauthenticated evidence that in no way is reliable but the content of which is probative? Should a forbidden factual premise or argument constitute a banned weapon in the dynamics of the now almost mythical arbitrator deliberations?

In what follows these questions are not answered. Yet, they are indirectly addressed. They must be.

The descriptive status quo of the presentation of evidence in ICA is not long-term sustainable. The single standard applying both (i) to evidence taking and (ii) to the presentation (admissibility and weight) of evidence has led to a black box scenario lacking in predictability, uniformity, and rooted in *ad hoc Free Proof*, which only yields uncertainty. Such approach furthers quantifiable inefficiencies, procedural inefficiencies, and cannot be conducive to *optimal efficiency*.

By having the "weight" requirement[16] arbitrators are compelled to pass judgment and to assess the quality of evidence and not just its quantity, although the latter

[15] Damaška, "Free Proof and Its Detractors," at 347.

[16] *See* IBA Rules, Prague Rules, Institutional Rules of the ICDR, SIAC, and ICC.

as well requires objective metrics beyond just personal belief. This "weight" of the evidence category requirement has been embraced, but not fully and clearly understood by the stakeholders. The elements comprising the weight to be accorded to evidence must be rendered intelligible particularly in the context of an arbitral culture that flouts uniformity and prizes *ad hoc* adjudication.

The extent to which evidence that cannot be contested remains opaque, by example in the form of cross-examination, is to be considered as to "weight," that is to say, a *qualitative* analysis. Is weight determined by the totality of circumstances? Does *reliability* constitute an element to be considered in *weighing* evidence? Should the credibility of the agent communicating probative evidence affect the weight of the actual evidence itself? Are the two truly related?

At present it is less than clear whether these considerations form part of the collective consciousness of ICA arbitral tribunals. They should.

There needs to be objective and reliable expectations on the part of all ICA stakeholders with respect to the concept of the *weight* to be accorded to the evidence. These expectations in turn should be based on reasonable approaches to evidence that are conducive to the principle that the probative force of evidence cannot be deemed so compelling by its own context and surrounding factual matrix to be beyond *ex ante* qualification by categorical legal rules.

A document that is not self-authenticating with a less than established chain of custody and a questionable provenance simply is not tantamount to reliable evidence to be accorded significant probative value (if at all) merely because of its content's propensity to prove the truth of a particular proposition asserted. The current ICA unbridled and unqualified *Free Proof* regime would apply no actual or metaphysical exclusionary rule to the document. Most likely it would be treated in *pari materia* with a counterpart lacking the requisite deficits while having the same probative evidentiary force.

In a regime where *admissibility* operationally is never challenged, ICA arbitral tribunals are inundated with purportedly probative but unreliable evidence in the form of witness testimony and documents lacking authentication (often dateless and without a signature). Even the most coarse aspirational rigor would invite arbitrators to engage in the not entirely futile task of disregarding such evidence as a matter of a categorical imperative notwithstanding its ostensible probative force.

Understandably, once such forbidden knowledge has reached the arbitral tribunal, mostly likely part of paradise has been lost, *but not all*. If the deficits of such tainted or unreliable evidence are discussed within the private confines of panel deliberations, then conceptual meaningful gains toward uniformity and reason-based objective expectations concerning the weight to be accorded to evidence is necessary, if not altogether existentially necessary. Even this much would contribute to mitigating the uncertainty that precludes *risk assessment* conducive to *optimal efficiency*.

Any new attitude toward probative evidentiary weight in the context of ICA would first necessitate as a point of departure embracing the principle that a *Free*

Proof system qualified by evidentiary principles or rules highlighting the extent to which evidence is reasonably reliable, and making provision for the party against whom *prima facie* unreliable evidence is being proffered so that ostensible deficits can be challenged and tested must. This much is necessary.

This initial foundational principle will not be readily accepted. The *status quo ante* represents a comfort zone that has not been challenged because of its inherent arbitrariness and conceptual deficits. Change will be resisted.

To be sure, the stale platitude will be raised that it was precisely the need for flexibility and informality that was conducive to rejecting the cumbersome rules of evidence that led to arbitration and not recourse to judicial proceedings.[17]

This "soundbite" has been the beneficiary of reflexive acceptance. In fact, however, much more important factors such as (i) party autonomy in selecting (ii) the applicable substantive law, (iii) the decision-makers, (iv) the arbitral institute, (v) the arbitral seat, (vi) the actual place of the arbitration, (vii) a binding and readily enforceable arbitral award pursuant to the New York Convention, and (viii) the certainty of finality in exchange for waiver of judicial appellate recourse and/or second instance *de novo* merits review, all come to mind before (if at all) considering the applicability of evidentiary regimes.

This latter consideration never seriously has been in any sort of contention. Certainly, sophisticated consumers of arbitral services do not select ICA over judicial proceedings on the ground that municipal evidentiary rules unduly restrict arbitrators from admitting all but evidence protected by a privilege, or in the rare instances that information is politically sensitive and, despite its probative force/value, cannot be disclosed.[18]

[17] *See* Green, "No Strict Evidence Rules," 533, 536 (addressing this concern and noting that "[e]ssentially, arbitrators need to balance concerns about informality, lack of legal therapeutic value, difficulties in obtaining witnesses, lack of legal representation, and the complexities of workplace disputes with the principles of supporting the evidence rules that exclude certain forms of evidence as reliable or because of policy reasons." While this statement was articulated in the context of domestic labor arbitration, the principle is equally applicable to ICA with some qualifications. A tempered approach is warranted and not an *ex ante* rejection of evidence rules on the theory that they will unduly stratify the proceeding.).

[18] The entire panoply of objections that "limit" admissibility are enunciated in Art. 9.2 of the IBA Rules, which reads:

> 2. The Arbitral Tribunal shall, at the request of a Party or on its own motion, exclude from evidence or production any Document, statement, oral testimony or inspection, in whole or in part, for any of the following reasons:
>
> (a) lack of sufficient relevance to the case or materiality to its outcome;
> (b) legal impediment or privilege under the legal or ethical rules determined by the Arbitral Tribunal to be applicable [citation omitted];
> (c) unreasonable burden to produce the requested evidence;
> (d) loss or destruction of the Document that has been shown with reasonable likelihood to have occurred;
> (e) grounds of commercial or technical confidentiality that the Arbitral Tribunal determines to be compelling;

Certainly it behooves all ICA stakeholders to have formal governing principles or rules that as a matter of form would preclude admissibility, but practically and operationally function to mitigate the effects of the "inadmissible" evidence on the arbitrators who cannot reasonably and altogether disassociate themselves from the "forbidden information" simply by calling it "inadmissible." Instead, the effects of having been exposed to inadmissible, but *possibly* highly probative content, can be adjusted for by not granting *any* weight to the evidence. This approach represents a more realistic scenario than assuming that after having tasted the fruit of the forbidden knowledge, somehow the panel would be able to take back the seductive bite. It cannot.

8.2 EXCLUSIONARY RULES OF EVIDENCE ARE NOT FOREIGN TO ICA

Contrary to popular arbitral culture, exclusionary rules of evidence are not *altogether* foreign to ICA. Again, the IBA Rules are helpful in this regard. By way of illustration, Art. 9.2(c) of the IBA Rules provides that at the request of a party or the arbitral tribunal *sua sponte* on its own motion any form of evidence (oral testimony, inspection, or document) will be excluded where it would cause an "unreasonable burden to produce the requested evidence."

This rule of exclusion both theoretically and practically is applicable to a scenario where the excluded evidence has probative force. Yet, notwithstanding even a high propensity to establish the proposition asserted as a matter of fact and law, the evidence would still be excluded if presumably on an objective basis (this much is not stated and cannot be completely assumed) the production of the evidence *somehow* would be too burdensome.

The Rule does not call for a balancing test pursuant to which probative value is assessed proportionally in connection with its propensity to establish the proposition to be asserted, versus the type of burden that must be overcome to satisfy production. Even though the Rule itself is silent with respect to any objective metric or reason-based balancing analysis, thus suggesting a strong likely penchant for *conviction intime*, it is still identifying a class of document (those that cannot be produced without surmounting a burden) that aprioristically will be excluded. While the *ex ante* evidentiary category of exclusion does not relate to authentication issues or questions having to do with the inability to test the reliability of assertions contained in the document, operationally the Rule is exclusionary because it renders technically inadmissible evidence irrespective of its qualitative probative force.

(f) grounds of special political or institutional sensitivity (including evidence that has been classified as secret by a government or a public international institution) that the Arbitral Tribunal determines to be compelling; or

(g) considerations of procedural economy, proportionality, fairness or equality of the Parties that the Arbitral Tribunal determines to be compelling.

Similarly, Art. 9.2(g) casts a broad and diverse exclusionary net. It grants the arbitral tribunal standing to exclude evidence, presumably irrespective of its probative qualities, based on "considerations of [i] procedural economy, [ii] proportionality, [iii] fairness or [iv] equality of the Parties that the Arbitral Tribunal determines to be compelling." The exclusion of relevant and material probative evidence on the ground of "procedural economy" represents a remarkable proposition. All the more so because there is no qualifying language applying to the term "procedural economy."

If such a term encompasses, by way of example, extending a hearing or otherwise delaying the procedural calendar, it is less than intuitive how such concerns would possibly outweigh the admission of probative evidence. This category resonates much like its permutation, *attenuated arbitral due process*. Here, the overarching principle of efficiency is deemed to outweigh the evidentiary effects of possibly relevant and material evidence. The exclusionary profile of the rule borders on draconian, and all the more so because it too lacks *any* reference to objective metrics.

The "proportionality" element of the rule ostensibly is more palatable but its clear aprioristic exclusionary effect remains ever present. Proportionality of course bespeaks a relationship of ratios. Thus, in a scenario, such as having the cost of production of the evidence at issue disproportionately expensive in relation to the amount in controversy, which also can be characterized as an efficiency issue, it may be conceptually more pliant to fathom *ex ante* exclusionary treatment.

Yet, the fact remains that relevant and material evidence having probative value is rejected based upon considerations *external* to the evidence itself. Such considerations modify what would be the fact-finder's direct cognitive assessment of the evidence, which in this scenario would be akin to ascribing no *weight* to evidence that otherwise is probative.

The third and fourth elements of the Rule, "fairness or equality," both are exclusionary and each presents different sets of challenges. Less so with "equality" (admittedly a category susceptible to measure), and the final element, "fairness," is a bedeviled term.

In some sense, the term "fairness" often serves as a catch-all category that can rear its head in circumstances that hardly lead to equity. Excluding evidence having substantial probative force on the ground that it would be "unfair" to a party, raises intriguing conceptual and ethical concerns from a purely analytical perspective.

These two components of the Rule are shrouded with the mantle of equity. More than just surface analysis, however, makes clear that a conceptual category serving an exclusionary purpose without a corresponding check or balance in methodology justifying the exclusion notwithstanding the probative force of the evidence, constitutes an important component of the Rule.

The third eloquent example of categorical exclusionary rule can be found in Art. 9.3. This provision reads that, "[t]he Arbitral Tribunal may, at the request of a Party or on its own motion, exclude evidence obtained illegally." The Rule also is quite remarkable. It renders possible excluding evidence that has not been legally obtained irrespective of the probative weight of such evidence.

In the field of Human Rights Law, in part as a reaction to the rise of totalitarian regimes that extracted "evidence" from prisoners pursuant to torture and the application of inhumane techniques, the evidentiary principle of excluding illegally secured evidence, independently of the evidence's probative force, understandably was universally embraced. Similarly, in the criminal law space a check and balance on a prosecuting State's use of evidence, again, independently of the probative quality of such evidence, is inextricably and rightfully linked to the legality of the means for securing such evidence.

It is somewhat more conceptually challenging, however, to justify the application of this policy-based principle in the context of ICA. An arbitral tribunal is charged with resolving a dispute. It is not empowered with the implementation of State or transnational social policy. The fruit from the poison tree, if probative, arguably may find its rightful place and weight in the proceeding so long as it is appropriately contextualized. The specificity of the operative facts matters.

Indeed, it is not altogether beyond man's wit to conceive of scenarios where as a matter of basic universal fairness such exclusion would favor the corrupt party to the detriment of a proceeding's merits. The systemic dismissal, for example, of a proceeding (in the ISDS context) where the Request for Production process was plagued by corruption actually constitutes a defense favoring the respondent host-State. The claims against the host-State are dismissed, notwithstanding its participation in the alleged corruption.[19]

Therefore, in sharp contrast to the thinking of "common arbitral culture," the application of aprioristic or *ex ante* exclusionary evidentiary principles simply are not foreign to ICA and, in fact, can be readily identified in the very IBA Rules when considered with care. Application of evidence rules and principles that temper, but do not altogether eviscerate a *Free Proof* approach will contribute to an over-arching ICA evidential architecture conducive to *optimal efficiency*.

8.3 THE QUALITY OF EVIDENCE MUST BE DISCUSSED WITH THE PARTIES

ICA evidentiary *adjudication* is a black box affair and radically *ad hoc*. In practice *all* evidence subject to evidence gathering is considered. There is no "admissibility screening." In effect, in the ICA domain of evidence gathering, that is, evidence deemed responsive to a demand for production in practice *almost always* will be the same as admissible evidence. Hence, in ICA "discoverable" or "discloseable" evidence equals admissible evidence.

[19] *See, e.g., World Duty Free Company v Republic of Kenya*, ICSID Case No. Arb/00/7, Award, October 4, 2006.

If for no other reason because the identical standard applies (relevant to the case and material to its outcome), and only *weight* theoretically is to be assessed at the presentation stage (see Chapter 4 in this volume). Once evidence is admitted its reliability *and* substantive importance theoretically are determined. Yet, technically the evidence now forms part of the record for "adjudication." Of course, how evidence is tested for reliability is shrouded in the mystery of subjectivity.

The non-arbitral panel stakeholders at no point, however, have any ability to engage in *risk assessment* with respect to that evidence. They are blessed only with the solitary understanding that because it meets the evidence taking ("discovery") standard, it therefore, constitutes admissible evidence. Any additional epistemic pronouncements concerning the *weight* of the evidence remains the subject matter of tea leaves.

Proposed principles for evidentiary assessment, including admissibility, and not just reliability and *weight*, must hold the arbitral tribunal responsible for articulating to the stakeholders the tribunal's views on the *quality* of evidence. The tribunal *should* be charged with the imperative of providing the parties with sufficient information so they may have "*some sense*" of how the arbitral tribunal views specific bodies or items of evidence in terms of their substantive probative value.

This much can be accomplished throughout the course of the arbitration. And should certainly constitute a procedural order priority item for purposes of discussion at the case management conference *prior* to the Final Hearing, and/or at any earlier time.

A discussion on the quality of evidence represents a basic proposition of universal standing. It is not partial to any legal culture or tradition. Consequently, adopting it merely requires the arbitral tribunal to engage in a transparent analysis of the evidence identified and/or presented, and to communicate these observations with sufficient coherence and specificity so as to render *risk assessment* possible.

8.4 EVIDENCE ADMISSIBILITY AND QUALITATIVE ASSESSMENT MUST BE BASED ON TRANSCULTURAL PRINCIPLES IN THE FORM OF RULES AND NOT STANDARDS

Rules fashioned for purposes of admissibility and the qualitative assessment of evidence must be transcultural. This proposition is simple and not a Pandora's box cloaked with the *non sequitur* mantle of the word "transcultural,"[20] much as the IBA and Prague Rules both purport to be. All members of the international arbitration community agree that principles such as:

[20] Wang, "Rethinking Evidentiary Rules," at 306. Professor Wang engages in a very similar analysis in the context of trial judges presiding over nonjury trials. The foundational premises of his analysis were helpful and appropriate in the development of this subsection.

(i) procedural transparency,
(ii) logical necessity,
(iii) the tendency to establish a factual proposition, or
(iv) a predicate from which a specific factual proposition reasonably or of necessity may be inferred,
(v) *qualitative* and *quantitative* assessment of the relationship between the evidence at issue (or body of evidence) and the proposition sought to be established, and
(vi) the authenticity or genuineness of the document, premise, or evidentiary proposition in question, i.e., the extent to which the evidence is that which it purports to be.

Of course, this list hardly purports to be exhaustive.

The organizing evidentiary principles need to be rules and not standards. This imperative is all the more applicable in ICA, that is to say, private international law, than in its ISDS treaty-based public international law counterpart. The application of rules would not allow for policies and potentially overbroad standards to cloud the determination of two very simple questions. First, should this evidence be deemed admissible and form part of the record such that its probative value and reliability may then be evaluated? Second, assuming the answer to the first inquiry to be in the affirmative, what is the reliability and, therefore, the quality of this item of evidence? A rule rather than a standard is far more apt to guide a tribunal through this analysis. On this point one commentator observed: "[W]hen umpire and evaluator are merged, rules that are actually standards may functionally become equivalent to a system without rules at all. And once again, this would likely be operationally true even if judges did pay greater lip service to the rules of evidence in bench trials."[21]

This principle is readily transposable from a trial judge presiding over a nonjury trial to an international arbitral tribunal. As arbitral tribunals are vested with seemingly unbridled inherent powers that are held in check mostly by a fictitious control system premised on the term "subject to agreement of the parties" (see Section 3.1).

8.5 EVIDENTIARY PRINCIPLES (RULES) MUST HOLD SACROSANCT THE INHERENT POWERS OF ARBITRATORS AND CORRESPONDING EXERCISE OF ARBITRAL DISCRETION

As discussed, having relinquished second instance merits review (see Section 1.2.2), much like subscribing to an attenuated iteration of due process protection that is not present in any legal system,[22] the checks and balance on the exercise of *arbitrator*

[21] Wang, "Rethinking Evidentiary Rules," at 305, citing to Mnookin, "Bifurcation and the Law of Evidence," at 141–142.

[22] *Id.*

discretion are not in the form of a *de novo* merits review. An arbitral tribunal cannot be compelled to apply substantive principles correctly under most, if not any, scenario. The administration of a simple operational set of evidentiary rules grounded in transcultural principles certainly is not meant to be an exception.

Instead, the self-evident and internal coherence of these principles should constitute the first layer of normativity that generally should suffice. In the outlier cases where the arbitral tribunal engages in a consistent and systematic disavowance of these rules sufficient to deny the parties arbitral due process (for example), then the prospect of rendering a flawed award should suffice to compel reasonable adherence.

Foundationally, however, the adoption of any such rules also would redound to the benefit of the arbitral tribunal because parties would be hard-pressed to flood the tribunal with evidence that is of little or no probative value. Similarly, parties are more likely to refrain from the strategic and tactical approach of producing evidence that is *relevant*, but not *material* (Section 4.3), in order to prejudice the tribunal's view of one of the parties.

Such examples can be readily imagined, particularly in areas of banking and finance where the operational conduct of a party in a separate and unrelated venture may be *relevant* to the dispute before the arbitral tribunal but not *material* to the dispute's outcome. Such evidence of prior conduct, however, almost inevitably would plant a seed of doubt in the tribunal's mind that the party who once engaged in such conduct is much more likely to have repeated it as may have been the conduct in the case *sub judice*. The rule on methodology would be one that emphasizes the exercise of discretion within fixed balancing parameters.[23]

[23] This point was ably articulated and developed by Professor Henry Zhuhao Wang. In the context of fashioning rules of evidence for trial judges presiding over nonjury trials, he states:

> When designing the new rules, trial judges' discretion should still be fully respected, but the new rules for bench trials should address inconsistency, common epistemic pitfalls, unpredictability, and unfairness. Considering these goals, most evidentiary rules designed for bench trials should be *admonition-style* rules that encourage judges to do the right thing in fact-finding. One good example of admonition-style rule in the FRE is FRE Rule 403, "Excluding Relevant Evidence for Prejudice, Confusion, Waste of Time, or Other Reasons": "The court may exclude relevant evidence if its probative value is substantially out-weighed by a danger of one or more of the following: unfair prejudice, confusing the issues, misleading the jury, undue delay, wasting time, or needlessly presenting cumulative evidence." This rule is concise, easy to understand, and easy to use. It provides a mechanism for trial judges to *balance* probative value and dangers of evidence. In this sense, it regulates process, not the results of assessment. And this rule uses the model verb "may," not "must." All these details reflect respect of the trial judge's discretion in fact-finding, while it still achieves the purpose of regulation – avoiding unfairness in judicial fact-finding. Another example of an admonition-style rule in the FRE is FRE Rule 807, "Residual Exception," which provides trial judges a mechanism to evaluate how reliable hearsay evidence is for admissibility purposes. Rather than telling judges what type of residual hearsay are admissible or not, this rule allows a trial judge to apply his or her discretion in balancing pros and cons of a piece of hearsay evidence while establishing the criteria for reliable hearsay for the judge to follow. (Emphasis in original)

Wang, "Rethinking Evidentiary Rules," at 305.

Pursuant to this approach arbitral discretion (inherent powers) are respected but in some sense empowered by providing the tribunal with a simple and basic framework within which to exercise its discretion. In turn, the exercise of this discretion is more than just a collective manifestation of will. It would be based on reasonable considerations of equity, fairness, transparency, and of course, efficiency.

8.6 THE PARTIES MUST BE EXHORTED TO USE THE *BEST EVIDENCE*

Notwithstanding the ubiquitous rote recitation that the arbitral tribunal shall determine the *admissibility*, *relevance*, *materiality*, and *weight* of the evidence (see Chapter 4), arbitral stakeholders simply are not doctrinally or culturally sensitized to *reliability* and *quality* of evidence analyses. At the initial case management conference that will yield the proceedings' first *Procedural Order*, the parties should be encouraged to present the "best evidence" available.

Such definition of best evidence must include more than just documents that are self-authenticating or the authentication of which is all but perfunctory. The *best evidence* should be evidence that most directly and proximately establishes a proposition or a factual basis from which the desired factual inference or conclusion can be had.

At this early juncture the arbitral tribunal and the parties would be well served by emphasizing the need to establish facts efficiently. The tribunal's disdain for cumulative evidence, as well as the need for the evidence presented to be the most relevant and therefore probative for the proposition asserted, should be pivotal. Put simply, the parties need to be placed on notice of the arbitral tribunal's expectations regarding evidentiary reliability and qualitative analyses.

As referenced (see Section 7.1), the IBA Rules, for example, heavily rely on the concept of relevance,[24] yet the Rules' definitional section is operational and by design not substantive.[25] It simply does not purport to define such essential terms as "relevant" and "material," among others.[26]

The obvious importance of the concept of *relevant evidence* renders it indispensable for ICA to aspire even to *process efficiency*, let alone *optimal efficiency*, where even a flexible working definition of relevance is not identified. This state of affairs cannot be countenanced. Each tribunal member theoretically may have a different understanding of the word, and therefore, of its definition.

FRE Rule 807 has a built-in full due process component that cleanses the evidence from any prejudicial effects, while at the same time rendering the evidence operational under the circumstances, and all within the trial judge's exercise of discretion. There are principles in this Rule that demonstrably preserve judicial discretion and at the same time sanitizes evidence from the prejudicial effect of free-standing evidence that has a foundational attribution that cannot be challenged.

24 Art. 2, ¶ 3(a), Art. 3 (b), Art. 3, ¶ 9, Art. 3, ¶ 11, Art. 4, ¶ 9, Art. 8, ¶ 6, Art. 9, ¶ 2(a), previously mentioned in Chapter 2, n. 44, are relevant to the case material to the outcome mentioned seven times.

25 Chapter 4, n. 9.

26 *Id.*

The need for a definition of relevance, even if only one that is semantical, is paramount.[27] The *OED* observes that the adjective "relevant" derives from the Latin *relevant-*,-ans, in turn from the present participle of the Latin *relevare*, to raise up, relieve, (in Medieval Latin) take up, take possession of (a fief), pay a relief for.[28] The modern usage of the adjective "relevant" has two entries. The first based upon Scots Law. "Legally pertinent or sufficient." A second entry, only marginally more helpful, defines this adjectival form of the noun "relevance," as "[b]earing on, connected with, or pertinent to the matter in hand."[29]

Certainly even so rudimentary an understanding as one premised on this adjectival part of speech, if collectively understood and shared, would be a very modest step in the right direction. Yet, it would border on unreasonable to assume that from a functional perspective, even if shared as an element of a collective consciousness, hardly would it provide substantive content to the appropriate ICA procedural and evidentiary rubrics (see Chapter 3).

Currently the epistemic-cognitive level of *admissibility* and *weight* considerations from a doctrinal perspective, at best only can aspire to a common and very general doctrinal understanding of relevance. More is compelled if efficiency by dint of uniformity and predictive value is sought. These predicates, *uniformity* and *predictive* value, are necessary elements of *risk assessment*.

Instead of a semantical *definition*, a *rule* providing for a *test* is indispensable. It is not here the intent to advocate in favor or against the importation of the FRE's test for relevant evidence and its limits. Reference to that Rule, however, may better explain a quality based relevance grounded analysis in the form of a Rule prescribing a *test* and *not* a general linguistic definition.

FRE Rule 401 is helpful. It provides:

Evidence is relevant if:

(a) it has any tendency to make a fact more or less probable than it would be without the evidence and
(b) the fact is of consequence in determining the action.[30]

[27] This principle needs some grounding and cannot be abandoned to the whim of ad hoc and fragmented conceptual categories arising from subjective personal experiences. This approach is rendered all the more problematic by the untested assumption that *somehow* all stakeholders share a common understanding of the concept. In fact, however, typically nothing could be farther the truth. Equally disconcerting is that a twin assumption that the stakeholders also are in unison in their knowledge of how to apply it and the extent to which relevance should not be subject to any exception. Here as well the assumption is fallacious.

[28] *Shorter Oxford English Dictionary*, 2: 2522.

[29] *Id.*

[30] Professor Graham in part observes:

> Evidence is relevant as defined in Rule 401 if the evidence has any tendency to make a fact more or less probable than it would be without the evidence, Rule 401(a), provided the fact is of consequence in determining the action, Rule 401(b). Rule 401(b) employs "fact is of consequence in determining the action" in place of the term "material," a term which has proved ambiguous.

The first part of the test **(a)** has three operational elements around which to structure the initial qualitative analysis to determine relevance. First, the term "any tendency" requires an initial determination on the *degree* of propensity. The "any" qualification itself will lead to an assessment that is qualitative.

Second, "to make a fact more or less probable" also requires reaching a settled understanding on the question of "probability" or "likelihood." This determination also will go directly to the strength of the evidence's probative character. Third, and finally as to this first part (a), "than it would be without the evidence"; the test for relevance necessarily requires examining different inferences as to a particular proposition with and without the evidence of concern. This introspection and thought experiment will represent a substantial advance toward more than just an unbridled *Free Proof* approach.

Analysis of subsection **(b)** provides for what is in effect a *materiality* analysis, but phrased in a manner that is universally more accessible than the term of art. A fact can meet all relevance strictures and principles and yet serve to be of no moment with respect to the underlying cause. Evidence of an enterprise's financial performance for years five and six, respectively, preceding its sale to a claimant alleging breach of contract presents an example on this point. Where the contract provides that only three years predating the sale are to be considered for purposes of assessing the value of the company is a helpful paradigm.

Certainly the company's financial performance for years *five* and *six* would have some mathematical tendency to prove the value of the company. Indeed, having years *five* and *six* would be more useful in proving the company's value than not having access to this information. Yet, however, these facts, that is to say, financial performance for years five and six, are inconsequential because a material term of

> Evidence, direct or circumstantial, is relevant when it possesses any tendency to establish a fact of consequence. Evidence affecting the weight accorded to such relevant evidence by the trier of fact falls within the concept of relevancy employed in Rule 401. Use of the phrase "fact is of consequence" in place of materiality serves to clarify that the breadth of admissibility of relevant evidence extends to facts not in dispute. Rulings on admissibility of evidence upon a point conceded by an opponent must be made by considering probative value in light of trial concerns such as waste of time and unfair prejudice, Rule 403. Rule 401 also makes clear that evidence which is essentially background in nature offered as an aid to understanding may be admitted. Such items include, for example, biographical information concerning a witness, charts, photographs, views of real estate, and murder weapons connected solely to the crime. [*Obviously, very unlikely in ICA.*]
>
> Relevant evidence may be either direct or circumstantial. Direct evidence is evidence where the sole inference which must be made to establish a fact of consequence is the truth of the matter asserted. Testimony such as "I saw X shoot B," is direct evidence as to a fact of consequence. Circumstantial evidence involves evidence offered to establish a fact of consequence where an inference in addition to the truth of the matter asserted need be made. Thus testimony that X fled the scene would be both direct evidence of flight and circumstantial evidence of the murderous act.
>
> Graham, *Handbook of Federal Evidence*, § 401, p. 2.

the sales contract at issue explicitly limits the years to be considered only to three years *predating* the company's sale.

Therefore, under FRE Rule 401(**a**) and (**b**), the evidence for years *five* and *six* simply are irrelevant, and therefore, inadmissible.[31]

In an ICA proceeding it is very likely that the financial data for years *five* and *six* would have been admitted. In fact, the arbitral tribunal may have deemed it appropriate under a number of potential scenarios to have considered years *five* and *six* notwithstanding the contractual clause to the contrary. The reasoning can be expressed in simple terms that are superficially attractive.

The tribunal, in its wisdom, may determine that one of the very central issues in the case concerns valuation, which constitutes the entirety of claimant's case-in-chief and respondent's defenses. In this connection, so the tribunal says, the greater the quantum of evidence of presale performance on the part of the enterprise, all the clearer the value of the company.

Moreover, the tribunal further reasons that the case before it is one of breach of contract. It so reasons based upon representations concerning the actual value of the company. And thus, under the circumstances of having a contractual provision excluding prior performance during years five and six, the tribunal reasons that the clause is draconian and exclusionary in nature. It further concludes that the clause cannot reasonably be justly enforced as its true purpose seems to be obscuring the company's *true* value as of the date of sale.

Free Proof would allow for such analysis, which may be right or wrong, but certainly it is in derogation of material terms of the contract. The three-year past-performance history also may comport with standard industry practice.

Certainly, a basic rule of relevancy that adjusts the scope of that term to fit within the conceptual framework of a legal proceeding will tend to contribute to the parties' expectations, as can be gleaned from the contractual clause at issue. And in this way contribute to predictability and *risk assessment*.

Depending on what the financial data for years *five* and *six* shows, a clear understanding that although within the purview of FRE Rule 401(a), *the subsection (b) prong simply cannot be met based upon contractual language that is indisputable.* Not knowing with geometric certainty whether the arbitral tribunal would consider the years *five* and *six* data based upon a banal semantical understanding of relevance

[31] FRE Rule 402 (General Admissibility of Relevant Evidence) prescribes:

Relevant evidence is admissible unless any of the following provides otherwise:

- the United States Constitution;
- federal statute;
- these rules; or
- other rules prescribed by the Supreme Court.

Irrelevant evidence is not admissible.
(Emphasis added)

that is exogenous to a legal proceeding, likely would render settlement impossible depending on the *unquantifiable risk* pertaining to this issue.

What constitutes the best evidence in the context of the proposed approach to the valuation of evidence in ICA proceedings is deeply connected to the extent to which *Free Proof* constitutes the polestar for evidentiary determinations. Pursuant to the *Free Proof* example, the data for years *five* and *six* may prove to be determinative. The FRE Rule 401(b) component, which is preceded by the conjunctive "and," if applied would likely exclude the years *five* and *six* figures as inconsequential in determining the action. Pursuant to this approach, both prongs **(a)** and **(b)** must be met. If met, the evidence is irrelevant. If irrelevant, it cannot be considered for any purpose, and therefore, it is inadmissible.

Under a rule of evidence approach to relevance that is not semantically grounded, the data for years *five* and *six* simply is not admissible evidence, let alone the *best evidence*.

The proposed rule on best evidence is one that encourages the parties to think about relevance in a legally probative way. It also encourages the arbitral tribunal to engage in uniform conceptual thinking on the subject.

The strict rule that the FRE codifies in Rule 1002 encourages that proof of a proposition, if pursuant to a writing, recording or photograph, should be undertaken with the original iteration of the writing, recording, or photograph.[32] The American-based "Best Evidence Rule" does provide for a copy or a duplicate as admissible, but only "to the same extent as the original unless a genuine question is raised about the original's authenticity or the circumstances make it unfair to admit the duplicate."[33]

8.7 THE RULE OF RELIABILITY AND DUE PROCESS: POLITICALLY CORRECT EUPHEMISMS FOR A HEARSAY RULE TO TEST RELIABILITY

Perhaps the most distinctive exclusionary rule identified with the Anglo-American law of evidence is the "hearsay rule." This rule simply finds no space in the continental or civil law systems in Europe and beyond.[34] The hearsay rule indeed has garnered the attention of scholars from non-common law jurisdictions who have found it to be of intellectual interest, but in some sense also an archaic and somewhat cumbersome (albeit fascinating) museum piece of little more than anthropological interest.[35]

32 FRE Rule 1002 (Requirement of the Original), states that "[a]n original writing, recording, or photograph is required in order to prove its content unless these rules or a federal statute provides otherwise."

33 FRE Rule 1003.

34 *See* Chapter 7, n. 2.

35 *See* Chapter 7, n. 6.

Viewed as the paradigmatic common law exclusionary rule that wrests from fact-finders their ability directly to evaluate evidence through the senses, experience, and knowledge of the evidence actually presented, the hearsay rule has drawn sharp criticism. Not all scholars, however, cling to surface critiques of the rule, which itself *should be* a litmus test for *weight* to be ascribed hearsay evidence in the context of nonjury trials and ICA. Professor Frederick Schauer in a discussion concerning the hearsay rule observed that,

> in all of these instances the evidentiary rule operates to exclude otherwise relevant evidence, and for almost all of these rules [hearsay rules, best evidence rules, character evidence rules, and propensity evidence rules] the exclusion is typically explicitly justified in terms of avoiding the risk of misleading … or preventing the [trier of fact] from mis-assessing the actual value of the evidence.[36]

Professor Schauer adds that "we have seen that judges sitting without juries often treat these exclusions and related requirements as being, at best, hints (or rules of thumb) *about how much weight* to give the evidence, rather than as genuine rules demanding categorical exclusion." (Emphasis added.) He does opine that the codified FRE evidentiary rubric, in rules such as hearsay, as well as issues of character and past acts, often are of value. With respect to the hearsay rule, for example, he states that:

> [] [O]nce we have put the likely fallacy of comparative juror cognitive incompetence to rest, the principal reason for rejecting a hearsay rule is eliminated as well. [Citation omitted.] In addition, and perhaps more importantly, the hearsay rule serves an important evidence-*generating* function, or, to put it differently, an important best evidence – in the non-technical sense of that term – role. [Citation omitted.] By excluding hearsay evidence (subject to all the usual qualifications, caveats, exemptions, and exceptions – or at least many of them), the hearsay rule compels the parties to search for more than less direct accounts. And to locate and bring forward the most immediate and cross-examinable witnesses. [Citation omitted.] Although an exclusion of hearsay will exclude some relevant evidence, such an exclusion will also compel the production of some better evidence, and it may well be that the aggregate value of the better evidence marginally developed will be greater than the aggregate loss of the relevant evidence marginally excluded.[37] (Emphasis in original)

More generally commenting on rules of evidence, which he viewed as unjustifiably exclusionary and themselves an obstacle to the equitable administration of justice inasmuch as he understood rules of evidence as also unduly altering the nature of evidence where they did not altogether exclude such evidence, Jeremy Bentham during the early part of the nineteenth century famously wrote that "almost every

[36] Schauer, "On the Supposed Jury-Dependence," 175–80.

[37] *Id.* at 179.

rule that has ever been laid down on the subject of evidence [is] repugnant to the ends of justice."[38]

Certainly, the hearsay rule is deliciously more complicated than FRE Rule 801 (Definitions that Apply to this Article; Exclusions from Hearsay) would suggest. Moreover, the very nature of "hearsay" is ubiquitous. Therefore, it cannot help but spawn its many exceptions, many of which are rooted in that wonderful term: human nature.[39] Indeed, FRE Rule 801(c) sets forth a "seemingly" pithy and straightforward definition of hearsay:

> (c) **Hearsay**. "Hearsay" means a statement that:
> (1) the declarant [the person who made the statement] does not make while testifying at the current trial or hearing and
> (2) a party offers in evidence to prove the truth of the matter asserted in the statement.

This ostensibly concise and plain definition, however, is subject (i) to statements that are not hearsay,[40] (ii) is subject to the exceptions to the rule against

[38] Jeremy Bentham, *Rationale of Judicial Evidence, Specially Applied to English Practice*, Vol. 4 (John S. Mill ed.) (Hunt & Clarke 1827).

[39] Indeed, the first two exceptions to the Rule against hearsay are five examples of exceptions based on what is believed to be known about human nature, and the manner in which members of our species act, react and think. Rule 803(i) (present sense impression), provides that "[a] statement describing or explaining an event or condition made while or immediately after the declarant perceived it." Here the underlying rationale is that the simultaneous articulation of an impression, as it is being experienced, likely constitutes an accurate account of what was seen or felt. The contemporaneity of the event and the statement, so it is believed, vests the statement with badges of truth and reliability. It would be unlikely for the "present sense impression" to constitute a deliberate misrepresentation because human beings simply do not think, act, or speak in such a way so as to render the impression deliberately false in keeping with the need to adopt to a rendition of the account to fit a subsequent scenario,

Similarly, Rule 803(s) (Excited Utterance) is defined as: "[a] statement relating to a startling event or condition, made while the declarant was under the stress of excitement that it caused." Of course, there is no *a priori* synthetic judgment that can be asserted regarding the veracity of an "excited utterance." The rule simply is premised on the belief that human beings assert propositions or display emotions truthfully in keeping with their experiences and personal traits, that likely will be accurate and non-agenda driven under specific circumstances and pursuant to particular ways. This exception is one such example.

[40] The unreliable nature of hearsay evidence was identified in the arena of empirical historical research by Thucydides (b. 471) in Bk. I., XVIII, 3-XX.2 of his *History of the Peloponnesian War*. In XX 20 he observes:

> Now the state of affairs in early times I have found to have been such as I have described, although it is difficult in such matters to credit any and every piece of testimony. For men accept from one another hearsay reports of former events, neglecting to test them just the same, even though these events belong to the history of their own country.

See also, Bk. I., XXI 3–XXII.4.

And the endeavor to ascertain these facts was a laborious task, because those who were eyewitnesses of the several events did not give the same reports about the same things, but reports varying according to their championship of one side or the other, or according to their recollection.

hearsay – regardless of whether the declarant is available as a witness in the proceeding at issue,[41] (iii) exceptions to the rule against hearsay when the declarant is unavailable as a witness,[42] (iv) hearsay within hearsay,[43] (v) attacking and supporting the declarant's credibility,[44] and (vi) residual exceptions.[45] Even a surface glance at this rubric governing statements, oral or written, articulated beyond the hearing and being offered to prove the truth of the matter asserted, bespeaks a very rigid and elaborate framework beset by exceptions and qualifications that envelop the very rule itself.

It rightfully would be heretical to suggest that ICA should adopt anything comparable to this framework. This suggestion hardly is the proposition being asserted. There is, however, compelling wisdom underlying the quality of evidence that constitutes hearsay, that is to say, offered as substantive proof but where the actual declarant is not present. A factual proposition incapable of being contested.

Thucydides notes that it is a human flaw that drives the human species to rely on hearsay evidence. He comments that "[s]o averse to taking pains are most men in the search for the truth, and so prone are they to turn to what lies ready at hand." Bk. I., XX. 2–XXI.2.

41 FRE Rule 803, Exceptions to the Rule Against Hearsay – regardless of whether the declarant is available as a witness sets forth twenty-three hearsay exceptions, a plurality of which address records and statements in specific kinds of records.

42 *See* FRE Rule 804. **Exceptions to the Rule Against Hearsay – When the Declarant is Unavailable as a Witness.**

This exception is notable because of ICA's increasing technical sophistication. Many, if not most, ICA proceedings involve the proverbial "battle of the experts." It has become apparent that party-appointed experts often speak with a "forked tongue" on the identical technical matters of valuation, resource extraction, intellectual property, and other similar questions that require technical expertise. Often, notwithstanding available privacy and confidentiality protections, these transcripts are available and certainly used to impeach technical experts whose only source of loyalty is to receiving compensation, and not to the subject matter of a testimony.

43 FRE Rule 805. **Hearsay Within Hearsay**, succinctly states that "[h]earsay within hearsay is not excluded by the rule against hearsay if each part of the combined statements conforms with an exception to the rule."

44 FRE Rulc 806. **Attacking and Supporting the Declarant's Credibility**, reads:

> When a hearsay statement – or a statement described in Rule 801(d)(2)(C), (D)), or (E)) – has been admitted in evidence, the declarant's credibility may be attacked, and then supported, by any evidence that would be admissible for those purposes if the declarant had testified as a witness. The court may admit evidence of the declarant's inconsistent statement or conduct, regardless of when it occurred or whether the declarant had an opportunity to explain or deny it. If the party against whom the statement was admitted calls the declarant as a witness, the party may examine the declarant on the statement as if on cross-examination.

This rule references those out-of-court statements under Rule 801 that are not hearsay, such as statements by a party opponent or a representative. Again, these are the kinds of statements, often found in documents, whether in the form of emails, formal communications, or a transcript, that may be particularly relevant in complex ICA settings.

45 *See* Rule 807. **Residual Exception When It Is the Rule.**

Rule 807 embodies considerable common sense and is worth noting as an operative methodology based upon virtually absolute flexibility and discretion, while safeguarding the parties' due process rights and protections.

The concern is best articulated in the form of a very simple question. Should an arbitral tribunal base a ruling on a statement attributable to a declarant who did not testify before the arbitral tribunal? Is there any benefit that may arise from an arbitral tribunal identifying evidence as hearsay? At least three approaches warrant consideration in explaining this question.

8.7.1 *The First Hypothetical*

First, there is an argument in favor of an unqualified *Free Proof* approach to hearsay. This approach enjoys an elegant rationale because of its simplicity. In a hypothetical example, respondent's witness, Mr. Tom, will testify that "then" CEO of Alpha Corporation, Mr. Jerry, had said in a private meeting between the two (Mr. Tom and Mr. Jerry) that Alpha Corporation would not distribute dividends for the next two years.

The tribunal accepts Mr. Tom's testimony without any qualification. And determines the veracity based on Mr. Tom's demeanor as a witness. In this scenario, the tribunal's reasoning is twofold. It initially subscribes to the theory that Mr. Tom's hearsay statement regarding Mr. Jerry's communication taking place outside of the hearing, and in every way uncorroborated except for Mr. Tom's recollection, is worth admitting into evidence.

In this hypothetical, Mr. Jerry is unavailable to testify at the hearing, and has long since left Alpha Corporation. Mr. Jerry is not a party to the proceeding. Put simply, the tribunal opines that the entire proceeding is better off knowing that Mr. Tom is of the opinion that Mr. Jerry had said that there would not be dividend distributions for two years, than the proceeding would be without having this information. For whatever it is worth. Mr. Tom *does* appear to be credible even though he has an economic interest in testifying as he has.

The tribunal then also reasons that, in any event, claimant is free to cross-examine Mr. Tom regarding his recollection of the hearsay testimony ascribed to Mr. Jerry. Likewise, the tribunal further finds that this cross-examination amply meets due process protection in favor of claimant warranted under the circumstances. It so believes notwithstanding claimant's inability to examine Mr. Jerry.

Claimant's view on the subject, however, is more than a shade removed from the tribunal's thinking. As to the initial claim that having been exposed to the hearsay statement actually does more good than harm, claimant opines that the statement is one that cannot be qualitatively assessed as evidence. It is not corroborated. And the only basis for its alleged existence on a most critical matter happens to be the partisan testimony of an adverse witness. Hence, so claimant reasons, the only fair and reasonable approach with respect to the hearsay statement would be to disregard it altogether unless corroboration is possible.

Aware that the arbitral tribunal itself is the fact-finder, claimant understands that whatsoever psychological and epistemic effect the hearsay statement may have had on the tribunal, the next best thing to not having been exposed to it would be for the Tribunal affirmatively to state that it would not accord any weight to the statement.

Claimant also has some thoughts on the tribunal's assessment of the extent to which cross-examining Mr. Tom concerning Mr. Jerry's hearsay statement redeems claimant's rights to due process, even attenuated due process in an ICA context.

Claimant's position on the question of cross-examining Mr. Tom and due process is clear enough. Here again claimant disagrees with the tribunal. Cross-examining Mr. Tom regarding the out-of-hearing statement ascribed to Mr. Jerry likely is near futile. Claimant's counsel in this instance, in the absence of collateral documents or witnesses, would be charged with the conceptually impossible task of proving a negative.

This position hardly bespeaks meaningful due process protection of any kind. It is claimant's position that due process, even in the ICA context, commands that claimant would examine Mr. Jerry himself. This view is all the more compelling where the tribunal likely would rely on the hearsay statement for purposes of meeting one of respondent's defenses or affirmative counterclaims. Claimant argues that allowing and relying upon Mr. Jerry's alleged hearsay statement without the ability to cross-examine Mr. Jerry, particularly where the hearsay statement can be case dispositive, constitutes an inarguable due process violation.

In this first scenario, pursuant to which unbridled *Free Proof* applies, the hearsay statement is admitted and accorded weight unless on cross-examination Mr. Tom's credibility generally, and on this issue in particular, is materially compromised. We do not have enough facts to know if such is the case. Under the facts of this hypothetical, however, meaningful impeachment on this issue is not possible. Therefore, the untested hearsay statement will turn out to be possibly determinative.

There is no empirical evidence suggesting that under this first scenario, the affirmative unbridled *Free Proof* approach arbitral tribunals realistically engage in qualitative evaluative/reliability analyses with respect to hearsay statements, oral or written. The arbitral awards, certainly those available in the ISDS space, rarely (if ever) engage in a sustained analysis on the reliability of evidence of this kind.

In this writing, it is suggested that according weight to untested evidence in the context of a proposition that is potentially case dispositive *should be* a violation of the due process rights of the party against whom the evidence is proffered. In fact, however, admitting such evidence is standard practice under the *Free Proof* rubric.

8.7.2 *The Second Hypothetical*

Second, the arbitral tribunal applies a strict hearsay standard and technically finds this part of Mr. Tom's testimony inadmissible and, therefore, does not accord *any* weight to the inadmissible evidence. The tribunal proceeds to do so under the theory that uncorroborated hearsay is unreliable and thus should find no resonance in ICA's evidentiary space. Respondent, understandably, takes issue with this approach. The tribunal further reasons that rendering the hearsay testimony admissible is tantamount to allowing a witness to testify without first having submitted a witness statement.

Respondent argues that formal rules of evidence are beyond ICA's ken. For this reason respondent further asserts, the arbitral tribunal's categorical exclusionary approach to evidence directly and explicitly violates, among other things, the essential elements of the arbitration clause, which in turn calls for the application of the IBA Rules as a supplementary guide for the tribunal.

The IBA Rules are silent on this kind of exclusionary approach to evidence (see Section 8.2). A strict reading of the IBA Rules establish a *Free Proof* evidentiary framework based on a single standard for (i) evidence gathering and (ii) admissibility, relevance, and materiality. Presumably, at least under one reading of the IBA Rules (so argues respondent), the category of *weight* cannot be severed from the initial three elements (admissibility, relevance, and materiality).

Lastly, respondent asserts that an exclusionary approach and a strict evidence rule-based evidential scheme is inapposite to at least two core ICA pillars: *flexibility* and *efficiency*. Respondent adds that respondent is willing to produce Alpha Corporation's current CEO, Mr. Jones, so that claimant may cross-examine Mr. Jones as to the purported hearsay statement as a policy that Mr. Jerry mentioned during the latter's tenure as CEO.

The arbitral tribunal forecloses the possibility of having claimant cross-examine Mr. Jones on the ground that Mr. Jones was not listed on the pre-hearing witness list. Therefore, so rules the tribunal, it would not be fair to allow Mr. Jones to be incorporated as a witness at this time. In this connection, the tribunal adds that if Mr. Jerry's hearsay statement is so central to respondent's defenses and affirmative counterclaim, then respondent should have identified this witness, rather than having the hearsay testimony presented through Mr. Tom. Respondent should have known that claimant would be unable to test the factual sufficiency of such critical evidence.

As to the contention that application of strict evidentiary rules and an exclusionary approach to evidence violates the arbitration clause at issue and hence the parties' expectations, the arbitral tribunal states that the IBA Rules, as well as the rules of the vast majority of arbitral institutes provide that absent the agreement of the parties, the arbitral tribunal shall determine every aspect of the conduct of the final hearing (Chapter 3 in this volume). Here, there has been no agreement between the parties. The arbitral tribunal additionally notes that applying substantive rules of evidence are not altogether foreign to ICA. In so ruling the arbitral tribunal points to the LCIA's Rules and to the English Arbitration Act as evident examples.[46]

The strict evidentiary rule-exclusionary approach based on hearsay is draconian and contrary to ICA core pillars and incident professional culture. While some of

[46] *See* LCIA Art. 21(vi); and Section 5.1 in this volume.

the arbitral tribunal's arguments have merit, particularly respondent's failure to list Mr. Jones as a witness expected to testify on this pivotal proposition, excluding the alleged hearsay statement appears to be as flawed as thoughtlessly affirming its admissibility, and according weight to this untested assumption.

The *Free Proof* approach, for different but profoundly related epistemic reasons, fares no better than the *exclusionary approach*. Both are rife with conceptual and doctrinal deficits.

8.7.3 A *Third Hypothetical*

The third and preferred approach is one that does not necessarily classify, as a matter of nomenclature or conceptual category, the out-of-hearing statement being offered to prove the truth of the matter asserted.

In this case, the Alpha Corporation would not distribute dividends for the next two years, as "hearsay." Instead, it is clear that the hearsay statement is unreliable because (i) in the hypothetical scenario posited the statement allegedly attributed to Mr. Jerry cannot be independently corroborated by collateral evidence and (ii) the factual sufficiency of this evidence itself cannot be tested.

Without recourse to the concept of "hearsay" or "a hearsay rule," simple logic and common sense lead to the necessary conclusion that the statement is *unreliable*. What, then, is an arbitral tribunal to do with such *unreliable* evidence that would allow for the equitable administration of law while safeguarding the foundational pillars of arbitration (at least some of them), and remaining within the bounds of arbitral culture?

Of course, there are many approaches to this query. One objective consideration would be to adopt a rule along the lines of FRE Rule 807 (Residual Exception). Paraphrasing that Rule to sanitize it from FRE legalese and internal self-references to the codified FRE, the proposed approach would constitute an operational balancing test requiring the tribunal to undertake a two-prong consideration.

First, the statement, whether oral or written, would be deemed admissible if it is "supported by sufficient guarantees of trustworthiness – after considering the totality of circumstances under which it was made and evidence, if any, corroborating the statement[.]"[47]

Applying this first prong to the hypothetical at hand, as crafted the alleged hearsay statement, or better yet alleged "unreliable statement," has no collateral corroboration. Hence, it cannot objectively be said to be cloaked with any mantle of "sufficient guarantees of trustworthiness." When *considering the totality of circumstances under which it was made*, all the record truly reflects is Mr. Tom's assertion allegedly purporting to narrate a private conversation, that is, there were no corroborating

[47] *See* Chapter 4, n. 68 in this volume.

witnesses. Likewise, we are not told of any confirmatory emails or other writings. This first prong is not met.

Before delving into the second prong, there is the flexibility of determining whether the first two prongs should be united by the conjunctive "and," or the disjunctive "or." If the former, then the inquiry is settled. The evidence would not be accorded any weight, but would be deemed admitted in order to serve the fiction of inadmissibility where in fact there is no "gatekeeper" issue as *always* is the case in ICA.[48]

Assuming for didactic purposes that the two prongs are joined with the disjunctive *or*, then the tribunal would inquire as to whether "it is more probative on the point for which it is offered than any other evidence that the proponent can obtain through reasonable efforts."[49]

Here again by design (of course) the hypothetical is bereft of any helpful facts. It is silent but for respondent's proposal to make Mr. Jones available for cross-examination and possible examination by the tribunal. This reasonable effort at corroborating the evidence would conclusively settle the matter.

The argument that respondent should have been more timely in raising it earlier and identifying Mr. Jones on the witness list is certainly meritorious, but outweighed by the probative value of the evidentiary proffer in the form of making the witness available for cross-examination and questioning on the part of the tribunal. The arbitral tribunal has the inherent powers to award claimant the costs and fees arising in connection with the preparation and actual cross-examination of this witness. The tribunal may also do so pursuant to the IBA Rules.[50]

Having worked through the hypothetical it seems that the proposed two-prong balancing test possibly yielded the fairest and most comprehensive resolution of the issue in keeping with the ultimate objective of having as perfect a record as possible for purposes of disposing of the case. Certainly reasonable minds may differ as to whether this outcome was the best possible resolution under the circumstances.

48 By "gatekeeper," reference is being made to a trial judge presiding over a jury trial and excluding relevant and probative evidence on grounds of hearsay or prejudice (fairness). The no gatekeepers status of ICA, as previously noted, is no different from that of a trial judge presiding over a nonjury trial. *See* Section 6.1 in this volume.

49 *Id.*

50 Article 9.8 of the IBA Rules on the Taking of Evidence in International Arbitration states:

> If the Arbitral Tribunal determines that a Party has failed to conduct itself in good faith in the taking of evidence, the Arbitral Tribunal may, in addition to any other measures available under these Rules, take such failure into account in its assignment of the costs of the arbitration, including costs arising out of or in connection with the taking of evidence.

> Certainly, the failure to disclose a witness may be deemed an act in violation of good faith. In fact, respondent in the hypothetical was relying on what it perhaps thought to be the "safest" methodology for proving the out-of-hearing statement, i.e., presenting it as hearsay evidence that was not susceptible to cross-examination. If in fact such was the strategy, and there certainly seems to be a sufficient factual record from which to draw such inference, then sanctions in the form of fees and costs pursuant to Art. 9.8 would be warranted.

It does seem superior to either the unbridled *Free Proof* approach or the strict evidentiary rule and evidentiary exclusionary methodology. A hybrid informed rule-based *Free Proof* approach would vest the presentation of evidence phase with more than just a vestige of reasonableness and predictive value, thus transforming it from a black box scenario yielding *unquantifiable risk*, to a formulation of adjudication that can be reasonably anticipated during any procedural juncture.

Carving out a conceptual category in the presentation and admissibility of evidence based upon the extent to which evidence is "reasonably reliable," while considering the due process rights of the party against whom the evidence is proffered, represents a significant step toward certainty, *quantifiable risk*, and, therefore, a greater likelihood of *optimal efficiency*.

8.8 CROSS-EXAMINATION HAS TO BE UNDERSTOOD AND EMBRACED AS A CROSS-CULTURAL METHODOLOGY CONCERNED WITH PERSUASION THROUGH THE PRESENTATION OF EVIDENCE

ICA has reached a sufficient level of internationalization (not *Americanization*) so as to recognize and integrate cross-examination, which in the common law world (particularly in connection with the US common law) is hailed as the "greatest legal engine ever invented for the discovery of truth…"[51]

Even though cross-examination forms an integral part of contemporary ICA proceedings,[52] cross-examination is far from having found its perfect workings in ICA. Indeed, as previously discussed, neither the IBA Rules nor the Prague Rules actually reference the nomenclature "cross-examination."[53] This omission bespeaks far less than full integration.

[51] *California v. Green*, 366 U.S. 149, 150, 90 S. Ct. 1930, 26 L. Ed.2d 489 (1970) (quoting 5 J. *Wigmore Evidence* § 1367 (3d ed.) 1940). This phrase likely is the most common and popular description of the workings of cross-examination.

Indeed, the U.S. Supreme Court has stated that "the principal means by which the believability of a witness and the truth of his testimony are tested[,]" is through cross-examination. *Davis v. Alaska*, 415 U.S. 308, 316, 94 S. Ct. 1105, 39 L. Ed.2d 347 (1974).

"[T]he right of cross-examination is included in the right of an accused in a criminal case to confront the witness against him." *Pointer v. Texas*, 380 U.S. 400, 404, 85 S. Ct. 1065, 13 L. Ed.2d 923 (1965). Indeed, it is settled US law that "[t]he right of cross-examination, though not absolute, is one of the most firmly established principles under Supreme Court law." *Cotto v. Herbert*, 331 F.3d 217, 248 (2nd Cir. 2003) (considering a petition writ of *habeas corpus* under § 2254. Hence, a denial of cross-examination without waiver … would be constitutional error of the first magnitude …. *Smith v. Illinois*, 390 U.S. 129, 131, 88 S. Ct. 748, 19 L. Ed.2d 956 (1968)[internal quotation marks omitted].

[52] *See* the next note in this chapter.

[53] *See* Section 4.2 in this volume. The late New York University Professor Andreas Lowenfeld as early as 1997 wrote on the then seismic incorporation of cross-examination into international arbitration:

> As to questioning witnesses, just a few years ago [pre-1997] there was significant controversy in the international arbitration community about whether interrogation should be conducted by

It may even be construed as an understatement to assert that the *art* of cross-examination is yet to find its perfect workings in ICA or its ISDS counterpart. This evidentiary process remains unsettled and somewhat embryonic. In fact, rudimentary questions linger. These questions create uncertainty that clouds risk assessment.

What is proper cross-examination as to form? Is it an expression of advocacy that should be restricted, or accorded expansive latitude as part of a complex process of simultaneously testing the veracity of the written word and the declarant's credibility? How "universal" or "international" is this methodology? Historically, is cross-examination strictly a product of Anglo-American law, or does it in fact enjoy European roots? This latter question matters because a visceral reaction against cross-examination in many instances is culturally driven "as a foreign precept" that, independently of its very own merits, somehow should not be embraced.

Other equally daunting foundational questions remain. Is there a corresponding framework of objections that arbitrators and counsel should follow? To the extent the answer to this inquiry is in the negative, is such *status quo* truly acceptable if the presentation of evidence in ICA is to be cloaked with uniformity and efficacy conducive to *optimal efficiency*?

Is a corresponding system of objections aimed at clarifying questions and thereby ensuring that witnesses are not misled, confused, or answering a question other than

> the arbitrators – on a model of the European judges – or by counsel. My view was that arbitrators could ask questions for purposes of clarification, but the kind of questioning designed to test a witnesses' veracity – that is a series of questions aimed at bringing out contradictions in the witnesses' testimony – was inappropriate for arbitrators, and particularly for party-appointed arbitrators. By now [1997], cross–examination by counsel is pretty well accepted in international arbitrations, and for the most part the continental lawyers have learned how to do it. Moreover, and almost as important, arbitrators have learned how to administer cross-examination: letting counsel do the questioning does not mean losing control over the proceedings or tolerating abusive behavior.

Andreas F. Lowenfeld, "Introduction: The Elements of Procedure: Are They Separately Portable?," 45 *Am. J. Comp. L.* 649, 654 (1997).

As of the time of this writing, the third quarter of calendar year 2025, while cross-examination forms part, and arguably an important part, of ICA hearings, cross-examination techniques, are still largely foreign to non-common law arbitral panels, even the most sophisticated of panels. In part such is the case because arbitral panels have encountered cross-examination empirically on an *ad hoc* basis. Moreover, most non-common law ICA arbitrators have not studied cross-examination, its techniques, underlying cross-examination theories, or even aspects of cross-examination such as collateral impeachment of witnesses, and the various more nuanced forms of impeachment. Indeed, with respect to this latter point, often seasoned and sophisticated civil trained arbitrators are unable to identify instances when the witness directly has been impeached, or even impeached by virtue of the cross-examination that previously took place that very day or earlier of another witness concerning a common point of inquiry. It is not far removed to state that not uncommonly civil law trained arbitrators are not sensitive to or lose track of *scope* qualifications concerning direct-cross, and re-direct examinations.

Despite Professor Lownfeld's then (1997) upbeat and promising descriptive narrative as to cross-examination in ICA, considerable work remains to be done.

the one posed, necessary and timely? Is there evidence of any kind suggesting that the practice of cross-examination, together with corresponding objections, "denaturalizes" ICA's "international" character?

The lack of definitive answers, and in most instances answers at all, to these queries is testimony to the need to develop a coherent framework. The exercise and practice of cross-examination in ICA cannot be subordinated to the particular cultural configuration of each *ad hoc* tribunal. This approach would only continue to contribute to the proliferation of uncertainty. Little, however, has been developed to protect against this *happenstance* and *piecemeal* application of so critical a component of the presentation of evidence.

The extent to which cross-examination remains as *ad hoc* in its rules as the very tribunals charged with overseeing its "rightful" application, has led to multiple uncertainties attendant to the very exercise of cross-examination itself. By way of example, tribunals' lacking experience with *any* form of cross-examination has rendered it a challenge for such rudimentary propositions as the identification of admissions, impeachment, and the collateral impeachment through the witnesses being interrogated of prior testimony by a different witness. Hence, material admissions are secured and impeachment has taken place, without the tribunal noting these extraordinary events.

Even mere *statements against interest* that do not necessarily rise to the level of impeachment often are misapprehended or not apprehended at all. Evaluating cross-examination requires a finely tuned ear that has more than just casual informal exposure to this complex science.

In this same vein, tribunals struggle to appreciate the *weight* to be accorded to admissions to predicate statements designed to lead to necessary logical conclusions. Well executed cross-examination will necessitate multiple concise factual predicates forming part of a particular thematic line of questioning that typically are based upon unassailable propositions that must be relied upon for purposes of establishing the final factual proposition giving rise to the specific premise sought to be established in the first instance.

Put simply, while it may be more readily apparent to an arbitral tribunal what the objective of a series of questions might be, it likely is less practical and accessible to a tribunal lacking extensive practice and having no *formal training* or *actual experience* with cross-examination to discern what weight to be ascribed to the multiple predicate questions leading to the principal proposition sought to be established.

It also follows that the lack of a uniform approach to and understanding of cross-examination too often tends to cause tribunals to limit the scope of predicate questions or even lose patience with the questioning. This deficit can give rise to troubling due process (even in the context of *attenuated arbitral due process*) and actual process legitimacy concerns.

Without a comprehensive understanding of cross-examination, it is not surprising for an arbitral tribunal of civil law trained arbitrators who themselves have never actually cross-examined a witness or defended a witness being cross-examined, to conclude that the predicate questions are not helpful and may actually be construed as misleading the witness.

8.8.1 *Cross-Examination's Actual Objective*

Cross-examination as a methodology for presenting evidence is far from being as effective as it should be in the context of ICA. Such has been the case in large measure because the most foundational aspect of cross-examination is misunderstood by practitioners who never have studied cross-examination, let alone engaged in the exercise of professionally cross-examining witnesses on a professionally habitual basis. Therefore, the nature of cross-examination itself leads to cultural and technical misapprehensions.

This confusing core defining element of cross-examination is susceptible to a lucid and very succinct explanation. Cross-examination is not a series of questions in the orthodox sense of the word "question." It has nothing to do with questioning a witness. Analysis is compelled.

The *OED*'s first entry defines the noun "question" as: "[w]hat is inquired (about)." The more expansive *first* entry definition develops the principle: "[a] sentence worded or expressed in a form such as to elicit information from a person; inquiry." Equally helpful in its verbal form, the *fourth* entry defines the act of questioning as: "[t]he stating or investigation of a problem; inquiry into a matter[.]"

Notably, however, the archaic form of the verb is identified as having meant, "talk," and "discourse."[54] Ironically, it is the archaic meaning of the verb "to question" that most accurately defines and explains cross-examination.

Cross-examination foundationally is contrary to the most rudimentary objective of a simple question. An inquiry or question, beyond the framework of a cross-examination, typically is posed as part of an effort to elicit information unknown to the person posing the question. In this traditional and contemporary nonjudicial form of the verb, the question reflects the examiner's need to learn specific information. This need-to-know is the question's prime mover.

In contrast, the questions posed by an examiner in cross-examination (hardly a mere inquisitive actor or questioning entity) are not mean to secure answers unknown to the examiner. In a very real sense, the declarant's *answer* to the cross-examination question is *almost* irrelevant.

In the context of cross-examination, questions are posed in order to extract responses that would allow the examiner to ask a question *with the objective of having the question itself serve as a declaration to be considered by the arbitral panel.* The true and actual *declarant* is the *examiner* and *not* the witness.

[54] "Talk" and "Discourse" *Shorter Oxford English Dictionary*.

It is the examiner who by virtue of leading questions or statements tantamount to leading questions is communicating facts to the arbitral tribunal, and in doing so the examiner is engaging the science of persuasion, and not eliciting information unknown to her. In the context of cross-examination, the witness is but a *pretext* for the questions posed, if cross-examination is to be properly performed.

This core counter-intuitive feature of cross-examination tends to render it all the more suspect to arbitrators, academics, theoreticians, and practitioners concerned with preserving a temperate and proportional contribution to international law from specific legal cultures so that the practice of international arbitration may constitute the arbitral exercise of all nations. Sustained analysis of the actual theory and practical application of cross-examination, as presented in the classical *continental* philosophy of Plato's writings, helps to render viscerally intelligible what otherwise may appear to be a disconcerting exercise between examiner and declarant.

8.8.2 *Cross-Examination and Plato's* Gorgias

The practice of posing questions that are not framed or raised by the need to know a particular answer and for the benefit of neither the examiner nor the declarant, is not at all novel. Moreover, contrary to "popular arbitral culture," it is hardly a construct of Anglo-American criminal and civil procedure. Its origins are deeper and firmly settled in Europe.

The principle of cross-examination as a methodology of *persuasion* pursuant to which the examiner is the *declarant*, and the declarant-witness a *mere pretext* for the examiner's "questions" with respect to which the answer is known *ex ante*, has its technical implementation and epistemic origins principally and most notably in Platonic dialogues. The practice was established in Plato's writings primarily, but certainly not exclusively, to persuade parties, in the case of Platonic dialogues, beyond just the declarant being examined.[55]

Classical cross-examination in Platonic writings often is a substantive monologue cloaked with the formal trappings of a dialogue. So, too, is elite cross-examination. Cross-examination is a *monologue* and not a dialogue.

In this sense cross-examination is perhaps the most effective form of *persuasion* and not an instrument of learning. And certainly not of learning the particulars attendant to a cross-examination line of inquiry. Cross-examination is a futile exercise and a blunder if the questions posed authentically sought an answer for epistemological reasons.

[55] It would require several lifetimes and many tomes to explain fully the workings of cross-examination in the context of the Platonic opus. The questioning that takes place in Platonic dialogue cannot be severed from Plato's epistemology. The examiner serves the role of a "midwife" who facilitates the declarant's articulation of propositions that are inalterable by space and time even though such premises often are contextualized by reference to concrete seemingly and deceptively banal examples.

The most eloquent and academically influential work on the rhetoric of cross-examination that presents the examination as a form of advocacy (persuasion), and thus, a methodology concerning itself with persuasion and not fact-finding, predates the common law by more than just a handful of centuries: Plato's most complete work on rhetoric, *Gorgias*, was written circa 380 BC. Consequently, the notion that cross-examination is a common law construct is (at best) but a half-truth. Its origins could not be more continental.[56]

An understanding and appreciation for cross-examination as a methodology of persuasion and not at all an inquiry, together with knowledge of its historical origins in Platonic works on dialectical examinations, may assist international arbitration in embracing cross-examination as a methodology that belongs to all cultures and hardly the offspring of the common law by itself.[57]

Greater appreciation of cross-examination as a means of *persuasion* and not *inquiry* will allow arbitrators to understand comprehensively the effects and objectives of cross-examination, as well as the necessary techniques that would allow a tribunal to grant a lawyer leave to cross-examine while the tribunal simultaneously retains control of the totality of the proceedings.

Regrettably, most of the writings on cross-examination in international arbitration omit mentioning, let alone emphasizing, cross-examination as a mode of argument and persuasion on the part of the examiner.[58] Although these contributions

56 *See* Plato's, *Gorgias*, W. R. M. Lamb translation, published as part of the Loeb Classical Library (Harvard University Press 1925).

This Platonic dialogue is rife with examples of cross-examination that

(i) controls the witness,
(ii) is tendentious in eliciting the desired answer known *a priori* by the examiner,
(iii) comports with the most sophisticated cross-examination techniques that lead to the witness, and
(iv) serves a threefold didactic objective that is aimed at (a) third-party listeners, (b) the declarant being examined, and (c) the dialogue's reader. Socrates, the lead examiner, does not use questions but statement-questions. In the alternative, he resorts to *tendentious questions and leading questions*. While certainly the analysis of the *Gorgias* in the context of contemporary cross-examination techniques is a study beyond the scope of this writing, practitioners and theoreticians concerned with understanding the theoretical underpinnings and practical application of cross-examination are encouraged to consult, read, and re-read this text. The text is a key component to appreciating the workings and uniformity of "authentic" cross-examination.

57 Analytically, however, the origins of the actual theory of cross-examination in continental Europe should not be relevant in the academic and professional decision to recognize cross-examination as a *sine qua non* of evidence presentation. The fact remains that cross-examination is an efficient methodology for presenting and contextualizing evidence that is deployed in common law systems, and as such simply must be acknowledged as a material part of the presentation of evidence in ICA. Lack of familiarity is not a cognizable basis for rejecting the incorporation of a peerless globally practiced methodology for the presentation and testing of evidence – its *quality* and *reliability*.

58 The writings on cross-examination, with few notable exceptions, mostly focus on different cultural consequences ranging from the most obvious contrasts between civil law and common law

are valuable in many respects, they do not serve the didactic role of actually explaining cross-examination as a transcultural phenomenon that has very little to do with posing questions to a witness. The absence of the term "examination," let

jurisdictions, to the somewhat subtler differences between UK cross-examiners applying the rule in *Brown v. Dunn*, 6 R.67 (H.L.) (1893). These writings certainly are helpful and represent meaningful contributions, but many fail to explain in the form of a sustained analysis the actual primary purpose of cross-examination as a methodology for presenting a party's case through an adverse witness, and securing admissions and different forms of impeachment. These writings also do not speak forcefully to the actual origins of cross-examination and the need to develop corresponding *objections as to form*, even though there is *some* cursory treatment pointing to substantive objections generally.

A descriptive analysis of the manner in which *some* civil law trained arbitrators react with trepidation toward cross-examination generally does not address the "800-pound gorilla" in the room, namely, that cross-examination properly performed provides the arbitral tribunal with a wealth of information that simply is not available without the formidable techniques first developed by Plato in the *Gorgias*, and more superficially and less comprehensively developed in the culture of US Continuing Legal Education lectures.

These contributions, however, merit reading and rereading. *See, e.g.*, Ignacio Gómez-Palacio, "International Commercial Arbitration: Two Cultures in a State of Courtship and Potential Marriage of Convenience," 20 *Am. Rev. Int'l Arb.* 235 (2010), asserting that in an unprecedented global environment international arbitration is a necessity destined to endure, and for this reason, common law and civil practitioners and consumers of arbitral services "must anticipate and pay attention to the degree of familiarity which the other party, coming from the common-law world, may have with regard to discovery, cross-examination and oral argument." The author limits the discussion on cross-examination to noting that:

> [t]he opposite [of direct examination] occurs in "cross," since the witness cannot anticipate the question, nor can the litigant who will conduct the examination anticipate what will occur on direct. To the foregoing must be added the fact that cross-examination is an aggressive questioning which to a significant degree seeks to reduce the credibility of the witness, who will need composure in order not to become confused.

Here it should be observed that neither direct nor cross-examination in ICA wrest from the witness the ability to "anticipate the question" nor from the arbitrator "who will conduct the examination anticipate what will occur on direct." Two propositions need to be clarified. First, in ICA, there generally is no formal direct examination in the technical sense of a party presenting a non-adverse witness to testify in a narrative owed in response to what would generally be open-ended questions. Instead, the fiction of having submitted a witness statement constitutes the substantive direct examination, with perhaps a five or six question perfunctory "direct examination" concerning the authentication of the witness statement, which often the very tribunal conducts.

Second, the scope of cross-examination generally is limited to the witness statement and its subject matter even though there is no such textual scope limitation in any of the rules, IBA or Prague. While there is no safety net for the examiner in the form of a deposition transcript, typically skilled cross-examination will be based on the *Witness Statement* and undisputed propositions contained in documents. Therefore, the examiner at all times will find herself on *terra firma*. So, too, will the witness who will have studied her witness statement, and all documents relevant and material to her witness statement. While cross-examination in ICA certainly lacks the light of certainty that a deposition transcript provides, both the examiner and the witness may find themselves "flying at night" but with a competent radar and GPS.

Elena V. Helmer, "International Commercial Arbitration: Americanized, 'Civilized,' or Harmonized?," 19 *Ohio St. J. on Disp. Resol.* 35 (2003) (noting that:

> [t]he scope of cross-examination in international arbitration differs from U.S. court practices as well. In the United States, cross-examination is usually limited to the scope of direct examination.

alone "cross-examination," in the IBA Rules and the Prague Rules is testimony to a misapprehension of this form of presenting evidence. Uniformity and predictive value will be maximized in the presentation of evidence once cross-examination

> In arbitration, because direct examination is often shortened significantly, cross-examination covers all of the issues the witness covers in his witness statement. And cross-examination is usually not as hostile as in the U.S. courts, which makes it less objectionable to Continental lawyers.);

Javier H. Rubenstein, "Perspectives: International Commercial Arbitration: Reflections at the Cross Roads of the Common Law and Civil Law Traditions," 5 *Chi. J. Int'l. L.* 303, 309 (2004) (the author states that: "the concept of adversarial cross-examination of opposing witnesses, ... is often one of the greatest sources of consternation for civil law trained counsel. This concern is understandable since such cross-examination is rarely, if ever, permitted in their [civil law jurisdictions] domestic courts." The author goes on to observe that in his opinion, cross-examination in ICA is blind because of the absence of *ex ante* deposition testimony, and "where counsel often have little assurance of knowing what a witness will say during the course of an examination." It is worth repeating that cross-examinations in ICA are hardly *impromptu* "blind cross-examinations." For the reasons previously stated, while indeed there is no assurance "of knowing what a witness will say during the course of an examination," the skilled examiner will be able to impeach a witness based on the witness statement and/or documents of record. Typically, every question that a cross-examiner poses is tethered to a document providing its answer that may be used to impeach the witness being examined.).

Peter Rosher, "Cross-Examination in International Arbitration," 2017 *Int. Bus. Law J.* 3, 203–224 (also known as *Revue de Droit des Affaires Internationales* (Thomson Reuters 2017)). This writing is particularly instructive because, among other things, the author asserts two very helpful propositions. First, after noting the broad schism dividing common law and civil law traditions on the taking of and presenting evidence, it is asserted that "international arbitral tribunals should have regard to the general rules and practice that usually accompany the cross-examination procedure in common law jurisdictions. However, if the approach in international arbitration is analyzed further, the common law approach cannot be applied wholesale to this forum." This assessment is prudent and captures a necessary and tempered approach.

Second, the commentator very accurately describes cross-examination as an undertaking that hardly concerns itself with eliciting questions in order to acquire knowledge of new information. The author writes that:

> Cross-examination should be used primarily to get the cross-examining party's side of the story across to the tribunal rather than to ask the witness for information. This is done by using short, leading questions that are simple statements of fact. Open-ended questions such as who, what, when, where, how, or why will allow the witness to explain their side of the story. Therefore, advocates often ask questions which must be answered "yes" or "no." (*Id.* at 208)

David J. A. Cairns, "The Premises of Witness Questioning in International Arbitration," in *International Arbitration and the Rule of Law: Contribution and Conformity*, ICCA Congress Series No. 19 (Andrea Menaker ed.) (Kluwer Law International 2017), 302–321. Without expanding, the author states that "[c]ross-examination has specific information functions including supplementing witness declaration that are direct testimony with information that has been omitted, to correct inaccuracies or misstatements in the declaration or oral testimony, to ensure facts are set in their proper contexts, and to identify and reconcile apparent contradictions." In fact, however, cross-examination is a vehicle of persuasion that should be deemed as akin to a *Summation* or *Closing Argument*. The author's observations are helpful, but in need of being contextualized. Impeachment clearly constitutes a foundational function of cross-examination.

The Accuracy of Fact Witness Memory in International Arbitration (ICC 2020), online at: https://shorturl.at/jeWbT (last accessed January 27, 2024) (stating that in light of the paucity of studies regarding the effects of cross-examination questions on memory acuity, "the Taskforce makes no

has been duly institutionalized rather than tolerated with skepticism rooted in cultural bias and misinformation.

recommendation with respect to cross-examination"); Rachel D. Kent, "An Introduction to Cross-Examining Witnesses in International Arbitration," 3 *TDM* 2 (April 2006) (observing that some arbitrators "will recognize the value of cross-examination, but will view the aggressive style of cross-examination prevalent in U.S. courts as repugnant"). Here it is important to note that the "aggressive style of cross-examination prevalent in U.S. courts" is somewhat of an extraordinarily general statement. Likely, it is influenced by dramatic Hollywood accounts, and not actual courtroom cross-examination. Indeed, there is no "prevalent" US courts style of cross-examination, as cross-examination varies in form depending on such non-exhaustive variables as: (i) the particular rules of court of the state or federal judge presiding, (ii) whether the proceeding is civil or criminal, (iii) whether the proceeding concerns an anti-trust litigation, a class action dispute, a personal injury case, a trust and estates dispute, or a child custody case. Put simply, the subject matter, venue, and particular applicable rules of court unique to each judge all factor into the cross-examination that takes place in US courts, and (iv) the extent to which a witness is hostile or recalcitrant (as opposed to just "adverse") also matters. For these reasons, it is virtually impossible conceptually to speak to any single modality of cross-examination as emblematic of a style "prevalent in US courts." Regrettably, many commentators on cross-examination in US courts have never stepped into a US courtroom and witnessed cross-examination in a complex federal court civil proceeding, let alone themselves actually cross-examined a witness in a US state or federal tribunal.

See also Tyler B. Robinson & Robert H. Smit, "Cross-Examination International Arbitration: A Class among Common Law Traditions," 29 *Am. Rev. Int'l Arb.* 105 (2018) (concluding that "given features of international arbitration that serve to distinguish from national court litigation, American and English/Commonwealth styles of cross-examination may best achieve their shared objectives by meeting somewhere in the middle. There is more that unites the two approaches than divides them. Yet the rule in *Brown v. Dunn* is a doozy of a difference."); Ragnar Harbst, "Cross-Examination," in *A Counsel's Guide to Examining and Preparing Witnesses in International Arbitration*, 30 (Wolters Kluwer 2024) (stating that:

> [b]y far the most important purpose of cross-examinations is to demonstrate that the witness' testimony is not safe to rely on [citation omitted]. Cross-examination can also be used both to have the other side's witnesses confirm parts of one's own story [citation omitted]. Within limits, cross-examination can also be used to elicit information from the witness [citation omitted]. And finally, cross-examination can be instrumental in reading and educating the tribunal [citation omitted].);

Henry G. Burnett & David Weiss, "Systematic Advocacy: A Guide to Cross-Examination in International Arbitration," 13 *Revista Brasileira de Arbitragem* 51, 99–132 (2016) (explaining some reasons why an examiner may want to pose questions to which the audience knows the answer); Laurence Shore, "Michael E. Schneider on Cross-Examination: A Respectful, Even Admiring Albeit Uneasy Reaction of a U.S. Lawyer," in *Stories from the Hearing Room: Experience from Arbitral Practice Essays in Honour of Michael E. Schneider* (Bernd Ehle & Domitille Baizeau eds.) (Wolters Kluwer 2015), 173–178 (concluding that while less than all accepting of the Schneider theses, the author:

> find[s] the tripartite foundation of the theses to be a compelling and enduring contribution to international arbitration: (i) the belief that the arbitrators, uniquely among the participants in an arbitration, are seeking the objective truth; (ii) the believe that the arbitral process must be structured so that the arbitrators can be put in the position of making sound decision in seeking the truth; and (iii) accordingly the arbitrators have a responsibility to resist the efforts of counsel to turn the process into a demonstration of counsel's forensic talents, and counsel have a responsibility, even as they represent their clients and demonstrate their talents, not to place obstacles in front of the arbitrators as they seek the objective truth.);

Samaa A. F. Haridi & Ilham A. Kabbouri, "Witness Testimony and Cross-Examination," in *International Arbitration: A Civil Law and Common Law Blended Approach? in The Plurality and*

8.9 WITNESS EXAMINATION OBJECTIONS AS TO FORM AND THE NEED FOR A CORPUS OF OBJECTIONS TO IMPROPER EXAMINATION QUESTIONS

The failure to understand and to embrace fully cross-examination as a transcultural methodology pre-dating the very common law itself has contributed to more than just a paucity of objections directed to the form of questions posed on cross-examination. There simply is no such rubric in either the IBA or Prague Rules.[59] This state of affairs is conducive to uncertainty. It commands attention.

Epistemically it follows that a misunderstanding of the role and workings of cross-examination would lead to an equally wanting framework of objections directed at correcting the posing of improper cross-examination questions as to form. Such objections do not go to questions of *admissibility*, *relevance*, *materiality*, or *weight*. Therefore, civil law-trained tribunals are at a loss when confronted with objections as to the form of the question. Yet, such objections are necessary and foundational to the dynamic of control of the proceedings by the Tribunal, the creation of a clear record, and to ensure that witnesses are not misled or otherwise responding to a question different from the one actually posed.

A tribunal that does not understand that the cross-examiner is acting as a *declarant* in seeking *admissions* and *impeachment* that are known to her *ex ante*, and that if (the tribunal) also is now confronted with a body of objections that do not at all relate to *admissibility*, *relevance*, *materiality*, and *weight*. In such instances, arbitral tribunals are not at all clear on how best to proceed. Should they altogether ignore the objection? Many of them do. They act as if no objection had been interposed, and look to the witness to answer the question.

Synergies of Legal Traditions in International Arbitration: Looking Beyond the Common and Civil Law Divide, Stavros Brekoulakis, Nayla Comair Obeid, & Claudia Pharaon eds.) (Wolters Kluwer 2024), chapter 11. (This analysis is very helpful, although I take issue with the assertion that international arbitration counsel educated and practicing mostly in common law jurisdictions assume that the scope of examining a witness narrows with each phase of examination, notwithstanding that the IBA Rules do not provide for scope limitations in Art. 8. Even though, to be sure, the IBA Rules do not provide for scope limitations, or as referenced do not even mention the term "cross-examination," the unwritten but general practice in ICA and even ISDS evidentiary hearings is that (i) a witness' testimony can only be held accountable for facts directly relating to its witness statement and (ii) the scope of examination narrows from direct to cross, cross to re-direct, and even furthermore if a re-cross is allowed. There is no authority for this proposition, but the incorporation of cross-examination into ICA does not exclude this critical feature. Without it witnesses would be overly exposed and a likelihood of burdening witnesses with questions with respect to aspects of a fact pattern that only tangentially, albeit still reasonably, relate to that witness' witness statement cannot help but constitute a model of inefficiency. The authors very ably, however, contextualize international practice, in part, by providing helpful overviews of witness questioning and cross-examination in France and Germany.); *see also* Kaj Hobér, "Cross-Examination in International Arbitration," in *Stockholm Arbitration Yearbook* (Azel Calissendorff & Patrik Schöldström eds.) (Wolters Kluwer 2019) 41–54; and John Fellas, "Cross Examination in International Arbitration," 254 *N.Y.J.L.* 26 (August 7, 2015).

59 *See* IBA Rules Art. 9.2(a)–(g) objections, which go to admissibility mostly on the grounds of (i) privilege, (ii) confidentiality or proprietary secrets, (iii) relevance, and (iv) burden.

Other tribunals do not know whether they should first allow the witness to try to answer the question, and then address the objection. Of course, these two approaches completely miss the point. If the witness has responded to a question that is proper as to its substantive content but impermissible because of its form at that point the harm has been done and likely is irreparable. Once a witness proffers an answer to a question that is substantively correct but formally impermissible, the witness' answer now forms part of the record.

Correcting that answer *a posteriori* technically would require striking the answer tendered, and instructing the examining counsel to rephrase the question in accordance with the objection so that the question can be correct as to form and posed to the witness again. All of these undertakings, however, are based on the assumption that the objection is well taken and therefore sustainable. Even the basic mechanics for processing an objection as to form are beyond the ken of many arbitrators.

A brief analysis of the purpose and types of form objections will make clear the appropriate corresponding mechanics. There is no finite list of objections to the form of a question because of the very reason for the objections themselves in the first instance. These objections are intended to correct the form of the question and thereby allow the question to be posed.

Again, it is not an objection that in any way concerns *admissibility*, *relevance*, *materiality*, or *weight*. The purpose of the objection is to correct the question so that the witness can properly answer the right question, that is to say, one that is clear and conducive to an answer that is not susceptible to being ascribed as an answer to a question that was not actually posed. The normative foundation for objection as to form is founded in the FRCP.[60] As briefly referenced, while there is no exhaustive

60 Fed. R. Civ. P. 30 (Depositions by Oral Examination) at subsection (c)(2), in part reads:

> An objection at the time of the examination – whether to evidence, to a party's conduct, to the officer's qualifications, *to the manner of taking the deposition, or to any other aspect of the deposition* – must be noted on the record, but the examination still proceeds; the testimony is taken subject to any objection. An objection must be stated concisely in a nonargumentative and nonsuggestive manner. (Emphasis added)

Fed. R. Civ. P. 32 (Using Depositions in Court Proceedings) at subsection (d)(3)(B), in part reads:

> (B) *Objection to an Error or Irregularity*. An objection to an error or irregularity at an oral examination is waived if:
>
> (i) it relates to the manner of taking the deposition, *the form of a question or answer*, the oath or affirmation, a party's conduct, or other matters that might have been corrected at that time [at the time of the interrogation] and
>
> (ii) it is not timely made during the deposition. (Emphasis added)

See e.g., *Cincinnati Insurance Co. v. Serrano*, 2012 WL 28071 *4 (N.D. Iowa 2014) (observing that Fed. R. Civ. P. 30(c)(2):

> provides that objections during a deposition are noted on the record, but that the deposition proceeds with the testimony subject to the objection. "An objection must be stated concisely in a non-argumentative and non-suggesting manner." [Citation omitted.] Timely objections during a

list of objections to the form of questions in large measure because of the vast empirical possibilities for defects as to form, the common law has identified common objections that may correct error as to form.[61]

The objection must be articulated "concisely in a non-argumentative and non-suggestive manner."[62] It would not be sufficient to register an objection merely by stating "objection to the form of the question," or any comparable permutation such as "objection to the form."[63] The objection should state its basis so as to alert

deposition must be made to avoid waiver of the objection if the objection "relates to the manner or taking the deposition, the form of a question or answer, the oath or affirmation, a party's conduct, *or other matters that might have been corrected at that time*." [Citation omitted.] However, objections to relevance or materiality of testimony are not waived [i.e., they are preserved] by failure to objection during the deposition. [Citation omitted.]

61 The Court in *State Mutual Automobile Insurance Co. v. Dowdy*, 445 F. Supp.2d 1289, 1293 (N.D.Okla. 2006) states:

Counsel is obligated to object to improper questions or run the risk of waiving the objection [*citing to* Fed. R. Civ. P. 32(d)(3)(B)] typical objections to the form of questions are:]

(1) ambiguous;
(2) vague or unintelligible;
(3) argumentative;
(4) compound;
(5) leading;
(6) mis-characterizes the witness's prior testimony;
(7) calls for a narrative;
(8) calls for speculation;
(9) asked and answered; and
(10) assumes facts not in evidence. [Citations omitted]

Once an objection to form is made, the examining attorney can ask another question in an attempt to overcome the objection or let the question stand. If the examining attorney lets the question stand, the deponent must answer the question (subject to the objection), but runs the risk that the question and answer may be stricken if the objection is sustained. Rule 103 of the Federal Rules of Evidence requires a lawyer making an objection to state the "specific ground of the objection, if the specific ground was not apparent from the context."

See also St. Luke's Episcopal Hosp. v. Garcia, 928 S.W. 307, 309 (Tex. App. 1996) (observing that "[o]bjections to the form of a question usually involve the following objections: '(1) assumes facts in dispute or not in evidence; (2) is argumentative; (3) misquotes a deponent; (4) is leading; (5) calls for speculation; (6) is ambiguous or unintelligible; (7) is compound; (8) is too general; (9) calls for a narrative answer; and (10) has been asked and answered.'" [Citations omitted]

62 Fed. R. Civ. P. 30(c)(2).

63 *Rakes v. Life Investors Ins. Co. of Am.*, 2008 WL 429060, at *5 (N.D. Iowa Feb. 14, 2008) (rejecting argument that an objection as to the form of a question should be limited to "objection to the form of the question," and observing that:

[t]he rule, however, is not so restrictive. Rather, it simply provides that the objection must be "stated concisely in a non-argumentative and non-suggestive manner." As the Court indicated at the time of the hearing, the general practice in Iowa permits an objector to state in a few words the manner in which the question is defective as to form (e.g., compound, vague as to time, misstates the record, etc.). This process alerts the questioner to the alleged defect, and affords an opportunity to cure the objection.);

the examiner and provide for an opportunity to cure the defect by articulating a remedial question.[64] The ground for the objection, however, cannot be presented in an argumentative and suggestive way so as to influence the witness' testimony. Therefore, the objection cannot constitute a "speaking objection."[65] ICA lacks this system of control.

The absence of any objections as to form further hampers the deployment of cross-examination in a dispute resolution framework that is yet to embrace fundamental structural features of this methodology of interrogation. The *status quo* in ICA has not institutionalized objections as to the form of questions and the consequences are evident.

First, the examiner is not duly controlled. Second, the witness is not protected. Third, an imperfect, and often deeply flawed, record is created. And lastly, the tribunal itself, particularly if not educated or trained on the particulars of cross-examination and the defense of a witness being cross-examined, likely also may be misled, confused, or altogether left with an unclear understanding of both the examiner's question and the witness' answer. A question as simple as "Did you sign the contract?" is ambiguous in at least three different ways if in fact the word "you" is not objected to on the ground of ambiguity or otherwise defined in a stipulation.

Absent the objection and additional context, there are three immediate possibilities that can be material to the very outcome of the case, let alone the proposition sought to be asserted. First, the word "you" can mean the witness in her capacity as a corporate representative. If so, it follows the testimony generally will be binding on what could be a corporate respondent. Follow-up questions such as "What was the policy thinking at the time that the contract was signed?" themselves can inherit

Security National Bank of Sioux City, Iowa v. Abbott Laboratories, 2014 WL 3704277 *602 (N.D. Iowa Jul. 28. 2014) (reversed on other grounds in *Security National Bank of Sioux City, IA v. Jones Day*, 800 F. 3d 936 (8th Cir. 2015) (articulating that:

> "form" objections are inefficient and frustrate the goals underlying the Federal Rules. The Rules contemplate that objections should be concise and afford the examiner the opportunity to cure the objection [citation omitted] while unspecified "form" objections are certainly concise, they do not alert the examiner to a question's alleged defect. Because they lack specificity, "form" objections do not allow the examiner to immediately cure the objection. Instead, the examiner must ask the objector to clarify, which takes *more* time and *increases* the amount of objection banter between the lawyers. Briefly stating the particular ground for the objection, on the other hand, is no less concise and allows the examiner to ask a remedial question without further clarification. (Emphasis in original))

64 *Id.*

65 *Breaux v. Halliburton Energy Services*, 2006 WL 2460748 at *2 (E.D. La. Aug. 22, 2006) (noting that objections that "suggest an answer to the witness as speaking objections … are prohibited during depositions"); *Cerda v. Cillessen & Sons, Inc.*, 2020 WL 4500721 *1 (D. Kan. Aug. 5, 2020) (proscribing speaking objections); and In Re: *Rezulin Products Liability* Litigation, 2001 WL 366420 at *6 (S.D.N.Y. Mar. 2, 2001) (holding that "[n]o speaking objections shall be allowed[,]" and adding the instruction that "[t]he objecting counsel shall not speak any additional words concerning the basis of the objection unless the examining counsel requests a clarification. Any clarification as to the basis of the objection shall be stated succinctly as possible, e.g., 'argumentative,' or 'ambiguous'").

the ambiguity of the predicate question. In the context of witness examinations mistakes multiply.

Second, the word "you" can refer to the witness in her individual capacity. Here as well, the point is central to determining whether in fact, by way of example, the hypothetical corporate respondent was taking a position that was not aligned with the witness' thinking on an issue relevant and material to the dispute. Of course, the more obvious consequence is that the witness' thoughts and actions cannot be imputed to the corporate respondent. In this very simple example, the word "you" can be used to impeach collaterally the corporate respondent (perhaps through its own executive) or to provide the corporate respondent with the defense (likely to be included in a post-hearing submission) that the witness' testimony, to the extent that it is adverse to the corporate respondent, is not binding.

Third, the word "you" can refer both to the witness in her personal capacity *and* as a representative of the corporate respondent.[66] This basic example concerns only one very simple question. By *design* it also only pertains to an equally simplistic objection. For these two reasons, the need to interpose objections as to form is all the more stark. As questions fraught with deficits as to form multiply throughout the course of a hearing, it does not become too great a feat to speculate on what the record of such examinations must look like in terms of answers that just do not correspond to the question posed, or that can mislead all stakeholders because the answer was premised on a defective question. It is equally quizzical to consider how the principle of efficiency can be used as a justification for the allowance of improper questions during the course of an evidentiary hearing.

Once a framework that allows for interposing objections as to form is agreed upon, examiners are placed on notice and, therefore, tend to articulate sharper and more direct queries, particularly within the context of cross-examination. The risk of somehow delaying or protracting the hearing because a handful of objections may be raised with respect to each witness, when carefully considered, is not a rational proposition.

To the contrary, certainty, expediency, and transparency are underscored when counsel participate in a hearing expecting to be taken to task when questions are not properly framed. Fashioning the clearest possible record can only lead to efficiencies, process transparency, and foster predictive value. These are the elements necessary for the kind of *risk assessment* conducive to *optimal efficiency*.

The *status quo* where objections to the form of a question are ignored or reluctantly embraced by a tribunal that itself likely is unaware of the very problem(s)

[66] It is not uncommon for the examiner to attempt to enter into a stipulation pursuant to which a witness is told that the word "you" refers to her in her personal and corporate capacity, and asked to distinguish if in either capacity the answer would be different. It is equally common for the invitation to be rejected. Typically, counsel defending a witness would like to place the onus on the examiner to ask a proper non-objectionable question with respect to every question, instead of shifting the burden to the witness.

plaguing the defective question, is indefensible against the charge that such state of confusion leads to process legitimacy concerns, compromises the integrity of the record, and generates *unquantifiable risk*. Change is warranted.

8.10 *FREE PROOF* IS PARTICULARLY UNRELIABLE WHEN EVALUATING THE QUALITY OF EXPERT EVIDENCE

The arbitral tribunal in ICA proceedings of course does not serve as a gatekeeper. The tribunal itself is the alpha and the omega in terms of determining admissibility and weight of the evidence. In this regard, and in some sense, all evidence technically is admissible because it finds its way to the arbitral panel. Therefore, the question of "*admissibility*" is in effect a question of the *weight* to be ascribed to a particular evidentiary proffer.

Inadmissibility in the context of ICA *should* translate into ascribing zero weight to the evidence deemed inadmissible. The inalterable epistemic challenge resides in the extent to which the item of evidence accorded zero weight may have a residual and even determinative effect on the tribunal's assessment of other evidence or the equities of the merits.

There is a considerable cognitive difference between inadmissibility in the sense of not having knowledge at all of the content of the evidence deemed inadmissible, and ascribing zero weight to evidence. The former has no effect on the possible assessment of any part of the dispute. The latter can, and often does, have consequential ramifications. Questions of admissibility and weight are rendered all the more complex in the context of ICA because the same dearth of evidentiary rules concerning fact witnesses is present in the context of expert reports and corresponding expert testimony.

Notwithstanding the ever-increasing role of technology and technical expertise forming part of modern ICA proceedings, there are simply no rules or standards governing,

- (i) the admissibility and qualification of a person or juridical entity as an expert in a *particular field*,
- (ii) the extent to which purported expert knowledge is based upon sufficient facts, data, or opinions,
- (iii) any metrics for securing the necessary assurances of trustworthiness that must be present if the explanative theory asserted to justify a factual proposition as evidentiary knowledge is conducive to a correct result warranting the arbitral tribunal's acceptance, i.e., a conclusion based upon reliable *premises* and *methodologies*,
- (iv) the explanative theory has been asserted consonant with the correct procedures,

(v) the witness is qualified as an expert by dint of skill, experience, training and/or education to proffer the expert evidence, and

(vi) the facts asserted purporting to constitute expert witness testimony or knowledge (the latter in the form of a report) will assist the arbitral tribunal in understanding the facts (evidence) of the case or assessing the veracity of a question on the merits.

There is no categorical approach to expert evidence of any kind in ICA. ICA lacks even a suggested approach to evaluating (a) experts and (b) expert testimony.

The consequence is clear. In an era that fuses technology with the ubiquitous presence of and knowledge globalization, arbitral tribunals assess expert testimony on complex financial transactions that often concern intricate methodologies in the form of synthetic leases, payment in bitcoin, AI, and the use of block chain technologies, as well as intricate technical resource extraction issues, and increasing biogenetics IP and commercial application disputes that include metagenomics sequential analyses having multiple potential biotech applications, all without any prescribed methodology for testing the legal sufficiency of the expert or the testimony. The ills of not having evidence-based principles to determine reliability and the quality of evidence, and the predicate question of the extent to which a proposed expert should at all be accepted as an expert, are all the more problematic in this context. ICA no longer is relegated to simple contractual disputes. ICA has outgrown and abandoned its original reason for being.

Subjectivity in the form of the arbitral tribunal's "personal impressions" and "intuition" regarding the expert's qualifications as an expert and the reliability of her testimony are determinative. There is no pretense at a rule or standard-based objective evaluation. Subjectivity rules.

Discussing this very issue but in the context of nonjury trials, one commentator has observed that "the FRE have been amended over the years in response to such challenges [technological and other developments the subject matter of which is foreign to fact-finders]."[67] This commentator provides an interesting example by noting that "in 2000, FRE 702,[68] "testimony by Expert Witnesses," was amended

[67] Wang, "Rethinking Evidentiary Rules," at 307, Chapter 2, n. 23 in this volume.

[68] F.R.E. 702 (Testimony by Expert Witnesses) reads:

A witness who is qualified as an expert by knowledge, skill, experience, training, or education may testify in the form of an opinion or otherwise if the proponent demonstrates to the court that it is more likely than not that:

(a) the expert's scientific, technical, or other specialized knowledge will help the trier of fact to understand the evidence or to determine a fact in issue;

(b) the testimony is based on sufficient facts or data;

(c) the testimony is the product of reliable principles and methods; and

(d) the expert's opinion reflects a reliable application of the principles and methods to the facts of the case.

to incorporate the *Daubert*[69] (and the follow-up case law applying *Daubert*[70]), a checklist for trial judges to use in assessing the reliability and helpfulness of scientific and non-scientific expert testimony [citation omitted]."[71] In this connection, it is noted that even though FRE 702 and 902 (Evidence that is Self-Authenticating) are "heavily influenced by 'jury thinking,' this 'phenomenon' plainly suggests that evidentiary rules about new forms of evidence and complex evidence are no longer based on the Jury Control Theory and hence should also be written into evidentiary rules for bench trials."[72]

This very analysis applies to an ICA arbitral tribunal. The incorporation of principles or rules similar to FRE 702 do not concern an aprioristic classification of evidentiary subject matter that precludes or detracts from an arbitral tribunal's ability to process evidence empirically. Instead, such rules create a reasonable and tempered relationship between the subject (arbitral tribunal) and the object (expert witness standing and proffered specialized knowledge) that allows for a reason-based relationship providing for a sanitized evaluation of the *quality* and *reliability* of the expert witness and the corresponding evidence. Such methodology would create a uniform non-*ad hoc* approach to expert testimony. And impose a minimum standard of requirements for purported expert witnesses.

The FRE approach sets forth a sequential roadmap for arbitral tribunals that also can easily be incorporated into a procedural order requiring the proffering party to meet the fundamental elements of FRE 702-style rule. Moreover, a standard methodology approach to the admissibility of an expert *as an expert*, as well as to the assessment of the expert testimony by testing what typically amounts to untested assumptions in standard ICA proceedings, certainly would further the very arbitral tribunal's ability to understand a technical opinion.

Too often rulings on expert testimony are based on the effects of persuasive advocacy arising from, for example, "hot tubbing," that is to say, the process by which competing experts are sequentially (almost simultaneously) invited to address the same question, or to offer contrasting points of view on specific propositions. This latter approach does little to tease from the evidentiary proffers the controlling principles offered by specialized knowledge.[73]

69 *See generally*, *Daubert v. Merrell Dow Pharms, Inc.*, 509 U.S. 579, 597 (1993).

70 *See, e.g.*, *Gen. Elec. Co. v. Joiner*, 522 U.S. 136, 146 (1997); *Kumho Tire Co. v. Carmichael*, 526 U.S. 137, 141 (1999).

71 Wang, "Rethinking Evidentiary Rules," at 307, *see* Chapter 2, n. 23 in this volume.

72 *Id.* at 307–308.

73 The admissibility of expert testimony, Rule 702, requires the trial court to make several preliminary determinations, Rule 104(a). The trial court must decide whether the witness called is properly qualified to give the testimony sought. [A proposition that would be heretical in the ICA context for no stated reason(s).] A witness may be qualified as an expert on the basis of either knowledge, skill, experience, training, or education or a combination thereof, Rule 702. The trial court must further determine that the testimony of the expert witness, in the form of an oral opinion or otherwise, will assist the trier of fact, i.e., be helpful, to understand the evidence or to determine a fact at

Having evidentiary principles comparable to those set forth in FRE 702 by design cannot limit or otherwise stratify the arbitral tribunal's exercise of discursive reasoning concerning the admissibility or assessment (weight) forming part of the evidentiary process stages because this approach does not entail an *ex ante* view of the subject matter to be analyzed. To be sure, if at all, it is inimical to categorical imperatives.

The *status quo Free Proof* approach to expert witnesses and evidence is but an anachronistic museum piece. A mere relic with the "legitimacy" (normativity) that stems from repetition and not born of discursive reasoning. It is time to change. A change that shall be conducive to *risk assessment* and *optimal efficiency*.

issue, Rule 702(a) [such an approach can only lead to more objective, and therefore fairer, results and should be considered in the ICA space]. Finally, the trial court must determine that as actually applied in the matter at hand, Rule 702(d) to facts, data, or opinions sufficiently established to exist, Rule 702(b), including facts, data, or opinions reasonably relied upon under Rule 703, sufficient assurances of trustworthiness are present that the expert witness' explanative theory produced a correct result to warrant jury acceptance, i.e., a product of reliable principles and methods, Rule 702(c). The explanative theory must be supplied by the expert; an opinion without analysis is meaningless. The proponent of the expert witness testimony has the burden of establishing the foregoing admissibility requirements to be more probably true than not. The weight to be given to expert testimony permitted by the court is for the trier of fact to determine....

Expert testimony is not limited to scientific or technical subject matter, but rather includes all areas of specialized knowledge. Thus, within the scope of Rule 702's concept of experts fall individuals, sometimes called "skilled" witnesses, such as bankers and landowners testifying as to land value, and others whose expertise is based largely upon experience.

When scientific, technical, or other specialized knowledge will be helpful to the trier in rationally evaluating facts, the traditional method of supplying data of this nature is the introduction of an opinion of an expert witness. Rule 702 provides that expert testimony may be "in the form of an opinion or otherwise," thus the expert may, but need not, testify in the form of an opinion. [She] may instead give an exposition of relevant scientific or other principles that may allow the trier of fact to draw its own inferences or conclusions from the evidence presented, or [she] may combine the two.

Graham, *Handbook of Federal Evidence*, at § 702:1.

Conclusion

Historical writings establish that, at minimum in connection with the enactment of the FAA in the US, efficiency is ICA's bedrock principle: not *party-autonomy* and not *arbitrator discretion*. The legacy, and current understanding, of *efficiency*, however, within the ICA rubric concerns what in this book, *Settlement and Risk Assessment in International Commercial Arbitration*, has been defined as *process efficiency*, namely, the efficiency that exclusively concerns itself with yielding a binding and enforceable award. It then is necessary to ask whether ICA has redeemed the broader promise of efficiency when less than 40 percent of all ICA arbitrations settle? If the answer to this query is in the affirmative, how then are merits-based determinations by arbitral tribunals more in keeping with the ICA principle of *party-autonomy*, rather than resolution by settlement pursuant to mutual accord?

If, upon reflection, the answer is in the negative, is there a principal reason or root cause why ICA settlements constitute the exception and not the norm? Assuming there is such a principal root cause, can it be identified and addressed?

Despite many shortcomings, judicial proceedings in both state and federal *fora* in the US enjoy an approximately 90 percent settlement rate. Both jury and nonjury trials meaningfully have declined in numbers where less than 3 percent of all trials are jury trials. Even though there are many factors that account for the high settlement rate in US litigation, a most salient feature appears to be the stakeholders' ability (i) to identify, (ii) to quantify, and (iii) to communicate risk early and at multiple strategic procedural junctures during the course of the proceeding. At the dawn of the proceeding, the parties know the value of their respective cases.

The ICA (i) self-disclosure, (ii) evidence taking, and (iii) evidence-presenting framework is anemic when closely examining the IBA, Prague, and major administrating institutional rules. This wanting state of affairs regarding the rules and principles that render *risk assessment* possible and therefore settlement probable, is compounded and made worse because by dint of having been designed to heighten *process efficiency* and yield a binding and enforceable award, ICA lacks a "settlement culture."

True, there have been minor gains of very recent vintage. The ICC, for example, has enacted settlement guidelines. And indeed, a handful of arbitral institutes provide for settlement provisions in their rules, as well as for mediation rules. Rules for expedited summary adjudications also are available. Also, it is now generally accepted that arbitrators have a duty to facilitate settlement. The "how" and not the "what," however, needs to be worked out.

Lamentably, however, these "settlement gains" exist in a vacuum, bereft of procedural and evidential rules that can render *risk assessment* possible. The kind of quality risk assessment that in turn would generate settlement probabilities, that is to say, the amicable resolution of disputes in a non-zero-sum-game context, thereby yielding *optimal efficiency*. To be sure, settlement, so it is here asserted, also constitutes a paradigmatic and most robust expression of *party-autonomy*. For this additional reason, it must be embraced as foundational to arbitral culture.

The rules contributing to self-disclosure and evidence taking can be readily refined to provide for an environment that promotes settlement during distinctive strategic procedural junctures in ways making possible far greater procedural transparency. The same standard applicable to *evidence taking* should not apply to the *presentation* of evidence. The *disclosure* standard cannot be one and the same with the criterion for the analysis of *admissibility* and *weight* accorded to evidence in support of a claim or defense.

Critical terms such as *relevant* and *material* must be accorded substantive content. Their application cannot be *ad hoc*. Objectivity is necessary if risk assessment and settlement negotiations indeed are to take place in the shadow of the law. The term *weight* must be conceptually enabled by way of evidential principles so that tribunals may evaluate the *quality* and *reliability* of evidence. Stakeholder expectations must be based on objective factors conducive to *optimal efficiency*.

The current unqualified *Free Proof* approach to the evaluation of *admissibility, relevance, materiality*, and *weight* is conceptually and doctrinally flawed. Leading to an unpredictable, (random) "methodology" with respect to arbitral tribunals' evidence assessment and epistemic understanding of the category "weight" (evidentiary reliability and qualitative analyses). Here as well, predictive value is necessary if settlement in ICA is to be anything other than a statistical improbability. The current understanding of settlement in ICA as a statistical improbability is unacceptable.

Finally, ICA stakeholders must embrace settlement as *optimal efficiency* and, therefore, as an integral molecular feature of ICA's fabric and tissue. Put simply, settlement as *optimal efficiency* must constitute a central feature of ICA.

Change is never easy. Yet, in many cases concerning the improvement of dispute resolution it is necessary. As a dispute resolution methodology ICA has lost its mantle of efficiency. General Counsel for the largest and most economically influential transnationals are reverting to domestic courts as the more *efficient* and predictable *fora* for cross-border dispute resolution. It follows that change to embrace *optimal efficiency* is existential to ICA, much as a mammal's fur coat must adapt its chromatic features to the changes in flora and fauna of its immediate habitat upon penalty of extinction.

> The woods are lovely, dark and deep,
> But I have promises to keep,
> And miles to go before I sleep,
> And miles to go before I sleep.
>
> Robert Frost, "Stopping by Woods on a Snowy Evening"

Frost's lonely traveler finds no respite, at least not within the confines of the *iambic tetrameters*. We are left with the image of a person alone with a horse, trekking the seemingly endless woods in furtherance of the redemption of an unknown promise. There is no hint that a place of rest is in sight, or of the possibility that the elusive promise itself will be redeemed.

We, too, are so placed in the pursuit of helping ICA redeem its promise. The concepts heralding change clearly are within grasp and in sight. Let us develop the arbitral culture to seize them. Lest we find ourselves left wandering in perpetuity, alone in the dark, and perhaps even in the snow.

Bibliography

ARTICLES AND OTHER AUTHORITIES

[2015] 1 Lloyd's Rep 423

Christian P. Alberti, "*Iura Novit Curia* in Commercial Arbitration: How Much Justice Do You Want?," in *International Arbitration and International Commercial Law: Synergy, Convergence and Evolution* (S. Kröll et al. eds.) (Wolters Kluwer 2011)

Richard G. Alleman, "Mind the Settlement Gap: A Call for More Effective Judicialization of International Commercial Arbitration," 38 *Arb. Int'l* 4, 231–248 (December 2022)

H. N. Aragaki, "Applicability of Rules of Evidence Where the Judge Is the Trier of Facts in an Action at Law," 42 *Harv. L. Rev.* 258 (1928)

Harry Baum & Leon Pressman, "The Enforcement of Commercial Arbitration Agreements in the Federal Courts," 8 *N.Y.U.L.Q. Rev.* 238, 239–249 (1930)

Klaus Peter Berger, "The Direct Involvement of the Arbitrator in the Amicable Settlement of the Dispute: Offering Preliminary Views, Discussing Settlement Options, Suggesting Solutions, Caucusing," 35 *J. Int'l. Arb* 5, 501–516 (2018)

Klaus Peter Berger & J. Ole Jensen, "The Arbitrator's Mandate to Facilitate Settlement," 40 *Fordham Int'l L.J.* 3, 887 (2017)

Piero Bernardini, "The Role of the International Arbitrator," 20 *Arb. Int'l* 113 (2014)

Hermann Bietz, "On the State and Efficiency of International Arbitration: Could the German 'Relevance Method' Be Useful or Not?" 12 *SchiedsVZ* 30, 121(2014)

Nigel Blackaby & Ricardo Chirinos, "Consideraciones Sobre la Aplicación del Principio Iura Novit Curia en el Arbitraje Comercial Internacional," 6 *Anu. Colomb. Derecho Int.* 77, 88 (2013)

Gordon Blanke, "The Use of National Civil Procedure Rules in International Arbitration," 9 *ERA Forum* 283, 283–290 (2008)

Gary B. Born, "Procedures in International Arbitration," (updated August 2022) in *International Commercial Arbitration*, 3rd ed., 1 (Kluwer Law International 2021)

Charles N. Brower, "Evidence before International Tribunals: The Need for Some Standard Rules," 28 *Int.'l L.* 47 (1984)

Chester Brown, "The Inherent Powers of International Courts and Tribunals," 76 *Brit. Y. B. Int'l. L.* 195 (2006)

Henry G. Burnett & David Weiss, "Systematic Advocacy: A Guide to Cross-Examination in International Arbitration," 13 *Revista Brasileira de Arbitragem* 51, 99–132 (2016)

Zechariah Chaffee, Jr. & Sidney Simpson, *Cases on Equity* (Published by the Editors 1934)

Seung Wha Chang, "Inherent Powers of the Arbitral Tribunal to Investigate Its Own Jurisdiction," 29 *J. Int'l. Arb.* 171 (2012)

Civil Justice Initiative, *The Landscape of Civil Litigation in State Courts* (November 11, 2015)
Kevin M. Clermont, "Litigation Realities Redux," 84 *Notre Dame L. Rev.* 1919, 1654–1655 (2009)
Marcus Commandeur & Sebastian Gößling, "The Determination of Mandatory Rules of Law in International Arbitration: An Attempt to Set Out Criteria," 1 *SchiedsVZ* 12, 12 (2014)
Giuditta Cordero-Moss, "General Report on Jura Novit Arbiter," in *Iura Novit Cura in International Arbitration* 477 (Franco Ferrari & Giuditta Cordero-Moss eds.) (Juris Publishing 2018)
Mirjan Damaška, *Evidence Law Adrift* 2 (Yale University Press 1977)
Mirjan Damaška, "Free Proof and Its Detractors," 43 *Am. J. Comp. L.* 343, 344–346 (1995)
Mirjan R. Damaška, *Crime, Procedure and Evidence in a Comparative and International Context: Essays in Honour of Professor Mirjan Damaška* (John D. Jackson, Máximo Langer, and Peter Tillers, eds.) (Hart Publishing 2008)
Kenneth Culp Davis, "An Approach to the Rules of Evidence for Nonjury Cases," 50 *A.B.A.J.* 723, 726 (1964)
Kenneth Culp Davis, "Hearsay in Nonjury Cases," 83 *Harv. L. Rev.* 1362 (1970)
Alexandre de Gramont, Michael D. Igyarto, & Tatiana Sainati, "Divergent Paths: Settlement in Us Litigation and International Arbitration," 40 *Fordham Int'l L.J.* 953, 964–966 (2017)
Debevoise & Plimpton LLP, "Protocol to Promote Efficiency in International Arbitration," available at: https://shorturl.at/DsGUa (2010) (last accessed March 18, 2019)
Decision 4 P. 100/2003, 22 ASA *Bulletin* (2004) No. 22, at 574 ff. especially fig. 5, at 579
Yves Derains, "Observations-Cour d'App de Paris (1 re Ch. C) 13 Novembre 1997 – Lemeur v SAR Les Cités Invisible," 1998 *Rev. Arb.* 711 (1998)
Yves Derains, "The Deliberations of the Arbitral Tribunal: 'Retour au délibéré arbitral,'" in *The Resolution of the Dispute: From the Hearing to the Award*, ASA Special Series No. 29, 16 (Markus Wirth ed.) (Association Suisse de L'Arbitrage 2007)
Diane Desierto, "Rawlsian Fairness and International Arbitration," 36 *U. Pa. J. Int'l L.* 4 939–993 (2015)
Radicati di Brozolo, "International Commercial Arbitration and Private International Law," in *Cambridge Compendium of Commercial and Investment Arbitration* 441 (F. Ferrari, S. Kroll, & A. Bjorklund eds.) 464 (Cambridge University Press 2020)
Michael Dunmore, "Increased Efficiency and Lower Costs in Arbitration: Sole Member Tribunals," IV *Indian J. Arb. L.* 1, 27–33 (2015)
David Earnest, Raúl Gallardo, Gardar Vidir Gunnarsson, & Tobiasz Kaczor, "Four Ways to Sharpen the Sword of Efficiency in International Arbitration," (2013) available at: https://shorturl.at/EqAa4 (last accessed March 18, 2019)
Melvin Aron Eisenberg, "Private Ordering through Negotiation: Dispute-Settlement and Rulemaking," 89 *Harv. L. Rev.* 637, 638–639 (February 1976)
Theodore Eisenberg & Charlotte Lanvers, "What Is the Settlement Rate and Why We Should Care?," 6 *Journal of Empirical Legal Stud.* 111, 112 (2009)
Rachel Engle, "Party-Autonomy in International Arbitration: Where Uniformity Gives Way to Predictability," 15 *Transant. L.* 323 (2002)
Facilitating Settlement in International Arbitration, Report, ICC Publication, https://shorturl.at/wrrFx (last accessed November 2023)
E. Allan Farnsworth "Legal Remedies for Breach of Contract," 70 *Colum. L. Rev.* 1145 (1970)
John Fellas, "A Fair and Efficient International Arbitration Process," *PLI Course Handbook*, International Arbitration, No. 10796 (2007)
John Fellas, "Cross-Examination in International Arbitration," 254 *N.Y.J.L.* 26 (August 7, 2015)

Diego P. Fernández-Arroyo, "Arbitrators' Procedural Powers: The Last Frontier of Party-Autonomy?" in *Limits to Party-Autonomy in International Commercial Arbitration* 202, 202–206 (Franco Ferrari ed.) (Juris 2016)

Cristina Florescu, "The Arbitration Agreement and Arbitrability: Towards Achieving Efficiency in International Arbitration," *Austrian Yearbook Int'l Arb.* 51–71 (2015)

Fabricio Fortese & Lotta Hemmi, "Procedural Fairness and Efficiency in International Arbitration," 3 *Groningen J. Int'l L.* 1, 110–124 (2015)

Susan D. Franck, "International Arbitration and Attorney-Client Privilege: A Conflict of Law Approach," 51 *Ariz. St. L.* 3.935 (2019)

Nora Freeman Engstrom, "The Diminished Trial," 86 *Fordham L. Rev.* 2131, 2137 (2018)

Emmanuel Gaillard & John Savage (eds.), *Fouchard, Gaillard, Goldman: On International Commercial Arbitration* (Kluwer Law International 1999)

Marc Galanter, "The Vanishing Trial: An Examination of Trials and Related Matters in Federal State Courts," 15 *Empirical Legal Stud.* 459 (2004)

Ignacio Gómez-Palacio, "International Commercial Arbitration: Two Cultures in a State of Courtship and Potential Marriage of Convenience," 20 *Am. Rev. Int'l Arb.* 235 (2010)

Michael Z. Green, "No Strict Evidence Rules in Labor and Employment Arbitration," 15 *Tex. Wesleyan L. Rev.* 533 (2009)

Lucy Greenwood, "Does Bifurcation Really Promote Efficiency?" 28 *J. Int'l Arb.* 2, 105–111 (2011)

Lucy Greenwood, "A Window of Opportunity? Building a Short Period of Time into Arbitral Rules in Order for Parties to Explore Settlement," 27 *Arb. Int'l* 2, 199–210 (2011)

H.R. Rep. No. 1829, 73rd Cong., 2d Sess.

Inka Hanefeld, "Limits to Party-Autonomy Imposed by European Mandatory Law," in *Limits to Party-Autonomy in International Commercial Arbitration* 402–413 (Franco Ferrari ed.) (Juris 2016)

Stutzer Hansjörg, "Settlement Facilitation: Does the Arbitrator Have a Role? The 'Referentenaudienz': The 'Zurich-Way' of Settling the Case," 35 ASA *Bulletin* 3, 589–608 (2017)

Ragnar Harbst, "Cross-Examination," in A *Counsel's Guide to Examining and Preparing Witnesses in International Arbitration*, chapter 8 (Wolters Kluwer 2024)

Samaa A. F. Haridi & Ilham A. Kabbouri, "Chapter 11: Witness Testimony and Cross-Examination in International Arbitration: A Civil Law and Common Law Blended Approach?" in *The Plurality and Synergies of Legal Traditions in International Arbitration: Looking beyond the Common and Civil Law Divide* (Stavros Brekoulakis, Nayla Comair Obeid, & Claudia Pharaon eds.) (Wolters Kluwer 2024)

Veijo Heiskanen, "Key to Efficiency in International Arbitration," 30 *ICSID Review* 481–485 (2015)

Elena V. Helmer, "International Commercial Arbitration: Americanized, 'Civilized,' or Harmonized?" 19 *Ohio St. J. on Disp. Resol.* 35 (2003)

HKIAC, www.hkiac.org/about-us/statistics (2022)

Kaj Hobér, "Cross-Examination in International Arbitration," in *Stockholm Arbitration Yearbook* 2019 41–54 (Azel Calissendorff & Patrik Schöldström eds.), chapter 3 (Wolters Kluwer 2019)

James Hope, "Why Choose Stockholm: Reflections of an English Lawyer after Two Years Practicing International Arbitration in Sweden," *Stockholm Int'l Arb. Rev.* 2 (2008)

House Report No. 96, 68th Cong., 1st Sess.

ICC Commission on Arbitration and ADR, Task Force on Reducing Time and Costs in Arbitration, p. 1, available at: https://tinyurl.com/yjfxz8rw (last accessed March 18, 2019)

ICC Commission on Arbitration and ADR in July 2023, launched guides on Effective Conflict Management and Facilitating Settlement in International Arbitration

ICC Commission Report Controlling Time and Costs in Arbitration (2012) p. 11

"ICC Dispute Resolution Bulletin," 2018, Issue 1

"ICC Dispute Resolution Bulletin," 2019, Issue 1

"ICC Practice and Procedure," 2018, Issue 1

ICSID_Convention.pdf (worldbank.org)

ICSID, https://icsid.worldbank.org/resources/publications/icsid-caseload-statistics (2023)

Malicorp Ltd v. Government of the Arab Republic of Egypt [2015] EWHC 361 (Comm)

Inter-American Convention of International Commercial Arbitration House Report No. 101-501

JAMS International Efficiency Guidelines 2011 for the Pre-hearing Phase of International Arbitrations, at www.jamsinternational.com/international-arbitration-efficiency-guidelines (last accessed March 18, 2019)

Nana Japaridze, "Fair Enough? Reconciling the Pursuit of Fairness and Justice with Preserving the Nature of International Commercial Arbitration," 36 *Hofstra L. Rev.* 4, 1415–1446 (2008)

Joanna Jemielniak & Stefanie Phisteer, "Should Arbitrators Know the Law? The Iura Novit Curia Principle in International Commercial Arbitration," *University of Copenhagen*, Conference of November 7, 2014 (2014)

Rodrigo Jijón & Daniela Páez, "¿Cabe la aplicación del principio Iura Novit Curia en el arbitraje comercial?" 5 *Revista Ecuatoriana de Arbitraje* 161 (2013)

Sabra A. Jones, "Historical Development of Commercial Arbitration in the United States," 21 *Minn. L. Rev.* 240, 243–244 (1928)

Judgment of 30 October 2008, 2009 *SchiedsVZ* 66 (Bundesgerichtschof)

Susan L. Karamanian, "Overstating the 'Americanization' of International Arbitration: Lessons from ICSID," 19 *Ohio St. J. on Disp. Resol.* 5, 27 (2003)

Gabrielle Kaufmann-Kohler, "Beyond Gadgetry: Substantive New Concepts to Improve Arbitral Efficiency," 5 *JWIT* 69–72 (2004)

Gabrielle Kaufmann-Kohler, "The Governing Law: Law or Fact?" in *Best Practices in International Arbitration: ASA Swiss Arbitration Association Conference*, January 27, 2006, Zürich, ASA Special Series (Markus Wirth ed.) 84 (Association Suisse de L'Arbitrage 2006)

Rachel D. Kent, "An Introduction to Cross-Examining Witnesses in International Arbitration," 3 *TDM* 2 (April 2006)

Jennifer Kirby, "Efficiency in Arbitration: Whose Duty Is It?" 32 *J. Int'l Arb.* 6, 689–696 (2015)

Laird C. Kirkpatrick, "Evidence Law in the Next Millenium," 49 *Hastings L.J.* 363, f.n. 11 (1998)

Stefan Kröll, "The Normative Framework on the Taking of Evidence," in *Handbook of Evidence in International Commercial Arbitration: Key Issues and Concepts* (Franco Ferrari & Friedrich Rosenfeld eds.) 23–39 (Wolters Kluwer 2022)

Zdeněk Kühn, "The Authoritarian Legal Culture at Work: The Passivity of the Parties and the Interpretational Statements of Supreme Courts," 2 *CYELP* 25, 25–26 (2006)

Karl H. Kunert, "Some Observations on the Origins and Structure of Evidence under the Common Law System and the Civil Law System of 'Free Proof' in the German Code of Civil Procedure," 16 *Buff. L. Rev.* 122, 141–143 (1966)

John H. Langbein, "The German Advantage in Civil Procedure," 52 *U. Chi. L. Rev.* 823, 829 (1985)

John J. Langbein, "Historical Foundations of the Law of Evidence: A View from the Ryder Sources," 96 *Colum. L. Rev.* 1168 (1996)

Alejandro E. Leañez, "The Future of the Anti-suit Injunctions: The Power of the Arbitral Tribunal to Issue Anti-suit Injunctions," 14 *Vindobona J. Int'l & Comm. L. & Arb.* 33 (2010)

Elisabeth Leimbacher, "Efficiency under the New ICC Rules of Arbitration of 2012: First Glimpse at the New Practice," 31 ASA *Bulletin* 2, 298–315 (2013)

A. Leo Levin & Harold K. Cohen, "Exclusionary Rules in Nonjury Criminal Cases," 119 *U. Pa. L. Rev.* 905, 908 (1971)

Andreas F. Lowenfeld, "The Party-Appointed Arbitrator in International Controversies: Some Reflections," 30 *Tex. Int'l L. J.* 59 (1995)

Andres F. Lowenfeld, "Introduction: The Elements of Procedure: Are They Separately Portable?" 45 *Am. J. Comp. L.* 649, 654 (1997)

Sam Luttrell & Isuru Devendra, "Inherent Jurisdiction and Implied Power to Stay Proceedings in Aid of Arbitration: A Nice Question," 32 *J. Int'l. Arb.* 493 (2015)

Pedro J. Martínez-Fraga, "Good Faith, Bad Faith, but Not Losing Faith: A Commentary on the 2010 IBA Rules on the Taking of Evidence in International Arbitration," 43 *Geo. J. Int'l L.* 387 (2011–2012)

Pedro J. Martínez-Fraga, "Developing Equipoise between Party-Autonomy and the Inherent Power of Arbitrator Discretion in the Gathering of Evidence in International Arbitration," in *Inherent Powers of Arbitrators* (Franco Ferrari & Friedrich Rosenfeld eds.) chapter 8, 209 (JurisNet 2019)

Thomas A. Mauet, "Bench Trials," *LITIG*, Summer 2002

Michael McIlwrath, "Faster, Cheaper: Global Initiatives to Promote Efficiency in International Arbitration," 76 *Arbitration* 532–537 (2010)

Sundaresh Menon, "Adjudicator, Advocate, or Something in Between? Coming to Terms with the Role of the Party-Appointed Arbitrator," 34 *J. Int'l. Arb.* 348, 351–354 (2017)

Sundaresh Menon, "Dispelling Due Process Paranoia: Fairness, Efficiency and the Rule of Law," 17 *Asian Int. Arbitr. J.* 1, 3 (2021)

Soia Mentschikoff, "Commercial Arbitration," 61 *Colum. L. Rev.* 846, 850 (1961)

Loukas Mistelis, "Article Special Section the 2008 Survey on Corporate Attitudes towards Recognition and Enforcement of International Arbitral Awards: The Settlement-Enforcement Dynamic in International Arbitration," 19 *Am. Rev. Int'l. Arb.* 377 (2008)

Loukas Mistelis, "Efficiency – What Else? Efficiency as the Emerging Defining Value of International Arbitration: Between Systems Theories and Party Autonomy," *Queen Mary University of London, School of Law Legal Studies Research Paper*, No. 313/2019

Jennifer L. Mnookin, "Bifurcation and the Law of Evidence," 155 *U. Pa. L. Rev. Penn. Umbra*. 134, 136 (2006)

Robert H. Mnookin & Lewis Kornhauser, "Bargaining in the Shadow of the Law: The Case of Divorce," 88 *Yale L.J.* 950, 968–69 (1979)

Edmund Morgan, "The Jury and the Exclusionary Rules of Evidence," 4 *U. Chi. L. Rev.* 247 (1937)

Michael Moser, "The 'Pre-hearing Checklist': A Technique for Enhancing Efficiency in International Arbitral Proceedings," 30 *J. Int'l Arb.* 155–159 (2013)

Margaret L. Moses, "Inherent Power of Arbitrators to Deal with Ethical Issues," *Loyola University Chicago School of Law, Public Law Research Paper*, No. 2014-016

Jus Mundi, "ICC Facilitating Settlement in International Arbitration" (2023), 4, https://shorturl.at/1JFgt (last accessed November 2023)

Dale Nance, "The Evidence Principle," 73 *Iowa L. Rev.* 227, 229 *passim* (1988)

Christopher Newmark, "Controlling Time and Costs in Arbitration," in *The Leading Arbitrators' Guide to International Arbitration* 81–96 (Lawrence Newman and Richard Hill eds.) (Juris 2008)

Mary Ellen O'Connell, "Lawful Self-Defense to Terrorism," 63 *U. Pitt. L. Rev.* 889, 895–896 (2002)

Mary Ellen O'Connell, "Rules of Evidence for the Use of Force in International Law's New Era," 100 *Am. Soc'y Int'l L. Proc.* 44 (2006)

Veit Öhlberger & Jarred Pinkston, "The Arbitrator and the Arbitration Procedure, *Iura Novit Curia* and the Non-passive Arbitrator: A Question of Efficiency, Cultural Blinders and Misplaced Concerns about Impartiality," *Austrian Yearbook Int'l Arb.* 101–117 (2016)

Brian J. Ostrom, Shauna M. Strickland, & Paula L. Hannaford-Agor, "Examining Trial Trends in State Courts: 1976–2002," 1 *J. Empirical Legal Stud.* 755 (2004)

William W. Park, "The Lex Loci Arbitri and International Commercial Arbitration," 32 *J.C.L.Q.* 25 (1983)

Jan Paulsson, "Delocalisation of International Commercial Arbitration: When and Why It Matters," 32 *Int'l & Comp. L.Q.* 1, 53–61 (January 1983)

Stefanie Pfisterer, "The Arbitrator as Settlement Facilitator," 24 *Am. Ren. Int'l Arb.* 649 (2013)

Wilson Pimentel, "Efficiency and Equilibrium in the Allocation of Costs," XII *Revista Brasiliera de Arbitragem* 59–67 (2015)

Karl Pörnbacher & Alexander Dolgorukow, "Reconciling Due Process and Efficiency in International Arbitration: The Arbitrator's Task of Achieving the One without Sacrificing the Other," LXI *Annals FLB – Belgrade Law Review* 3, 50–62 (2013)

J. J. Prescott & Kathryn E. Spier, "A Comprehensive Theory of Civil Settlement," 91 *NYU L. Rev.* 59, 77 (2016)

Queen Mary School University of London, *2015 International Arbitration Survey: Improvement and Innovations in International Arbitration*, pp. 5, 10, available at: https://shorturl.at/lIT4i (last accessed June 22, 2023)

Queen Mary University of London, *2008 Corporate Attitudes and Enforcement of Arbitral Awards*, p. 5, available at: https://arbitration.qmul.ac.uk/media/arbitration/docs/IAstudy_2008.pdf (last accessed June 24, 2023)

Paul Radvany, "The Importance of the Federal Rules of Evidence in Arbitration," 36 *Rev. Litig.* 469, 511–512 (2016)

Alan Redfern, "The Jurisdiction of International Commercial Arbitrator," 3 *J. Int'l. Arb.* 19, 27 (1986)

Andreas Respondek, "Five Proposals to Further Increase the Efficiency of International Arbitration Proceedings," 31 *J. Int'l Arb.* 4, 507–513 (2014)

Restatement (Second) of Conflicts of Laws § 187 (1971)

Jorg Risse, "Ten Drastic Proposals for Saving Time and Costs in Arbitral Proceedings," 23 *Arb. Int'l* 3, 5 (2013)

Tyler B. Robinson & Robert H. Smit, "Cross-Examination International Arbitration: A Class among Common Law Traditions," 29 *Am. Rev. Int'l Arb.* 105 (2018)

Janet A. Rosen, "Arbitration under Private International Law: The Doctrines of Separability and Compétenz de la Compétenz," 17 *Fordham Int'l. J.* 599, 610 (1993)

Freidrich Rosenfeld, "*Iura Novit Curia* International Law," in Jura Novit Curia *in International Arbitration* 461 (Franco Ferrari & Freidrich Rosenfeld eds.) (Juris Publishing 2018)

Peter Rosher, "Cross-Examination in International Arbitration," *International Business Law Journal* 2017 3, 203–224 (also known as *Revue de Droit des Affaires Internationales* (Thomson Reuters 2017))

Javier H. Rubenstein, "Perspectives: International Commercial Arbitration: Reflections at the Cross Roads of the Common Law and Civil Law Traditions," 5 *Chi. J. Int'l. L.* 303, 309 (2004)

Paola Sánchez, "Introducing Efficiency into the 2010 IBA Rules on Evidence: Does This Create a Back Door for Introducing Additional Inefficiencies into the System?" 1 *International Commercial Arbitration Brief* 1, 3–4(2011)

Paul L. Sayre, "Development of Commercial Arbitration Law," 37 *Yale L. J.* 595, 597 (1928)

Frederick Schauer, "On the Supposed Jury-Dependence of Evidence Law," 155 *U. Pa. L. Rev.* 165 (2006)

Maxi Scherer, "The Fate of Parties' Agreements on Judicial Review of Awards: A Comparative and Normative Analysis of Party-Autonomy at the Post-Award Stage," in *Arbitration International* Vol. 32, Issue 3, 437–457 (William W. Park ed.) (2016)

Anne-Veronique Schläpfer & Marily Paralika, "Striking the Right Balance: The Roles of Arbitral Institutions, Parties and Tribunals in Achieving Efficiency in International Arbitration," 2 *BCDR Int'l Arb. Rev.* 2, 329–342 (2015)

S. Rep. No. 1049, 73rd Cong., 2d Sess.

Senate Report No. 536, 68th Cong.1st Session at 8

S.R. 91st Cong., 2nd Sess., No. 91–702 (Calendar No. 695) Foreign Arbitral Awards at 8

Steven Shavell, *Foundations of Economic Analysis of Law* 412 (2024)

John Sheldon & Peter Murray, "Rethinking the Rules of Evidentiary Admissibility in Non-jury Trials," 86 *Judicature* 227 (March–April 2003)

Laurence Shore, "Chapter 22: Michael E. Schneider on Cross-Examination: A Respectful, Even Admiring Albeit Uneasy Reaction of a U.S. Lawyer," in *Stories from the Hearing Room: Experience from Arbitral Practice Essays in Honour of Michael E. Schneider*, 173–178 (Bernd Ehle & Domitille Baizeau eds.), (Wolters Kluwer 2015)

Statement of Mr. Charles L. Bernheimer, Chairman Committee on Arbitration. Chamber of Commerce of the State of New York, New York City, Joint Hearing before Subcommittees on the Judiciary, Congress of the United States 68th Congress, 1st Session on S. 1005 and H.R. 646, January 9, 1924, pp. 6–7

Thomas Stipanowich & Zachary Ulrich, "Commercial Arbitration and Settlement: Empirical Insights into the Roles Arbitrators Play," 6 *Penn State Yearbook on Arbitration and Mediation* 1 (2014), Pepperdine University Legal Studies Research Paper, No. 2014/20

Takne Sugiahra, "The Principle of *Jura Novit Curia* in the International Court of Justice: With Reference to Recent Decisions," 55 *Japanese Y. B. Int'l L* 77 (2012)

The Accuracy of Fact Witness Memory in International Arbitration (International Chamber of Commerce 2020), available at: https://shorturl.at/jeWbT (last accessed January 27, 2024)

The Landscape of Civil Litigation in State Courts

Lester C. Thurow, "The Zero-Sum Solution: An Economic Political Agenda for the 80s," in *The Zero-Sum Society: Distribution and the Possibilities for Economic Change* (Simon & Schuster 1985)

"U.S. District Courts–Judicial Business 2020," U.S. CTS, www.uscourts.gov/statistics-reports/us-district-courts-judicial-business-2020 [https://perma.cc/3ZSX-G2GQ] (last accessed November 6, 2022)

"U.S. Judicial Business Report 2020"

United Nations Convention on the Recognition and Enforcement of Foreign Arbitral Awards (New York Convention) (New York, June 10, 1958)

United States Department of Justice, Office of Justice Programs, Bureau of Justice Statistics, Civil Justice Survey of State Courts, 1992. Inter-university Consortium for Political and Social Research [distributor], 2011-11-02. doi.org/10.3886/ICPSR06587.v5

Albert Jan van den Berg (ed.), *Planning Efficient Arbitration Proceedings: The Law Applicable to International Arbitration*, ICCA Congress Series, No. 7 (Kluwer 1996)

V. V. Veeder, *The Historical Keystone to International Arbitration: The Party-Appointed Arbitrator: From Miami to Geneva*, Proceedings of the ASIL Annual Meeting 107: 387–340 (Cambridge University Press 2013)

Sir Paul Vinogradoff, "Aristotle and Legal Redress," 8 *Col. L. Rev.* 7, 548–560 (November 1908)

Gerhard Walter, *Freie Beweiswürdigung* 69–73 (Mohr 1979)

Henry Zhuhao Wang, "The Fate of Evidence Law: Two Paths of Development," 24 *E & P* 3, 329–348 (2020)

Henry Zhuhao Wang, "Rethinking Evidentiary Rules in an Age of Bench Trials," 13 *U.C. Irvine l. Rev.* 263, 302–303 (2022)

Irene Welser, "Efficiency: Today's Challenge in Arbitration Proceedings," *Austrian Yearbook Int'l Arb.* 151–166 (Kluwer Law International 2014)

BOOKS

2 *Blackstone*, Bk. 3, pp. 15–17

6 *Moore's Federal Practice* – Civil Section 26.23, citing to Manual for Complex Litigation Section 11.481, 4th ed. (2004)

9 A. Fed. Prac. and Proc. Civ. § 2411, 3rd ed. (Wright & Miller 1999)

Georges Abi-Saab, "The International Court as a World Court," in *The International Court as a World Court, in Fifty Years of the International Court of Justice: Essays in Honor of Sir Robert Jennings* (Vaughan Lowe & Malgosia Fitzmaurice eds.) 3–16 (Cambridge University Press 1996)

Robert Ardey, *The Territorial Imperative* (Atheneum Publisher 1966)

Aristotle, *Rhetoric*, Bk. 1, Ch. 13, 1374b

Jeremy Bentham, *Rationale of Judicial Evidence, Specially Applied to English Practice*, Vol. 4 (John S. Mill ed.) (Hunt & Clarke 1827)

George A. Bermann (ed.), para. 4.2.2; and also Jean-Louis Delvolvé, Gerald H Pointon, and Jean Rouche, *French Arbitration Law and Practice: A Dynamic Civil Law Approach to International Arbitration*, 2nd ed. (Kluwer Law International 2009)

George A. Bermann (ed.), *Recognition and Enforcement of Foreign Arbitral Awards: The Interpretation and Application of the UN Convention by National Courts* (Springer 2017)

Gary B. Born, *International Commercial Arbitration*, 3rd ed. (Kluwer Law International 2020)

W. W. Buckland, *A Text-Book of Roman Law from Augustus to Justinian*, at 527–528 (Cambridge University Press 1921)

David J. A. Cairns, "The Premises of Witness Questioning in International Arbitration," in *International Arbitration and the Rule of Law: Contribution and Conformity*, ICCA Congress Series, No. 19, (Andrea Menaker ed.), 302–321 (Kluwer Law International 2017)

David D. Caron & Lee M. Caplan, *The UNCITRAL Arbitration Rules: A Commentary*, 2nd ed. (Oxford University Press 2013)

Donald L. Carper, John A. McKinsey, & Bill W. West, *Understanding the Law* 187 (2002)

Zechariah Chafee (Jr.), Sidney Post Simpson, 1 *Cases on Equity, Jurisdiction and Specific Performance* 552–553 (1934)

Bing Cheng, *General Principles of Law as Applied by International Courts to Tribunals* 299–301 (Stevens & Sons 1953)

John Chong & Michael J. Moser, *Hong Kong SAR Asia Arbitration Handbook* 189–198, 241 (2011)

Julius Henry Cohen, *Commercial Arbitration and the Law* (Hardpress Publishing 1918)

Graham Cook, A *Digest WTO Jurisprudence on Public International Law Concepts and Principles* ¶ 725 (Cambridge University Press 2015)
Mirjan Damaška, "Evaluation of Evidence," in *Evaluation of Evidence: Pre-modern and Modern Approaches*, ASCL Studies in Comparative Law (Cambridge University Press 2019)
Martin Domke, Gabriel Wilmer, & Larry E. Edmonson § 1:2 *Domke on Commercial Arbitration* (West 2023)
Caroline E. Foster, *Signs and the Precautionary Principle in International Courts and Tribunals: Expert Evidence, Burden of Proof and Finality* (Cambridge University Press 2011)
Philippe Fouchard & Berthold Goldman, *Fouchard, Gaillard, Goldman: On International Commercial Arbitration* (Kluwer Law International 1999)
Michael H. Graham, *Handbook of Federal Evidence*, 9th ed. (Thomson Reuters, November 2023 update at § 702:1)
Michael H. Graham, *Handbook of Federal Evidence*, 9th ed. (Thomson Reuters 2020–2023)
G. W. F. Hegel, *The Phenomenology of Spirit*, translated by A. V. Miller (Oxford University Press 1977)
William Holdsworth, A *History of English Law* 519–520 (Methuen 1938)
Chantal Joubert, *Judicial Control of Foreign Evidence in a Comparative and International Context* (Rozenberg Publishers 2005)
Julian D. M. Lew, Loukas A. Mistelis, & Stefan M. Kröll, *Comparative International Commercial Arbitration*, 28 (Kluwer Law International 2002)
Henry Summer Maine, *Village-Communities in the East and West*, 7th ed. (John Murray 1895)
Pedro J. Martínez-Fraga, *The American Influence on International Commercial Arbitration: Doctrinal Developments and Discovery Methods*, 2nd ed. (Cambridge University Press 2019)
Michael Mcilwrath & John Savage, *International Arbitration and Mediation: A Practical Guide* (Wolters Kluwer 2010)
Peter Nicolas, *Evidence: A Problem-Based and Comparative Approach* 3–50 (Carolina Academic Press 2009)
Oxford English Dictionary (OED)
Oxford English Dictionary, 5th ed., Vol. 2 (2002)
PCJ International Commission of the River Oder Case (1929)
Plato, *Gorgias*, W. R. M. Lamb translation, published as part of the Loeb Classical Library (Harvard University Press 1925)
Plato, *Republic* BKVI (509D–513E)
Max Radin, *Handbook of Roman Law* 308 (West Publishing Company 1927)
Redfern and Hunter on International Arbitration (Nigel Blackaby KC, Constantine Partasides KC, and Alan Redfern eds.), 6th ed. (Oxford University Press 2015)
Restatement of the US Law of International Commercial and Investor-State Arbitration, approved in May 2019
William Shakespeare, *Love's Labours Lost*
Shorter *Oxford English Dictionary*, 5th ed. (Oxford University Press 2002)
Collin Tapper, *Cross and Tapper on Evidence*, 6th ed., ed. C. Tapper (Oxford University Press 1985)
James Bradley Thayer, A *Preliminary Treaties on Evidence at the Common Law* (Little, Brown & Co., 1898)
Thucydides (b. 471) in Bk. I., XVIII, 3-XX.2 of his *History of the Peloponnesian War*
Lester C. Thurow, *The Zero-Sum Society: Distribution and the Possibilities for Economic Change*, 11–12 (Basic Books, Inc. 1980)

Sir Paul Vinogradoff, 2 *Historical Jurisprudence* 50, 146 (1922)
3 *Wigmore* §§ 774–778
5 J. Wigmore *Evidence* § 1367, 3rd ed. (1940)
John Henry Wigmore, A *Treatise on the Anglo-American System of Evidence in Trials at Common Law*, 2nd ed. (Little, Brown & Co. 1923) § 4b
Williston on Contracts, 6 *Contracts*, rev. ed. (1938) Section 1927A (p. 5392 n. 9)
Yearbook of Commercial Arbitration 2005, 557 (Oberlandesgericht Köln)

Index